D1598887

The BaSotho kingdom emerged and consolidated in the dramatic and dangerous environment of nineteenth-century South Africa. Elizabeth Eldredge provides a rich description of local agriculture, iron-working and craft industries, bringing out the resourceful responses of the BaSotho to the challenges of drought and famine, and explaining the dynamics of the competition for land. During the colonial period, regional economic integration increasingly influenced local production, land use and internal politics, and drew the BaSotho into the regional migrant labor system. Throughout these turbulent years, the overriding interest of the BaSotho was the pursuit of security. Dr Eldredge analyzes the epic struggle which bound together rich and poor, chiefs and commoners, and men and women in a largely successful effort to sustain this fragile and innovative society in the face of political threats and environmental challenges.

A SOUTH AFRICAN KINGDOM

AFRICAN STUDIES SERIES 78

GENERAL EDITOR
J. M. Lonsdale, *Lecturer in History and Fellow of Trinity College, Cambridge*

ADVISORY EDITOR
J. D. Y. Peel, *Professor of Anthropology and Sociology, with special reference to Africa, School of Oriental and African Studies, University of London*

Published in collaboration with
THE AFRICAN STUDIES CENTRE, CAMBRIDGE

A list of books in this series will be found at the end of this volume

A SOUTH AFRICAN KINGDOM

The pursuit of security in nineteenth-century Lesotho

ELIZABETH A. ELDREDGE

Michigan State University

CAMBRIDGE
UNIVERSITY PRESS

Published by the Press Syndicate of the University of Cambridge
The Pitt Building, Trumpington Street, Cambridge CB2 1RP
40 West 20th Street, New York, NY 10011–4211, USA
10 Stamford Road, Oakleigh, Victoria 3166, Australia

First published 1993

Printed in Great Britain at the University Press, Cambridge

A catalogue record for this book is available from the British Library

Library of Congress cataloguing in publication data

Eldredge, Elizabeth A.
  A South African kingdom: the pursuit of security in nineteenth-century Lesotho /
Elizabeth A. Eldredge.
      p.   cm. – (African studies series)
  Includes bibliographical references.
  ISBN 0 521 44067 X
  1. Lesotho – Politics and government – To 1966. 2. Lesotho – Economic conditions –
To 1966. I. Title. II. Series.
DT2630.E44 1993
968.85 – dc20   92–31675   CIP

ISBN 0 521 44067 X hardback

CE

To David
and
to Michael and James

Contents

Illustrations

Tables

Acknowledgements

The fieldwork on which this book is based was supported by an Oesau Fellowship from the History Department at the University of Wisconsin-Madison, a grant from the Vilas Foundation, and a Fulbright grant for doctoral research. Funds for additional research were provided by York University (Toronto).

I am indebted to Mr. Malete Mokhethi of Mashai, Qacha's Nek District, for his invaluable assistance with interviews and SeSotho transcriptions in 1981 and 1982. I am also grateful for the assistance of Mr. Malefetsane Marabe on subsequent research trips in 1988 and 1989.

Many people have provided generous hospitality to me and my family during our visits to Lesotho. I am particularly grateful to Lois and Molapi Sebatane and to Mpoetsi Lemeke for sharing their homes with us. Aline and Albert Brutsch have made work with archival materials in Morija thoroughly enjoyable. Albert Brutsch, David Ambrose, and L. B. J. Machobane have generously shared their expertise on the history of Lesotho. I would also like to thank Robert Edgar, who provided advice and assistance in the later stages of manuscript preparation. Father David Wells S. S. M. assisted with archival materials from the Society of the Sacred Mission in Modderport, and has always provided generous moral support. I am indebted to Mr. Robert Kukubo for his assistance with materials at the BOLESWA collection in the library of the National University of Lesotho; Father Frank Bullivant at the OMI archives in Rome, Italy; and the staff of the archives of the Société des Missions Evangéliques in Paris.

As always, I am especially grateful to Jan Vansina for his unfailing support.

Finally, I pay tribute to my wonderful family. This work would not have been possible without the countless contributions of my husband, David N. Plank, and the loving patience of our sons Michael and James.

In the end this work rests on the contribution of the old people of Lesotho, who allowed their knowledge to be recorded for posterity. I hope that their contribution to the writing of their history will help to forge a brighter future. *Kea leboha le ka moso.*

Abbreviations

BR	Basutoland Records
BBNA	Blue Book on Native Affairs
CRA	Colonial Report – Annual (Great Britain)
JME	Journal des Missions Evangéliques
OMI	Oblats de Marie Immaculée
PEMS	Paris Evangelical Missionary Society/Société des Missions Evangéliques de Paris
SANAC	South African Native Affairs Commission

Note on orthography and terminology

I have chosen to use the official SeSotho orthography of Lesotho instead of the SeSotho orthography in use in South Africa, in accordance with the choice of modern BaSotho to retain their own orthography. The spellings of names and places reflect this choice.

In the SeSotho orthography of Lesotho, the letter *L* followed by *i* or *u* is pronounced as a *d*; when followed by other vowels it retains the ordinary English pronunciation of *L*. The vowels *o* and *u*, when followed by *a* or *e* and sometimes another *o*, serve as consonants sounded as *w*. Similarly, the vowel *e* when followed by *a* or *o* and sometimes another *e* serves as a consonant sounded as *y*. Clicks are represented by *g*, *c*, and *x*. An apostrophe before *m* or *n*, as in *'me* or *'na* indicates duplication of the consonant (*mme* or *nna*). The consonant *h* does not form a new sound when it follows *p* or *t* as in *ph* or *th*, but indicates the *p* or *t* are aspirated in pronunciation.

I have avoided the use of word stems as words; such use of stems in place of full words would not be acceptable in English usage, where full compliance with word transitions, such as from England to English or Britain to British, is standard. As in other Bantu languages, word changes in southern Bantu languages often occur before the stem, which can be confusing for readers accustomed only to European languages. To alleviate confusion I have adopted a system used by other scholars by which the stem is capitalized in the middle of the word. This should make changes from singular to plural, and differences between group names, easier to identify. For example:

Sotho:	word stem
SeSotho:	language and customs
MoSotho:	person
BaSotho:	people
LeSotho:	nation

Group names are particularly problematic in the ambiguity of their meaning. Thus the term BaSotho could refer to anyone speaking the SeSotho language, or it could refer to a member of the nation of Lesotho. I differentiate between SeSotho-speaking peoples, who might or might not belong to the nation called Lesotho built by Moshoeshoe from 1824; and the BaSotho, by whom I mean those people who gave their allegiance to Moshoeshoe and Lesotho, and their descendants, among whom are included people speaking numerous languages and dialects. Similarly I distinguish between IsiZulu-speaking peoples, some of whom became BaSotho, and the AmaZulu people of the nation built by Shaka. The distinction is more ambiguous for the IsiXhosa-speaking peoples and the SeTswana-speaking peoples. Again, various IsiXhosa and SeTswana-speakers became BaSotho by virtue of their incorporation into Lesotho under Moshoeshoe, but the terms AmaXhosa and BaTswana cannot be used to designate people belonging to a single specific polity in the region. I therefore try to designate the specific polity or political context where appropriate. Because there were numerous polities which were composed primarily of SeTswana-speaking peoples, they are sometimes distinguished by separate group name (for example, BaTlhaping, BaRolong), and sometimes designated collectively as BaTswana when the specific sociopolitical distinctions are not relevant. It should be noted that chiefdoms and kingdoms throughout the region, whether dominated by AmaXhosa, AmaZulu, BaSotho, or BaTswana, included peoples of various origins speaking various language. Processes of amalgamation and accultur-ation accompanied ongoing political changes among all southern African peoples in the eighteenth and nineteenth centuries.

The descriptive term I use to designate Lesotho changes, varying from chiefdom to kingdom to nation to colony according to the historical context. The BaSotho have referred to Lesotho from its origins as their *sechaba*, which translates as nation, and this seems generally the most appropriate term for the polity established by Moshoeshoe. On the other hand, when Moshoeshoe's chiefdom incorporated other chiefdoms after 1824 Mosh-oeshoe became the *morena o moholo*, or paramount chief, distinct from subordinate chiefs within Lesotho, and the polity can appropriately be termed a kingdom. During the colonial era the kingdom persisted in the status of the colony of Basutoland, so the term kingdom has the advantage of remaining appropriate for the entire history of Lesotho. I apply the term nation in most contexts, however, because it draws attention to the dynamic role played by the BaSotho in shaping their political and economic destiny in a changing political context, independently of any one chief or king. By using the term nation I suggest an underlying allegiance and loyalty to the polity which survived Moshoeshoe and his heirs in the paramountcy, as well as the colonial era, to shape the modern nation of Lesotho. At the same time the term nation implies dynamics which have allowed the incorporation of people of diverse origins, and therefore also suggests the potential for broader regional incorporation based on wider regional ties and loyalties.

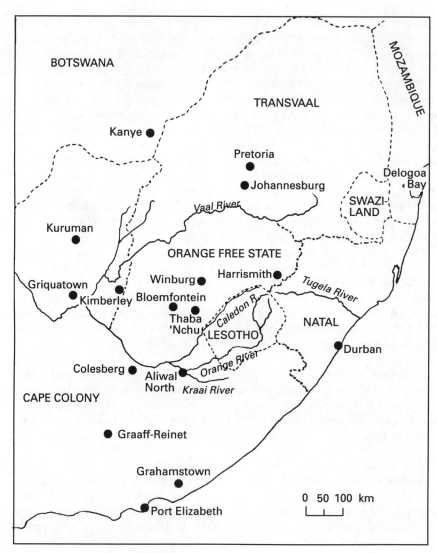

Fig. 1 Southern Africa

1

Introduction

Throughout the nineteenth century the health and livelihood, and sometimes the very survival, of every person living in the region of Lesotho were continually threatened.[1] Recurrent droughts created food scarcities and posed the threat of famines, and large-scale migrations of both Africans and Europeans posed the threat of wars, dispossession, and death or servitude. This climate of insecurity was pervasive. It shaped the choices and actions of individuals, households, chiefs, and nations in the region of southern Africa.

Before the 1820s SeSotho-speaking peoples were scattered in small chiefdoms along the upper Caledon valley, united by ties of language, culture, and traditions of origin. They practiced mixed agriculture and traded sporadically with their neighbors in every direction; only occasional cattle raids disrupted the tranquility of the region. The chiefdoms of SeSotho-speakers occasionally incorporated individuals or families of SeTswana, SePedi, or Nguni-speaking origins through intermarriage or clientship relations, which intensified cultural and economic interchanges. Because of these contacts, political consolidation among their SeTswana-speaking and SePedi-speaking neighbors beginning in the eighteenth century had repercussions for SeSotho-speaking chiefdoms.

Internal change and sociopolitical consolidation in the southern African interior can be traced back at least to the mid-eighteenth century. A process of consolidation among SeTswana-speaking chiefdoms, emerging from competition over land, cattle, people, and trade, had begun by about 1750 and intensified beginning in the 1790s.[2] Internal sociopolitical and economic dynamics originated changes, but competition intensified and the consolidation process accelerated with the arrival of violent new forces emanating from the expanding Cape Colony. Beginning in the late eighteenth century both San-speakers and SeTswana-speakers were pushed out of their southern territories by various groups of Khoi, European, and slave descent, who sought out the best springs and fertile areas along the Orange River.[3] Joined and often led by escaped European criminals, Khoi and "Bastard" intruders from the south were fleeing the enforcement of increasingly restrictive labor laws which reduced supposedly free blacks to the status of unprotected

1

slaves. Resisting their own victimization, these groups moved beyond the Cape frontier and inflicted devastating raids on the southernmost SeTswana-speakers, reducing them to indigence in the 1790s. Notorious European, Khoi, Kora, and Bastard marauders depended on access to guns and ammunition from the Cape Colony for hunting and self-defense. In exchange they traded cattle which they raided from their northern neighbors. Growing settler demand for slaves spawned increasing slave-raiding across the northern frontier over the first three decades of the nineteenth century, following a pre-existing pattern of enslavement of Khoi and San by Europeans in the Cape Colony dating from the emergence of so-called "apprenticeship" as early as 1721.

Just as confederations of BaTswana chiefdoms were emerging they were faced with population compression caused by the northern movement of San- and SeTswana-speakers who were pushed away from southern springs and fertile Orange River sites by Khoi, Kora, and Bastards. At the same time the BaTswana confederations were challenged by several ecological disasters, including successive droughts in the late eighteenth and early nineteenth century, which resulted in food scarcities and at least one devastating famine at the turn of the century. Oral traditions attribute conflicts over crops and cattle around 1820 to the intensification of competition for food resulting from these droughts.

In 1822 migrants fleeing from incorporation into the Zulu state under Shaka further disrupted political and economic stability in the region. Political consolidation east of the Drakensberg paralleled that in the interior, and emerged from increasing competition over trade networks, fertile land for cultivation, cattle, and people.[4] Pre-existing patterns of competition intensified at the turn of the nineteenth century as a result of drought-induced food scarcity and famine, giving dominant groups both an opportunity and incentive to increase further their wealth and power. Emerging leaders such as Dingiswayo attracted followers with the promise of wealth and security generated from agricultural and pastoral production as well as trade to Delagoa Bay. They built up their military potential based on their growing constituencies, and forcibly expanded their control over weaker neighbors. These processes were well under way by the time Shaka came to power, and growing popular insecurity prompted allegiance to a leader who promised wealth derived from raiding as well as from production. Conflicts arising from food scarcities further interrupted food production and prevented economic recovery, and hunger accompanied the disruptions spawned by migrating chiefdoms seeking a place to settle. Slave-raiding by Europeans and their allies in the Delagoa Bay region and on the Cape frontier intensified these conflicts and perpetuated regional instability.

Destitute refugees from the east crossed the Drakensberg mountains and raided the inhabitants of the Highveld and upper Caledon River Valley for standing crops and cattle beginning in 1822. Their initial attacks prompted the young Moshoeshoe, son of a minor BaSotho chief, to form alliances with neighboring SeSotho-speaking groups and to seek refuge in the mountains. Aware of the vulnerability of his people, however, Moshoeshoe sent out scouts to find a better refuge, and they located a large flat-topped mountain further south. In June or July of 1824 Moshoeshoe led his people more than seventy miles in three days to take up residence on this mountain fortress. The weather was bitterly cold, and stragglers were attacked and captured by starving groups who, according to oral tradition, resorted to cannibalism in their desperation, but the move proved to be a stroke of genius. Thaba Bosiu, the "mountain of night," was almost invulnerable, and it is from this move that the creation of the BaSotho nation can be dated. Now able to protect people, cattle, and crops, Moshoeshoe attracted followers with his open generosity and warded off subsequent invasions. When the first European missionaries arrived in 1833 they found a nation at peace and on the threshold of prosperity.

After a decade of wars accompanied by chronic hunger and frequent famines, the BaSotho were eager to resettle the lands of their parents in order to expand agricultural production and to build up their stores of food. As a consequence the BaSotho economy expanded so rapidly that the BaSotho were soon supplying surplus food to both their African and European neighbors. At the same time, however, Boers in the Cape Colony were becoming bitterly frustrated with British rule, which imposed new restrictions on land tenure, deprived them of their slaves, and prevented continued expansion eastward into the land of the AmaXhosa. Discontent which had been evident as early as 1831 manifested itself in the Great Boer Trek, when approximately fifteen thousand Boers and their dependents migrated north across the Orange River between 1834 and 1845.[5] By the early 1840s, many of these Boers had settled along the southwestern fringes of lands which had belonged to the forefathers of the BaSotho. As they slowly moved northeast, early Boer settlers acknowledged Moshoeshoe's authority over this land and sought his permission to settle. Later both Boer settlers and the British who were expanding their area of control were more aggressive, however.

The revival of prosperity in Lesotho was therefore short-lived. The BaSotho lost over half of their arable land to the Boers in successive wars in the 1850s and 1860s. British colonial rule stabilized the country's borders after 1868, and the discovery of diamonds allowed the BaSotho initially to profit from selling their surplus grain and their labor at the Kimberley mines in the 1870s and early 1880s. Over time, however, the redirection of production to meet the demands of the capitalist economy fostered the economic dependency of colonial Basutoland, and encouraged direct intervention by the British to strengthen the economic ties between the BaSotho and the mines, especially with regard to labor recruitment. In the long run, then, the BaSotho became trapped in the migrant labor system abroad, while at home no amount of effort could compensate for the lost land. By the beginning of the twentieth century Lesotho was no longer even self-sufficient in food production, and exploitation by chiefs increased to exacerbate the plight of the poor.

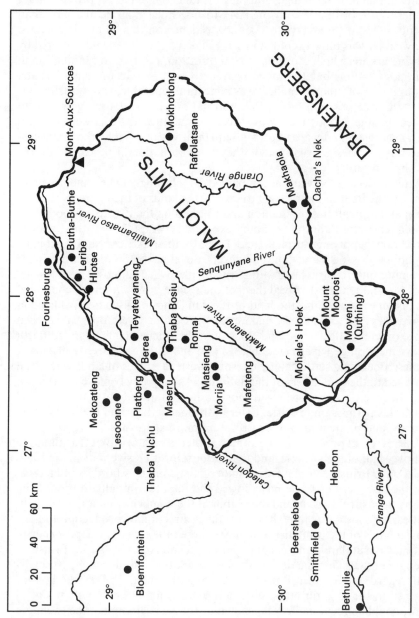

Fig. 2 Lesotho

In Lesotho, economic as well as political developments at the local and national levels can best be explained with reference to the pursuit of security. In interpreting the events and developments of the nineteenth century, an emphasis on security rather than mere physical survival signifies a recognition that the exploitation of resources to meet material needs is governed by the social system which structures and limits the abilities of individuals or groups to exploit these resources. The pursuit of security helps to explain the motivations of subordinate groups who willingly accepted the authority of Moshoeshoe. For them physical survival was contingent on the achievement of security in a political context which could protect their access to productive resources. Constrained by regional politics, individuals and groups often chose clientship under a MoSotho chief in preference to more severe servitude or total deprivation under a less generous ruler, African or European.

The motives of the dominant groups in Lesotho were also shaped by the pursuit of security. Given the regional context of struggle, first among Africans during the 1820s and subsequently between Africans and Europeans, the motivation of dominant groups within African societies cannot be reduced solely to a desire to exploit subordinate groups within their own societies. Chiefs also sought to achieve security from outsiders by consolidating their control over larger and larger groups of subjects, but they could broaden and sustain this popular base only by accumulating and reallocating wealth in such a way as to attract supporters. Harsh exploitation would only have driven clients away. Both dominant and subordinate groups thus achieved a measure of security through clientship relations.

Because societies in southern Africa did not develop in isolation from one another, implicit underlying "class" struggles and gender struggles were not allowed to play themselves out. Subordinate groups identified their interests not with those of their counterparts in other societies but with those of their rulers, to whom they were bound by linguistic, cultural, and political ties. When subordinate groups perceived a threat from the foreign societies with which they struggled, they tolerated the injustices of their own societies in pursuit of security against the external threat. The imperatives of national unity thus undercut class struggle here as elsewhere in the modern world.

The driving force of pre-colonial societies in southern Africa was the accumulation of people. People were necessary for increased and intensified agricultural production, and for the production of tools and weapons and other implements useful for survival. People were also necessary for military protection against neighbors who might covet the resources of production on which a society depends, notably land, livestock, and people, all of which were sometimes lost in war. The greater the intensification of agriculture, the more specialization in production could be sustained, allowing for both innovations in military organization, such as maintaining a standing army (comprising men no longer needed in food production), and innovations in military technology.

The events of the 1820s in southern Africa necessitated the restructuring of societies to meet the needs of many hungry, desperate people. Military advances upset the prior balance between neighboring societies, compelling all societies to adjust or risk conquest or dispersal by a stronger neighbor. The new nation built by Moshoeshoe offered security and potential prosperity to the people living in the area which became Lesotho. Land of varying quality was readily available, but access to land was of little use when people could not protect their crops and cattle from marauders. In the beginning it was primarily the safety of the natural mountain fortress of Thaba Bosiu which Moshoeshoe had to offer; as his followers increased, security was found in numbers. In addition Moshoeshoe redistributed wealth by loaning cattle to his followers, and attracted by this promise of wealth people placed themselves under his governance.

Power, wealth, and gender in nineteenth-century Lesotho

I begin with a survey of regional settlement patterns and trade relations before the 1820s to demonstrate that cultural and economic contacts across wide areas were not new with the arrival of Europeans, but rather were pre-existing and created a local dynamic for change. This chapter provides an important context for understanding subsequent political and economic relationships between the BaSotho and their neighbors, since early trade patterns among SeSotho- and SeTswana-speaking peoples indicate that these societies were already engaged in surplus production for exchange in the eighteenth century. In this context I then examine the demographic and political setting as the BaSotho nation emerged in the 1820s, and changes which ensued with the advent of European settlers bordering on Moshoeshoe's territory beginning in the 1830s. The political and economic fortunes of the BaSotho were intricately interwoven, tied as they were to control over land.

Agriculture provided the productive base for BaSotho social and political organization. I examine not only BaSotho success in cultivation and the raising of livestock with the aim of producing food, but also the politics which created situations of food scarcity and famine during times of environmental stress. It is important to establish that BaSotho agricultural prosperity was already evident to the French Protestant missionaries when they first arrived in Lesotho in 1833 and was not merely a function of the subsequent integration of the BaSotho economy into the regional European economy. Evidence that sophisticated techniques of agricultural production such as intercropping, crop rotation, and pasture rotation were traditional among the BaSotho demonstrates that they had long since been taking conscious measures to maximize output and obtain surpluses. The arrival of a European market for food did not initiate the production of surpluses among the BaSotho; it merely created a new outlet for surpluses which had previously been stored or exchanged with Africans elsewhere. The BaSotho experienced a boom in agricultural production in the middle decades of the nineteenth century. High levels of production were achieved initially because of high labor inputs supplied voluntarily by the BaSotho, and later by technological innovations as well. The explanation for the hard work and productivity of the BaSotho in the nineteenth century lies in their shared historical memory. During the 1820s every MoSotho had faced starvation, including the wealthier members of society. The BaSotho who survived the 1820s learned to produce as much food as possible, to store against future need. If the memory of the 1820s receded over the decades, the memory of starvation was renewed by recurring famines which resulted from the interaction of natural factors, such as droughts, with human factors, such as wars and dispossession.[6]

Throughout the nineteenth century the ways in which the BaSotho managed their resources and organized themselves politically continued to be determined by their responses to threats to their survival. When the BaSotho failed to provide for themselves and found themselves in want, it was the result of politics. Early suffering from famine, and the failure of the BaSotho to sustain self-sufficiency in food production by the end of the century, were the result of political struggles with Europeans which interrupted food production during wars. These wars eventually left the BaSotho with insufficient land resources when the country's colonial boundaries were fixed, so that the economic success which had been predicated on the expansion of cultivation was precluded by the disastrous outcome of the struggle for land. With the advent of formal colonial rule politics continued to interfere with BaSotho efforts to achieve and sustain self-sufficiency in food production, as the BaSotho were compelled to sell their dwindling food supplies under adverse market conditions in order to pay colonial taxes.

In addition to agriculture, the BaSotho engaged in a variety of local craft industries. Important regional productive activities prior to the European arrival included an iron industry involving mining, smelting, and smithing; pottery; weaving; and the manufacture of leather goods and wooden implements. These activities were central to the working of African economies, and the undermining of local specialization in craft production has been explained in various ways. Indicating both the complexity of patterns of the production and exchange of locally-produced goods, I demonstrate that the process of import substitution was selective and deliberate on the part of the BaSotho. The adoption of European commodities did not reflect the emergence of "artificially induced wants," but rather the consumption of imported goods represented a rational choice based on labor time in production, opportunity costs, and transaction costs. In noting which locally-produced items continued to be made long after cheap European imports were available, and which were replaced by imports, the logic which governed local manufacturing is clear. The partial decline in specialization reveals this phenomenon not as a simple, inevitable result of competition from European goods, but rather as a deliberate choice by Africans who selected what to continue producing themselves (custom-made luxury goods) and what to purchase from Europeans (generic, labor-intensive goods). This selective process on the part of producers and consumers demonstrates deliberate African initiative "in pursuit of security," in this case economic security.

Internal patterns of social and economic stratification changed as internal BaSotho politics changed. The economic boom of the mid-nineteenth century benefitted the chiefs by increasing their personal wealth, but chiefs were not the sole beneficiaries of agricultural expansion. The benefits of economic growth were widely shared among all segments of the population. Economic expansion, achieved through voluntary inputs of labor, was not mandated from above by Moshoeshoe, nor was the boom in production the result of coercion by chiefs. As the threat of invasion by other Africans receded, the BaSotho became less dependent on the protection that Moshoeshoe had provided, and they were able to move about freely. Moreover, people could accumulate wealth through their own enterprise and not solely through clientship relations with chiefs. Many people acquired livestock by selling grain, tobacco, salt, cosmetics, and craft goods which they produced themselves.

The chiefs were not able to monopolize wealth, which limited their control over their subjects. Moreover, the power, wealth, and prestige of a chief were determined by the number of his followers, so the extent to which a chief could exploit his followers was constrained by the ability of his people to emigrate. Chiefs were motivated to attract and retain followers through generosity and fairness because a chief's wealth increased through the payment of tribute in labor and in kind. The ability to move away from a chief's domain served as a source of leverage for commoners over their chiefs.

The capacity of the chiefs to coerce and exploit their followers was thus distinctly limited, and cannot explain why the BaSotho worked so hard. Furthermore, evidence from slave societies indicates that oppressed people who do not directly benefit from their own efforts engage in passive resistance by working slowly and sabotaging work efforts. Consequently economic growth in Lesotho can be attributed mainly to individual initiative rather than to chiefly control. Economic decisions were taken at the level of the household, and it is therefore appropriate to examine household economy in order to identify the dynamics of economic expansion.

Later in the century, however, as people became impoverished following the loss of arable lands to the Boers, the chiefs were increasingly able to exploit their people. Most obviously, the fixing of the colonial boundaries of Lesotho after 1868 circumscribed the area available for BaSotho expansion, which hindered and eventually eliminated the ability of people to move away from exploitative chiefs. In addition, the continuing threat of European expansion, including the plans of the Cape Colony to expropriate more BaSotho land, encouraged the BaSotho to continue to support their chiefs. Only the chiefs could provide effective resistance to Europeans. The influences governing the political and economic decisions taken by households and by chiefs consequently changed. As the chiefs increasingly collaborated with the colonial authorities and labor recruiters from abroad, the people were unable to resist.

BaSotho relations with their chiefs were moderated by a political discourse among commoners and intellectuals, and not by a hegemonic ruling class ideology.[7] BaSotho repetitions of platitudes about the positive roles of chiefs in the late nineteenth century appeared merely to have reflected the perpetuation of an ideology of dominance, but the reality was tested and explicitly explored by BaSotho intellectuals who called into question chiefly rights and popular obligations throughout the nineteenth century. The turning point at which the relations between the BaSotho and their chiefs were revealed most explicitly was the Gun War of 1880–81. Working from false assumptions in her earlier work, Kimble depicted the steady acquisition of guns in the period prior to the war as a Bakoena conspiracy to consolidate their internal political dominance.[8] Since guns can easily be turned against rulers when their possession is so widespread, however, popular acquiescence if not enthusiastic support for chiefs was implied in popular participation in the accumulation of guns, which were then turned not against their chiefs but against their colonial rulers. The subsequent consolidation of power by the chiefs and their gradual betrayal of popular interests does not negate the fact that as late as the 1880s the BaSotho consciously chose to support their chiefs. Oral traditions reveal the dynamics which explain this support. The persistence of popular support for chiefs in this period cannot just be attributed to the ideological hegemony of a ruling class, but rather cultural continuity over time with regard to popular attitudes towards, and perceptions of, chiefs which were consciously accepted, not unconsciously received. Where tradition persisted, it was the result of the ongoing test of reality, and it was molded and reinvented to meet the changing needs of the BaSotho.

Woven into my analysis of politics and wealth in nineteenth-century Lesotho is evidence of gender relations and the many roles of women which elucidates many facets of the internal dynamics of BaSotho society. The demand for people necessitated the protection of the existing society and its perpetuation through reproduction. Hence women played a central role in the process of achieving wealth and power, and social and economic stability, growth, and prosperity. The evident value placed on reproduction created a clear incentive to protect and control women, operating as an incentive both to maintain them in good health and to subordinate them to male social controls. Women were also valued for producing the daily food requirements of their families, a task which has sometimes been subsumed under the category of reproduction. As women cared for and raised their children, they imbued in them social and cultural values which were the ideological glue binding the society together; hence women reproduced culture and reproduced the social relations dictated by that culture. In other words, women played indispensable roles in biological reproduction, daily reproduction (which can also be categorized as production), and social reproduction.[9]

Through their children, women reproduced descent lines, and reproduced political relations which rested on alliances between lines of descent. In other words, the notion of reproduction can be extended even further, into the realm of politics: women not only reproduced the social relations internal to their societies, they also reinforced old and forged new political relations between societies, serving as core components in political networks from which emerged chiefdoms on larger and larger scales.

Women's productive roles were also critical. As the primary laborers in arable agriculture, women in particular actively promoted economic expansion. Women and children suffered disproportionately during times of food scarcity, since they had little control over food supplies. Pre-colonial BaSotho were surplus producers, and women regularly invested their labor voluntarily in order to produce surplus grain. Surplus grain was critical for food security, especially for women and children. In times of drought, the value of livestock declined dramatically relative to grain because grain was an efficient food which could feed many people over a long period of time, whereas livestock were perishable, and meat is an inefficient food source relative to grain. As livestock began to perish, men drove them far afield to find better pastures, and ate those animals which happened to die. The women were left to fend for themselves, and if they did not have stores of grain at hand they had to survive on the tiny amounts of grass seed which could be foraged during droughts. Thus women had a strong incentive to produce surplus grain for storage against future shortages. For this reason women actively supported the expansion of cultivation, in spite of the fact that they shouldered most of the burden of agricultural labor. Women also acquired food which they controlled themselves by producing and trading surpluses from their work in home industries such as pottery, weaving, digging salt, and making cosmetics. When their own work was finished, women worked in the fields of their neighbors and were paid with baskets of grain. The hard work performed by women seeking to accumulate food for themselves and their children constituted a central dynamic generating economic growth in nineteenth-century Lesotho.[10]

Beyond the sustenance of the family, however, surplus grain had other important uses. Food was money, and grain was a primary means of obtaining livestock through exchange. Hence the surplus grain produced by women was converted through trade into livestock, especially cattle, which was a primary measure of and source of wealth among the BaSotho. Cattle as well as smaller stock could be traded for a variety of valuable goods and services, and cattle were exchanged in the form of bridewealth for women. Hence through a circular process, women's labor produced surplus grain which was exchanged for cattle which was exchanged for women; men were merely the brokers controlling the social and economic relations embedded in the bridewealth system, reflecting women's fundamental importance because of both their reproductive and productive functions in BaSotho society.

The case of Lesotho is unique in southern Africa in several ways. Further from the domains of early white settlers, the BaSotho remained less affected by the European intrusion longer than did the AmaXhosa and other neighbors to the south. The boom in agricultural production in Lesotho began at least a decade before the BaSotho were integrated into the regional European economy. It also occurred long before the area available to the BaSotho for cultivation was circumscribed, so that new lands could still be brought under cultivation. As a result, economic prosperity was widely shared among the BaSotho. In addition, a dramatic increase in the production of grain by the BaSotho occurred before the adoption of the plow, before Christian influences were significant, and without a transition to individual land tenure. Given that the number of Christians in Lesotho was minute throughout the nineteenth century, the boom in production from the 1830s and the adoption of the plow and other innovations from the 1850s onward cannot be attributed to Christian influences related to an emphasis on individual rather than communal interests. Neither individual land tenure nor Christianity, which have been emphasized in studies of successful peasant producers elsewhere in southern Africa from about 1870, were linked to the rapid expansion of agricultural production and marketing in Lesotho which occurred earlier in the century. The BaSotho retained their political independence for decades after economic relations were established with white farmers, so that a boom in the sale of grain to whites preceded rather than followed white colonial rule.

Like Swaziland and Bechuanaland, Basutoland came under British colonial rule, which buffered the BaSotho from some of the direct effects of white rule experienced across the border, including almost total land dispossession. While the British protected the remaining lands of the BaSotho from further white encroachment, however, they subjected them to direct taxation, failed to provide external financial support for development, and bolstered the chiefs whose exploitative activities often went unchecked as long as they served colonial administrative ends. Because of the British colonial system the experience of the BaSotho diverged in several ways from that of their neighbors who were brought within the boundaries of South Africa. On the other hand, the story of the decline of production in colonial Basutoland closely paralleled the fate of other Africans in the region. In Lesotho as elsewhere the decline in agricultural output was linked to disadvantages deliberately imposed on African producers by white settler governments across the border, which favored white farmers over African farmers and created a labor supply for the emerging industrial economy of the twentieth century. This book therefore ends with an examination of the dilemma faced by the BaSotho once they had lost their political and economic independence and had come to rely on economic returns accruing from the migrant labor system. In a vicious cycle economic depression and political oppression reinforced each other, and prevented the BaSotho from ever reclaiming the economic prosperity and popular leadership which they had known in the nineteenth century.

Historiography and theoretical issues

The purpose of this book is to retrieve evidence about the people who came to belong to the BaSotho kingdom of Moshoeshoe in the nineteenth century, and to analyze this past in terms of historical theories about southern Africa which have not yet been tested in an empirical context. The dependency theory approach adopted by Bundy, with its emphasis on the European connection as the primary dynamic for change in African societies, fell far short of explaining the intricacies of internal pre-colonial political, economic, and social relations within African societies.[11] The focus of Marxist scholarship has inevitably been oriented towards the point of intersection between pre-colonial and capitalist societies in southern Africa, drawing attention away from further explorations into the workings of pre-colonial society.[12] The study of pre-industrial, pre-capitalist societies in Africa has involved a search for the principles and mechanisms underlying the organization and operation of society and the dynamics which generate change in such societies. The theoretical dilemma of Marxist work on pre-colonial African societies has hinged on whether these societies were comprised of classes in the classic Marxist sense, which stood in a special relation of production to each other and to the forces of production, and which reproduced themselves as classes. Whether or not one accepts the formal definition of classes as applicable, it is necessary to explain evident disparities in wealth and power in these societies. Where there was clearly unequal wealth, and unequal control of and access to the forces of production, how did this inequality first emerge? Where there were discernible power relations around a centralized political authority at any level – village, district, or state, on what were these power relations based? The anthropological debate has considered but not resolved the questions of economic determinism, and of kinship writ large as a constituent of infrastructure (or base) as well as superstructure in social organization.[13] Fundamental to all these questions is the problem of identifying the basis and origins of sociopolitical and socioeconomic stratification, and of assessing the ability of upper social strata to maintain ideological hegemony in order to perpetuate their dominance (such as through an ideology of kinship).

Jeff Guy, arguing from a theoretical rather than empirical base, has continued to pursue these issues with regard to the history of southern Africa. His goal is "to derive from the evidence a set of social principles" which reveal "the essential organising features" that play "a dynamic role at the centre" of pre-capitalist societies in southern Africa.[14] Guy challenges the prevailing assumption that cattle and women were a dominant social goal merely because their accumulation and distribution were a means for obtaining security and authority. He argues that "we cannot continue merely to equate cattle and followers with power and social strength. We have to ask *why* was this so? ... The drive to accumulate, and the association of accumulation with power and wealth, cannot just be assumed as an unproblematic, universal social feature."[15]

Guy agrees that "it is quite correct to identify, as many analysts have done, the drive to control human beings as a factor of the greatest significance."[16] However, he argues that the goal was not accumulation *per se*, but the accumulation of labor power, that is, the productive and creative potential of people.

Guy argues that because men controlled cattle and women were denied possession of cattle, married men controlled the whole productive process, while women and children formed a subordinate class whose labor power was expropriated by their husbands and fathers. According to Guy this created a relation of exploitation based on male rights to the means of production in the form of cattle and land which allowed for the accumulation of labor power by men through their control over cattle, wives, and daughters. Guy agrees with other scholars, if for different reasons, that "redistribution" was not egalitarian in its goals or effects, but rather increased a chief's control over labor power.[17]

According to Guy, the goal of accumulation changed over time, as had the ultimate aim of production. But if, as Guy has argued, the goal was to accumulate labor-power, we must ask to what end, if not as the source of social and economic and political security both within a given society and in the context of struggles between competing societies? Underlying Guy's analysis is Meillassoux's argument that the driving force behind the organization of power relations in society was control over reproduction, with implied ultimate goals of achieving social (and, perhaps, political) control as well as material wealth, which seems like a circular, if not tautological, argument.

Meillassoux has argued that material wealth such as gold can only reproduce wealth if reconverted into the instruments of life, that is, women, thereby suggesting that the reproduction of wealth is indeed the end goal, and women the means of achieving these ends.[18] He argues that social control derives from the management of reproduction, implying that social control is the ultimate aim of society and control over women merely the means for achieving an ultimate goal of social control, that is, political power. The theoretical challenge posed by Meillassoux and taken up by Guy in the context of southern Africa thus remains unresolved by either of these scholars. The internal dynamics of southern African societies prior to European contact remains a fertile ground for exploration.

My goal is to identify change in pre-capitalist BaSotho society in order to come closer to an understanding of the dynamics behind those changes, and to determine when possible the level of consciousness governing those changes. I infer from human actions and choices the underlying motivations, in order to shed light on the dialectical relationship between human ideas and material conditions in history. What was the role of human agency, whether individual leadership or conscious collective action, in directing political and economic change in nineteenth-century Lesotho? What was the role of gender in defining or creating power relations at all levels of society, and in mediating economic change? And what was the role of external influences in serving to affect human agency, such as through the diffusion of innovative technology or ideas?

I eschew both mechanistic economic determinism and environmental determinism as historical explanations. My focus on the economy reflects a belief that people organize themselves in such a way as to maximize the production of wealth from which derives their physical well-being and basic survival. The environment is not the exclusive determinant of human prosperity since it is the use that humans make of their environment which determines levels of productivity. The environment does impose natural constraints which cannot be overcome by deliberate human action, however, and these constraints must be recognized. The failure to take into account the variability of the geographic environment has limited the applicability of theoretical formulations concerning the forces of production in southern Africa. In the study of Africa, low population densities have led to the assumption that labor rather than land has been the most important determinant of and constraint to the level of productivity and that control over land was therefore insignificant in understanding issues of economy, wealth, and political dominance. But not all land is the same. There has historically been considerable competition over the most favorable sites for settlement in Africa, whether because of the fertility of the land, water resources for land and people, mineral resources (especially iron, gold, and copper), or defensibility of the site. Differences in the favorability of settlement sites based on these factors gave clear advantages to certain groups over their neighbors. The desire to control these sites generated among neighboring groups an underlying, implicit competition and an incentive for contesting control over them. In addition, advantageous sites could increase the potential of their inhabitants to dominate neighboring groups.[19] Fertile, well-watered land sustains a larger population density, iron provides the means for technological superiority in cultivation and war, and prestige goods provide the means to attract people or acquire tools and weapons. The wealth of the community derives from the quality and attributes of the land they control, as exploited by the community.

Given variability in the quality of land resources, the relations between neighboring groups had an ongoing and decisive effect on how societies organized themselves for purposes of defense (if they controlled the best site) or attack (if they coveted their neighbors' site of settlement). Competition between societies began with the advent of permanent settlement for cultivation if not before, and there is no period in which we can assume settled agricultural societies enjoyed the luxury of security from attack. Hence it is a mistake to analyze the dynamics governing such societies solely in terms of their internal economic and social relations. An analysis of external trade and politics are indispensable in an analysis of internal sociopolitical dynamics and the distribution of wealth and power.[20]

It is here that I diverge from the conclusions of both Meillassoux and Guy regarding the incentives for accumulating people under a centralized authority. A large population is necessary for military strength given equal levels of military technology, and it is also necessary for economic prosperity. It is simplistic to assume that people were valued only for their productive capacities rather than for the military and economic security that derived from strength in numbers and combined social wealth.[21] To seek the driving forces in society only in internal socioeconomic relations ignores the dynamics of competition and struggle between societies. Even in modern capitalist societies, the drive to accumulate people, or "labor power," is an explicit goal justified on the basis of national interests with regard to military defense and economic strength. In pre-capitalist societies as well, defense against outsiders was as important as internal social and economic relations in determining political and economic decision-making on the group and individual levels. Only wealth and power provided the means for ensuring military security in the context of ongoing, endemic competition for natural resources, and security was indeed a primary motive force for the people of southern Africa.

To explain the dynamics of change in nineteenth-century BaSotho society I combine an analysis of the broader regional setting, including settlement patterns, trade patterns, and political relations, with an examination of the local patterns of production and exchange underlying the organization of wealth and power within BaSotho society. An analysis of internal social dynamics has to include a consideration of gender and reproduction in shaping power relations at various levels of society. Furthermore, to take into account human agency as a factor shaping BaSotho history, we must seek to recreate the perceptions and motivations of the BaSotho in pursuing various courses of action. I conclude that the BaSotho were motivated by the pursuit of security, be it military, political, economic, or social, and that this explains the actions of leaders and followers, men and women, rich and poor, and allows us to explain apparent inconsistencies in the behavior of people who seem to be acting against their own interests at times. The pursuit of security explains why people with divergent and even strongly conflicting interests sometimes found common ground.

Lesotho in the nineteenth century

The nineteenth-century history of the BaSotho has not yet been adequately studied. Both Thompson and Sanders, who centered their studies on the personality and leadership of Moshoeshoe, provided excellent analyses of the political forces at play in the region up to 1870.[22] Their work has been supplemented by several studies by Sandra Burman on the period of Cape Colony rule in the 1870s.[23] Before publishing two articles on the colonial period, Judy Kimble attempted a Marxist analysis of pre-colonial Lesotho in her Master's thesis, "Towards an Understanding of the Political Economy of

Lesotho: the Origins of Commodity Production and Migrant Labour, 1830–1885."[24] Kimble's thesis, a theoretical Marxist construction of the period, is replete with footnotes to Marx but lacks a substantive empirical foundation. Her work on the colonial period is meticulous and empirically sound, but flawed by her theoretical assumptions about class relations which she posited but never demonstrated or substantiated in her earlier thesis. Kimble therefore incorrectly depicted an all-encompassing Bakoena ruling family dominance in political, social, and economic relations reaching back to the formation of the BaSotho nation in 1824 and controlling all aspects of the political economy of Lesotho throughout the nineteenth century. Kimble did not examine the basis of power relations, but took them for granted. She failed to acknowledge that power was mediated by people and popular choice, and read backwards in time the unchallenged dominance of chiefs, supported by the British, in the late nineteenth century, to assert its existence throughout the pre-colonial period.

Evidence shows that the Bakoena ruling family held no monopoly on wealth, the assumption on which Kimble predicated her conjecture of their supposed monopoly of power. Rather, to the extent that centralized political authority was accepted by the BaSotho, it was not because of an overwhelming dominance of the Bakoena internally but because of the overriding threat of first Africans and later Europeans externally. My work therefore explicitly challenges Kimble's assumptions and conclusions concerning the pre-colonial period in BaSotho history. Kimble raised important questions about class-based conflicts of interest within BaSotho society, in contrast to Thompson and Sanders who gave little attention to the divergence of interests between ruler and ruled. On the other hand, the international politics of the time made the congruence of chiefly and popular interests depicted by both Thompson and Sanders more determinant than their conflicting interests. Kimble failed to explore the dynamics of internal relations in the context of the broader regional setting for the nineteenth century, when the BaSotho were still evidently supportive of their chiefs.

At issue in the explanation of economic and sociopolitical change in nineteenth-century Lesotho is decision-making by individuals and groups which enhanced long-term social, economic, and political security in ways which were sometimes and sometimes not economically rational in a western sense. Indeed, they were sometimes not obviously rational from a political perspective, for example, in the acceptance of sociopolitical subordination and even oppression as the price paid for personal or national security in a threatening political environment. The factors creating a climate of insecurity for the BaSotho changed, notably at two important junctures, the disruptions of the 1820s and the advent of colonial rule. However, there was significant continuity in the mindset of the BaSotho which was governed by the pursuit of security in an insecure setting, reflecting a deeper constant in their history.

Lacking the benefit of hindsight, the BaSotho did not gain a sense of security from external threats during the colonial period even though in the end the British preserved the colonial boundaries and prevented any further expropriation of BaSotho lands. More salient to the BaSotho perspective was not the end result, which they could not take for granted, but the fact that during the period of Cape Colony rule a plan was made to expropriate land, and the BaSotho continued into the twentieth century to believe it was an ongoing possibility since the British continued to entertain the idea of turning Basutoland over to South Africa for incorporation. Similarly, the slight presence of the British in terms of magistrates and politics appeared to constitute minimal colonial rule involving little intervention, much less any threat to BaSotho security. Once again the perspective of the BaSotho was colored not by the actual limits to the British presence, but rather by the explicit threat of force which the British issued regularly in order to ensure BaSotho compliance to colonial rule. More than once the British threatened to bring in colonial forces, and they did so during the Gun War, strengthening the credibility of later threats in the eyes of the BaSotho. At other times the British threatened to abandon the BaSotho to the Boers. These threats of the use of greater force were much more important in the shaping of a BaSotho sense of insecurity than the actual minimal presence of British rulers. The BaSotho were compelled to devote considerable attention and energy towards warding off British threats, insecure even though the British ultimately maintained the integrity of Basutoland's boundaries.

2

Settlement and trade patterns before 1830

The formation of the BaSotho nation under Moshoeshoe and the expansion of production and trade did not constitute a dramatic departure from the past. There were always tendencies to amalgamate and divide, and to trade and raid, causing the transfer of ideas and goods between separate sociopolitical groups, and these tendencies were merely amplified during the upheavals of the 1820s. Continuous communication and trade, however irregular or infrequent, had always allowed for the transfer of cultural patterns and the diffusion of innovations across the region of southern Africa. It is important to establish the extent and nature of early demographic and trade patterns in order to explain the apparent cultural continuity evident over a long period between SeTswana- and SeSotho-speaking peoples scattered over a wide geographic area. Evidence of such cultural continuities in turn indicate that the formation of the BaSotho nation of Moshoeshoe in the 1820s was not a revolutionary political development, but reflected long-standing practices of incorporation and amalgamation among SeTswana- and SeSotho-speaking peoples. In order to discredit the white settler mythology which portrayed Africans as incapable of peaceful political development and nation-building it is important to establish that processes of state formation in southern Africa pre-dated the turmoil of the 1820s, and were stimulated by both internal and external features of the economic and social organization of southern African peoples. Patterns of settlement and trade were shaped by environmental factors, such as regional ecological variations, and were reinforced through the manipulation of kinship through marriage.

The patterns of production and trade which characterized the BaSotho economy after the formation of the nation under Moshoeshoe in the 1820s reflected older forms of Sotho-Tswana patterns of production and exchange. Demographic upheaval generated new patterns of contact and new relationships of tribute and exchange in the 1820s, but the disruptions lasted only a dozen years and did not fundamentally alter patterns of sociopolitical organization. There was a radical difference in scale between chiefdoms of southern SeSotho-speaking peoples before the 1820s and the nation which later emerged under Moshoeshoe, but political chiefdoms on a larger scale existed among both SeTswana-speaking groups and northern SeSotho-speakers in the earlier period. Strong cultural similarities between SeSotho-speaking groups and SeTswana-speakers centuries after their dispersal and division, such as the observance of totems (emblems) and preference for cousin marriage, indicate a lack of isolation which would have been evident in independent divergent cultural developments. Apparently the cultural similarities arising from the mutual origins of SeSotho- and SeTswana-speaking peoples were reinforced by on-going interchanges that included trade relations, which in turn explains the continuity in regional social and political structures.[1]

Sometime before the fifteenth-century SeSotho-speaking peoples had separated from SeTswana-speaking groups and moved south into the Southern Highveld from a series of east–west ridges stretching from Kanye to east of modern Pretoria. Archaeological and historical evidence based on oral sources show agreement with regard to the origins and dissemination of the SeSotho-speaking peoples, and link the early Iron Age peoples of the Southern Highveld to the later inhabitants of Lesotho.[2] Like the SeTswana-speakers who lived in large, compact settlements of several thousand inhabitants, the BaFokeng and BaKoena settlements built by SeSotho-speaking groups in the fifteenth or sixteenth centuries were relatively large, containing approximately 100 units and over 1,000 people. A tendency towards larger social and political amalgamations was therefore already present among the SeSotho-speakers centuries before the emergence of Moshoeshoe's nation in the 1820s. The Pedi state also incorporated a large population of northern SeSotho-speakers over a large area in the eighteenth century.[3] However, as SeSotho-speaking groups moved south towards present-day Lesotho, they formed smaller settlements. This is because as they moved south into the area of the Caledon River and modern Lesotho they encountered terrain that offered the variations necessary for a mixed economy repeated within limited geographic areas and favoring small-scale clusters or people, so an ecological impetus for large sociopolitical organization was absent.[4] Under the new conditions seasonal transhumance involving the entire society, as practiced by SeTswana-speaking groups, was no longer necessary. Instead small-scale sociopolitical organization based on residence in small scattered villages reduced travel times to and from fields and pastures. Architectural differences arose between the two groups because of differences in climate and availability of building materials. Cultural differences between Sotho and Tswana groups reflect environmental factors rather than isolated historical development, and communications and trade contacts continued, although on a limited scale.

The dissemination of metal goods demonstrates that the Iron Age societies were linked by a loose but extensive trading network. Evidence of regional trade before the 1820s is sparse. What evidence there is suggests a relay pattern in which articles of trade were passed from group to group, rather than being carried long distance by traders from their points of origin. Early travellers to the area were led to believe that most groups traded with their immediate neighbors, but knew little or nothing about groups further away whose territory did not border on their own. Burchell, who visited the area in 1812–14, wrote that

> It seems to be a common maxim with all the nations of the Interior, to oppose the wishes of any strangers desirous of visiting the tribes beyond; always giving as a reason for doing so, that it is dangerous to travel among people so cruel as they represent them to be; but their real motive is, the desire that no tribe but themselves shall reap the advantage to be derived from trading with strangers.[5]

The distribution of iron and copper goods formed the primary impetus for regional trade. Unfortunately, Iron Age chronology in the region is still tentative because the archaeological data is inadequate and the historical evidence relating to iron-working and trade refers only to the more recent period. From oral tradition, it has been estimated that the BaRolong branch of the BaTswana had mined and smelted iron since the thirteenth century.[6] They may have been major suppliers of iron goods to the whole region from very early times. The earliest evidence from Europeans confirms that in the seventeenth century some BaTswana were trading (selling) iron goods, although they may not have made these themselves.[7] This is an important indicator that the transfer of technology and trade in iron goods was ongoing in the region, which in turn suggests that other goods were traded, if on an irregular basis.

The BaTswana were certainly trading in many goods by the eighteenth century. By 1778 the BaTlhaping were making annual trips to trade with the Khoi on the Orange, bringing copper ornaments, copper and iron beads, knives, assegais, axes, and awls, as well as tanned skins, tobacco, ivory spoons, and glass beads. In exchange they received cattle.[8] As the BaTlhaping did not work iron themselves at that point, they must have imported it from elsewhere. A member of the first European expedition to visit the BaTlhaping in 1801 reported that the copper rings worn by the chief came from the BaRolong.[9] Other travellers indicated that the BaTlhaping received their copper rings and beads from the Damara in the west and from the BaNgwaketsi to the northeast.[10] By 1812 the BaTlhaping were learning to work iron themselves.[11]

Iron-working may have disseminated to the southern SeSotho-speaking groups in the Caledon Valley and the area of Lesotho either from the BaRolong (BaTswana), or from the AmaHlubi and MaZizi (Nguni) in the Tugela River region across the Drakensberg mountains. According to oral traditions, the BaTlokoa and BaFokeng traded hoes to the BaKoena and other SeSotho-speakers in exchange for cattle, but the origin of these hoes is uncertain. The AmaHlubi and MaZizi were also said to have crossed the mountains to trade with the BaKoena as early as the seventeenth century, bringing knives, spatulas, and hoes to exchange for animal skins, cattle, and tobacco.[12] Copper goods may also have percolated down into the region of Lesotho from the northeast. Oral traditions about the copper miners of Musina (Messina) state that the BaPedi and "all the tribes of the Sotho" came to trade for copper at Musina.[13]

The circulation of beads as currency is another indication of the level of trade in the region. Beads were useful as a circulating medium because they were fungible, could not be easily obtained, and could be given different values according to their sizes and colors. Thus, like gold and silver, cowries, cloth, salt, and metal rods elsewhere in Africa, beads facilitated the relay trade system in which groups who traded directly with one another but did not need each other's trade goods accepted compensation in beads that could be used elsewhere to obtain the goods they did need.

Beads functioned as a circulating currency in the interior of Southern Africa, and as early as 1731 it was evident that different types of beads had different exchange values. The earliest beads in demand were red, while later white and then blue and yellow beads had greater value.[14] This was evident to Burchell on his journey to the BaTlhaping in 1812. He carried mostly small black, white, and blue porcelain beads for trade because he was told they were the most in demand, and also had some red beads, which proved to be "less acceptable."[15] The Griqua of Griquatown traded beads and tobacco to the BaTlhaping for cattle, and from them Burchell learned the "usual relative value" of the various beads, so he would know how to bargain.[16] He noted about the BaTlhaping that "In begging for any trifling gift or remuneration, they never asked for *sekhaka* (beads); these being considered more especially as *money*, to be employed only as the medium of trade with distant tribes, and for the purchase of the more expensive articles . . ."[17]

In the region of Lesotho itself beads were known but relatively rare when the first missionaries, Casalis and Arbousset, arrived in 1833. Casalis wrote that beads were still *almost* unknown when they arrived, although a traveller in 1840 noted that many of the Basotho wore "strings of small beads around their heads, necks, arms, and legs."[18] It is possible that the paucity of beads observed by the early missionaries reflected the recent impoverishment of the people, and that beads had previously been in wide circulation. In fact, another traveller reported in 1834 that "*beads* will be found in estimation with the Bashootoo . . . but they will not readily pass at the Missionary stations and among the Bastards, etc. unless they be of a superior quality."[19] The sophisticated understanding on the part of the BaSotho of the relative (exchange) value of beads of different colors certainly implies regular exposure to and use of beads over a longer period. According to oral tradition, beads were introduced into Lesotho during the time of Mohlomi, chief of the BaMonaheng (BaSotho), who died an old man in 1814, and was renowned for his travels to distant places.[20] The early beads were therefore called "beads of Mohlomi." Other traditions report that the beads came from the MaZizi during the reign of Shaka's father, Senzangakona, which would have been at about the same time. The early beads were blue, white, and red, and were used as ornamentation by the wealthy.[21]

The oral evidence about beads in Lesotho accords well with other historical and archeological data. The earliest beads found in Southern Highveld sites were blue, green, and black, and were made sometime before the eighteenth century. They were rare in the Southern Highveld and apparently did not disseminate as far as Lesotho. This indicates that the inhabitants of Lesotho were not yet trading in beads before the eighteenth century. However, white beads and dark blue beads from the late eighteenth century and the nineteenth century similar to those used by Burchell were found in early nineteenth-century Southern Highveld sites, and were present in Lesotho. The white and blue beads described by a MoSotho writer in 1910 may have been of more recent origin, but he also reported the use of red beads, which indicated trade in an earlier period. Plain opaque red beads were used in the region in the eighteenth century, but were not manufactured after the eighteenth century and apparently were no longer in circulation in the nineteenth century. This suggests that the red beads reported in Lesotho were of eighteenth century origin, which corresponds with the date of introduction suggested by the oral evidence cited above. Furthermore, as beads were made in a wide variety of other colors in the late nineteenth century and early twentieth centuries, the failure of Sechefo to mention beads of other colors of recent import suggests that his information reflected an earlier period.[22]

Clearly the predecessors of the BaSotho living in the region of Lesotho before the 1820s were at least marginally involved in the trade networks of the larger region, and were not entirely isolated from their neighbors. The diffusion of iron and copper goods and the diffusion of iron-working technology, the presence of imported beads throughout the area, and the dissemination of new crops such as maize and tobacco, suggest on-going contacts of separate chiefdoms with their immediate neighbors, which allowed for the diffusion of culture and innovation. It is difficult to ascertain the extent of these contacts, and the degree to which they were continuous over time. The BaSotho retained historical traditions of their ancestry not only from the Ntsuanatsatsi area, but also from the hilly country further north which was the earlier focus of Sotho-Tswana dispersion. By the time the missionaries arrived in the 1830s, the BaSotho had regular contacts with their neighbors to the north and northeast, although these may have come about as a result of demographic changes in the 1820s. On the other hand, cultural similarities which persisted through the centuries are evidence of continuous links and trade relations between Sotho-Tswana groups in the region.

Early Sotho-Tswana and Nguni peoples were motivated to trade because of the uneven geographical distribution of certain natural resources, primarily iron. There is little variability in the topography, climate, and vegetation of most of the inhabited regions of southern Africa, and agricultural and household production consequently show strong uniformity throughout the region. This may partially explain why there was no stimulus to the development of periodic markets as elsewhere on the continent, where neighboring groups in different ecological zones traded a variety of different products on a regular basis.

At least by 1833 the BaSotho were maintaining a network of communications and trade with their African neighbors, which can be confirmed from written European sources. Because this was after the 1820s, there is some ambiguity as to the extent to which old relations were being reaffirmed or new relations were being established, but clearly a network of communications had previously existed. Describing routes of communication leading from Lesotho, a missionary wrote that

> There exist two points at which the Bassouthos have free communications with the other tribes. In the southeast, one opening in the Malutis [Drakensberg mountains] allows them frequent communications with the Matabele and the Bakhoni [Zulu and other Nguni] ... the second point of communications is to the northeast. There the Bassoutho communicate with the Zulus of Panda (in the north of the colony of Natal) and with another nation of considerable size, also Bassoutho properly speaking, who are sometimes called the northern Bassoutho, sometimes the Basseli, sometimes the Maaoa [BaPedi].[23]

In fact Moshoeshoe exchanged ambassadors with his African neighbors, and he defended the practice, stating that "... people come to me from nearly all the Tribes living in South Africa, and that is one way of communicating with one another."[24]

On a trip to the north of Lesotho in 1836 two French missionaries, Arbousset and Daumas, encountered many neighboring peoples, and from them learned of local contacts with other groups in the region.[25] The BaSotho were in contact with the AmaSwazi, at that time known as the BaRaputsa, under Sobhuza I, who ruled from 1816 to 1836. The BaRaputsa traded with the "Makasana", another Nguni group, who produced iron hoes and copper earrings, collars, and bracelets. This may have been one source for the copper ornaments already in Lesotho before the arrival of the first missionaries.[26]

The BaSotho also had strong links with the BaPedi, or northern Sotho. In 1844 some travelling Swazi told the missionaries at Morija that several chiefs of the northern Sotho called themselves subjects of Moshoeshoe. At about the same time, a group of BaPedi arrived at Morija "to arrange certain matters regarding peace and commerce with the subjects" of Moshoeshoe.[27] Any earlier contact between the BaPedi and the southern Sotho groups was almost certainly disrupted when the AmaNdebele broke up the BaPedi kingdom about 1823, sending the BaPedi chief Sekwati fleeing north with survivors to the Soutpansberg. The new alliance between Sekwati and Moshoeshoe was presumably established after Sekwati returned home in about 1829, when he was in the process of consolidating the remnants of the northern Sotho into a new kingdom.[28] As late as 1868, a British official

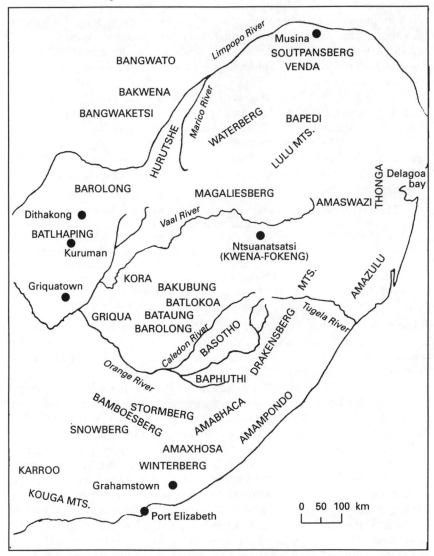

Fig. 3 The distribution of peoples in Southern Africa, *c.* 1830

reported that the BaPedi worked for Moshoeshoe when they passed through Lesotho on their way to work in the Cape Colony and Orange Free State. They also gave Moshoeshoe the "chief's portion" of their salary when they passed through the country on their return home.[29]

Contacts between the BaSotho and BaPedi were important, because the BaPedi were in contact with the various SeTswana-speaking groups, and with Thonga traders who brought copper, beads, and cloth from Delagoa

Bay to people in the interior. The BaPedi received beads indirectly from the Portuguese via trade with their neighbors.[30] The presence of these beads throughout the region indicates ongoing trade contacts which dated back to the eighteenth century. The BaPedi may also have traded in iron implements, for they had a widespread reputation for forging pickaxes which were "twice as heavy as those of the other bechuana and the caffer tribes we have known, and twice as good," from iron which was plentiful.[31] Their familiarity was apparently limited to contiguous groups, which indicates that trade occurred in relays rather than over long-distance networks, but they facilitated the dispersion of goods south to the BaSotho.

The BaSotho also traded with groups to the northwest of Lesotho before the arrival of the missionaries in 1833, but these contacts may have been of more recent origin. In 1829 European travellers encountered BaSotho trading with the BaHurutshe far to the northwest.[32] Among the remnants of the BaTlhaping which remained at Kuruman after 1835 were some BaSotho among the various BaTswana groups, although it is not clear when or how they had come to be there.[33] Moshoeshoe also traded with the "Makoata," who lived beyond Mekuatling, at least since 1826, when he began sending skins and the feathers of rare birds acquired from the Makoata to Shaka.[34] Closer at hand, Moshoeshoe maintained relations and had a marriage alliance with villages of remnant "Lighoyas," or Hoja, the BaKubung branch of the BaRolong, most of whom had been absorbed under the BaTaung.[35] Members of the BaSotho party travelling north with the missionaries Arbousset and Daumas in 1836 gave salt and tobacco to these BaKubung in exchange for iron implements and copper bracelets.[36]

Southern Sotho trade links with Nguni-speaking groups across the Drakensberg had existed for several centuries, involving the import of iron goods, cloth, and perhaps beads.[37] During the 1820s Moshoeshoe also established a new trade relationship with Shaka. This has been characterized as a tributary relationship with the Zulu state, but Moshoeshoe received compensation in kind for the goods he sent. By entering into the trade arrangement, Moshoeshoe acquired for his people something akin to "most favored nation" status with Shaka, merging economic and political motives as do modern nations. Explaining this alliance, which he still honored in 1861, Moshoeshoe himself wrote that "I was still very young when Chaka did choose me as his servant to procure him Ostrich feathers, skins, and other ornaments used among the Zulu, and so I did since that time, and as a compensation the Chief of the Zulu is wont to send me cattle."[38]

Moshoeshoe's son Nehemiah described the establishment of the agreement (which according to Ellenberger's calculations occurred in early 1826) in more detail. The passage is revealing with regard to the prevailing regional relations at the time:

> Moshoeshoe had already heard that the Mankoane and the Mahlubi feared Chaka. He heard Chaka did not need cattle for tribute, he wanted feathers of the ostrich and the blue [Stanley] crane and the skins of wild cats. He ordered

25

Moshoeshoe to trap cranes for him and he would give cattle for the feathers. The Makaota who were living [by means of] animals were ordered [to provide] ostrich feathers. They brought them to Thaba Bosiu where they were bartered. They killed the wild cats as they were also ordered. All these things Chief Moshoeshoe sent to Chaka; he said he wanted Chaka to take him under his wing. He sent his man named Khoho, who was sent to pay tribute. Khoho was well received by Chaka. Chaka said to Khoho: if Moshoeshoe continues to do thus there will be no one who can kill Moshoeshoe, because Chaka himself was the chief of all the chiefs on earth ... Khoho was given fifty head of cattle.[39]

Exchange in these goods was carried on in an unofficial capacity as well. A MoSotho refugee from Mzilikazi who had fled into Dingane's (Zulu) territory used his contacts with his compatriots in Lesotho to procure ostrich feathers, wings of cranes, and leopard skins to sell to the Zulu for use as military ornaments, but his village was later destroyed by Dingane after he traded with the AmaSwazi enemies of the AmaZulu.[40]

The formal relationship between Moshoeshoe and the Zulu state continued after the death of Shaka. When Moshoeshoe's ambassador, Khoho, found Shaka murdered, he "... quickly returned with sixty head of cattle which came for Moshoeshoe. Then Dingane said liked his MoSotho a lot."[41] In 1835 Casalis wrote that the subjects of Dingane "circulate peacefully in the country of Moschesch, where they come to exchange tobacco, iron hoes, and assegaies for the skins of panthers [leopards] and otters, ostrich eggs, and sheep and goats."[42]

The BaSotho also received cattle and copper collars and bracelets from the AmaZulu.[43] The trade was bolstered by the formal tribute relation, but the two were not synonymous. In 1871 Chief Molapo received threats from Cetshwayo and feared the AmaZulu would invade because the news of Moshoeshoe's death had not been properly reported to Mpande, the Zulu king, and because an offering of tribute had not been sent when Letsie succeeded to the Paramount Chieftancy. As the Lieutenant Governor of Natal explained to the High Commissioner, Moshoeshoe "was always considered a Zulu vassal by the Zulu kings, and in all his communications with them he acknowledges this position. In former times he paid irregular tribute ..."[44]

Moshoeshoe's relations with his Griqua and Kora neighbors to the West were not so peaceful. The depredations of the Griqua and Kora against the BaSotho started with raiding in the mid-1820s, and they continued even after the arrival of the missionaries in 1833. The Griqua and Kora attacked the BaSotho to raid their herds. In addition they formed "commandos" against the "Bashutas" to murder the men and women and take the children, who were sold as slaves to farmers.[45] In counter-attacks, the BaSotho retrieved their herds and acquired their first guns, as well as horses. The BaSotho immediately recognized that they were at a disadvantage without guns and horses, and they sought to remedy this through trade as well as raiding. Moshoeshoe purchased three guns for the extraordinarily high price of fifty oxen each from a Griqua who came to Thaba Bosiu.[46]

After the BaRolong moved into the area around Thaba 'Nchu in 1833–34, they also established trade relations with the BaSotho. They prepared and sewed furs which they exchanged for the cattle and grain of the BaSotho. By the mid-1830s, BaSotho trade with their neighbors was flourishing. After the BaSotho harvested a good crop in 1836 Arbousset wrote: "here are the neighboring tribes who come to get provisions for themselves among [the BaSotho]."[47] In 1838 he reported that BaRolong, BaTlhaping, and Griqua came daily to buy sorghum with cattle.[48]

The BaSotho were ready to take advantage of trade contacts with their neighbors as soon as peace was re-established in the region. The BaSotho reacted to the destruction and deprivation of the 1820s by striving to ensure that they would never again be subject to such hardship and deprivation. They built a nation militarily capable of defending itself against neighboring Africans, and they immediately applied themselves to the production of huge grain surpluses. Part of the surplus grain was stored for use in times of scarcity, and the rest was used to buy livestock. No longer concentrated into large defensive settlements, the people of the new BaSotho nation of Moshoeshoe, speaking SeSotho, SeTswana, IsiZulu, and IsiXhosa, were ready to reoccupy the lands from which they originally hailed to expand both arable and pastoral production. The people who owed their allegiance to Moshoeshoe had come from far and wide, and it only remained for Moshoeshoe to establish his authority over the lands of his new followers.

3

Political consolidation and the rise of Moshoeshoe in the 1820s

Kinship identification and non-kin incorporation were the building blocks of power and wealth among the early SeSotho- and SeTswana-speaking peoples. Kinship was an ideology which promoted a sense of mutual interest in a community and served to mask a reality of differentiation and conflicting interests in the distribution of wealth and power. Lines of descent were important bases for self-identification, but they were not the operative factor in the contest over the distribution of resources. The natural environment created a natural competition over the most favorable settlement sites even in the context of low population densities relative to overall land resources. The advantages of certain sites – water, fertile soil, iron, gold, natural physical defenses – stimulated competition for control over favorable sites, and served to attract followers to those who held them. Those who settled in advantageous areas were subsequently able to compound their advantage, since the accumulation of people under their control increased their ability to protect the site militarily and to exploit its resources with human labor, generating wealth which they could expropriate and manipulate. Inequality and dominance were therefore present from the time of permanent settlement. The local balance of power could only shift with a shift in the factors which initially conferred dominance: increased population, new sources of wealth (for example from trade), or changes in military strategy or technology. Chiefs and leaders used various strategies to acquire followers and increase their polity's strength in numbers, and they manipulated production and trade to obtain access to strategic goods such as iron tools and weapons, and to increase their wealth with which to attract new followers. The retention in the oral traditions of the BaSotho of information about migration to favorable riverine settlement sites, and about the dissemination of iron-working technology and iron goods, is evidence that the BaSotho of the nineteenth century implicitly recognized the importance of these factors in motivating their SeTswana- and SeSotho-speaking ancestors.

The balance of power between competing groups with similar military technologies rested on population size, making the accumulation of people a driving imperative in pre-colonial southern African societies. Most modern scholars have seen oral traditions as reflecting a process of division because the early separations of subordinate branches of a chiefdom under competing sons of the ancestral chief are recorded. However, equally evident and yet unacknowledged by modern scholars are the processes of amalgamation which are so evident in the oral traditions of the BaSotho. They contain countless accounts of SeTswana- and SeSotho-speaking groups with various kinship affiliations settling together and co-mingling and eventually merging under a single name associated with a chief's name or the *seboko* of the chief.

There were environmental factors at work creating incentives for amalgamation. If competition was initially fostered by inequality in land resources, where land resources were relatively homogeneous the population naturally dispersed, whereas where land resources differed dramatically the population congregated around desirable sites. The divergent settlement patterns in southern Africa in the past confirm this pattern. Homesteads in the fertile and better-watered areas to the east of the Drakensberg mountains and along the southern coast were small and scattered, towns of the SeTswana-speakers in the dry areas of the west had populations of up to 15,000 people, and villages of SeSotho-speakers in the intervening region of the Caledon River Valley were of moderate size, averaging perhaps 200 people. Critical resources such as water in the dry areas to the west gave those who controlled springs a basis for domination and others an incentive to submit themselves to domination for the privilege of gaining access to the water. Early settlers on the highveld chose settlement sites based on the availability of iron and copper, and in the 1820s settlement sites on mountains were chosen because of their defensibility. Initial inequalities in wealth and power tended to be perpetuated, however, even as resources were shared among those who joined the original settlers. The most powerful, who retained control over the better-watered land, produced surplus grain more readily. They allocated available lands which were further from the sources of water to the newcomers, hindering their ability to accumulate surpluses. Pasture privileges would similarly be allocated unevenly. Newcomers had to offer tribute either once or on an ongoing basis, further reinforcing socio-economic inequalities.

Whoever controlled the most fertile land and best pastures could translate wealth in food into social strength, since grain was commonly exchanged for livestock and livestock was the primary means of obtaining wives. In BaSotho oral traditions the original settlers at any given site seem generally to have retained their political and economic advantages, using marriage and clientship to absorb newcomers who scattered and were absorbed across the region. The newcomers nevertheless also had the opportunity to build their wealth over time through their labor in the fields, and through the loaning of their labor to others for a return in kind. The original identity of incorporated groups continued to be acknowledged socially but in politics their kinship identification became invisible, submerged beneath the identity of the dominant group.

With the accumulation of people a primary sociopolitical goal, it was economically and militarily rational for chiefs to ensure the basic welfare of anyone who chose voluntarily to join them, thereby also ensuring their loyalty, but there was a countervailing tendency to perpetuate dominance rooted in socioeconomic inequality. The early oral traditions of the BaSotho suggest just such an historical pattern. For example, when small parties of BaFokeng joined the Maphetla and Mapolane already residing near Thaba Tsoeu in the southern part of modern Lesotho, about 1730 or 1740, "these Bafokeng were nicknamed Maja-poli ("eaters of goat") because they were too poor to eat beef."[1] These newcomers clearly remained distinct from the wealthier prior settlers on account of their poverty. This is a pattern repeated throughout world history, as rich people tend to wield power by virtue of their wealth, and do not often need to migrate, whereas the poor and less powerful tend to migrate to seek greater opportunities for themselves. Where all good land is already under the control of others they have the option of trying to impose their own control by force, or of submitting to the resident authority in order to gain access to the land. By definition the poorer migrants are not likely to be able to overcome a settled group unless they have exclusive access to superior weaponry, and the option of incorporation on subordinate terms was more common among Africans in pre-colonial southern Africa.

Leaders emerged because they facilitated the process of ensuring group dominance, from which insiders benefitted to a greater or lesser degree relative to outsiders or newcomers. These leaders accumulated more followers through various strategies. Lines of descent provide a natural basis for ties based on blood and the presumption of kin-based loyalty, and they were indeed an important basis for identification among SeSotho- and SeTswana-speaking peoples. Mutual identification based on a common line of descent did not automatically imply or confer real power relationships within that line of descent, however, in spite of an ideology which asserted them. Descent groups were based on lines of descent traced back through the male line to a given ancestor in the past. The relevance of such descent groups to contemporary politics was conditional and variable rather than fixed, however. Whereas the ideology of the power structure used kinship terms to define an ideal allocation of power based on generation, age, and gender, in practice positions of leadership were conferred on the basis of personal ability to command allegiance because of either leadership qualities or patronage ties, rather than on the basis of rules of inheritance. Time and again the oral traditions of the related SeSotho- and SeTswana-speaking peoples tell of younger brothers assuming dominance over elder ones, and of junior lines of descent assuming dominance over senior lines. For example, although the descendants of the senior son of Monaheng (Ntsane) were always given precedence in circumcision and other feasts to mark his genealogical seniority, Ntsane did not succeed his father in the chieftainship.[2] When the chief of the BaTsueneng died, the people chose his younger son

Khiba over his elder son to become chief because of the younger son's "reputation for wisdom and courage."[3] Similar shifts of power took place among Moshoeshoe's ancestors whose great-uncle Thamae gained dominant influence over his elder brother, Moshoeshoe's grandfather Peete. Later Peete's children Libe and Mokhachane regained their father's lost power from their uncle Thamae, only to see leadership eventually fall to the younger brother, Mokhachane, who was Moshoeshoe's father. The ideology of kinship and seniority in descent provided an explanation and justification for inequality and domination, but on the ground power politics played themselves out differently each time an heir succeeded, and each time one group was incorporated into another.

The SeSotho- and SeTswana-speaking people recognized descent through the male line, and there is no record of there ever having been a matrilineal reckoning of descent. The patrilineal reckoning of descent was advantageous because it permitted groups to incorporate people easily and quickly. In matrilineal descent groups, in which inheritance passes between men according to the mother's descent line, the descent group can grow only at the rate of the natural reproductive rate of women born into the descent group. In a patrilineal descent group women are obtained from the outside, so there is theoretically no limit to biological reproduction. On the other hand, it is only possible to take advantage of this feature of patrilineality if polygamy is practiced, for if men can marry only one wife then the number of women who can be acquired to reproduce the descent line will still be limited, this time by the number of men born into the descent group. Polygamy thus went hand in hand with patrilineality as instruments to speed the growth of descent groups.

Settlement patterns only partly overlapped with descent groups, but it was on the basis of settlement that leaders built and wielded power. In practice leaders made considerable use of ties based on common descent as they consolidated their power. The breadth or depth of the descent group identified for such purposes varied according to the strategy appropriate to the specific needs of the leader, however. It was sometimes useful to call upon the members of a limited line of descent in which membership was obvious, because it spanned only two or three generations. Such "lineages" tended to have limited decision-making powers and were subject to external power factors even in such matters as the allocation of land, but they were important in that people readily identified themselves with such limited descent groups.

Identifications based on descent became blurred over time, however. The original settlers on a site were known by their line of descent, and where two branches of a descent group remained in the same area, the senior line of descent was identifiable according to the seniority of the ancestors to whom descent was traced. But such seniority became irrelevant when the junior descent line moved away, or if the junior descent line in fact took power, which happened when the designated heir was particularly incompetent or

31

when the head of the junior descent line was particularly ambitious and popular. The original relationship of the two lines was remembered, but became irrelevant to the allocation of power. Junior descent lines often moved away and members of other descent lines often joined a settlement, so that "lineages" became less important than broader descent groups, based on tracing descent to a more distant ancestor, in claiming identification. Even as various "lineages" broke away from each other, they retained their identification with their original ancestor and the emblem or totem, *seboko* (pl. *liboko*), associated with that descent line. Although this broader descent group is normally designated by modern scholars as a clan, among the early SeTswana- and SeSotho-speaking peoples the term clan is inappropriate insofar as it connotes a corporate group with delegated responsibilities and powers in a real setting. In the eighteenth and nineteenth centuries, identification with group membership based on the totem and ancestry of the group remained significant socially but not politically. Since *liboko* were based on recognized genealogies, the status conferred upon each was based on the original relationship between the ancestors founding the *liboko*. This relative status was honored ritually in circumcision practices, and it in turn conferred ritual authority to senior lines and, by transference, members of senior *liboko*. As people from different lines of descent and different *liboko* travelled around and settled in mixed groups over time, leaders exercising power in the context of settlement groups could play upon *seboko* loyalties and relationships as well as "lineage" loyalties and relationships in constructing and reinforcing a power base. Such loyalties could not be taken for granted, however, and ancestral status recognized in ritual carried prestige but no guarantee of social or political status.

If lines of descent could not provide guaranteed loyalties, obedience, and authority, then ideological authority had to be bolstered in other ways. Leaders and dominant groups continually manipulated their wealth to increase their following and ensure their power. Outsiders could join a chiefdom voluntarily, offering loyalty, service in the military, and tribute in labor and in kind, but they were induced to do so only when incorporation into the chiefdom offered clear benefits. These might include access to better land than could be had elsewhere, access to the means for increasing their wealth, such as loan cattle, or even access to protection from outsiders. The incorporation of outsiders was cemented through intermarriage, ensuring bonds of family loyalty in the next generation. Because of the blending of descent groups in the context of mixed settlement over time, the actual identification of descent groups became blurred. Unless outsiders had enough strength to conquer the original settlers of an area, they had to join the chiefdom on terms of subordination and with lesser access to the natural advantages of the area. As the dominant group the original settlers tended to have greater wealth and the means to acquire more women, so that their descent group overshadowed any incoming descent groups who continued to identify themselves separately. In other words, a chiefdom became identified with its dominant descent group in spite of its heterogeneous origins and even when the population of the dominant descent group constituted a minority. The consolidation of chiefdoms in the late eighteenth and early nineteenth century led to the identification of these chiefdoms in terms of *liboko*, in spite of the fact that they comprised people of diverse origins and were based on the manipulation of many factors besides kinship in the consolidation of power. The boundaries of groups incorporated politically into chiefdoms were amorphous and continually changing in terms of popular composition. Processes of disintegration and amalgamation were speeded in the first three decades of the nineteenth century, during which time chiefdoms became closely identified with individual leaders and bore little resemblance to the descent group names by which they might be known. The tremendous confusion in identifying a group of people incorporated under a single leader is evident in the work of scholars such as Legassick and Lye, who have struggled to trace the processes of fission and fusion among SeTswana- and SeSotho-speaking peoples in the eighteenth and early nineteenth centuries. Legassick appropriately adopts the term "confederation" to refer to unified groups which, although known by their *liboko*, a totem or symbol associated with a line of descent, in fact constituted amalgamations of SeTswana-speakers from various *liboko* and sometimes even outsiders such as Kora, under the leadership of a single chief.[4]

Through these processes a balance of power was maintained between rulers and their followers. In the early nineteenth century chiefs acquired and increased their power by using their wealth to accumulate followers. They accomplished this directly through the payment of bridewealth to acquire wives whose progeny would bring natural population growth. They also accumulated followers indirectly by offering newcomers land which bound them through obligations of tribute and service, and by offering them loan cattle which bound them through ongoing patron–client obligations. However, chiefs were constrained in their exercise of power by the moral suasion and influence of their councillors who mediated on behalf of popular opinion, and by the people themselves who could emigrate away from an oppressive chief. For people who moved into the fertile Caledon valley and surrounding lands, the option of emigrating away from oppressive chiefs was readily exercised because water resources were fairly well distributed and the fertility of the land was relatively equal over wide areas. This encouraged population dispersal, as the incentives to submit to domination were small and the rewards of seeking sociopolitical independence potentially great. To the west, in contrast, where water was scarce, SeTswana-speaking chiefs built large followings settled in towns of 10,000 people or more. The opportunity for large-scale political consolidation further east among the related SeSotho-speaking peoples came only when the relative balance of power was disrupted, giving one group the means and opportunity to dominate and others the incentive to submit. Once the balance was tipped, an ambitious chief could consolidate his power and build a nation using traditional strategies for accumulating people.

In the 1820s Moshoeshoe expanded his chiefdom by taking advantage of growing disparities in wealth, and by implementing traditional political practices of SeTswana- and SeSotho-speaking peoples. Throughout the early part of the nineteenth century, low population density in southern Africa meant that productivity was limited more by human and animal resources than by land. The socioeconomic basis of political power therefore rested on the control of labor and the ownership of livestock as well as land. When a European traveller described what he called the "state of society" of the BaTlhaping in 1814, he described the socioeconomic basis of power which was evident among the BaSotho two decades later:

> ... from the possession of property, the distinction of men into richer or poorer classes has followed as the natural consequence. Those who have riches, have also, it seems, power ... According to this scheme of society, the chief will always be the richest man; for once arrived at supreme authority, he holds within his own hands the power of obtaining property.[5]

Chiefs acquired some wealth through fines or confiscation, which were the usual forms of punishment, but a more effective means for a chief to rapidly increase his herds was to plunder the cattle of adjoining peoples. After cattle had been captured in battle, they were distributed to subordinates. At the heart of BaSotho unification was a patronage system, *mafisa*, in which a rich cattle-owner loaned one or more head of cattle to a poor man without any of his own. Each man who took cattle into his keeping became responsible for the care and well-being of the animals, and received in exchange the right to the milk produced and to some of the offspring. Moshoeshoe was not the first to use the *mafisa* system to attract followers. The system was traditional among the BaTswana, and groups such as the BamaNgwato used *mafisa* to build large BaTswana chiefdoms in the nineteenth century.[6] For the chief or wealthy cattle-owner the system provided numerous advantages. His herds were cared for with labor provided by his clients. His risks were diversified because his livestock were spread over a wide geographic area; if a portion of the country was affected by drought or an epizootic, only part of his herd would be adversely affected. Finally, the interests of the men to whom he loaned cattle were bound to his own interests; they became his political and military allies.

The *mafisa* system offered advantages to the poor man as well. He enjoyed all the advantages of having cattle except power or influence: he fed his family with the milk, he plowed his fields with the oxen, and he used the animals for transport. Furthermore, once the cattle were under a man's care, they could not be taken back from him except for "grave reasons."[7] He was given a portion of the natural increase to keep as his own, with which he built his own herd. The loan of the cattle was seen as a loan made in generosity. The BaSotho did not perceive the *mafisa* system as exploitative; instead they saw it as a successful welfare system which eliminated extreme poverty. Socioeconomic inequalities remained, but in fact wealth was redistributed in a permanent way, since a destitute person could acquire his own livestock through *mafisa* arrangements.

Elderly informants interviewed in Lesotho in 1981–82 defended the socioeconomic system of the past despite the inequalities in wealth that it engendered, because it also provided for the poor and protected the indigent from destitution.[8] Because Moshoeshoe used the *mafisa* system to provide for his people, he is remembered as a generous chief; his generosity is recounted even today by old people in Lesotho. Comparing Moshoeshoe to his uncle, Libe, one of my informants related that: "[Libe] was not generous; he did not have the goodness which attracted the nation to lay down for him; it was for this that others said they loved Moshoeshoe because he felt sympathy, and others said he knew the customs. Others said they loved him because they loved animals."[9]

Usually the people who lost a battle were deprived of their cattle by the victorious chief. Moshoeshoe's son Nehemiah Sekhonyana indicated that his father was motivated by a generosity which was *not* customary when he returned captured cattle to the original owners instead of keeping them for himself, thereby bringing more people under his authority.[10] Casalis explained that the chiefs used their wealth to support their people:

> From the products of their herds they must feed the poor, procure weapons for war, and elicit and secure alliances which it is necessary for them to contract with neighboring nations. The idea of a tax has not yet come to them. All of their ability is directed towards maintaining and augmenting, if possible, the resources which they already possess.[11]

Because wealth reinforced power, it was necessary for chiefs to limit the wealth of others so as to maintain an effective monopoly on wealth and power. In 1837 Casalis claimed that "The power of the chief is absolute. With the exception of some individuals who have succeeded in conserving their cattle in the last wars, the people depend entirely on Moshesh and his sons for the means of subsistence."[12]

Casalis pointed out the subtle way in which the *mafisa* system was at once generous and self-serving; it increased the chiefs' influence without diminishing their wealth:

> Such is at bottom the great social bond of these peoples. The sovereigns instead of being maintained by the community are their principle purveyors. In certain cases ... the subjects receive part of the booty [from raids]. The chiefs, after having first taken their share, distribute the remainder. These acts of largesse are rare. Wealth, in being displaced, would compromise too much the stability of power.[13]

Another missionary, E. S. Rolland, writing "Notes on the Political and Social Position of the Basuto Tribe," viewed the place of generosity within the system more cynically: "The great secret of his power consists in his wealth, the possession of which enables him to confer favours upon his immediate followers, and thus the hope of favours to come will induce them to do his bidding."[14]

Certainly wealth reinforced power, but this missionary's assessment dates from almost fifty years after Moshoeshoe incorporated his followers into a nation, and does not explain the dynamics of his original achievement of wealth and power. Moshoeshoe's early influence came from his abilities in raiding cattle; from these early cattle raids his people acquired wealth. Subsequently Moshoeshoe preserved his wealth in cattle at a time when the herds of surrounding peoples were being decimated or destroyed by Nguni invaders. With these herds Moshoeshoe attracted and retained followers.

Women also took advantage of the protection offered them by Moshoeshoe. Women were extremely vulnerable in times of conflict, and frequently found themselves captured and abducted by force.[15] In normal times all women would be subject to control by their male kin, but would enjoy the benefits of their protection. During the 1820s many women found themselves victimized when their male kin were unable or unwilling to protect them. One informant described the life story of his paternal grandmother, who placed herself under Moshoeshoe's protection when she found herself alone. He explained:

> I should be right about this information, my father's mother was not married. Indeed I am right. She was a Matabele [of Nguni origins] who was captured in the wars with Chief Moshoeshoe in Natal there at Tjopu. So she was not yet married, then she gave birth to my father and other children not being married. You understand, the man who fathered the child did not marry her although the child was his. She came here with her children and migrated into Lesotho; being a stray person of Moshoeshoe, she was a person of Moshoeshoe, a child of Moshoeshoe, and she always went to be examined at Moshoeshoe's and then later by Letsie, and then by Lerotholi.[16]

This MoSotho woman's story is interesting not only because it suggests a degree of independence and autonomy from male kin when she first placed herself under Moshoeshoe, but also a continuing autonomy throughout her life. According to her grandson she voluntarily left the man with whom she lived (who was not the father of her children), and she apparently never did marry. This level of independence from the control of male kin was the result of her separation from her kin by birth, and of her refusal to submit to male control in marriage. Instead she gave direct allegiance and fulfilled her obligations directly to the Paramount Chiefs during her lifetime. There is no indication that she ever received an allocation of land, however, and she apparently lived first with the man whom she did not marry and later with her adult son.

Moshoeshoe allocated land to his male subjects for cultivation. The allocation system used by Moshoeshoe when "placing" new adherents was also based on the traditional Sotho-Tswana system of land tenure. Villages were formed when Moshoeshoe gave a man and his followers twenty to thirty head of cattle, assigned a place for the construction of their residences, and allocated land for cultivation. The chief had full rights over land and others used it on sufferance. The chief decided where houses and kraals were to be built, allotted land for cultivation, and could dispossess anyone and expel them at his pleasure. As every chief needed to attract and retain followers, however, the expropriation of a man's fields by a chief was relatively uncommon until Lesotho became over-crowded in the 1880s, when there were no new fields available for allocation. As long as a man continued to live in the area and cultivate his fields, the fields remained his and were traditionally passed on to his family through inheritance.[17]

Although chiefs controlled the allocation of land within their jurisdiction, it was not control over land that gave them their power, for people could easily emigrate and resettle under another chief or on empty land if a chief was too abusive or exploitative. Economic productivity, as well as military strength, depended on population size. People offered their allegiance to a chief because he provided them with protection and with livestock through the *mafisa* system. Because land was plentiful, chiefs competed for subjects, giving chiefs a strong incentive to show generosity.

The means by which Moshoeshoe built his nation had important ramifications for the subsequent history of the country. Insofar as the initial offering of allegiance to Moshoeshoe was voluntary, people retained the option to move beyond his jurisdiction. Since Moshoeshoe's power was dependent on his ability to mobilize military forces and to appropriate surpluses from production, it was in his interests to retain followers. Moshoeshoe extracted tribute in the form of labor, but it was provided by his followers in exchange for benefits which he provided to them. People willingly contributed labor to certain fields of chiefs which were designated as *masimo a lira* ("fields of the enemy") until the 1880s because the product of these fields was used for soldiers, travellers, and the indigent. A missionary observed that "The mosuto chief possesses to the supreme degree this quality of ... hospitality ... such that in Basutoland there are never any poor; nowhere anyone who dies of hunger ..."[18] Similarly, the military service required of subjects cannot be seen as merely reflecting the ability of chiefs to subordinate their subjects, when military security was a primary interest of the subjects themselves. Taxes, that is, payment in kind, were only collected in rare circumstances, such as to pay the bridewealth of the senior wife of a chief who would bear the new heir for the nation, to pay a war indemnity, or to pay a rainmaker from whose services the whole nation would presumably benefit. While no one likes to pay taxes, apparently the burden in Moshoeshoe's time was not onerous and the benefits were evident, for the BaSotho say, "*Lekhetho ke boroko le khotso*," or "taxation is sleep and peace."[19]

Moshoeshoe encouraged the expansion of arable and pastoral production, and consolidated his own wealth and influence through arrangements involving tribute labor and *mafisa*. Both commoners and chiefs benefitted from economic expansion, however. Many BaSotho had been incorporated into Moshoeshoe's new nation by accepting *mafisa* cattle, and many young men were married through the provision of cattle for bridewealth by Moshoeshoe and other chiefs. At no time did Moshoeshoe or the ruling BaKoena family have a monopoly over wealth in cattle, nor did chiefs control all the cattle of the country through *mafisa*. The provisions governing a *mafisa* relationship in fact ensured that livestock ownership would become even more widespread, as clients who accepted loan cattle into their care received the offspring periodically as animals of their own. Every married man who gave his allegiance to a chief was entitled to three fields (per wife) until overcrowding prevented this at the end of the century. Therefore every married man had the opportunity to invest his own labor and that of the members of his homestead to increase agricultural production and trade his surplus for livestock. Socioeconomic stratification was perpetuated through this system since wealthy men could afford to acquire more wives, entitling them to more land and returning to them greater surpluses and wealth. Through the efficient allocation of labor, however, every homestead could increase its material wealth, and many did. When Moshoeshoe ended the practice of "smelling out" witches, this was not just a symbolic abolition of a superstition. The identification of so-called "witches" had been the means by which chiefs had traditionally prevented the accumulation of wealth by others, since anyone who seemed to acquire too much wealth might be assumed to have done so through witchcraft, or in any event could be accused of trumped up witchcraft charges as an excuse to confiscate their property. The ending of the practice of smelling out witches therefore had the effect of allowing people to accumulate wealth openly without fear of persecution and confiscation. As migrants returned to Moshoeshoe's kingdom in the 1830s and 1840s with livestock they had accumulated through service in the Cape Colony, they did not have to give up their livestock to Moshoeshoe but were allowed to keep them.[20] The kingdom of Moshoeshoe was a land of opportunity even for the poor and disadvantaged. Harking back to the past which continues to provide a symbolic contrast to the present, elderly informants remember not a falsely glorified social and economic equality but rather a system which provided for the poor. One man explained,

> Thus it was for people long ago; a poor person was never seen. In those days of yesterday. Because even if someone had nothing people were all alike even if he still had nothing. If I have cattle, when the cattle go up to the countryside there, your child goes with his little tin and his little dish [and helps take care of the cows]. When the cows are milked there a second drawing of milk is done for him ... even if I had nothing, I stayed on my field which was plowed, it was still plowed.[21]

When asked how food was used up, another informant replied,

> In our stomachs here, and to feed people; food was eaten at that time; there was not a person about whom it was said this is a poor person, even when there was no cow at your home you still ate milk, you still had your fields plowed for you

... Now today you say the BaSotho of before were bad people who did not know God. There was no person who was hungry, you could find a person without a cow but his leather bags still stood full of thick milk.[22]

Implicit in these descriptions is clear socioeconomic inequality, yet the presence of poor people did not mean they were left indigent by society, nor that they had no opportunities for advancement. A sense of social responsibility was not merely associated with kinship, according to informants. Villagers took care of each other:

> But I can say well there was indeed no great hardship. I say that because people of those days helped each other. They felt sympathy for each other. Even if there is no cow; then the village has them, the village still has other people who have cattle. Others plowed for them and transported their crops from the fields for them. With the animals of the village here. They never said that he has no cow. His child still received milk and was given a cow or two which he could milk [and care for]. When someone slaughtered a cow here or a sheep, it was not said "that one doesn't have a sheep, so his child cannot have meat"; the child was still called. People ate at the courtyard and [a person without animals] came to eat meat here. And this person, like that, who has children and does not have animals, his children can still look after the animals of these other people.[23]

The chief was ultimately responsible for the welfare of those who lived under his jurisdiction, and the food from the fields which were plowed and harvested "by the nation" through work-parties for the chief was designated to feed the poor as well as strangers and visitors from elsewhere, and soldiers in times of war. Hence the fields which appeared to benefit the chief and were worked by his people, in fact benefitted the whole society.

As the number of chiefs within Lesotho multiplied at the end of the century the BaSotho came to resent their labor obligations to chiefs, and many court cases from this period involve the punishments meted out by chiefs to people who refused to fulfill their labor obligations on the *masimo a lira*. Some chiefs tried to exploit the system by insisting that the people work their personal fields as well, but the produce from the *masimo a lira* continued to be used to feed the people when in need, as most chiefs continued to fulfill their obligations to supply food to travellers and to their indigent followers. As one informant explained,

> Now this field, this one of the chieftainship, that is like the one of my grandfather [who was a chief], it was one which was plowed by the nation and it was said to be the field of the enemies. It was his field, there below the white place [on the cliff] up to here, it was one field of his there that was called [a field] of the enemies which was plowed by the nation in work parties [*matsema*]. When the chief ordered that people should plow this field they plowed. When it was said it was "of the enemies" like that, it was of the chief, that is to say that people who arrived at the chief's place were offered hospitality with the food from that field, as was the whole nation when they come to the chief's instead of to their own homes. Whereas the chief used it [the food from this field] it was only used *for* the nation itself.[24]

Moshoeshoe's nation was based on the winning of popular allegiance and from this the consequent right to control the land from which these people hailed, which was contrary to the western notion that land is conquered and from this derives the right to rule the people on it. Africans recognized the right of Moshoeshoe to control the land of the people who had placed themselves under his rule, and hence it is on the basis of ancestral land holdings that BaSotho claims to land rights were based. By the early 1840s the BaSotho were being challenged by encroaching Europeans over their land rights. Only by identifying which land was previously occupied by BaSotho is it possible to determine the extent to which the BaSotho were deprived of land by immigrating European farmers. It is difficult to identify the BaSotho with reference to either political boundaries or language, however, and thereby define the limits of their occupation of land. On the one hand, the geographic boundaries of Lesotho changed continually through the nineteenth century, and many SeSotho-speaking peoples found themselves living outside the political boundaries of Lesotho as the land area of the country contracted over time. On the other hand, while the majority of peoples who came under the government of Moshoeshoe were SeSotho-speaking peoples, various Nguni groups who spoke IsiZulu or IsiXhosa were also incorporated into his kingdom. It is only in the historical context of the formation of the BaSotho nation of Moshoeshoe that the term BaSotho can be defined. For the purposes of this history, BaSotho is used to refer to those people who owed allegiance to the government of Moshoeshoe in the nineteenth century, and to their descendants since then. This definition includes non-SeSotho speakers who placed themselves under Moshoeshoe and adopted the SeSotho language over time, as well as SeSotho-speaking peoples who had been governed by Moshoeshoe but later became tenants in the Conquered Territory of the Orange Free State or elsewhere in white-ruled South Africa.

Moshoeshoe claimed that the BaSotho had land rights in the territory which had been inhabited by the forefathers of the BaSotho. In the early 1820s the people inhabiting the region of Lesotho and its vicinity were grouped together in highly concentrated populations inhabiting isolated hills and mountaintops for defensive purposes, and the plains which they had previously inhabited lay apparently vacant. This temporary concentration of peoples, which left wide areas uninhabited, led the first European observers in the area to believe that the lands were open for settlement. In fact, prior to the disruptions of the 1820s, largely caused by European-sponsored Griqua and Kora raiding against the African inhabitants of the interior, many of the lands which became parts of the Cape Colony and Orange Free State later in the century had been inhabited by the ancestors of the BaSotho.

Moshoeshoe described the political situation governing the area before 1818 in a letter to the "Secretary to Government" concerning the implementation of an 1843 Treaty with Great Britain establishing new boundaries for Lesotho:

Previous to the year 1818 the country defined in the treaty together with the parts at present occupied by the Chief Sikonyela were exclusively *known* and *owned* by the Mayaiya, the Machoachoa, the Bamonageng, the Baramokheli, the Batele or Batlakoana, and the Baphuti. These tribes went by the general name of Basutos, spoke one language, had the same habits and customs, intermarried, and considered each other as having had, at some remote period, one common origin. Only, each governed itself separately, and no supremacy existed between the Chiefs than that produced by the influence which talent might occasionally give to one of them.[25]

Moshoeshoe went on to explain that as a result of the wars of the early 1820s the chiefs of the Mayaiyana, the Batele, and the Makhoakhoa had perished, and many people fled to the Cape Colony and elsewhere to take refuge. He continued:

All that remained in the land sought my protection and acknowledged my authority; thus I became entrusted, by the desire of the people, with the government of the whole Basuto country ... thus my title to rule Basutoland rests, first, on my being born Sovereign of a great portion of it, and secondly, on my having become the acknowledged Chief by the original proprietors of the remainder.[26]

The building of national loyalties, the creation of a national identity of belonging to the BaSotho nation, was readily understood by the participants themselves as the nation was being forged. When Moshoeshoe was accompanied by Arbousset on a trip across his domains to the northeast, they encountered a new subject of Nguni origins. This Mokanana, of the MaZizi, told Arbousset's MoSotho guide that "I am of Setebele origin; but I am already a Mosotho in my ways, and even in language. I recognise you, my friend. I have seen you at Thaba-Bosiu. The Makakanas are no longer foreigners in your country. I too am a Mosotho calf!"[27] Arbousset reported the man's response when challenged about his loyalty to the Zulu king Dingane: "'Dingane, I served him for a while; I have also served his father,' answered the old man. 'But both of them have been the death of me. Believe me, friend, Dingane is nothing to me any more, nor to my family. We are Basotho.'"[28]

The MoSotho guide who had ridiculed the old man accepted his words, noting logically that "I needn't say anything about the hatred towards Dingane of Zulus who have migrated from their country to this one."[29] Emigration was recognized as a form of political resistance, of "voting with one's feet." Conversely, immigration required the adoption of allegiance to Moshoeshoe and the BaSotho nation at large. Moshoeshoe's subjects came from many places, represented many descent groups, and spoke a variety of languages. The BaSotho enjoyed tangible benefits when they offered their allegiance to Moshoeshoe. Moshoeshoe indeed represented the interests of his followers as he extended his influence as far as possible over the territories from which they hailed.

4

The land of the BaSotho: the geographic extent of Moshoeshoe's authority, 1824–1864

The legitimacy of Moshoeshoe's claim to territory rested on a fundamentally different principle of rule than that to which Europeans subscribed. Contrary to the European notion of conquering land and then ruling all the people on that land, Africans in the region recognized Moshoeshoe's right to rule over all areas of land which belonged to the people who offered him allegiance, including the land which they had recently abandoned in light of the turmoil caused by drought, migrations, and the frontier raids of Griqua, Kora, and Europeans. The land which came under Moshoeshoe's jurisdiction by virtue of the allegiance of the land's "original proprietors" to the new BaSotho nation was far more extensive than the area subsequently incorporated into colonial Basutoland. Areas came under contention on the south, southwest, west, and northwest borders of Moshoeshoe's country. The territorial claims made by Moshoeshoe are well-documented, but it is further possible to establish the validity of his claims based on prior occupation. This is important because white South Africans have traditionally denied the previous occupation of these areas by Africans, and have continued to assert their right to these lands based on a false claim of prior occupation.

Ancestors of the BaSotho had inhabited lands to the southwest and west of modern Lesotho which Europeans claimed had been either empty or inhabited only by the San. When the first Europeans explored the area, BaSotho were living on the Kraai River near Buffel's Vlei (Aliwal North), and at Koesberg near Hebron. Boers visiting the area in the early 1820s were told by San about "Koes" living in Koesberg, "Koes" being the Khoi word for black people.[1] On 2 September 1823, Field Cornet A. Pretorius found "Koes" living on the Kraai River, and reported seeing 1133 huts, although this was probably a recording error and he probably saw 113 huts.[2] The lower figure is more in keeping with typical settlement patterns in the area, but still represented a significant population in one place.

These unidentified black people could have been either a branch of the BaMonaheng BaSotho, or BaPhuthi, who later came under Moshoeshoe's rule. Boer witnesses stated that they had first met the BaMonaheng chief Mojakisane in about 1825, and gave him the Dutch name April. In 1835 Sir

Benjamin D'Urban entered into an agreement with Mojakisane, referred to as the "Bechuana Chief Kaptyn." The agreement received Mojakisane under the protection of the British Government within the new limits of the Colony Territory, which were extended to the Kraai River. The territory east of the Kraai was designated as the "Territory of the Basuto Chief Moshesh," and specific kraal (village) locations were cited for the BaSotho chiefs Lipeane, Mokwena, and Mojakisane, as well as the BaPhuthi Chief Moorosi.[3] Although the treaty was revoked by Lieutenant Governor Stockenstrom on 5 December 1836, it still stands as evidence that Mojakisane's people and other BaSotho were residing there at that time.

Some BaSotho were driven out of the southwest by the AmaNgwane as they swept into the area in the early 1820s, but they returned in 1827. Other BaSotho were driven out of the areas around Herschel and Quthing by AmaBaca invading from the southeast.[4] Chief Kama of the AmaGqunukhwebe sought Moshoeshoe's permission before settling at Herschel. Other evidence also demonstrates that Moshoeshoe's authority over this area, which was known as Kamastone and later became the Wittebergen Native Reserve, was recognized by both Africans and Europeans. A British Bluebook from 1842 (concerned with negotiations by the Wesleyan missionary Shepstone to establish a mission at Kamastone) showed the Kraai River as the boundary of the BaSotho, and Herschel was not included in the Cape Colony until the issuance of "a summary proclamation and without reference to Moshesh" in 1849.[5] The names of all the rivers and hills in the area are SeSotho names, and Orpen insisted that the BaSotho, with the San and BaPhuthi, were the only people to occupy the country between the Kraai and the Orange.[6]

The BaPhuthi under Moorosi were also incorporated into the BaSotho nation of Moshoeshoe. The ancestors of Moorosi's people were three Nguni-speaking groups, the MaZizi, the MaPolane, and the MaPhetla, who had migrated into the region during the seventeenth and eighteenth centuries, and who were slowly adopting the SeSotho language and customs. These people eventually moved into the southern portion of Lesotho, where they were decimated and dispersed in the first wave of Nguni attacks in the early 1820s. A few found refuge among the San and lived by raiding Nguni cattle until they eventually drew the attention of Moshoeshoe in 1825. Moorosi told Orpen that "Moshesh surrounded them on their mountain and forced them to surrender and he had ever since been under Moshesh."[7] This evidence about the BaPhuthi, with that about the BaMonaheng, suggests that Moshoeshoe's claims over land as far to the southwest as Aliwal North were politically justified.

Moshoeshoe also claimed jurisdiction over the land stretching west to Thaba 'Nchu. The French missionaries encountered the BaRamokhele (BaSotho) chief Moseme at Thaba 'Nchu when they first entered the area in 1833; he informed them that he was under the government of Moshoeshoe and gave them a guide.[8] The following year BaRolong under Moroka, who were seeking refuge from their invaded lands north of the Vaal, sought permission from Moshoeshoe to settle at Thaba 'Nchu. Under the influence of the Wesleyan missionaries who settled with them, the BaRolong later claimed that they had purchased the land from Moshoeshoe and were therefore independent from his governance.

On the one hand, Moshoeshoe placed the BaRolong at Thaba 'Nchu according to established BaTswana and BaSotho customs which did not permit the alienation of land, and accordingly the BaRolong were subject to Moshoeshoe for as long as they stayed. For the purposes of this argument, however, it is only necessary to recognize that Moshoeshoe's *original* claim to the land was never questioned, only the extent to which he had given up that right when he accepted the gifts sent as tribute by the BaRolong. Furthermore, BaSotho continued to live at Thaba 'Nchu in considerable numbers. When the BaRolong challenged the 1843 Treaty between Sir George Napier and Moshoeshoe which set the boundary of Moshoeshoe's territory at Thaba 'Nchu, Casalis wrote to the Civil Commissioner of Colesberg that there were 189 BaSotho villages in the vicinity of Thaba 'Nchu which recognized Moshoeshoe as their principal chief.[9] It was to the advantage of the Boers to foster divisiveness between the groups in the region, however, and the land inhabited by Moroko's people was taken from Moshoeshoe in subsequent treaties.

Eventually the land was also taken from the BaRolong, most of whom took refuge in colonial Basutoland. Since most BaRolong were eventually assimilated by the BaSotho, the early debate over the ownership of the land becomes moot. Because the area was occupied by the ancestors of BaSotho of various origins, including BaRamokhele and BaRolong, Moshoeshoe's claims of authority over this land were justified according to the criteria of prior occupation.

The territory northwest of the Caledon River was also an area of dispute in the early nineteenth century. One of the first areas affected by the disruptions of the 1820s, it was raided by BaTlokoa under 'Manthatisi in 1822, followed by the AmaHlubi under Mpangazitha, and the AmaNgwane under Matiwane. After wandering around the area for several years, raiding for food on both sides of the Caledon, the BaTlokoa eventually settled on two mountains not far from Butha-Buthe, where Moshoeshoe's people had their stronghold before moving south to Thaba Bosiu. At the same time that Moshoeshoe began building his strength from his new fortress at Thaba Bosiu in 1824, the BaTlokoa used similar methods to incorporate the people living near them into their nation. When the French missionaries Arbousset and Daumas first visited the BaTlokoa in 1836, they found a population of 14,000 spread over 80 to 100 square miles, speaking the same language as the BaSotho and differing from them "in but few respects."[10] The people who had been absorbed by the BaTlokoa included BaFokeng (BaSotho) and remnants of the Nguni who had followed them into the region. Moshoeshoe considered the BaTlokoa invaders, and he eventually defeated them and regained control over the area in 1853.[11]

West of there, the Wesleyan mission station among the Griqua at Lesooane was surrounded by BaSotho villages when Backhouse saw it in 1840. The BaSotho in this area included the BaKubung ("Hoja"), whom Daumas found living with other BaSotho and Nguni refugees when he visited Mekuatling in 1837.[12] SeSotho-speaking people, who already referred to themselves as BaSotho, were living in this area around Mekuatling as early as 1824, when they fled to find refuge with the Griqua after being attacked by Korana.[13] It was here that Moshoeshoe formally "placed" the BaTaung under Moletsane, when they requested refuge in 1838, having fled their homeland north of the Vaal several years earlier. Apparently Moshoeshoe's political connection with the remnants of the BaKubung and other scattered BaSotho gave him jurisdiction over this area and areas further to the east where the BaTlokoa were considered invaders in Moshoeshoe's land. This authority was evident when the BaTaung sought Moshoeshoe's permission before they resettled at Mekuatling. Furthermore, when a MoSotho chief at Mekuatling, Ramatlaping, began fighting with nearby Nguni, the dispute was taken to Moshoeshoe for settlement, and he imposed a fine in cattle on Ramatlaping.[14]

Unlike the BaRolong and the BaTlokoa, the BaTaung never questioned Moshoeshoe's authority over the region. As early as 1851, Moletsane sought permission to return to his homeland between the Sand and the Vaal, but permission was denied by the British government and he was forced to remain.[15] Concerned with over-crowding in the area, he wrote to the High Commissioner of Mekuatling in 1864 that "As friend and ally of the Great Chief Moshesh, I have lived many years in the district of Mekuatling, which is a territory belonging to the Basuto Chieftain."[16]

Moshoeshoe's authority extended even further to the northwest. Beyond Mekuatling lived the "Makaota" who supplied Moshoeshoe with ostrich feathers and valuable skins which were sent to Shaka as tribute. Later evidence places BaSotho in the Winburg area in 1848. On the order of the Magistrate of Winburg (Biddulph), the BaTlokoa were invited to attack the two BaSotho villages in order to clear the Winburg area of BaSotho and make room for Boer farms.[17]

The authority of Moshoeshoe in the northeast was somewhat ambiguous. In 1853 Casalis informed the British Resident, on behalf of Moshoeshoe, that Chief Witsie (Oetse) was independent of him. The "Makhoakhoa" living near Witsie did acknowledge Moshoeshoe's authority, however.[18] Several years later, five AmaZulu chiefs placed themselves under Moshoeshoe and settled in "Witsieshoek," also suggesting Moshoeshoe's authority over the area.[19] This was not an area Moshoeshoe ever claimed during border disputes, however, and it was never included within the negotiated boundaries of Lesotho.

Many groups, large and small, were incorporated into the new nation of the BaSotho under Moshoeshoe. A "List of Refugee Chiefs in Basutoland as supplied by Moshesh to Sir Philip Wodehouse" from 1864 includes the names of thirty-two groups.[20] The nineteenth-century nation-state of Moshoeshoe was not characterized by ethnic, linguistic, or cultural exclusiveness. Political unity and stability was achieved among a population which included not only SeSotho-speaking groups, but also many thousands of BaTswana, AmaZulu, and AmaXhosa. This multi-ethnic unity was achieved not by force, but peacefully through the voluntary allegiance of people to the nation. The ultimate viability of the nation was threatened not from within but from without. When Moshoeshoe wrote the list of refugee chiefs for Wodehouse in 1864, his purpose was to defend his claim to lands the Europeans had taken. He called it "a correct list, showing the true extent of Basutoland which has been taken away by the white men."[21] As he noted the people, he noted the areas from which they came. Hence he listed:

> Molitsane, whose country is on the Valsch River, and whose people have fallen on my hands. Tlalele has also been driven into my lands. Makume has been obliged to immigrate into my country. Patsa is also on my hands. Mahoete, Magoana, Maiane, Tsele, Nkokoto, Ra-Mootsi, Tsele, Letuka, the Basia, ditto. The Baphuting, Ratsebe, beyond Harrismith. The Makholokue have also taken refuge with me. The Bathlakuana under Makatse, and the Batsitsi, have also been driven in. The Matluite, the Mankuane, the Batsunyane, the Baphole, Geketsi, the Bafokeng, are all refugees with me. Now the Bamonageng are coming in. Pehabane from Harrismith. Ramakaatsa from Winburg. Ratloodi from Ditsoeneng. Thaane from near Winburg. Mesoboya. The tribe of Lephui. Mamohale and Moroko.
>
> These are the names of the principal Chiefs whose lands are now occupied by the Boers, there were independent Chiefs besides unlike Morosi and Molitsane.[22]

Moshoeshoe strove in vain to protect the land of his followers from the onslaught of European settler expansion. With eloquence he made a plea which remains unresolved to this day:

> By the preceding list of [recently] deserted lands we explain and clearly maintain that this country belongs to us Blacks. We are now crowded together, and we ask why we should be further molested. Having taken so much country, are the white men not content? I point to the deserted Villages of the many Chiefs I have mentioned, and I ask *if the the ruined walls do not prove that those lands are theirs?* If the day of equitable settlement has come, have these people not a right to be restored to their old habitations? All these Chiefs are now in my Country, and I say behold and judge between us.[23]

5

The European intrusion and the competition for land, 1834–1868

By the 1830s territorial competition had been largely resolved between the BaSotho and their African neighbors, but the struggle for land between the BaSotho and their European neighbors had just begun. The land of Moshoeshoe was a fertile reservoir compared to the dry surrounding lands. Ongoing European demand for the land of the BaSotho was created by the need for extensive grazing lands as well as the desire for more fertile land for grain production. The European frontier economy was exclusively pastoral, and the Boers required huge land holdings to support their large herds of cattle and sheep. At the same time, because they did not grow their own food, the white farmers depended on trade for grain which they purchased primarily from the BaSotho who were very successful farmers. It was impossible for the Boers to intensify the use of their own land through the adoption of arable production because the land of Transorangia was infertile and the climate was arid. Only by forcibly expropriating the fertile land of neighboring Lesotho could the white frontiersmen begin cultivation and end their dependence on trade with the BaSotho for meeting their basic food needs. The European desire for BaSotho land was further fueled by two exacerbating factors: lengthy and repeated droughts which brought white herders to the brink of starvation, and increasing land speculation which artificially raised the value of land in the region.[1]

The quality of the land in the Orange Free State was much poorer than that in Lesotho to the east. When the Catholic missionary Gerard first saw the Orange Free State, he noted that while the area was rich in sheep, cattle, and horses, the land was very barren, and the stony soil resembled that of the plains of the Karroo desert. In stark contrast was the fertility of the lowlands of Lesotho. In 1834 Andrew Smith visited Moshoeshoe at Thaba Bosiu and wrote:

> From the village of the chief a few excursions in the neighborhood proved the superiority of this country over most of the other districts of South Africa. The lower slopes of the hills were covered with fine grass, the valleys and plains had more the appearance of meadows than common pasture ground ... Many of the valleys contained small streamlets and an abundance of good soil existed

for the purposes of cultivation ... The appearance of trees of considerable size such as we observed here in the ravines of the mountains was a pleasing novelty to all of us, as, with the exception of willow trees along the banks of rivers, we had seen nothing which had a claim to be characterized as anything but a shrub since leaving Graaff Reynet.[2]

Boer farmers had been migrating across the Orange River from the Cape Colony with their herds in times of drought since the early 1830s, and political disaffection from the British Government prompted some Boers to emigrate from the Cape Colony as early as 1834. Following the Sixth War between Europeans and AmaXhosa in 1834–35 this trickle of emigrants turned into a massive migration of Boers into Transorangia. While most of these continued on to Natal to settle, many remained in the Transorangia area, and many others returned to this area from Natal following the British annexation of Natal in 1843.

Boer pastoralism and expansionism

The Boers first intruded into Moshoeshoe's territory because of their need for more grazing lands. They herded both cattle and sheep as their main product for exchange and profit. The demand for beef and cattle products had diminished and cattle herding, especially at such great distances from the Cape market, was no longer profitable. At the same time, the continued demand for wool in Great Britain ensured the profitability of wool-producing for the Boers. In 1852 wool accounted for £230,000 of total combined Orange River Sovereignty exports to the Cape Colony, England, and Natal valued at £256,000.[3] According to the 1856 Census, whites in the Orange Free State owned 27,552 horses, 137,164 head of cattle, and 1,231,849 sheep and goats.[4]

The initial response of the BaSotho towards the Boers who entered Lesotho was to treat the white newcomers as they would any of their African neighbors who chose to live on BaSotho lands under the sovereignty of Moshoeshoe. All BaSotho lands were inalienable, but any group of people could apply for permission to use an area of land. Thus Moshoeshoe explained to the British Secretary of Government in 1845 that:

The selling, or renting of lands, has been hitherto a practice wholly unknown to us and I believe to all Bechuana nations ... Our system is that whenever people wish to establish themselves on unoccupied spots, they apply to the principal Chief of the country for permission ... *As long as the people choose to remain on the spot it is considered as theirs*; but whenever they move another party may come and take possession, provided they previously make due application to the Chief. I could not, according to the custom of my tribe, alienate any portion of my territory without the consent of the people.[5]

Moshoeshoe tried unsuccessfully to impose this system on Boer settlers intruding in the area. In 1839 he informed the lieutenant governor that for eighteen months white farmers had been residing in his territory, and that he had never received any acknowledgement from them of his authority, in spite of the fact that he had sent them a "Circular" informing them of their temporary rights to graze on his land.[6] White farmers who arrived in the area over the next few years did acknowledge his authority, however, as indicated by the fact that they did apply to Moshoeshoe for permission to settle and use grazing lands. The very fact that settlers requested his permission to settle indicates that Moshoeshoe's claims over the land were recognized.

The testimony of these settlers in fact bears out Moshoeshoe's claim that they had been granted rights to *use* the land, but had not been granted ownership or the right to sell or transfer the land to other farmers. Eighty-three farmers seeking British protection for their land claims signed a petition stating that when they first arrived in the region between the Caledon and Orange Rivers, "... after having been informed that Moshesh claims that territory, we, with a view of acting amicably, requested his leave to occupy it and he gave the places for always ..."[7]

When British officials were trying to sort out land claims during the period of the Orange River Colony, 1848–54, they received depositions from white farmers who were seeking titles to their land. In one case the applicants' claim stated:

> Your memorialist further sheweth that in the year 1842 the Chief Moshesh placed him on the Farm, giving him his Written Authority, and granting *him* the full and free occupation thereof in Perpetuity, the said farm being at that time beyond the line marked out by His Excellency Sir Peregrine Maitland ...[8]

Both of these statements support Moshoeshoe's claims that the farmers had been granted rights to use the land for as long as *they* remained settled there, but not rights of ownership. Since the terms reflected traditional BaSotho land tenure practices, the right of occupation was not transferrable to others, and even heirs would have been required to reapply for the right to the land. The same system of land tenure had been applied to the white settlers as was in force for all BaSotho living in the territory of Moshoeshoe, and indeed according to SeSotho and SeTswana customs in general. The white farmers sought to take advantage of these lenient terms of land tenure, and the right to permanent occupation was interpreted as equivalent to land ownership. Thus in 1854:

> ... the Boers residing on that frontier were averse to any more exact demarcation of those extensive tracts of country, from a sense of the advantages of trusting to availing themselves again of the fair, and even liberal, spirit in which Moshesh was accustomed formerly to grant lands to them on the easiest tenure possible ...[9]

The intentions of the farmers were obvious to contemporary observers. Cattle raiding both by white farmers and by Africans was common, with each side claiming their actions to be only retaliating in kind. But the Boers had clearly aggressive intentions with regard to territory, and trumped up charges against the BaSotho to win sympathy for their hidden cause, that of taking the land. In 1856 a British Agent revealed these underlying motives of the Boers:

> ... there is something hollow and deceptive in the present negotiations between the Free State and Moshesh. The great object which these Frontier Boers have in view ... is at bottom, *the new line*. This cattle matter serves to introduce the subject ... but the grand point to be gained is the Land.[10]

Wars, treaties, and dispossession

The Boer pastoral economy thus generated an insatiable thirst for land in the interior, just as it had on the Eastern Frontier until white expansionism had been diverted northwards by AmaXhosa resistance in the 1830s. The missionaries began complaining about the encroachment of Boers on BaSotho lands as early as 1839. At that time a French missionary characterized the migration of the Boers as a "scourge," noting that "this beautiful country is almost constantly traversed by the caravans of these emigrants, a large number of whom have already settled in its neighborhood."[11] Complaints to the British government from missionaries and from Moshoeshoe himself finally led Sir George Napier to issue a proclamation prohibiting "any of her (Majesty's) subjects to molest, invade, or injure any of the native tribes, or to take or maintain unlawful possession of any of the lands to those tribes belonging ..."[12] But even Napier already recognized that such a proclamation was useless. In a letter to Lord Stanley about the Boer emigrants, he wrote that:

> ... their [European] population increased by additional immigrants from the Colony, until it has reached so considerable a number as to make the possession of a part of the territory of Moshesh not only desirable but, in their consideration, a necessary appendage to their possessions ... a return to the Colony with quantities of cattle and no farms whereon to graze their herds is not a practical measure even were they willing to adopt it ...[13]

In spite of his apparent pessimism regarding British ability to control Boer expansion, Napier entered into the first British territorial treaty with Moshoeshoe in 1843. According to this treaty, the British recognized BaSotho sovereignty over the land between the Orange (Gariep) and Caledon Rivers, plus a strip of territory from 25 to 30 miles wide along the north side of the Caledon. The impossibility of forcing the Boers to recognize this treaty immediately became apparent. At Beersheba, well inside the BaSotho territory as recognized by the 1843 Napier treaty, the French missionary Rolland complained about Boer intentions to take over the area:

> But all the proclamations and all the threats of the Government have produced no other effect than to aggravate the exasperation of the farmers and to render our situation more critical ... the Boers are spreading the report that the country is their own, and now and then, threaten to expel us: they are only seeking a pretext to do so ... At present, they speak of nothing less than fixing

their limits on the other side of the Caledon, about three-quarters of the way between Beersheba and Morija.[14]

To defend the interests of the Boers, Governor Maitland altered the Treaty in 1845 so that certain lands within Lesotho became "alienable," thereby giving official British sanction to the permanent retention by the Boers of lands on which they had been allowed (by Moshoeshoe) to settle.

Continued problems between the Boers and BaSotho inspired Sir Harry Smith to annex all of the land between the Orange and the Vaal Rivers to Great Britain so as to impose direct control over the area. At this time Smith ordered the British Resident at Bloemfontein, Henry Warden, to establish a new boundary line which would not require any Europeans to abandon the lands on which they were settled. Warden moved the new western boundary of Lesotho east approximately 40 miles in 1849, with narrow corridors remaining to connect the Beersheba and Hebron mission stations to Lesotho. The British also tried to establish boundaries between the African chiefdoms in the newly-annexed territory, and Warden favored the land claims of Moshoeshoe's African neighbors at the expense of Moshoeshoe when drawing boundaries.[15] The new line thus officially separated from Lesotho the land held by Moroka, Sekonyela, and the Griqua north of the Caledon, all territory which Africans recognized as falling under Moshoeshoe's authority.

In 1854 the British decided for financial reasons to abandon the territory north of the Orange, leaving the BaSotho and their African neighbors to deal directly with the Boers. The fact that the Boers continued to claim extensive lands not occupied by any whites and still occupied by BaSotho meant that boundaries were constantly in dispute, and the Boers found it impossible to enforce their claims. At the time of the British abandonment, Orpen writes that:

> ... every inch of the Smithfield District had originally been recognized by Treaty to belong to Moshesh, that it was at this time in occupation, both by Boers and by upwards of ten thousand Basutos, and that throughout the greater part of it no boundaries of any farms had been defined by any authority and all were in dispute and a very great part was claimed by land speculators holding land that had never been occupied by any Europeans ... There was, now, no part of the boundary with Basutoland not disputed and disputable for similar reasons.[16]

Orpen commented on the difficulties of enforcing the Warden boundary and removing the BaSotho from land designated as Boer lands: "I believe that all the above-mentioned Basuto had been a considerable time on the spots mentioned and that their fathers before them had occupied these spots until they had given way before attacks from Sikoniela during Warden's time."[17]

Given that the borders had been left undefined in practice, with a mixture of Boers and BaSotho each occupying land claimed by the other, it is not

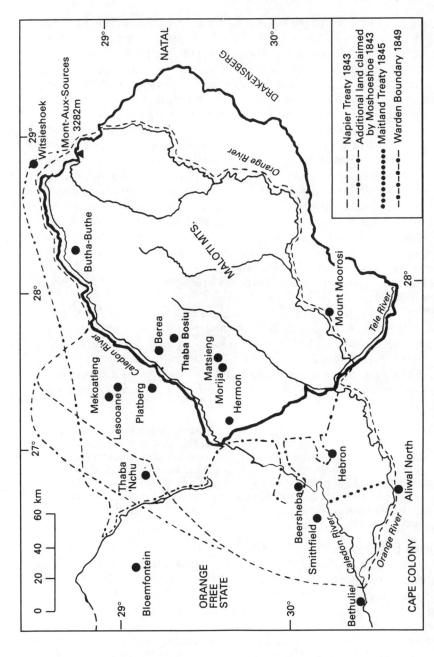

Fig. 4 The changing borders of Lesotho, 1843–1849

surprising that a major war was not long in coming. Relations between the Orange Free State and Moshoeshoe had been precarious since Jacobus Boshof had replaced Josias Hoffman as Orange Free State President in 1855. War was long anticipated, as the Boers sought to enforce the Warden boundary and to compel Moshoeshoe to discipline his subordinate BaSotho chiefs who were engaged in frequent raiding. War broke out in March 1858, and by May Moshoeshoe's strategy brought victory to the BaSotho, allowing them to recoup some of their earlier territorial losses when a new border was drawn in the Treaty of Aliwal North.[18]

BaSotho cattle raids served as the justification for Boer aggression in 1865 and 1866, but it was the desire to free themselves from dependence on BaSotho grain which prompted the Boers to conduct successive campaigns against the BaSotho, and to wrest from them more than half of Lesotho's arable land. In 1866 the Boers defeated the BaSotho and imposed the Treaty of Thaba Bosiu, under which the BaSotho lost all of their land north of the Caledon. The western boundary of Lesotho was once more pushed east, 25 to 30 miles east of the Warden line, or about 40 miles east of the line established by the 1858 Treaty of Aliwal North. Once the BaSotho had harvested their crops they refused to abandon their lands to the Boers, and the fighting was renewed. Finally in 1868 Great Britain annexed Lesotho to the Crown and negotiated the Second Treaty of Aliwal North with the Orange Free State on 12 February 1869. This Treaty was considerably more favorable than that of Thaba Bosiu had been with regard to BaSotho claims, but it still deprived the BaSotho of any lands north of the Caledon and of much of the area to the west between the Caledon and Orange Rivers. With the incorporation of Molapo's Reserve in April 1870 and the territory of the BaPhuthi under Moorosi south of the Orange River in 1872, colonial Basutoland's final borders were fixed.[19]

European land speculation

Land speculation also intensified European competition for BaSotho land. Most if not all of the land speculators who bought land in the area after the annexation of the Orange River Sovereignty in 1848 were British. An understanding of the extent to which land speculation influenced British policy on the frontier is important as an illustration of the functioning of British imperialism. In addition, the fact that land speculators were at the forefront of frontier expansion and the expropriation of BaSotho lands contradicts white claims to the land based on prior occupation, since the land held by white land speculators had not yet been occupied by any Europeans and was indeed fully occupied by African farmers. The white speculators had no trouble gaining European titles to vast tracts of African land, since the African occupants were legally invisible. These speculators never intended to occupy their "new farms" themselves. Instead they touted the attributes of these fertile "farms" to lure more whites to the frontier,

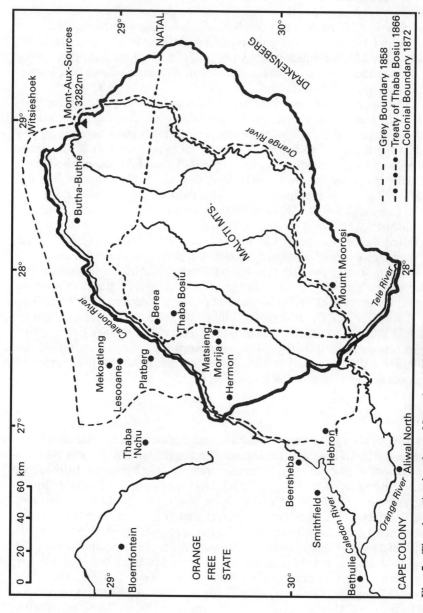

Fig. 5 The changing borders of Lesotho, 1858–1872

selling them areas which they had never seen, much less staked out. The speculators pocketed huge profits, leaving the Boers and the BaSotho to "resolve" their conflict over right of occupancy in the series of wars which left the BaSotho devastated and dependent on British intervention in 1868.

The white population of the Orange Free State in 1856 was 12,829, of whom 2,709 were able-bodied men.[20] The estimated land area of the Orange Free State as defined by the Warden boundary was 38,250 square miles.[21] There were 1,265 farms with a total area of 11,000,000 acres in 1854, yielding an average of 8,696 acres per farm.[22] While most of these farms were granted in the period of the Orange River Sovereignty and were supposed to range from 6,000 to 12,000 acres, many extended over 40,000 acres.[23] A title to land was obtained by making application to a Land Board, and costs or fees amounted to very little: approximately £1 to £15 *per farm*. Because these absurdly low fees encouraged land speculation, the Orange Free State Volksraad imposed a fee of £5 on each unoccupied farm, which led to the evolution of the "bywoner", or tenant system. Since a farm had to have a white resident, speculators would allow Boers lacking the money to buy land themselves to settle on their farms.[24]

Most land was owned by land speculators. Orpen, who surveyed land in the Orange River Sovereignty for the British government in the early 1850s, wrote that in 1850 "land was, at that time, being given away right and left, or sold at public sales at £20 for a farm."[25] In 1853, the total number of British owning farms was 139, but there were only 34 British farmholders actually occupying their farms.[26] In 1854 Orpen sent an anonymous letter to the *Zuid Afrikaan* saying that

> There is ground sufficient for about a thousand new farms in the country ... Nearly one third of the farms in this country are unoccupied and in many instances a large tract is entirely in the hands of speculators, and has not a single occupant. In a part of the district of Harrismith, there are nearly two hundred farms adjoining each other of which only three are inhabited. Even in the immediate neighborhood of Bloemfontein there is a block of about 20 farms, some of which are about 30,000 acres in extent.[27]

Land speculators had a decided influence on British policy, both directly and indirectly. The British Resident wrote to the High Commissioner in 1850 that "There are many Land Speculators in the Country, and in the Caledon District Mr. Charles Halse takes the lead. Any arrangement, however desirable it may be for the native population, if it thwarts the views of Land Speculators, the most extravagant statements get abroad."[28]

But British officials were quick to recognize the potential profits to be realized in land speculation, and they were soon buying land as well. Sir George Clerk, pointing out that Napier's treaty indicated that the BaSotho had a just claim to lands in the West, wrote:

> I find much even for Mr. Green, the British Resident, to investigate and to learn regarding the tenures and extent of large tracts of country claimed by

our land speculators residing in the Smithfield district, among the foremost or the most advanced of whom I regretted to hear was its Civil Commissioner.[29]

Green, British Resident and Treasurer General, was not likely to conduct an objective investigation, however, since he owned 164,124 acres of land himself. Percy Crause, who served in several offices including Registrar of Deeds and Acting Auditor of Accounts, owned 29,434 acres. The four Civil Commissioner/Resident Magistrates each owned between 9,000 and 42,000 acres, the Crown Prosecutor owned 9,000 acres, and even the Clerk to the Civil Commissioner owned 30,000 acres. Perhaps most significant of all was the fact that Major Warden, who instigated the 1851 attack on the BaSotho, owned five farms totalling 14,031 acres. Warden's aggressive attack on the BaSotho, which Moshoeshoe tried so judiciously to ward off, was clearly motivated by the promise of personal profit from land speculation. A successful conclusion of war would have secured the safety and value of his farms and brought him spectacular profits. Instead the success went to the BaSotho, ultimately causing the British officially to withdraw from Transorangia. In a last ditch effort to secure some personal gain Warden and dozens of others, including other British officials, submitted claims for compensation to the British Government because of supposed financial losses incurred after the Orange River Sovereignty was abandoned in 1854, since they claimed that land values had declined. The British magistrate was unimpressed, and their claims of having suffered personal financial loss as a result of government action were rejected on the basis that they owned the land for speculation only.[30]

The profits to be realized in land speculation were enormous. During the period of British rule, between 1848 and 1854, land values rose astronomically. Farms purchased in the years 1848 to 1850 sold for double or triple their price after only two years; it was not unusual for the price of a farm to increase *ten times* or more in only two or three years. In spite of landowner fears that values drop after British abandonment, farm prices continued to rise. A farm of 16,600 acres purchased in 1857 for £300 sold in 1861 for £3,500, and another purchased for £375 in the late 1850s sold for £2,525 in 1861.[31]

White claims to these lands at that time seem ludicrous in light of the fact that not only were the lands unoccupied by whites; they were in fact densely inhabited by BaSotho, who had ancestral claims to them. Thus in 1861 the Rev. J. Daniel wrote:

> The people of Paulus Moperi are occupying something like 60,000 morgen [120,000 acres] of the Free State territory in the district of "Senekal" (Wittebergen). The whole country east of Leeuw and Doorn Kops is now in possession of the Basutos. In this tract are farms which have been bought by farmers for as much as £1,000 sterling each.[32]

The speed with which newly conquered territory continued to be sold was astonishing. In April 1868, a year before the Second Treaty of Aliwal North established the final boundary between the Orange Free State and the newly protected Basutoland, the President of the Orange Free State wrote to the High Commissioner that

> The ceded territory, after having been inspected at a cost of several thousand pounds, was laid out in farms ... Between 300 and 400 farms have already been sold by public auction, large sums have been paid by the purchasers, titles have been issued and registered, money has been advanced, and mortgages have been passed and registered, and several farms have changed owners by sale and transfer.[33]

This land, some of which had been sold and resold, was still occupied by BaSotho, and it was not possible for Free State forces to expel them. This gave the BaSotho and British the leverage necessary to negotiate the Second Treaty of Aliwal North, which was significantly better for the BaSotho than had been the Treaty of Thaba Bosiu, but the greater part of the arable land of the BaSotho was lost for posterity. In the context of this gradual dispossession, the stagnation and eventual decline of BaSotho agricultural productivity became inevitable.

6

Food and politics: feasts and famines

The study of food is essential to the study of politics. Hunger is a driving force, and the most significant political revolutions in modern history began with food riots initiated by starving people, most notably women trying to feed their children.[1] As elsewhere in world history, many open contests of war in nineteenth-century southern Africa were fuelled by hunger. The re-creation and analysis of sociopolitical developments in this region thus hinges in part on an understanding of the natural environment and human uses of natural resources. However, hunger and famine are usually the result not of absolute food shortages, but the inequitable distribution of food in times of food scarcity. Therefore whenever political events were driven by hunger, the underlying explanation for the hunger itself lay in sociopolitical factors determining the human response to a given environmental crisis such as drought.

The nineteenth century brought radical political changes to the SeSotho- and SeTswana-speaking peoples. However, these changes, involving the creation of larger African sociopolitical formations and the contest between African and European societies, cannot be attributed to environmental factors. Rather, environmental factors mediated political developments, as people competed with each other while trying to cope with social stresses brought on by environmental crises. The first part of this chapter is devoted to recounting the food production strategies of the BaSotho in the nineteenth century, to provide a context in which to understand their periodic vulnerability to food scarcity and famine in times of drought. The second half of the chapter provides an analysis of the interaction between drought and sociopolitical factors which shaped the fate of the BaSotho in the nineteenth century.

Food production, 1830–1900

The gradual transformation of the food production system in Lesotho in the nineteenth century reflected the adaptability of the BaSotho which had become necessary for survival during the years of wars and famine. The capacity of the BaSotho to adjust to changing circumstances was in evidence throughout the century. The BaSotho responded to a changing physical and social environment characterized by a diminishing land area, increasing population, and migration into lands with unfavorable topography. They adopted new crops, new breeds of livestock, and innovations in technology, and they responded to changing market incentives.

Prior to the 1820s, the food production system of the ancestors of the BaSotho included hunting and gathering, cultivation, and stock-keeping. During the disruptive period of wars and migrations, livestock were raided or killed off and people were frequently forced to move before they could harvest their crops. Both stock-keeping and cultivation were interrupted in the 1820s and many people once again relied primarily on hunting and gathering for their subsistence. Only those people who occupied mountain strongholds with large plateaux were able to raise crops and livestock successfully during this period.

The advent of peace in about 1830 brought new changes in the food production systems. The BaSotho intensified their efforts at cultivation and rebuilt their herds of livestock. Through heavy inputs of labor the BaSotho had already achieved a dramatic increase in production before the advent of the missionaries and more than a decade before European markets were available to stimulate BaSotho production. Then in 1833 the missionaries brought new crops, new animals, and new technology. The intensification of production, with increasing emphasis on cultivation over stock-keeping, initially occurred spontaneously as the BaSotho sought food security. Not until later, in the 1840s and after, did the BaSotho further respond to the market incentives created by exchange with Europeans in the Cape Colony and Orange Free State. The steady increase in population density also necessitated the continued intensification of cultivation.

Land resources

Eventually the ability of the BaSotho to sustain agricultural growth was severely limited by the quality of the land area left to the BaSotho when the boundaries of the country were finally fixed in 1872. Of the total land area of colonial Basutoland, only 28 percent was suitable for cultivation. Of the remainder, 66 percent comprised the mountain range at an altitude of approximately 7,000 to 10,000 feet. Approximately 12 percent of the land area of Lesotho was unsuitable for either pastoral or arable use, and 60 percent of the total was suitable only for grazing.[2]

Erratic rainfall, ranging from 20 inches to over 40 inches annually, frequently caused damaging deluges alternating with prolonged droughts throughout the country. The growing season in the mountains was short, and there could be unexpected frosts or snow even in January (mid-summer) at the higher altitudes.[3] Temperature extremes hindered both cultivation and stock-keeping. Cold weather killed livestock during severe winters, and crops were killed by both blistering summer heat and unexpected summer frosts.[4] For example, many livestock were killed by the cold in the winter of 1852, and in mid-summer 1863 frost destroyed the wheat crop. In the winter of 1884 the temperature fell to 21 degrees Fahrenheit at night, and in May 1902 a missionary reported three consecutive nights at 1 degree Fahrenheit.

Soils in Lesotho suffered progressive erosion and depletion over the course of the nineteenth century.[5] Soils with the highest fertility in Lesotho also tend to be stony or impermeable, and the hill and mountain slopes create severe drainage problems.[6] The deep ravines which criss-cross the country today, caused by severe erosion, were already a problem in the nineteenth century. A missionary described these *dongas* in 1873 as already 20 feet deep and 30 to 40 feet wide, and getting larger every year from the rain.[7]

As the expanding population used trees and shrubs for building purposes and for fuel the country was denuded, accelerating soil erosion. In 1836 willows 28 to 30 feet high bordered the Orange and Caledon Rivers.[8] In 1845 Morija mountain was still covered with trees, and there was an abundance of shrubs for firewood in the ravines. By 1872, though, the forests at Qeme and Korokoro mountains were nearly exhausted, and there were scarcely any willows remaining along the rivers. A MoSotho writer lamented in 1884 that a dark forest at Thaba Bosiu had been cut down for building.[9] By the 1880s and 1890s trees had all but disappeared, and could only be found in remote mountain areas and at mission stations and magistracies where new trees had been planted. In 1902 many of the remaining trees were killed by snow damage and frost, suggesting that severe winters may previously have contributed to the destruction of trees and shrubs.[10]

The BaSotho were clearly aware of the physical properties of their land and the need for land management, exercising deliberate care in their allocation of land for cultivation and grazing. The care of pastures and the conscientious allocation of pasture land became more and more important during the nineteenth century as the amount of land under cultivation increased and the area of land available for grazing steadily diminished. In 1859, Casalis wrote that every village chief regularly set aside pastures for winter grazing.[11] The Governor's Agent in Basutoland, Charles D. Griffith, writing on "Native Basuto Custom" in 1872, referred to the system of *maboella* by name, and described it as the marking of a tract of grazing land in December each year which was reserved for use in the winter. He explained that as severe frosts killed almost all grass, without the reservation of pastures there would have been no pasturage in winter.[12] The assistant commissioner for Mafeteng imposed a fine in 1905 on a European trader whose cattle had been found grazing on reserved pastures, and wrote that to his knowledge the system of reserved grazing had been in effect since 1890.[13] Numerous informants also indicated that the system of pasture reservation, *maboella*, was not practiced when they were very young, but was introduced more recently.[14] In fact the system was older, but may have only been common in more densely populated areas.

By the end of the century the BaSotho were using a complicated system of pasture rotation, in which herds migrated seasonally into the mountains. In the spring the BaSotho burned off the old grass in the pastures to allow the new grass to grow in quickly and thickly. The practice of burning off old pasture grass was traditional among the BaSotho. The earliest missionaries observed the practice when they first arrived. They noted that it enriched the soil, and that when the rains came the new grass appeared.[15] The practice was necessary because the old grass grew nearly six feet high and became dry and inedible before it was burned at the end of the winter. Burning ensured early pasturage and cattle thrived on the new grass, but it also destroyed the roots of sweet grass varieties and kept the grass rank and sour and unsuitable for sheep.[16]

Fields were reserved until the grass was thick and had started scattering seeds, so that a new crop of grass would be assured later on. Following good rains, the grass appeared after only a week, and cattle were allowed on it after about two months. The cattle, which were thin after the winter, grew fat quickly on the new grass in those pastures where they were allowed to graze. The areas where thatching grasses grew were reserved throughout the year, and in addition some pastures were set aside as reserved grazing grounds (*maboella* or *letobo*).

Between late October and late December, when the plowing was finished, the herd-boys drove the cattle and smaller livestock to cattle posts for summer grazing in the mountains. Sometimes the hardier sheep and goats were left at the cattle-posts year-round. During the summer, each family was allowed to keep two or three milking cows or smaller animals at home. These grazed in specified areas, since most of the lowlands were cultivated, or were pastures reserved for roofing grasses or winter grazing. The animals remained in the mountains until the first frosts in April or early May, when they were brought down and allowed to graze on the stubble where crops had been harvested from the fields. In addition, the pastures reserved for winter grazing were opened, to feed the cattle until the new grass appeared in the spring. In August, on certain days designated by the chief, women cut thatching grasses and the herdboys then allowed the cattle to graze on the remains. Men burned the pastures again after the roofing grasses had been cut.

Each chief appointed a caretaker of the pastures, who enforced pasture rotation and observance of *maboella*. The caretaker was called the *mobehi oa leboella* or *mophuthi oa maboella*, the one who announces the reserved grazing, and he received for his services the right to larger amounts of thatching grass, which was controlled by the chief.[17]

Population

The population which had to be accommodated on the land grew steadily over the century. As early as 1846 pastures on the frontiers of Lesotho were

61

said to be better because the central districts had too great a concentration of population.[18] Early population estimates show a dramatic increase in the population of the Morija district from approximately 4,000 people in 1837 to 20,000 in 1848. In 1845 British Commandant Gideon D. Joubert estimated that there were 50,000 to 60,000 people under Moshoeshoe's rule, and an additional 1,000 BaTaung under Moletsane and 10,000 BaRolong under Moroka. Three years later the population under Moshoeshoe numbered 80,000. This may have been exaggerated: later estimates put the population of Lesotho at 70,000 in 1852 and 80,000 in 1855.[19]

The 1850s and 1860s were a period of demographic turmoil because of the fluctuating borders of Moshoeshoe's country. After the BaSotho defeated the BaTlokoa in 1853 Sekonyela fled with a band of refugees to the Cape Colony, while those who earlier had fled from the BaTlokoa into the Berea District of Lesotho returned to the territory west of the Caledon. In 1858 the residents from the Beersheba mission station took refuge in Moshoeshoe's country at Hermon, Matatiele, Botheta, and Morija. Droughts in 1858, 1861, and 1862 sent people from drier areas in the Cape Colony and Orange Free State into Lesotho seeking better land.[20] In the 1860s, the population from around the Bethulie mission station fled to Morija and Hermon, the BaTaung under Moletsane fled to Siloe and Berea, and Lebenya's people moved from Hebron to Paballong and Matatiele. In 1860–61 AmaSwazi refugees migrated into northern Lesotho.[21] The BaMonaheng and "upwards of 4,000 people" from the Koesberg area moved into Lesotho at the invitation of Moshoeshoe in 1869, as well as Bastards from the Platberg area, who settled at Bokhate.[22]

Because of this tremendous influx of refugees, the population in Lesotho in 1865 was an estimated 180,000; although the first census taken in 1873 reported a population of 127,323, observers suggested that a more accurate estimate would be 200,000.[23] The census figures may have been inaccurate because the population was still unsettled in the aftermath of the wars, famines, and diseases which had plagued the country for the previous ten years. A Catholic missionary explained the extensive immigration in the 1860s:

> The issue of this war has changed the configuration of the country. A consider-able part of the state of Moshesh has been annexed to the Free State. It is the portion situated on the right bank of the Caledon ... But as the Boers do not like to have Kafirs under their rule, very different is that from the English in Natal, all the Basutos who occupied the conquered territory, that is *more than half the nation of the Basutos* are obliged to leave the land which they inhabited to come and establish themselves on the left bank of the Caledon.[24]

Extensive immigration continued in the 1870s and 1880s. Sekonyela's grandson Lelinguana took the remnants of the BaTlokoa from the Herschel District of the Cape Colony into the mountains of Lesotho after being defeated by Colonial troops in 1880 during the Gun War. After the BaRolong lost most of their land at Thaba 'Nchu in 1886, thousands migrated *en masse* into the area around Hermon in Lesotho. Also in the late 1880s, there was extensive immigration into the Leribe District of BaSotho families who had been working in the Cape Colony and Orange Free State and who were returning to Lesotho with their livestock.[25] Thousands of AmaXhosa from the Transkeian territories immigrated into Lesotho in the late 1880s, and the annual Colonial Report for 1895–96 reported migration into the Qacha's Nek District from both Natal and the Cape Colony.[26] The official census of 1891 reported a total population of 218,902, and the annual Colonial Report of 1894–95 estimated the population at 250,000. If anything these figures were low, for the official census of 1904 showed the population of Lesotho had increased to 347,731.[27] Even this later figure may be low, as people tried to evade census-takers to avoid being taxed. Immigration into Lesotho can only be understood with reference to the regional context. Immigration was extensive not because the opportunities within the country were great, but because residence within Lesotho offered security which was not available across the borders in the British colonies and the Boer Republics. No matter how crowded the country became, or how exploitative BaSotho chiefs became, allegiance to these chiefs was considered preferable to the insecurity and oppression to which Africans were subject elsewhere.

The rapidly expanding population residing within the boundaries of colonial Basutoland was gradually pushed further and further into the mountains. As early as 1879 a missionary reported that the country was almost plowed over, and predicted that shortly the fields would become "ungrateful and fruitless."[28] In 1886 a British official noted that the whole face of the country up to the mountain slopes was a vast corn field, and that many people were actually plowing in the mountains.[29] In 1878 Moshoeshoe's nephew Maluke migrated with his people to the upper Orange River, and during the Gun War (1880–81) entire villages emigrated from the plains into the mountains. Mabille estimated that there were more than 600 villages between the sources of the Orange River and Mount Moorosi in 1885.[30]

Reports from the late 1880s indicated that every available piece of ground on every plateau and in every valley had been plowed under. Each time a member of the royal family was "placed," or given authority over a new area, he took his followers to settle with him. In this way, the mountain areas of the country filled up quickly. In 1890 Paramount Chief Letsie sent his son Rafolatsane with his people into the mountains to enforce his authority over Lelinguana's BaTlokoa, and then Letsie's heir Lerotholi placed his son Makhaola as chief over the entire region. Shortly after that two of Letsie's other sons, Kloli and Nako, established themselves with many people in the hills and valleys of the Majhalaneng, a mountain area which was previously uninhabited. Similar reports document the populating of the valleys of the Maphutseng and Quassing Rivers in the 1890s, and at Qomoqomong a missionary was surprised to find fifteen scattered hamlets of 350 to 400 people each. These people were cultivating fields and using pastures at an altitude of over 6,000 feet.[31]

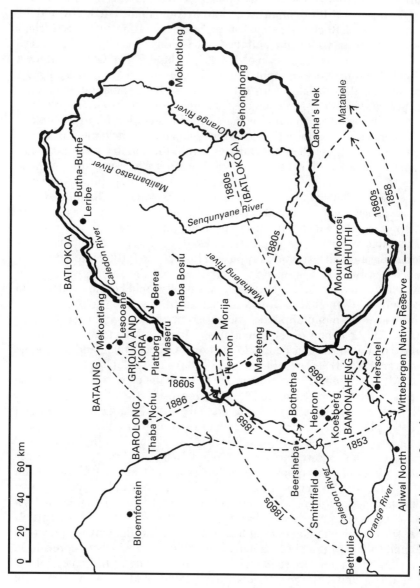

Fig. 6 Migration into Lesotho

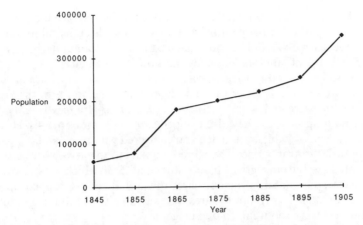

Fig. 7 Estimated population of Lesotho, 1845–1905

The negative effects of over-population were already being experienced in the 1890s. A missionary wrote that most fields had been cultivated steadily for half a century and were exhausted.[32] New generations could no longer be provided with fields of their own, and land and grazing disputes became common. Because land suitable for cultivation was all allotted, when leading chiefs died the inheritance became a potent source of contention.[33]

Hunting and gathering

While the human population increased, the size of the wild animal population declined steadily in Lesotho over the course of the nineteenth century. During the 1820s agriculture was completely disrupted and most livestock were killed off. Game became the mainstay of the BaSotho diet, along with gathered roots and vegetables. At other times hunting provided an important supplement to the diet of the BaSotho. The BaSotho carefully dried, cut and stored the meat from an antelope, which could amount to 200 lbs. from a single animal.[34]

Wild game constituted a plentiful source of food early in the century. Large herds of wildebeest, springboks, and blesboks were commonly found in the lowlands in the 1830s.[35] Most common was the letsa (pl. *matsa*), the vaal or grey reebok. But by the 1850s game in the lowland districts of Lesotho was already rare, for there were no more forests to serve as retreats for the wild animals, which had migrated further into the mountains. In spite of this, hunting parties continued to find game in the central region of Lesotho, and in the Orange Free State, where the BaSotho often sought permission to hunt.[36]

Hunters could still find large game in the mountains of Lesotho at the end of the century, but it became more and more scarce over time. By 1880 elands, reebok, and hartebeest were scarce in the mountains, and each year

65

hunters had to go further into the "innermost reaches" of the mountains to find game.[37] Earlier in the century leopards, lions, cheetahs, hippopotami, jackals, hyenas, wolves and baboons had roamed the mountains, but by 1900 only a few kinds of antelope, monkeys and birds remained.[38]

The BaSotho hunted in various ways. When men hunted in large groups, they used spears, bows and arrows, and later guns. The points of the arrows were sometimes treated with "medicine" (*moriana*). Hunters usually used dogs for hunting as well. They also trapped game by various means. Hunters often dug a *lemana*, which was a deep hole covered with reeds and plants and grass, in order to trap game. They lured animals to the area where the trap was located by burning green plants, the smoke of which was known to attract game. The BaSotho made snares out of flat rocks propped up with two poles or sticks. Traps and snares were especially useful during famines when hunters were too weak to pursue game.[39]

People also ate locusts, which were dried and stored for future consumption. The BaSotho customarily gathered invading locusts in massive quantities early in the morning when the dew on the locusts' wings prevented them from flying. The BaSotho dried the locusts, pulled off their heads and wings, and ate them dry or made them into porridge. Locusts frequently caused severe crop destruction, but they also provided relief from the very famine they precipitated. In 1851 locusts swarmed at the Bethulie mission station for over two months, and people ate little else for several months of the year.[40] The BaSotho also fed locusts to animals, who grew fat on them.[41] The use of arsenic spray to destroy locusts while still in the crawling stage prevented much crop destruction after the turn of the twentieth century. Spraying was necessary because the destruction of harvests by locusts was frequent and severe, and spraying reduced times of food scarcity caused by locust invasions.

The BaSotho consumed countless varieties of wild roots and vegetables to avoid famine during droughts and crop failures. They threshed the tiny grains of *moseeka* grass to make the food most commonly eaten during famines. People collected this grass by the mountains, and subsisted on it, along with roots and tubers, when their corn was gone.

Cultivation

Before stationary settlement became temporarily impossible and arable agriculture impractical in the 1820s, the ancestors of the BaSotho practiced mixed agriculture and cultivated numerous crops. The gradual return to peace and stability brought renewed opportunities for arable agriculture, while the years of confrontation with starvation created an incentive for heavy labor inputs to expand agriculture quickly. In 1836 Arbousset and Daumas observed that the BaSotho and BaTlokoa were better agriculturalists than were "the greater part of the bechuana tribes."[42] The BaSotho successfully expanded cultivation over the next few decades.

Chiefs allocated two or three fields to every man when he married. In return every man who had been allocated fields owed his allegiance to the chief and among other things was obligated to work at the chief's work-parties, *matsema* (sing. *letsema*), when certain designated fields of the chief were cultivated. The number and size of fields allocated to a man changed over time and varied according to several factors. In the early days fields were small, like gardens. Frequent migration discouraged the BaSotho from investing the large amounts of labor time that were necessary to dig up large fields by hand. Once settlements became permanent, however, people began enlarging their fields, and beginning in the 1850s the adoption of the ox-plow made it possible to plow much greater areas than previously. In addition, the fertility of the fields declined over time, so that it became necessary to plow larger areas to achieve the same output. Because the soils of the country frequently differed, a person was not commonly given a big field in one place. Instead he was given a few acres in one place and a few in another so that everyone shared the most fertile areas. This protected a family from losing their whole harvest if one area was ruined.[43]

After the introduction of taxation during the colonial period, every tax-payer was entitled to a field. As the land became crowded, however, this became impossible and young men had to pursue their claims aggressively to be allotted a field.[44] Polygamists were traditionally allocated two to three fields per wife while there was still sufficient land. This reinforced the unequal distribution of wealth, since only rich men could afford several wives.

A man was entitled to keep his fields until he died or moved away, but according to the codified customary laws of Lerotholi (1903), if a man left a field unused for more than one year, "especially at this time of shortness of fields," the chief had the power and right to take it and give it to another person.[45] A man's fields were inherited by his wife and children when he died, or by the sons and unmarried daughters if his wife also died.[46] Thus a woman did sometimes inherit fields with which she was expected to support herself, her children, and her grandchildren.[47] In theory, fields that were cultivated continuously stayed in a family indefinitely, but in practice fields were often re-allocated when the owner died, and his heirs kept only part of his fields.[48] A widow was rarely allowed to keep all of her husband's fields since it was assumed she needed fewer fields because there was one less mouth to feed. Because the remaining fields were generally divided among several sons, land-holdings became progressively smaller.

The BaSotho grew a wide variety of foods in their fields, thereby hedging against individual crop failure while also diversifying their diet. Millet or sorghum (*mabele*), often called "Kafir corn" by nineteenth-century writers, was the staple food of the BaSotho. Oral tradition says the BaSotho first acquired sorghum from their Nguni neighbors to the south.[49] It was particularly useful in Lesotho because it grew easily even when there was not much rain. The BaSotho grew four varieties of sorghum, plus two related varieties of sweet reed (*ntsoe*) which they consumed in enormous quantities.[50]

Maize (*poone*), also called "mealies" by Europeans, is said to have come from the Portuguese on the east coast, via the Nguni. Casalis speculated, however, that it entered the region simultaneously from the Mozambique coast and the Cape Colony.[51] Before the Europeans came to Lesotho, there was only one variety of maize, and at first the BaSotho just planted maize on the edge of sorghum fields, since it was not very important in their diet. The BaSotho did not use maize for brewing until the twentieth century, because it was not thought to "strengthen the body" like sorghum did; however, they allowed cattle to graze on the stalks and they used the cobs for fuel. Maize also did not fare as well in Lesotho as did sorghum. Maize needs a lot of rain while growing or it will dry out, but after it has grown too much rain will cause it to turn yellow. Eventually, however, the BaSotho grew seven varieties of maize.[52]

In addition to grain, the BaSotho traditionally cultivated several vegetables, including pumpkins, calabashes, watermelon, and beans. Pumpkins (*mekopu*) were difficult to grow because they need a lot of rain and shade so they will not be burned by the sun. In addition to the one variety traditionally cultivated, the BaSotho adopted two more from the Europeans. Calabashes (*mehope*) could be eaten when very small and then used to make tobacco boxes, or grown larger and used as vessels for fetching, pouring, and drinking water. There were three varieties of watermelon (*mahapu*). One was usually only to feed animals, one was eaten by people, and a third rare variety was made into "bread" or jam. The BaSotho traditionally grew two varieties of beans. Like sorghum, beans grew well even in drought conditions.[53]

The French missionaries introduced several new foods to the BaSotho after their arrival in 1833. Of these they promoted wheat the most aggressively because they believed that the cultivation of wheat for exchange with their European neighbors was the best way to integrate the BaSotho into the regional market economy, and so to achieve a higher "degree of civilization."[54] The cultivation of wheat was difficult in the central lowland districts of the country, however, because of the dryness of the climate. The first wheat crop planted by the French Protestant missionaries in 1835 failed and was abandoned. Fifteen years later their annual report indicated that wheat would scarcely succeed except with irrigation, and subsequent observers agreed that wheat only grew where it was possible to water it regularly from springs or rivers. In 1844 irrigation became a subject of discussion at the annual missionary conference. According to the missionaries Moshoeshoe resisted the dispersal and resettlement of people in areas suitable for irrigation because of his concerns for maintaining more concentrated settlements necessary for defense and security.[55]

In spite of this, the missionaries continued to promote the new grain. The BaSotho resisted these efforts, both because millet required much less moisture than wheat and was much more successful, and because they did not develop a taste for wheat so that it did not take on an important role in their own diet. Furthermore, although there was a market for wheat, the BaSotho became involved in market exchange with the Europeans by selling corn, cattle, and other livestock, so that there was no distinct market advantage attached to the cultivation of wheat. In the 1840s the missionaries reported that near some of the mission stations the BaSotho were beginning to grow wheat, but as late as 1891 an Anglican missionary wrote that wheat was just beginning to be extensively grown in the central districts.[56]

In fact, the widespread adoption of wheat cultivation came only as the BaSotho moved into the mountain districts of the country. Wheat was more successful there than in the lowlands because of greater annual rainfall, and it required a much shorter growing season than sorghum and maize, which were ruined by early frosts in the mountains. Reports of abundant wheat harvests thus began to appear in the 1870s and 1880s, when more and more people were moving into the mountains and cultivating wheat because it was best suited to the new environment. At the end of the century the traditional crops of sorghum and maize were still more widely grown than wheat by the nation as a whole, but in the mountain districts the people had come to depend almost entirely on wheat for subsistence. In 1887 the Colonial government distributed seed wheat to improve the class of the cereal in Lesotho.[57]

The missionaries introduced several other foods which proved successful when grown in Lesotho, and which the BaSotho readily adopted into their diet. Potatoes were successful from the outset, and their use spread throughout the country, as they also did well in the mountains. Fruit trees were also an important contribution of the missionaries. In addition to vine shoots for grapes, they brought cherry, peach, orange, fig, and apple trees.[58] By the 1850s the BaSotho had begun planting fruit trees and vines, and in 1877 Maeder reported that in one month he had distributed 400 fruit trees, in addition to poplars and willows. Other foods brought by the Europeans and adopted by the BaSotho in the nineteenth century included two new varieties of pumpkin, and several new varieties of corn and beans, peas, lentils, and oats.[59]

Tobacco had spread into the region of Lesotho before the arrival of the first Europeans in the 1830s. The cultivation of tobacco was labor intensive. The BaSotho delegated the work of cultivating tobacco to old people; it was thought that tobacco grown by a young person would be weak and tasteless. The seeds were planted near the house, and when the first shoots appeared the seedlings were transplanted into a small walled enclosure, a process requiring considerable time and care. Once harvested, tobacco was dried in the sun, rolled in leaves, and smoked in a pipe or mixed with aloe ashes and water to be used as snuff, especially by women.[60] Indian hemp, *Cannibis sativa* (*matekoane*), had also been grown in the region for a long time. It was generally smoked in a pipe, and was a regional article of exchange.[61]

Pastoral production

The ancestors of the BaSotho were also herders. Most people lost their livestock during the 1820s, and the dramatically unequal distribution of cattle wealth which resulted became the basis for the new sociopolitical order. When the missionaries first arrived in the 1830s the BaSotho were primarily agriculturalists, for they had lost most of their cattle during the previous ten years of wars. In the late 1820s and early 1830s they had begun to rebuild their herds through raids, as they had done in the past, but gradually cattle raiding was abandoned. Instead, by reaping large crops the BaSotho were able to trade for livestock with their African neighbors beginning in the early 1830s. Arbousset emphasized the success of the BaSotho in acquiring livestock and diversifying their economic production:

> The Baralong, the Bahlaping, and the Griquas come daily to buy grain and to supply this nation with cattle; it was hitherto very poor in the latter ... Since our arrival in this little state, no fewer than 1,500 head of horned cattle, 40,000 sheep, 35,000 goats, 200 horses ... have been imported.[62]

In 1845 the BaSotho still did not possess many cattle, but the fact that the BaSotho were exporting surplus cattle to the Cape Colony in the 1850s suggests that they had been very successful in increasing their herds.[63] According to census data, by 1875 the BaSotho possessed 217,732 cattle including oxen, which had increased to 320,934 in 1891.[64] Observers in the 1890s were impressed with the number of cattle in the country, and overstocking had become a problem before the onset of Rinderpest in 1896.[65]

The primary importance of cattle, beyond their socioeconomic value, was the production of milk. Cattle were rarely slaughtered for their meat: chiefs killed them for feasts, and occasionally an old animal would be slaughtered by a family at the beginning of winter. This was the logical time to kill an animal, because forage in pastures was scarce and weak animals were likely to die anyway. It was also a time when meat could easily be dried and stored to supplement the food supply for several months. Cattle were also used for transport, and after the introduction of the plow they were needed for cultivation. The BaSotho made ointment from cow's milk, and prepared fuel from cattle dung.

The BaSotho also kept large herds of sheep and goats. In 1834 a European traveller observed a village with goats but no cattle, a situation which must have been common at that time.[66] Goats fared better than sheep because the sheep did not thrive on the sour grasses in Lesotho. Certainly the production of milk, as well as meat, constituted a strong incentive for keeping goats. Traditional "fat-tailed" sheep were kept for meat, and sheepskins were used for clothing. Wooled sheep were gradually introduced from the herds of the

AmaXhosa and BaTswana. These sheep were red and black, and were smaller than the white part-merino wooled sheep of the Boers, but they needed less care during severe weather than did the fat-tailed sheep.[67] By 1858 a new commerce in wool had begun, and by the 1870s the sale of wool was helping to compensate for a reduction of trade in grain during years of poor harvests.[68] In 1875 census data indicated that the BaSotho possessed 303,080 sheep and 215,485 goats.[69]

The French missionaries introduced pigs into Lesotho soon after their arrival in the 1830s. The BaSotho at first thought pigs were detestable, but soon herd-boys and women began to look after them, and the BaSotho added pork to their diet. Those that kept pigs on the mission stations "felt much less the loss of their cattle than they would otherwise have done" after the wars with the Europeans.[70] The census showed that the BaSotho owned a total of 15,635 pigs in 1875. BaSotho women fed pigs with grain which had been infested with weevils, and slaughtered them for meat. They also sometimes made ointment from pig's fat. Some BaSotho refused to eat pork, but others regarded pigs as the "salvation" of the BaSotho.[71]

The BaSotho acquired horses in raids on the Kora and Griqua beginning in the early 1830s. Ellenberger reports that the first horse owned by Moshoeshoe was sent to him by Moorosi, but a letter in the *Graham's Town Journal* in 1845 offers a lengthy story suggesting that the first horses were brought into the area by a Prussian traveller and botanist, Zydensteicker (Seidenstecher), in 1829 or 1830. In 1845 horses were still few and of inferior quality in Lesotho.[72] By 1861 the number of horses in the country had increased significantly, and by the time of the 1875 Census the BaSotho possessed 35,357 horses. This figure more than doubled to 81,194 in 1891.[73] When first introduced horses were primarily valuable for raiding, as the BaSotho were at a great disadvantage in conflicts with mounted Kora and Griqua until they acquired horses of their own. Later the BaSotho used horses primarily for travelling, and sometimes as pack animals, although oxen remained the primary beasts of burden.

Animals were widely distributed among the population by the end of the nineteenth century. Data from eighty informants indicates that over 90 percent of their families owned cattle at the turn of the century, but a disproportionate number of wealthy families may have been represented in the pool of informants. It is also possible that informants may have been reluctant to reveal the poverty of their fathers, which would have been implied by not owning cattle. In either case the figure may be distorted to show a higher proportion of families owning livestock than actually did. Nevertheless these data reinforce the hypothesis that as the nineteenth century had progressed disparities of wealth had decreased because people were able to acquire cattle wealth through means other than the *mafisa* system. They sold crops or worked on farms and in the mines outside the country in order to earn the money to buy cattle. However, at the beginning of the twentieth century there were still great disparities in the numbers of cattle held by each household. Some households owned only one or two animals, while some chiefs owned hundreds of head of cattle, sheep, and goats.

The advent of Rinderpest in 1896 further altered the distribution of wealth in the country. Some areas were adversely affected more than others, because some chiefs refused to allow inoculation in their districts. Both chiefs and commoners saved many of their cattle in districts where herds were inoculated, while chiefs and commoners elsewhere lost their entire herds. This altered the geographic distribution of wealth, and commoners from some districts found themselves temporarily better off than chiefs in other districts.[74] In those districts where entire herds were lost, however, chiefs were able to mobilize other resources to generate income, and they quickly rebuilt their herds.

A large proportion of households also owned other livestock at the end of the nineteenth century. If the data from my informants is representative, more than half of all families owned sheep, although the size of family flocks ranged from just a few sheep to hundreds. Information from my informants shows that 40 percent of their families owned goats, 38 percent owned horses, and 18 percent owned pigs. These figures, like those for cattle ownership, may not reflect the general population if a preponderance of informants were wealthy, and the percentage of households which actually owned these varieties of stock may have been smaller. The data do reflect the relative popularity of the various breeds of livestock, as confirmed in census figures from 1875.

Donkeys were apparently introduced at the beginning of the twentieth century. In a journey through the mountains in 1909, Segoete observed that people owned both donkeys and mules (*esele* or *tonki*, *mulete* or *'moulo*), but these were probably rare.[75] Only 19 percent of the informants reported the presence of donkeys when they were children, and several conceded that they were rare, while 14 percent stated explicitly that there were no donkeys at all in Lesotho when they were little, and that they had come only recently.[76]

The BaSotho also kept poultry. They already had chickens when the missionaries arrived, but Casalis and Arbousset introduced ducks, geese and turkeys. Eggs were consumed by the household and sold to others, and the birds were frequently slaughtered for meat. BaSotho women fed poultry with coarse grain left over from grinding.

Environment, politics, and food, 1802–1902

The BaSotho clearly used their natural resources carefully and deliberately for food production. They diversified production, combining pastoralism with cultivation and integrating the two systems of production in a careful seasonal allocation of land use. They diversified their livestock holdings and their crops. They adopted techniques of planting which ensured the best use of diverse soil types and conditions and the rejuvenation of the soil. Implicit in their activities is a conscious understanding and use of the environment, and an intentional maximizing of outputs achieved with their knowledge and a high input of labor. Most significantly it is clear that the BaSotho deliberately produced food surpluses above and beyond their immediate consumption needs. Contrary to modern western assumptions about non-western agricultural societies, people such as the BaSotho had strong incentives to produce food surpluses and did so regularly. Most obviously, the regular and frequent appearance of droughts in southern Africa prompted the BaSotho to produce and store surplus grain for consumption during periods of food scarcity. Surplus production was the most successful strategy for famine avoidance in an area plagued by droughts.

In spite of their efforts, however, the welfare of the BaSotho was continually challenged by the disruptions in production caused by environmental problems and political disturbances, sometimes related to each other, which caused food shortages and sometimes famine. In the history of this region in the nineteenth century it is possible to trace and analyze how the effects of ecological crises such as droughts were determined by the human responses to those crises. As scholars have shown with regard to modern famines, famines are not the direct and inevitable result of food shortages. Rather, famines result from the failure, whether deliberate or unintended, of people to intervene in ways which would ensure the equitable distribution of scarce food supplies, such that no one would starve.[77] In times of war, both Africans and Europeans fighting in southern Africa often deliberately induced famine by the wholesale destruction of enemy crops and foodstores, so as to weaken their resistance. Ironically, however, those wars themselves were often sparked when droughts made evident the inadequacy of land resources held by a group of people. Hence drought often fuelled war, and war in turn brought crop destruction and further reduced food supplies, resulting in famine. This scenario recurred in the vicinity of the SeSotho-speaking peoples time and again in the nineteenth century, setting them against both African and European neighbors in a struggle which became increasingly desperate by the middle of the century.

Political stability and economic prosperity in Lesotho in the nineteenth century were adversely affected by droughts, wars, famine and epidemics, locusts, and epizootics, as indicated in table 1. The incidence of drought was high throughout the century: in addition to the frequent droughts lasting less than a year, Lesotho suffered from a prolonged drought in every decade but one. Prolonged droughts caused crop failure and the death of livestock from starvation, and prompted the migration of people and animals in search of food. In addition crops were devastated by periodic locust invasions, although the arrival of locusts during droughts actually brought some relief from famine.[78] Because of accelerated population growth, the decline in traditional hunting and gathering activities, the limited potential for arable agriculture because of the decline in the area and quality of available land, and the sale of agricultural surpluses, over time the BaSotho became less

Table 1. *Incidents of drought, famine, and disease in nineteenth-century Lesotho.*

Drought	Famine	Disease	Migration/Wars
1800–03	1802–04	—	migrations
1812	—	—	(Xhosa Frontier War)
1816–18	1818	—	Shaka's campaigns begin in 1817 AmaZizi immigration 1818 AmaHlubi & Matiwane immigrations 1821–22
1826–28	1826–28	—	Matiwane migration 1827
1834	—	—	(Xhosa Frontier War, Boer migrations)
1841–43	1841–43	typhus yellow fever	Boer immigration
1851–52[a]	—	—	British/BaSotho wars, June 1851 & Dec. 1852
1858–59	1858–59	typhoid dysentery	Boer/BaSotho war
1860–63	1862–63	smallpox	
1865	1865–66	typhoid	Boer/BaSotho war 1865, 1866, 1867
1877–80[b]			Gun War 1880–81
1883–85	1883–85	smallpox	Civil War 1882–85
1887 partial	—	whooping cough	—
1890 partial	—	typhoid measles	—
1895–98	1896–98	dysentery typhoid influenza smallpox	Civil War 1898

[a] Orange Free State
[b] Cape Colony and Orange Free State

successful at generating surplus food for storage and consumption during droughts.

Amartya Sen has provided an incisive conceptualization of the social process involved in the creation of famines. Sen's concept of entitlement is useful in explaining how socioeconomic and political factors induced famines during droughts. Sen defines the term "entitlement" as the ability of people to command food, and explains why famine is not necessarily a function of food supply but is rather a function of the legal access people have to the food which is available. Famines can and do occur even when sufficient food supplies are present. Famines affect those segments of the population who have no entitlement to the food which is available, hence Sen indicates that one must examine the socioeconomic and political factors determining food distribution in order to understand the origins of famine.[79]

The experience of the SeSotho- and SeTswana-speaking peoples in the early nineteenth century can only be understood with reference to their interaction with an environment which was frequently plagued by drought. Droughts before 1800 are difficult to trace. However, the most common reaction to a food shortage caused by drought was migration, either temporary or permanent, in search of food, which could take people long distances where the effects of the drought was widespread. Therefore reports of migrations before the nineteenth century may suggest periods of environmental crises such as droughts, since migrations are not undertaken without compelling reasons. Oral traditions of migrations must always be treated with care since they may be a metaphor for internal social or political changes rather than an accurate recording of a physical migration. However, the migrations recorded in the early traditions of the BaSotho correspond sufficiently to the archeological record and include specific references to people which suggest relative accuracy for the seventeenth and eighteenth centuries. Evidence of migrations supports the logical assumption that droughts were not new to southern Africa in the nineteenth century.

It is easier to trace droughts which Europeans witnessed, beginning with the devastating drought of the turn of the nineteenth century which adversely affected the entire region. The whole area of southern Africa, from the Cape Colony to the east coast, suffered a severe drought from 1800 to 1802 or 1803. Europeans in the Cape Colony lost so many cattle from the drought that cultivation using draught animals was hindered and food became scarce. The Cape government sent an expedition north to trade for cattle and for the first time Europeans went far enough to encounter SeTswana-speaking people.[80] Ellenberger summarized oral reports he collected about this drought:

> This took place in the year 1803, the year of the terrible famine which was called by the name Sekoboto. It was a time of disaster and death. Family ties were suspended as well as those between chiefs and people, and the starving people gave themselves to any one who could keep them alive. Owing to the long drought there were [sic] no grain and hardly any milk or leguminous plants. Old men who went through it in their youth have related that never before or since has there been such a famine. People grew so weak that they could only crawl or stagger about. Men could not maintain their families, and turned off their younger wives to fend for themselves, with freedom to join themselves to any one who could keep them. Mokotjo and his relations as well as other of the people managed to exist on a kind of meal made of beef liver which was first boiled, then dried and minced fine. It was made into a kind of paste with milk when procurable, and made a sort of substitute for grain.[81]

The Africans in the interior of the region suffered famine as a result of this drought because there was an absolute and severe decline in food availability in the region and trade networks carrying food did not yet exist to alleviate the shortage. So severe was the drought that even the families of wealthy chiefs were adversely affected. The family of a chief of the BaTlokoa survived only by slaughtering large and small animals daily, an option only available to the very wealthy who had extensive herds which could survive over a period of a year or more after much livestock had perished from starvation.[82] Thus entitlements determined who survived widespread food scarcity during this drought, as the possession of large numbers of animals represented a direct food entitlement not available to the poor. Even within wealthy households entitlements determined the distribution of food among members of the same family. The famine was called the "famine of the female servants" by SeSotho-speaking people, as polygamists "freed" their wives to marry again since they could not feed them, that is, men turned their junior wives out of their homes to fend for themselves or starve. The appropriate unit of analysis for identifying entitlements was smaller than both the community and the household, for women and children had lesser entitlements to food within households, making them more vulnerable to famine in times of food scarcity.[83]

In the 1810s drought and other natural disasters affected southern Africa. A drought occurred in 1812 and led to food scarcity but no recorded famine, presumably because of traditional strategies of famine avoidance, including consumption of stored grain and migration to obtain food by trade. According to oral tradition, the Mapolane at Maphutsing were short of grain in 1811 or 1813 or 1814, but they nevertheless collected some to give to the travelling chief and healer Mohlomi whose people were in need.[84] Drought recurred in 1816–18, and grain crops were destroyed by rust in 1816. In 1817 many cattle in the region died of a plague which was called the "Lefu la ma-Motohoana."[85] Shaka's earliest campaigns were reported to have taken place between 1817 and 1820, in the aftermath of severe regional losses from the crop rust and cattle epizootic. In 1818, perhaps as a result of natural disasters and accompanying political turmoil, "very many" MaZizi came into Lesotho from the area of the Tugela River, some to trade and many to settle.[86]

Droughts, famines, and raiding for standing crops and stored grain were reported across the region for the early 1820s.[87] "About the year 1821," before the arrival of the AmaNgwane and AmaHlubi from the east in 1822, the BaTsueneng chief considered it necessary to send armed guards out with their herds during a severe drought. The chief's relative, who along with his followers was keeping the herd, refused to return the cattle, but the stock was retaken forcibly by the chief's son, and the women and children were the first to concede and return to the chief.[88] In 1822 the younger brother of the MaKhoakhoa chief Lethole was driven to steal grain from a new ally, the young chief Moshoeshoe.[89] The same year the BaMolibeli went to extreme measures to hide their grain at the top of some precipitous rocks by hauling it up with ropes. So precious was grain at this point that their allies betrayed the hiding place to Matiwane and the AmaNgwane who took it for themselves. The BaMolibeli then travelled to Peka and got enough grain to avoid famine, returning home to sow a crop which they reaped in 1823.[90] The MaKhoakhoa were suffering from famine at the time, prompting their men to go out foraging for food in spite of a recent successful raid for cattle against the BaSia, which left them vulnerable to attack from former allies, the MaTlotlokoane of Sepetja, whom the Makhoakhoa had just betrayed.[91] The BaTlokoa kept secret stores of grain at Sefate, and some BaHlakoana finally fled to Makhoarane near modern Roma after their stored grain was seized by Makhetha.[92] Some of the MaKholokoe were driven by starvation to migrate to Zululand where they put themselves under Shaka, and "there under a strong ruler, they got a little rest, and remained quietly for about four years until the death of Chaka in 1828."[93]

Written European sources confirm these incidents of drought which caused regional food scarcity, exacerbated conflicts, and prevented stable settlement, cultivation and recovery. When Moffat first arrived among the BaThlaping BaTswana in 1820 he discovered that "years of drought had been severely felt."[94] In August 1824 Thompson found some Kora who were literally starving to death and attributed their starvation to extreme drought.[95] Moffat reported in 1826 that there had been "several successive years of drought, during which water had not been seen to flow upon the ground; and in that climate, if rain does not fall continuously and in considerable quantities, it is all exhaled in a couple of hours."[96]

The effect of this drought was food scarcity and famine. Before the rain finally came in 1826 Moffat observed that "the cattle were dying from want of pasture, and hundreds of living skeletons were seen going to the fields in quest of unwholesome roots and reptiles, while many were dying with hunger."[97] The drought was felt over a wide area, for Griqua hunters visiting as far north as the BaNgwaketsi had to take a detour on their way home to Griquatown because of the drought.[98]

Interpretations of the conflicts in the interior of southern Africa in the 1820s have falsely attributed war and devastation to the ruthlessness of Zulu raiders in the so-called "*mfecane*" or "*lifaqane*" which has blinded historians to the interaction of human and natural factors which were responsible for the misery experienced by the African population. Systematic slave and cattle-raiding by the Griqua and Kora, sponsored and supported by white frontier farmers who supplied the weapons and ammunition and purchased the slaves and cattle, prevented SeSotho- and SeTswana-speaking groups from resettling once they had been uprooted in migrations induced by severe drought and a competitive search for food.[99]

As a result of these disruptions Moshoeshoe set about deliberately acquiring horses, guns, and missionaries to serve as a military and political balance and protection against the raiding Griqua and Kora who had wrought such destruction on the BaSotho for several decades. With political stability the BaSotho pursued their age-old practice of producing grain surpluses to store for times of need. The consumption of stored grain apparently prevented famine among the BaSotho following a drought in 1834, but in later decades their strategies for avoiding famine began to break down and they succumbed to famine more easily when drought was prolonged. From this time on the association of political crises and wars with drought is apparent as there were no wars which occurred independently of drought. Drought did not cause these wars, rather these early conflicts between BaSotho and Boer were manifestations of a continuous struggle for control of land, and conflict became overt during periods when drought brought the two groups into more direct competition for additional grazing and arable lands. The BaSotho enjoyed exceptionally productive years in the 1830s, but this was followed by drought, locusts and epidemics of typhus and yellow fever in 1841–43. Notably good years followed again in 1844–46. Attacks on the BaSotho by the British in June 1851 and December 1852 occurred during the course of an extended drought in the Orange River Sovereignty which lasted from 1849 to 1852.[100] The drought did not extend into Lesotho, and the BaSotho did not suffer from crop failure, famine, or epidemic disease at this time. It is significant that the war alone was not sufficient to induce famine conditions among the BaSotho.

A serious cattle disease appeared again in 1852. Lungsickness (pleuropneumonia) entered the Orange Free State and Lesotho from the Cape Colony in 1855, devastating the herds of both Boers and BaSotho in 1856 and 1857.[101] This catastrophe provoked cattle raiding between the two groups. Another drought in 1858 was followed by a Boer–BaSotho war in 1858, which culminated in the Treaty of Aliwal North. Once again the BaSotho suffered famine in 1858–59, because the depredations of war exacerbated the food shortage caused by drought. In this war the Boers deliberately destroyed BaSotho crops, and most BaSotho lost their cattle.[102] Epidemics of typhoid and dysentery occurred at this time.

Two dry years in 1860 and 1861 were followed by the drought of 1862, which was known for generations as the "great" drought, or "red dust," when the Caledon River ceased to flow for the only time in memory.[103] It was reported that not a trace of vegetation could be found, and tens of thousands of animals died from hunger, thirst, and disease.[104] Sufficient rains fell in 1863 and 1864, but locusts destroyed the crops in both years, so that there was no real recovery from famine before drought recurred throughout southern Africa in 1865. The BaSotho suffered from lengthy epidemics of smallpox, typhoid, and typhus.

Significantly, however, their Boer neighbors suffered as well. So severe was the drought that draught animals could not survive the route from the Cape and food supplies could not be transported. As a result the Boers experienced famine for the first time in 1863. Having made a transition from herding cattle and Cape fat-tailed sheep to the herding of wooled (part-merino) sheep, the Boers could not depend on their livestock as a food supply and were totally dependent on trading for the grain of the BaSotho. In 1863 a French missionary reported that in the Orange Free State "hunger is beginning to make itself felt everywhere," whereas the BaSotho were still living on stored grain.[105] The Boers coveted the more fertile land of the BaSotho, and took it by force in the wars that were fought over the next few years.

In the 1860s, the BaSotho ability to resist militarily was undermined by the devastation wrought on them by famine and disease. Crops were destroyed either by drought or locusts in every year from 1860 to 1865 and again in 1867. Many livestock died of starvation during the drought of 1860–63, and the movement of livestock in search of pasture led to the spread of a lungsickness epizootic described as "affreuse" in 1864.[106] Missionaries reported that entire herds were dying and feared that the cattle herds might be entirely annihilated. Another epizootic killed more than half the sheep and horses in some areas in 1865.[107] Thousands more cattle died over the two years 1864–66: an estimated 20,000 to 30,000 cattle had died from hunger and thirst in the Thaba Bosiu district by September 1865.[108] A smallpox epidemic occurred in 1861, and typhus and typhoid reached epidemic proportions in the period 1866–68. A missionary reported in December 1868 that typhus had been in the country for ten months and had already killed more people than had the war.[109] The famine and disease conditions which prevailed in the mid-1860s and which prevented an effective BaSotho military defense against the Boer intrusion, was deliberately fostered by the Boers who raided BaSotho cattle and standing crops in 1865 and pursued a policy of total destruction. Adele Mabille, wife of a missionary, described famine at Thaba Bosiu and its causes in 1865:

> You must remember that the Boers had burnt all the villages and carried off the maize and mabele, burning that which they could not take away with them. Their [the BaSotho] cattle had been seized. Thus began a long time of suffering which lasted for over three years ... Famine made terrible ravages among us. These poor wretches dug up the bones of the cattle which had thrown themselves from the rocks at the time of the siege, to try to find yet some remains of tendon or skin. In the early morning at dawn, girls and women were seen leaving for the fields to try to gather some grains of grass (moseke) or some roots. They came back at night with a tiny handful of these seeds which they made into broth for their little children.[110]

Under these debilitating conditions, the BaSotho signed the Treaty of Thaba Bosiu in 1866, ceding to the Boers approximately two-thirds of their arable lands. It was called "The Peace of the Sorghum," and once crops were harvested the BaSotho resumed fighting.[111] The BaSotho were able to prevent the Boers from occupying the ceded land, but they could not defeat them. Only under the duress of severe famine and epidemic levels of disease, as well as Boer depredations, were the BaSotho finally compelled to request protection from the British Crown, which was granted in 1868.

The experience of the BaSotho during their first three decades of contact and conflict with Europeans, from the mid-1830s through the mid-1860s, vividly demonstrated that drought could play a significant role in politics, and that famines were governed by human factors, caused by war and used

79

in war. Droughts did not create the competition between Europeans and Africans which was constant, but they determined the timing of overt conflicts. Once a conflict broke out, the Boers took by force the food and livestock which they could not obtain through legitimate means of production or trade, and deliberately induced famine by destroying that which they could not take for themselves. Their ultimate goal was to obtain the land which would give them the capacity to produce their own grain, giving them a direct entitlement to food and eliminating their dependency on trade entitlements controlled by the BaSotho. Since food was politics, so also land was politics.

Land and politics were similarly intertwined in the colonial period. The early colonial years of Basutoland, from 1868 through the late 1870s, were drought-free and the BaSotho economy experienced a period of relative prosperity. However, the region experienced a serious drought in 1877. Lesotho suffered from the same great drought which was reported throughout southern Africa. By October 1877 the missionaries in Lesotho were reporting that "In the [Cape] Colony the large and small livestock are dying like flies. Already they have announced a famine and the price of food has risen in consequence."[112] Once again, however, the Europeans across the border were suffering far more than did the BaSotho, and once again the white settlers coveted the more fertile land of the BaSotho. In July 1880 the Anglican missionary reported from Leribe that "During the last few years a sufficient rainfall has given them [the BaSotho] good harvests, while in the Free State the crops have been destroyed by drought. They have thus had a ready market for their corn, and they have grown rich in oxen."[113] The British colonists to the south were also suffering, and when they decided to apply the disarmament act to Basutoland they also decided to expropriate the fertile southern part of Basutoland for redistribution to white settlers. The last attempt to expropriate BaSotho land came yet again in the wake of an unsettling drought, but this time the BaSotho successfully defended their borders in the Gun War of 1880–81.[114] The BaSotho continued to suffer the social consequences of political turmoil, however. Coinciding with a lengthy period of drought, the Civil War of 1883–85 caused a famine and in turn promoted a smallpox epidemic. Measles appeared in 1888, and whooping cough and typhoid appeared in 1889 and 1890, following partial droughts in 1887 and 1890.[115]

The 1890s saw a particularly disastrous chain of events. Locusts destroyed crops in 1892, 1893, 1895, and 1898. The country suffered a prolonged drought from 1894 through 1898. The Rinderpest cattle epizootic entered the country in 1896, and internal migrations caused by the drought accelerated the spread of the disease among the cattle. At the end of the century, the BaSotho lost 80 percent of their cattle during the Rinderpest epizootic. Famine was severe by 1898, when once again a civil war broke out. Food production was interrupted during the civil war between Masupha and Lerotholi in 1898. The war intensified the destructive effects of drought and

Rinderpest, and epidemics of typhoid fever, smallpox, influenza, and dysentery ravaged the population.[116]

A partial drought caused crops to fail in the southern districts of the country in 1899, but harvests were notably successful in the years 1900 to 1902. The cattle population recovered dramatically during these years, with imports accounting for most of the increase. During the Anglo-Boer War (1899–1902), livestock of all varieties entered Lesotho, as the British traded cattle to obtain horses from the BaSotho, and many Boers took refuge in Lesotho with their animals. The introduction of herds from across the border led to the appearance of "every variety of equine and bovine disease in South Africa."[117] Rinderpest reappeared in a milder form and was controlled through inoculation, but cattle mortality was high from lungsickness. Thousands of horses died from scab (*Brandzickte*), and the winter of 1902 was so severe that many animals died from exposure to the cold and snow. In 1902 severe frost in March and April killed the crops, and a drought lasted through the year until November. For the first time food, valued at over £25,000, was imported into Lesotho in 1903.[118] Regional politics entailing war and dispossession, colonial rule and taxation, had undermined the once successful BaSotho agricultural economy. The BaSotho continued to sell their grain to meet an increased tax burden, so that grain continued to be exported, but Lesotho, once the grain basket of the Cape Colony and Orange Free State, was no longer self-sufficient in food production.

7

The rise and decline of craft specialization

Individual households in nineteenth-century Lesotho were not entirely self-sufficient in the production of household goods. Labor requirements determined the level of demand for specialization in each craft industry. Specialization naturally arose in crafts demanding a high degree of skill. Labor intensive activities such as the preparation of skins were also organized using labor from outside the household unit. In addition, sometimes it was inefficient for every household to engage in some labor-intensive activities requiring few or no specialized skills, such as the digging of salt and red ochre and the preparation of ointments.

Before the nineteenth century, iron-workers who smelted and smithed locally-mined ore were the main specialists in the economy of SeSotho-speaking communities. The high level of skill witnessed by early European observers in activities such as the preparation and tailoring of skins suggests that specialization in other crafts had also been present for a long time. When local and regional trade patterns were disrupted in the 1820s, however, craft production declined as households devoted their energy to basic food production.

In the early 1830s, permanent settlement and the boom in BaSotho agricultural production set the stage for renewed craft specialization. As trade links were re-established between the BaSotho and their neighbors, specialization and internal exchange were stimulated in the local economy. Prosperity brought increased local demand for hunting weapons, agricultural tools, woven granaries, more substantial housing, fancier leather clothing, and articles of conspicuous consumption, including copper and brass jewelry. Increasing demand for craft products stimulated the local production of these goods. Subsequently the integration of the local economy with the Europeanized regional economy transformed the BaSotho economy, however. At the end of the nineteenth century, opportunity costs and transaction costs determined the degree to which specialization in a given craft survived or declined.

Local crafts and industries, 1830–1910

Iron-working

Iron-working was the most important local industry in nineteenth-century Lesotho. The presence of iron-working in Lesotho has been largely ignored to date, perhaps because the historical sources are relatively obscure and archaeological evidence is lacking.[1] Written and oral sources nevertheless demonstrate that the BaSotho mined, smelted and smithed iron and copper in the period before European penetration into the area.

Small iron ore deposits were plentiful in Lesotho. Arbousset discovered an iron ore site in a valley near the Caledon River in 1836. In the northern Maloti mountains, he found Nguni-speaking refugees from Natal extracting iron ore and making iron hatchets and hoes which were traded to the BaTlokoa and BaSotho.[2] Arbousset first observed the BaSotho themselves smelting iron in 1839. Five leagues from the mission station at Morija he discovered a huge hill from which the BaSotho were extracting iron ore. He wrote: "These stones contain much iron oxide. The indigenous people have already exploited all of the deposits which are found on the surface, with a depth of only several feet. They smelt the iron in the same place ... "[3]

Other nineteenth-century travellers and missionaries also testified to the presence of iron deposits throughout the country.[4] Oral evidence confirms the presence of many surface deposits of iron ore in Lesotho in the nineteenth century, but there is no indication of any deep sub-surface mining.[5] There is also no evidence about mineral rights or the organization of labor for mining, but surface mining would have required only a minimum of organization.

The origin of the copper used by smiths in Lesotho is not clear. In 1864 Orpen observed smiths using "native" copper which he believed had been dug in Lesotho.[6] Martin also indicated that a copper alloy, which she identified as brass, was made using locally-dug ore as late as 1904.[7] The lack of any more direct evidence of local copper deposits suggests that the BaSotho relied on obtaining copper from outside Lesotho through long distance trade networks. European observers regularly identified brass as well as copper objects which were made by local smiths, but in the absence of further evidence it must be assumed either that the brass was of European origin, perhaps mixed with local copper, or that the Europeans were confusing some other yellow-toned copper alloy with brass.

Fuel for smelting iron, although not abundant, was available to the BaSotho. Some BaSotho iron-workers may have taken advantage of coal deposits which were present in some parts of the country, as was asserted in a letter to the *Graham's Town Journal* in 1833.[8] BaSotho sources indicate the use of charcoal in the smelting process. Evidence from Lesotho suggests that trees and fuel did not become scarce until the mid-nineteenth century, so it is a mistake to assume that the area was always treeless, preventing iron-working.[9] Two early BaSotho writers, Sekese and Sechefo, each specified the use of charcoal from the olive and "Leucosidea sericea" trees for smelting purposes.[10]

By the nineteenth century, if not before, the BaSotho had the technology for smelting iron. It is not clear exactly how and when the BaSotho acquired this expertise. Archaeological studies may eventually generate new evidence about the dissemination of iron-working technology in southern Africa, but conclusions based on the limited historical evidence now available are tentative at best. The evidence, taken exclusively from oral traditions and the genealogies derived from them, suggests that the various groups of SeSotho-speaking peoples, including the MaPhuthing, BaTlokoa, BaKoena and BaFokeng, began receiving iron goods from Nguni-speaking groups to the east in the early seventeenth century, at about the time that a MaZizi (Nguni) clan first crossed the mountains to settle in the area which would become Lesotho. By the end of the seventeenth century the MaPhuthing were working iron themselves, having learned smelting and smithing from the third MaZizi clan to come across the mountains, the BaPhuthi. Iron goods diffused throughout the region in the eighteenth century, through trade networks among the SeSotho-speaking peoples.[11] The art of smelting and smithing spread as well, so that the BaSotho of the nineteenth century were able to produce their own iron goods, using locally-mined iron ore.

The role of the blacksmith was vital to nineteenth-century BaSotho society, for it was the smith who provided tools for agriculture and weapons for war. The smith was referred to as *lelala*, blacksmith, derived from *bolala*, smithy, or alternatively as *setei/setehi*, one who forges, from the verb *ho tea*, to beat, forge, or hammer.[12] The smith enjoyed a high status in BaSotho society. Informants and written nineteenth-century sources report that some smiths were chiefs, indicating that smiths were socially accepted and respected.[13] Casalis described the smith as the only laborer in BaSotho society whose work was elevated to the status of an art. He wrote that: "All recognize in the smith an exceptional character. He is more than a worker, he is the *ngaka a tsepe*, the doctor of iron. They say that, in order to succeed in this occupation, he must submit to mysterious purifications and drink the juice of certain plants. A long apprenticeship appears to be necessary . . ."[14]

The prevalence of iron smelting in nineteenth-century Lesotho is demonstrated by the fact that ten of my informants born at the end of the century were still able to describe aspects of the smelting process when interviewed in 1982. They explained that iron ore stones were crushed, heated on a very hot fire, and then beaten to get out impurities. Bellows (*mefutho*) were made of ox skin bags with an ox horn attached in the front and a stick handle attached to the back. The bellows blew into a clay structure in which the iron was smelted.[15]

Other descriptions of the smelting process are provided by European observers. In 1841 Backhouse visited a local smith:

> Each bag [bellows] is terminated by a cow's-horn with the point cut off, and these pipes terminate in one of clay, in an arched wall of the same material.

Between this and a smaller wall, about six inches distant, a charcoal fire is placed. The blast is well maintained; and the rougher work is effected by means of hard stones on others of large dimensions, and the finer with hammers of their own making.[16]

Casalis also described the smelting process which he himself observed. He indicated that apprentices participated in the work, and that the iron produced was of varying quality:

We found there a circular hearth on which is heaped up a large quantity of carbon and a little ore. From the center extend, like so many rays, a large number of pipe nozzles made of baked clay. These pipes, by their length, allow for some vigorous apprentices to blow with all their might without being annoyed or distressed by the heat. As soon as the fusion has taken place and the metal coagulated, they beat it and submit it to more consecutive heatings to separate out the impurities [foreign materials]. In spite of this work, the people complain that the iron is often mixed with cinders and dirt. In return, however, the pieces without any slag have almost the strength of steel, which is no doubt acquired immediately when the carbon first comes into contact with the ore.[17]

These oral and written reports are in basic agreement as to the types of furnace and bellows employed in smelting, and they seem to confirm that charcoal was used in the process.

Other descriptions from the nineteenth century offer more details about smelting by the BaSotho, but the evidence is inconsistent. Sekese and Sechefo indicated that the iron was melted in the process.[18] Laydevant, a Catholic missionary who arrived in Lesotho in 1914, collected oral reports about a smith who lived during the time of Moshoeshoe, and wrote a similar description of smelting which describes the production of molten iron.[19]

Evidence that the BaSotho were making guns and cannons later in the century indicates that BaSotho technology was capable of producing enough heat to generate molten iron. However, most iron goods made by BaSotho smiths were not cast from molten iron. Instead the iron or "bloom" was produced below the melting point of iron and then hammered to remove the remaining impurities; it was then ready to be worked.

It is surprising that so many witnesses reported the use of molten iron since it must have been uncommon. The inconsistency in the evidence about molten metal may arise from linguistic confusion, or from a failure to distinguish between the smelting and smithing processes. The SeSotho word *tsepe* is used to designate iron, but also refers to the broader term metal, thereby encompassing both copper and brass. Copper is more specifically referred to as *tsepe e khubelu* or "red metal" and brass as *tsepe e tsehla* or "yellow/brown metal," but the color specification may be easily omitted, thus causing confusion. BaSotho smiths did melt down copper and brass and cast them in molds. Some of my informants who provided descriptions of smelting may have remembered only this process, and may have failed to identify properly the metal involved.

Most of my informants interviewed in 1982 were aware that the iron implements used by the BaSotho of previous generations were of BaSotho origin, and more had witnessed the smithing process than had witnessed the smelting process. This suggests that smelting was probably abandoned much sooner than smithing, when imported European iron became readily available to the smiths. Informants identified smiths in what are now the districts of Maseru, Leribe, Butha Buthe, Mohale's Hoek, Quthing, and Qacha's Nek, indicating that at the end of the nineteenth century smiths were found all over the country.[20] European observers in the nineteenth century also identified smiths located throughout the country.[21]

During the wars of the 1820s and subsequent wars with Europeans, the smith's role in providing iron weapons was critical for the BaSotho. The spear, with an 8 inch blade and 4 foot shaft, was used in hunting and in slaughtering domestic animals long after it became obsolete as a weapon of war. BaSotho smiths also manufactured barbed spears, battle axes, and square or round-blade spears used for hunting animals. The BaSotho also learned new techniques from European smiths, and according to both contemporary European written sources and surviving informants, the local smiths manufactured cannons, guns, and bullets.[22]

The tools manufactured by local smiths were also important in agriculture and household production. The hoe, *mohoma*, with an oval blade 10 inches long and 7 inches wide, was the most important of these tools. The BaSotho manufactured hoes from locally mined iron as late as the end of the century.[23] Smiths also manufactured pick-axes, spades, sharp tools for use in harvesting, and later knives and plows. Among other tools in general use were axes, razors, and several tools used in the preparation and sewing of skins. A small iron spatula, worn on a chain around the neck, was made for scraping sweat off the face, or for cleaning out the nose.[24]

BaSotho smiths also smelted and worked copper and brass, primarily for ornamentation and jewelry. On this trip through the country in 1840, Backhouse was most impressed with the breastplate of thin brass, *khau*, used in war: "Breastplates of [brass] ... worked so smooth and bright, that they would not disgrace a Birmingham manufactory, are also made by this people, for use in war.[25]

Also impressive was a brass or copper collar, three or four centimetres wide, which was worn around the neck by both men and women. Martin saw these collars made in the 1890s:

> The brass neck ornaments are made out of the native metal, which is dug out and melted, and then poured into a hollow previously made in a large flat stone, and this forms it into a ring large enough to encircle a woman's neck. Before the metal is cold it is polished with round smooth stones, while still soft it is cut through at one end, and gently forced open until the woman is able to insert her neck.[26]

Casalis noted that the BaSotho worked copper and knew how to draw it out into wire, which is indicative of a high degree of skill.[27] Brass earrings, bracelets and leglets were commonly worn by the wealthy. Brass or copper buttons and brass ornaments were used to decorate women's skirts.[28]

The preparation of animal skins

Preparing and sewing animal skins was the labor of men in BaSotho society. This was the logical extension of the convention that any activity related to animals was the responsibility of men. The scraping and tanning of skins was a long and arduous process, but groups of men worked together while enjoying food and beer prepared by women.

In 1834 Smith observed that "softening skins or making karosses (skin blankets) form a considerable portion of the labour of the men."[29] It took five to six days for several workers to prepare and tan a single skin. Every man needed enough skins for blankets and clothing for each member of his family, as well as for various leather bags and straps. Therefore men worked long hours in the winter months in order to provide every man with a sufficient number of skins. Sewing articles from the skins involved even more time.

The work was done in an outdoor courtyard where men could gather around a large ox skin. After the skin had been left to dry in the sun for several days, two or three men spent several days scraping the inside of the skin with an adze. The skin was then dampened in one of two ways: it was either put into water to rot or buried in the ground and covered with wet mud for several days. In addition it was covered with a paste made from petrified ox brain, *lebejana*, to aid in the softening process and prevent cracking. After this the hard labor of softening the skin began, as several men working together went through a rigorous process of continually folding, beating and fraying the skin. This "fraying" process took seven or eight men one day or night for a single skin and resulted in a soft nap across the entire surface of the skin. The skin was then smeared with tallow, *tsoto*, or with dregs of beer to prepare it for the final tanning process, *ho ngoaela*. Friends were invited to help with tanning. It took one to two days for four or five men to tan a large skin.[30]

The early stages of skin preparation did not involve specialized skills, but were extremely labor intensive. The preparation of a single skin in the processes described above could take twenty-four man-days of work. These extensive labor requirements necessitated the organization of labor for this work outside the household unit. The provision of labor generally involved arrangements of reciprocity rather than payment for services. However, food was provided to the workers by the owner of the skin, and he did not incur a direct obligation to offer his labor in return for the services he received.

Additional time and specialized knowledge, training, and skill were also required for the sewing of skins into garments, which further necessitated the recruitment of labor from beyond the household. A tailor was *sesehi*, "one

87

who cuts," and he could specialize in making one of a variety of items. His tools were simple: a sharp pin of wood or iron, *lemao*, used as an awl to punch holes, and a thread of sinew, *lesika*. This sinew was taken from a tendon in the hip or back of a leg of an ox.[31]

Tanned skins were sewn into many things. Some tailors specialized in making large skin karosses or blankets. Widdicombe observed that; "The neatest of European furriers could barely hold their own against the Basutos and Bechuanas in the dressing of the skins of wild animals, and the preparation of these robes of fur so justly and universally admired by all who have seen them."[32]

Tailors also made various articles of leather clothing for wear by men and women. After being sewn, clothing was often decorated. A woman's skirt was pricked with iron pins to produce an artificial fur, *mohlono*, which hung down in fringes; it was then bordered with beadwork, and decorated with brass ornaments and buttons. Designs were also embedded into karosses and articles of clothing. After a design was meticulously hammered in with pegs, a colored ointment was poured on the skin and the designs were hammered in, never to come out once the blanket dried. These designs were difficult and time consuming to imprint. More often the skins were merely dyed with ointment made either from *masa* or red ochre, which was smeared on with a stone, giving the skins a reddish color.[33]

The BaSotho made numerous other leather articles. A traditional grain bag held approximately two muids (406 lbs.) of grain, but later bags were made the size of the imported European cloth bags and held only one muid. A milk bag was made from a calf by cutting a hole at the scrotum and removing the whole carcass through the hole, leaving the skin as a bag. The BaSotho used hard, raw oxskins to make shields. They cut the skin into a round shape, pointed at the top and bottom, with a handle on the side, and white-washed it with a white soil, *mokoetla*. Men also made leather straps and thongs which were commonly used for tying grain bags onto oxen and for various other purposes. Small bags were made for holding food, medicines and herbs, and razors. Bellows for smelting and smithing were also made with skins. After horses were introduced the BaSotho learned to make saddles.[34]

The extent to which a family relied upon a specialist for making their leather goods varied. One informant specified that her grandfather and grandmother tanned skins, the women of the household tanned sheep and goatskins for the children's use, her grandfather made grain bags, and her father bought leather skirts for her mother from "those who did tanning."[35] It was common to rely on a master tailor to make a woman's skirt, and certain men specialized in cutting and tailoring these skirts. Some tailors specialized in making shoes, while old men often specialized in making karosses or blankets. The specialists were generally paid in some way: food such as beer often served as compensation.[36]

The manufacture of goods from plant fibres

Both men and women made goods from various kinds of reeds and plant fibres, and the gender division of labor in this craft was determined by the nature of the item being produced. Reeds needed for productive purposes were carefully protected and could only be cut under a chief's order. On a designated day all of the women under the chief's jurisdiction gathered and harvested grass for the chief; the following day they kept what they cut for themselves. Both men and women made long flat ropes of rushes or reeds, which were used for making baskets and for roofing and fencing purposes.

Men wove huge grain baskets or granaries, *lisiu* (sing. *sesiu*), with these flat ropes. The granaries had to be ready at the time of the harvest, so much of the labor of weaving fell to the old men who did not help in the harvesting process itself. The work required skill and training, and not everyone knew how to make the *lisiu*.[37] In the household of one of my informants two uncles were given this job, and the father of another informant wove *lisiu* for other people.[38] An individual "basket" granary held from nine to thirty-six bushels, and could be six feet or more in height.[39] Men also made articles of clothing from plant fibres for their own use. For their heads they wove conically shaped grass hats, and to protect themselves from rain they made a covering from long grass.[40]

Women wove smaller articles, also by hand. These included small baskets used for winnowing or for carrying food on the head, and floor mats for sitting and sleeping and for catching meal which fell from the grinding stone. Women also wove door coverings, sieves or filters for straining beer, and straw spoons for skimming flies from the beer. They also made ropes from the hair of horses' tails.[41] The manufacture of these items did not require highly-specialized skills or extensive labor time, and they were produced by women within the household.

Some women specialized in making skirts from plant fibres, however. From the age of three years, girls wore a short skirt, which also served as an underskirt for women wearing leather clothing. To make these skirts, the women gathered wild marigold in February and March when the plants were still green, and peeled the fibres off the stems. The fibres were twisted into strands which were sewn thickly to a leather belt. Finally the skirt was smeared with oil to protect it, and those who could afford them sewed beads onto the bottom edge as decoration. Most women made these skirts themselves, but because the process was time-consuming, some women bought them from specialists.[42] Other articles of clothing made by and for women included fringed ropes made from plant fibres, which were wound into dresses and leggings.[43]

Pottery

Making pottery was women's work. A certain amount of specialization developed in pottery production for two reasons. First, deposits of potting clay were not evenly distributed throughout the country. Clay, *letsopa*, was dug from deposits found along river banks or in ditches; a *morafong* was a digging or mine.[44] The people who lived in those places which lacked clay deposits, such as mountain areas, were forced to purchase clay pots from people who lived elsewhere. Second, the successful production of pottery was difficult, which stimulated specialization even in areas where clay was readily available.

Every woman learned to make pots as a young girl, but the production of well-made, unbroken pots was difficult. The clay was allowed to dry thoroughly, and ground to a powder on a millstone. It was then mixed with ground up pieces of old broken pots and with water, and kneaded for a long time. The clay was then moulded into a pot, which was polished with smith stones until dry. To add designs to the earthenware, the woman ground small black stones into a powder and applied it smoothly. The finished pot was covered with cow dung which was molded over the clay to make a small furnace or oven, and this was baked over a fire overnight until it turned gray. The most common large pot was used for cooking food, and rested over a fire on three stones. Other pots were used for brewing beer, transporting water, keeping and serving porridge and drinks, milking, holding fat, and as chamber pots.[45] The largest variety of pot was used for beer at feasts and could reach three feet in height.[46]

The manufacture of pots was a fairly labor-intensive process. Two days were required to mold pots, which were then left to sit for several days. Another two days were needed to polish and finish the pots, after which they were baked. From an entire batch of pots, only two or three would come out unbroken.[47] The high rate of breakage probably occurred because of the baking or firing method which was used. On this reckoning, four days of labor would yield only two or three pots. The time and care required in the process therefore led to specialization and trade in pots in spite of the fact that every woman learned this craft when young. Specialists presumably had a higher success rate than nonspecialists, and produced better pots. Several European observers in the nineteenth century were impressed with BaSotho skill in the manufacture of pottery. One missionary described the pots made by BaSotho women as perfectly regular in their lines and of the greatest elegance.[48] Ellenberger noted that the techniques used required artistic talent: "Pottery was baked in the open air in a fire of dried cow-dung, sheltered from the wind. Much skill and art were required."[49]

The production of salt and ointments

Some women specialized in the digging of red ochre, and sold it to others. Women dug red ochre not only from surface deposits, but also sometimes from deeper mines.[50] The women mixed red ochre with milk and animal fats to make ointments which they then sold locally. In addition women dug salty minerals from deposits to use for seasoning food. This "salt" was referred to as *lenyekethe*, but a discrepancy in the descriptions of *lenyekethe* indicates that it was probably a term used to designate several minerals, all of which had a salty taste.[51] These deposits were apparently located throughout the country, which explains why salt, of great importance in trade elsewhere on the continent, was not widely traded among SeSotho-speaking peoples over long distances. On the other hand, *lenyekethe* was traded locally. One of my oldest informants from Leribe District was known by the nickname Raletsoai, "father of salt," because his mother dug and sold salt locally.[52] He explained in detail:

> There was not yet seasoning which was called *letsoai* [salt], but from kinds of precious stones in the ground there were still minerals which were eaten. They were dug by people who it was said sold *likama* [sing. *sekama*, antimony] and other minerals like that. [It was] *sekama* which was for ointment they made, that is they put the ointment on plaited hair; now there were still people who sold things like that. That is, things [minerals] that were found in the salt licks of animals because they noticed the rocky side of a ditch when it was of that kind of mineral. They dug it and took it around and then sold it; if it was quite a lot it was worth a goat; it if was twice that much it was another goat; these minerals were sour. So they used them in very many ways; some people used them even in medicine to cure with them, such as to make someone well so that he should not die; until finally it was food to which people became accustomed, until the time when they gave it up because white people arrived with salt [*letsoai*] of another kind; whereas it is said they also got their kind of salt from the ground.[53]

Raletsoai thus noted with irony that there was no apparent reason for the BaSotho to adopt a new kind of salt, supplied by white traders, in preference to the old kind of salt provided by BaSotho women, since both kinds of salt were dug from the ground.

Building

Men and women cooperated in the building and maintenance of houses. Traditional dwellings were made of reeds and grass mats in the shape of beehives, with a long low entryway.[54] These were replaced by larger huts made of poles or large sticks from the trunks of small trees, cut and planted upright close together to form the walls of the circular enclosure. This kind of house was the *mohlongoafatse* or *mohlomafatse*, predecessor to the stone "rondavels" or round houses adopted later in the century.[55] It was the responsibility of women to cut grass and reeds for weaving and thatching, and women built the reed and grass enclosure, *seotloane*, around the court-yard of the home. According to one European observer in 1861, the women also built the houses themselves.[56] The women plastered the inside and outside of the walls with a mixture of dung and mud, and both men and women roofed the house with reeds and grass. Women continued to be responsible for maintaining the house and re-plastering the walls frequently,

91

at least several times a year. When asked about women's work, plastering or smearing, *ho lila*, was always one of the first jobs mentioned by informants because of the large amount of time it required.[57] Often the women embellished the walls with artistic designs in colors or in patterns etched into the plaster.

Gradually European influence inspired a transition to stone houses, and by 1888 grass huts had been mostly replaced by stone huts.[58] The transition to stone houses created a demand for the skills of stone cutters, and building became a specialized trade of men.[59] The work of women in building decreased because their work in cutting and setting up poles for walls was no longer required. In addition, it was no longer necessary to plaster the outside of the house, although the inside floor and walls had to be plastered on a regular basis, and some women continued to decorate the outside of their homes with plastered designs. The new stone houses lasted longer and required less maintenance than the old huts, to the benefit of both men and women. However, cutting stones and setting them together was skilled labor, and it became necessary for many homesteads to hire special stonecutters to build their homes. The construction of stone houses therefore involved a large initial investment either of the labor time of men from the homestead or of household resources to pay a builder. As settlements became more stable, larger investments in the building of more permanent homes became worthwhile. Members of the household continued to roof their houses with reeds and grass, however, and men constructed the stone cattle kraals of the homestead.

Wood-working

Carpentry and carving were men's work. The carpenter, *sebetli* or *mobetli*, used only a spear and a very hard grinding stone. Spoons, wooden dishes, and wooden milking pots were the most common items carved from wood. Also carved from wood were knobkerries or sticks used as weapons. Pipes and spatulas were carved from horn or bone. Musical instruments were also crafted from wood.

Men also made several kinds of agricultural implements from wood. Hoes of wood had been used before the introduction of iron tools, and could still be found in the nineteenth century.[60] Other wooden items were nineteenth-century innovations copied from European implements. The yoke, used to harness oxen for plowing, was carved of *cheche* wood.[61] Wood was used to construct parts of plows, which also had iron components. Sledges for dragging loads behind oxen were made of wooden poles bound together in a triangular shape.[62] The cultivator or harrow was made with heavy wooden teeth.

Some men were apparently very skilled at carving. The bowls, pots, and spoons made by BaSotho men were described as being "most attractive" by a European observer.[63] There is no evidence that carved household goods were sold locally, however, and it is most likely that these products were manufactured by the men of the household. There was apparently little specialization in wood-working, perhaps because of the scarcity of wood in Lesotho.

The decline of specialization in the late nineteenth century

The division of labor and the allocation of labor time changed in response to changing levels of demand for the products of craft specialists. The adoption of innovations, the availability and rising use of imports, and BaSotho participation in the regional wage economy, all affected the demand for locally-produced goods. It has generally been assumed that Africans adopted European imports because they acquired new tastes inculcated by the Christian mission ideology of the superiority of the trappings of western "civilization." The view that the adoption of western imports reflected the adoption of Christian values was naturally propagated by the missionaries who needed to claim every possible sign of success in order to win continued financial support from back home. Hence when Africans began to wear western clothing missionaries reported this as a sign of the success of Christian missionary doctrine. Relying on these missionary interpretations of early changes in the use of imports, most scholars have assumed as well that Africans began to wear western clothing because their tastes had changed, and that like the missionaries they believed western goods were superior to their own. Following from this logic, western scholars have implicitly accepted the missionary claim to be working their magical transformation in the minds and hearts of Africans, who by adopting "civilized" clothing voluntarily must have been adopting western tastes. As missionaries were the sole representatives of western civilization for long periods of time in the years of early contact, then, westernization in consumption has been taken as the result of Christian influence, and as a measure of Christian influence.

According to this logic first used by the missionaries for their own public relations purposes, evidence of the extensive use of imported goods in Lesotho in the nineteenth century suggests that the BaSotho were quickly influenced by Christianity. A closer examination of further evidence, however, reveals how hollow the old missionary claim was, and how misled modern scholars have been in accepting the missionary vision of African motivations. The number of BaSotho who were actively engaged in mission activities in the nineteenth century serves as a gauge of the percentage of BaSotho who might have been considered "Christianized" with regard to ideological beliefs. In fact the numbers of BaSotho Christians were still tiny at the end of the century. The Paris missionaries had been the first to arrive in 1833, but their church grew very slowly. Thompson has discussed the dilemmas which Moshoeshoe and his people faced in the early years of missionary work, and Perrot has noted the relationship between clothing and attitudes which was assumed at various times.[64] Drawing from missionary reports, Perrot comments that "the adoption of elements in the European lifestyle accompanied conversion; one could almost say that this was the sign of it [conversion]."[65] Perrot presents the evidence that this was indeed the belief of the missionaries, including the revealing quote from the missionary Rolland that "civilization makes progress in the same proportion as Christianity. All those who seek God and convert also wish to dress like the European and adopt as many customs as possible of civilized peoples."[66] At the same time, Perrot is aware of the ambiguities of this position, and traces the vagaries of Christian influence in the early years of the Paris missionaries. On the one hand, the missionaries wrote that "when one sees a MoSotho build himself a nice [convenable] house, one knows that his intention is to seek God."[67] But Perrot noted that it was in fact the chiefs who were building European-style houses. In the early years Moshoeshoe wished to associate himself with any advantages accruing from the missionaries, whom he had originally recruited because of the potential advantage they would bring in foreign diplomacy. For this reason Moshoeshoe acquiesced to many missionary tastes even when they were not his own: as Perrot notes, he did not live in the European house he had built, but preferred his traditional home.[68] Certainly there was an initial association between western clothing and Christianity, as Christians were expected to wear western clothing to church. The early companions of the missionaries were Moshoeshoe's sons and their companions, who were placed at Morija to learn what they could, and the earliest conversions came from the BaSotho elite, including many of Moshoeshoe's relatives.[69] But the situation changed when the first glow of mission promise wore off and the BaSotho found most of Christian ideology incompatible with their lifestyle, beliefs, and social order. Then, as the BaSotho reacted against Christianity beginning about 1848, they initially (if temporarily) threw off their western clothing, symbolizing their rejection of Christianity.[70] From then on it was social outcasts who were attracted to the mission stations, where they received Christian charity and western clothing. Christianity and the trappings of western "civilization" were no longer only associated with the privileged and wealthy chiefs, but also with the poor and indigent who had been socially rejected for some reason.[71] The missionaries themselves were generally regarded as a necessary evil because of their usefulness in foreign affairs.[72] Attendance at mission events and conversion to Christianity remained minimal relative to the total population throughout the nineteenth century, as the statistics show. There were a total of 151 baptized members of the Paris Evangelical Mission church in Lesotho in 1843. The total number of adult Christians in the PEMS church, including communicants and catechumens, grew from 393 in 1843 to 13,733 in 1894. Communicants, or those with church membership, numbered a combined total of 19,577 in the 1904 census for the PEMS, Anglican, African Methodist Episcopal, Roman Catholic, and Seventh Day Adventist churches.[73] Given the population statistics for BaSotho residing within the changing borders of the country, the number of adult BaSotho Christians as counted by the missionaries rose from 0.5 percent of the population in 1843 to a mere 5.6 percent in 1904.[74] Congregation sizes were larger than official membership figures, totalling 50,878 for all churches in 1904. Even this figure only produces a total of 14.6 percent of BaSotho participating in Christian churches as late as 1904.

The low conversion rate to Christianity indicates that the widespread adoption of European imports was not confined to those influenced by Christianity nor was it primarily the result of Christian influence. The indirect influence of the missionary example might be considered important, except that the missionary connection has often acted as a disincentive to adopt western ways. In 1864 Chief Molapo prohibited the wearing of European clothing as a symbolic rejection of the hypocrisy of western "civilization" as experienced by the BaSotho in the midst of a desperate struggle against "Christians" across their borders.[75] A missionary wife in the 1860s complained that after she dressed a young girl servant in European clothing the mother refused to allow the girl to continue working for her, for fear the girl would become a Christian.[76]

If the rise in use of imports in place of locally-made goods cannot be attributed to a popular adoption of a new western taste and ideology arbitrated by Christianity and missionaries, then alternative factors must explain the rising BaSotho use of imports. In fact the decline in the use of locally-made goods was selective and uneven in its effects, and was primarily determined by the efficiency and economy of local craft and household production. Taste has been a factor in the consumption choices of the BaSotho, but westerners have been wrong to assume that the BaSotho preferred western goods based on taste in style and culture. On the contrary, the evidence demonstrates that when taste mediated the choice between local products and imports, local goods generally won out. Also important was the quality of an item, in terms of function and durability. When they could afford it the BaSotho chose the higher-quality product, which was sometimes locally-made and sometimes an import. When they could not afford it the BaSotho chose the cheapest good, which was generally the import. Thus several factors accounted for the different degrees and rates of decline in specialization in various crafts, with economic factors determining the choices of most BaSotho who could not generally afford the luxury of choice based on taste or quality.

In nineteenth-century Lesotho the household was the main unit of production, and households generally produced for their own consumption. However, when the cost of producing a certain item was high in terms of the acquisition of specialized skills or large labor inputs, the household could not always produce that item for itself. In this case a contract was entered into with persons outside the household, who would supply the needed goods as part of a negotiated exchange. Goods which required minimal skills or labor continued to be produced within the household. In this way, specialization arose in the manufacture of selected items within each craft.

95

Smiths were the exclusive practitioners of their craft, but other crafts were learned and practiced both by specialists and within households.

When a buyer entered into a contract, however, he incurred certain transaction costs.[77] In the context of nineteenth-century Lesotho, such "costs" variously included the amount of time (days or weeks of intermittent bargaining) necessary to negotiate the "contract," uncertainty and delays in the delivery of the product, buyer obligations to provide the raw materials necessary in the production process, and uncertainty and fluctuations in price.[78] Transactions with craft specialists were therefore governed by what is termed "relational contracting": negotiated agreements between the buyer and the seller. Relational contracting is an alternative to the contracting which governs impersonal standard market exchange, in which the identity of buyers and sellers is irrelevant to the transfer of standard goods at set prices. Relational contracting is appropriate for idiosyncratic transactions in which commitments by specific partners is important because investments in production are high. Such investments can be high because production involves specialized physical capital (for example, tools), human capital (skills), or the manufacture of individualized, customized products which cannot be sold to another buyer. In addition, transactions may be idiosyncratic because of the involvement of family or personal relations.[79]

The concept of transaction costs and relational contracts governing exchanges help to explain why specialization declined rapidly in certain crafts at the end of the nineteenth century, while specialization in other crafts survived. Over the course of the nineteenth century, idiosyncratic transactions became less important in Lesotho as demand increased for standardized goods, and as transactions were less often governed by family or personal relations.

Europeans noted the disappearance of local crafts at the end of the nineteenth century.[80] One observer wrote in 1906 that:

> Blacksmiths are becoming rare. They used to melt the ore and forge their iron and copper. Nowadays, they buy iron and grass from the stores and – except spatulas ... lancets, knives, bracelets, and imitations of European articles, which they make with primitive tools – they do not think it worth while to make what they can buy cheaply ...
>
> The mill stone ... is perhaps what will survive after many other things have been forsaken. The plough is superseding the hoe, and the pick is only now used for weeding the fields. Clay jars are being replaced by iron pots and tin buckets and cans. The rifle has long superseded the assegai and other weapons which are now very rare and difficult of acquisition ...[81]

Smelting declined quickly because the smith's production costs were high: ore and fuel were scarce and difficult to acquire. At the same time, imported European iron could be purchased easily from traders. The standardized nature of iron bars or rods made them appropriate for simple market exchanges, because they did not need to meet individualized specifications.

The demand for the labor of smiths changed according to the nature of the items they were able to manufacture. Some items, such as battle axes and copper shields, became obsolete. The use of other items, such as tanning tools and small spatulas, declined over time. Smiths learned to make new items, however, including guns, bullets, plow parts, and knives. The steady demand for hoes for weeding meant that BaSotho smiths continued to manufacture them even after the introduction of European hoes and plows used for field preparation.

The inability of local smiths to produce these standard goods at set prices and with low transaction costs for the buyer deprived them of the ability to compete effectively with traders offering the same goods through the market. If a buyer wanted an iron tool made by a local craftsmen, he had to take the time to negotiate a contract, he often had to supply fuel and/or iron for the work, and he had no guarantee as to when the item would be finished. The purchase of the same iron tool from a trader offered an attractive alternative. At the same time, local producers could not offer competitive prices for their goods because their costs for raw materials and labor could not be reduced when more cheaply-made European products were introduced.

Specialization in the smithing of other iron, copper, and brass goods survived the arrival of traders and the emergence of market exchange conditions, however. In the production and acquisition of non-standardized goods relational contracting remained appropriate for both the specialist and the buyer. There is no evidence that spears were ever imported, and these were used well into the present century for slaughtering animals. Iron spears therefore remained an important product of local smiths. In addition, items which were made to individual specifications continued to be purchased from local craftsmen. Jewelry made by local craftsmen continued to be in demand, because it was made to specification with regard to quality, size, and design. Nevertheless, imports of European jewelry and wire partly undermined the demand for locally-manufactured jewelry.

The local manufacture of leather goods was similarly affected by changing market conditions. Traditional leather shields, important at the beginning of the century, became obsolete with the advent of guns. Late in the century imported cloth bags and leather straps rapidly replaced locally manufactured leather grain bags and straps because efficient and impersonal market exchange was appropriate for the purchase of such standardized items.

In addition, the manufacture of such items from animal skins was increasingly uneconomic because of the high opportunity cost of not participating in the regional wage economy. Approximately twenty-four man-days of labor were required for the preparation of a single oxskin, and additional labor time was required for tailoring and sewing the skin into garments or bags. A person who wanted a new skin blanket therefore had to recruit laborers and provide them with food and beer while they worked, and then pay a tailor to sew the blanket. At the beginning of the twentieth century, a man could earn fifty to sixty shillings a month as a migrant worker at farms or mines in the Orange Free State and Transvaal. The price of imported cotton and wool blankets at that time ranged from 10 shillings to 30 shillings according to the quality of the blanket. Although wool blankets were less durable than their locally-made leather counterparts, a man could purchase two to five wool blankets with the wages earned in the time it would take to manufacture a leather blanket. In the context of such high opportunity costs, it was far cheaper for a buyer to purchase an imported blanket from a trader.

On the other hand, prestige items, including karosses made from wild animal skins and intricately decorated skirts, could only be made by BaSotho specialists. Often the skins were provided by the buyer, and the garments were individually tailored for size and design. Because these were luxury goods, the wealthy were willing to bear the high costs of having local craftsmen custom tailor these items for their use. The continued demand for such expensive locally-made leather clothes indicates the value placed on them by the wealthier and more influential BaSotho, whose prestige rested on the clothing they wore.

Weaving was only partly affected by changing economic conditions at the end of the nineteenth century. For the most part, woven granaries fell into disuse as grain was stored in bags inside huts and excess grain was sold. There were regional disparities in the decline in use of the huge woven granaries, however, and they can still be found in more remote mountain areas. There are several reasons why people living in the mountains continued to use woven granaries long after they had become obsolete in the lowlands. Fewer people from the mountains left the country as migrant laborers, because of the greater distances to be travelled and a lack of information about opportunities. Men in the mountains were therefore more likely to remain at home and pursue traditional activities, such as weaving, than were men in the lowlands. Second, there were few traders in the mountains, so that imported goods, including bags for storing grain, were not readily available as substitutes for locally made goods. In addition, the scarcity of traders in the mountains meant that a larger proportion of surplus grain was stored by the household, requiring the larger and more permanent storage facility provided by the woven granaries.

The manufacture of other woven goods persisted throughout the country. Women continued to weave small baskets, sieves, and mats. These items were not generally sold by traders, and there was no demand for imported substitutes. The manufacture of small woven goods required little skill and a minimal amount of labor. In addition, because women had few alternative opportunities in the wage economy, the opportunity cost of making these goods was small. Cloth skirts gradually replaced woven grass skirts, but the cash or grain surplus of the household was more likely to be used to buy men's clothing because men determined household purchases, and because employers in South Africa required that migrant workers wear western clothing.

Wood-working persisted for similar reasons. Items such as dishes and spoons were replaced by imports to some extent, but because they were easy to make they continued to be produced locally. Tool handles, yokes, and plow parts were also easily made with a minimum of skill and time. Local craftsmen continued to make traditional musical instruments.

Given the high labor cost of producing pottery, it is not surprising that the local production of clay pots was easily undermined. Pots were made to standard rather than individual specifications, and imports could easily serve as substitutes for locally-made pots. Many households already purchased pots from local specialists, so the transition to buying pots from traders was easy. Traders sold iron cooking pots, which were substantially more durable than their clay counterparts made locally. Tin pails came to replace water pots for similar reasons. BaSotho women continued to manufacture clay pots which met special needs, however, such as the huge pots used for brewing beer. The high profitability of brewing beer for sale made the investment of labor time in making brewing pots worthwhile.

Finally, the local digging of salt and red ochre and the manufacture of ointments declined at the end of the nineteenth century. Cheap imports were available and competed with the local products. European traders sold imported salt and packets of red ochre, and petroleum jelly, referred to as "vaseline" as early as 1901, replaced ointments made from milk and animal fats.[82] Other factors came into play as well. Red ochre deposits, like iron deposits, were gradually used up. The same may have been true of local deposits of salty minerals. When informants were interviewed in 1982, only those people living in the northern lowland districts and the mountain areas remembered that locally-dug minerals had been used for seasoning instead of imported salt. This suggests that either there were fewer deposits in the southwest lowland districts, or that the earlier availability of imported salt in that area had undermined the local production of salt at an earlier date.

In Lesotho at the beginning of the twentieth century, purchasing certain standardized goods through the impersonal market system was both appropriate and economical, and market exchange through traders, governed by classical contracting, came to supplant idiosyncratic local transactions involving these items, governed by relational contracting. The decline in the manufacture of specific craft items occurred after imported goods of standard specifications became available and freed consumers from the cost of making individual arrangements for such goods. Once most needs of most people could just as easily be met with standardized goods, the way was paved for the operation of an open market-based economy.[83]

Opportunity costs, transaction costs, and the more remunerative allocation of labor in the local and regional economies were important factors determining the degree and rate of decline of craft production in nineteenth-century Lesotho. In addition, consumers were also compelled to purchase imported goods because of the inability of local craftsmen to keep pace with local demand. European traders supplied the BaSotho with massive quantities of goods at competitive prices. In fourteen months in 1856–57 a merchant at the Morija mission station sold 7,300 knives and 1,500 hoes.[84] Local smiths were not equipped to manufacture iron goods in such quantities. Furthermore, the changing relation of supply to demand lowered the value of the goods produced by local smiths. Similarly, tailors were put out of business by traders who imported cotton, wool, and leather clothing and shoes. For the years in which statistics are available at the beginning of the twentieth century, wearing apparel and cotton and woollen goods accounted for over half of the value of all imports.[85] Imports of cloth grain bags, wooden utensils, iron pots, salt, and ointments similarly undermined local industries.

BaSotho craftsmen continued to make some products locally. Standardized European imports of iron tools, clothing, blankets, and jewelry did not meet the demand for customized products made to buyer specifications by local tailors and smiths. Imports were not available as substitutes for some goods, such as spears, small woven articles, carved sticks, and musical instruments. Small woven and carved articles were easy enough to make so that there was no incentive for people to buy them from outside the household, either from local craftsmen or European traders. Nevertheless, craft production and specialization in Lesotho declined dramatically at the beginning of the twentieth century.

Craft specialization and the level of sophistication of production techniques in nineteenth-century Lesotho were at best rudimentary in comparison with other areas of Africa. However, political consolidation and peaceful settlement following the wars of the 1820s allowed for the production of a food surplus which in turn made some degree of economic specialization possible. Agricultural prosperity initially stimulated specialization in craft production, as demand for the goods of local craftsmen increased. Eventually, however, local production of many goods became uneconomic in a context of higher opportunity costs and competition from cheap imports. Local industries and specialization in craft production declined, and at the beginning of the twentieth century the BaSotho came to rely on the purchase of foreign imports and participation in the regional wage economy.

8

The allocation of labor, 1830–1910

Within the homestead unit of production, headed by a married man with one or more wives each with her own household, the allocation of labor revolved primarily around the gender division of labor. In addition labor was allocated to some extent on the basis of age. Over the course of the nineteenth century, the division of labor between men and women changed, first in response to the introduction of the ox-drawn plow and in response to market opportunities for grain, and subsequently in response to the participation of BaSotho men in the regional migrant labor system. These changes in turn had ramifications for the allocation of labor time by women, and for the age-based division of work within households.

The sexual division of labor changed considerably after the introduction of the ox-plow, and surprisingly little after men began to work as migrant laborers in South Africa. Instead, other changes were made in the allocation of work to compensate for the loss of men's labor. Men continued to be available on a seasonal basis to fulfill critical tasks in agriculture. Women worked hard to sustain agricultural production while men were away, but they had always worked hard. At the same time that women took on more work in cultivation, they gave up other work related to the production of household goods. Other members of BaSotho households, that is old people and children, also took on more work when men left as migrant laborers. Thus both men and women struggled to maintain the economic viability of their homesteads in the face of diminishing returns to the investment of additional labor time, and they employed numerous strategies in meeting this challenge.

The BaSotho strategies for organizing labor were similar to those evident across the region, including the gender division of labor as well as the ongoing re-allocation of labor to meet market demands for food and labor in South Africa. Lesotho was unique mainly in that it was one of the first areas to be influenced by the introduction of the ox-drawn plow and the commoditization of agriculture, long before the introduction of colonial rule and the migrant labor system. Changes in the gender division of labor which were fostered by the introduction of the plow and by the commoditization of agriculture occurred independently from direct colonial influence, and can be attributed to the initiative of the BaSotho themselves. In addition, the advent of the plow in Lesotho occurred while open land was still plentiful, allowing much more land to be brought under cultivation and increasing the agricultural workload. In other areas of southern Africa the plow arrived later, after available land was already circumscribed, so that the plow diminished rather than increased the workload of men and women.

The gender division of labor within the homestead

Food production

Men hunted for big game in large groups, which were arranged by the chiefs who appropriated part of the kill at the end of the hunt. Such hunts usually took place in the winter. As big game became more and more scarce, fewer and fewer large hunts were organized, and men tended to hunt individually or in small groups for small game.

Gathering was traditionally women's work, as wild greens, fruits, and vegetables were mostly consumed by women. The work generally fell to girls, young unmarried women, and old women, but men and boys who were off herding livestock often gathered wild roots and vegetables for themselves. Wild roots and vegetables were an important dietary supplement and helped women avert starvation during droughts and crop failures.

Men and boys cared for cattle, sheep, goats, horses, and donkeys. Generally older boys cared for the cattle and horses, and little boys looked after smaller animals. Because the herd-boys drove the cattle and smaller livestock to cattle posts for summer grazing in the mountains and remained there until the first frosts in April or early May, the labor of the young men and boys was not available to help during the heavy labor seasons in agriculture: weeding, bird-scaring, and early harvesting.

Women cared for pigs and poultry, and occasionally took care of sheep, goats, and donkeys as well. Pigs were referred to as *likhomo tsa basali*, "the cattle of women," because they were always cared for by women.[1] It was forbidden for women to associate with cattle, and this restriction was justified by the belief that the fertility of the cattle would be adversely affected by contact with women during their reproductive years. Men certainly believed that women generated intense and potentially destructive power through heat when they were fertile, but it is questionable whether the restriction on women handling cattle was fundamentally ideological in origin, or whether ideology merely provided a justification for limiting women's access to a major source of wealth.

Gender divisions also determined the allocation of labor in cultivation. The BaSotho used a lunar calendar to determine the appropriate times for agricultural activities.[2] Table 2 shows the annual agricultural calendar of the BaSotho. Men and women cooperated in the work of cultivation. Women

Table 2. *Agricultural calendar*

August	September	October	November	December	January
PLANT	PLANT	PLANT	WEED	WEED	BUILD HUTS for bird-scaring

Sorghum ————————————— Sorghum forming ears; ears spreading
Sweet Reed   Sweet Reed ripe
Pumpkins   Pumpkins: many leaves   Pumpkins forming
Calabashes
Watermelon

        Maize   Maize flowers; Green corn eaten
        Beans   Bean pods forming
        Peas   Pea pods forming
        Lentils
        Potatoes

                    TRANSPLANT
        Tobacco   Tobacco
        Wheat: in
          mountains

                   BIRD-SCARING ——— CUT & THRESH ———————————
Winter Wheat: Winter Wheat   Winter Wheat
  grows quickly; makes heads; grains out; ripens ——— ripe ——————————
                                          BIRD-SCARING
Winter Sorghum: Winter Sorghum:
  comes up quickly   forming ears ——————————— grains out

February	March	April	May	June	July

     BREAK UP UNPLOWED LAND   PLOW FIELDS UNDER
BIRD-SCARING ————————————————————— HARVEST   HARVEST
                                      THRESH   THRESH
                    Sorghum hardens   Sorghum ——————
HARVEST
Sweet Reed
Pumpkins eaten   Pumpkins firm   Pumpkins
             Watermelon firm   Watermelon
                            Calabashes
Green maize eaten ——————— kernels harden —— Maize ————————————
Beans eaten   Beans firm   Beans
Peas eaten   Peas firm   Peas
                  Lentils firm   Lentils
                            Potatoes
                            Tobacco
                 HARVEST
                 Wheat in mountains
                                PLANT   PLANT
                                Winter Wheat ———— Winter
                              (lowlands)   sorghum

used hoes to prepare fields for seeding, but men assisted in field preparation when virgin land was first being prepared for cultivation and it was necessary to use spades to "cut" the fields, dig out lumps, and make furrows.[3] Men broke up unplowed and previously uncultivated land in March and turned the soil over again when planting began. They turned over fields which were already under cultivation in June and July as the crops were harvested and cleared out of the fields. According to Moshabesha and Jankie, before the advent of the plow both men and women went to hoe the fields at planting time.[4] It is significant that the BaSotho initially expanded dramatically the area of land under cultivation and achieved a boom in agricultural production in the 1830s through 1850s with the use of hand tools only. This reflects the readiness of the BaSotho, both men and women, to engage in hard work to produce more food for both consumption and exchange.

Men participated more in field preparation after the introduction of the ox-drawn plow, as women were not allowed to associate with cattle. Men therefore became involved in the annual plowing of old fields, in addition to the occasional clearing of new fields. The advent of the plow reduced male labor time used for clearing virgin land, but the overall workload of men increased because they now had to prepare fields which had been previously cultivated, in addition to any virgin fields which were being brought under cultivation. The ox-plow was readily adopted by the BaSotho beginning in the 1850s, and by the 1890s there was a ratio of approximately one plow to twenty people.[5] The ready availability of plows and the numerous arrangements for the exchange of labor between homesteads suggests that by the end of the century virtually every family had access to a plow.[6]

Before the introduction of plows it had taken two people approximately one week to hoe a small field by hand, so that if a woman did not have help it took her two weeks per field.[7] After the introduction of the plow, most families continued to maintain these small fields, *serapanyana*, which were the sole responsibility of the woman of the homestead. If a man had more than one wife each generally had her own small field or fields. The men, taking over responsibility for plowing with oxen, also brought much larger fields under cultivation. In the middle of the nineteenth century the size of an average family's holdings therefore increased, until further extensions became impossible as the land within the boundaries of Lesotho filled up. These new fields of greater dimensions took two to three days to cultivate with a single plow, while the largest fields took about one week with an ox-plow.[8] With the advent of the plow the labor time of men involved in field preparation initially increased, while the labor time for women, still involved in preparing the smaller family fields by hand, remained the same.

The overall agricultural labor time of women increased dramatically, however, because women had primary responsibility for the rest of the field work. August and September were the months in which most crops were planted. Traditionally everyone in the household helped with the sowing; the seeds were sprinkled on the surface of the soil by hand until the field was covered. Then as the first sprouts appeared, the long and difficult labor of weeding began. Weeds became plentiful in November, and weeding became the time-consuming preoccupation of women. The early missionaries complained about the long labor of weeding required in sorghum cultivation, and they used this argument to promote wheat which required no weeding. Sorghum fields had to be weeded "perfectly" two or three times between sowing and reaping, and had to be thinned and pruned as well. Women did this work using the traditional hoe or short thick sharpened sticks.[9] Occasionally work-parties (*matsema*) were held for weeding fields, but generally the women of the household did it themselves, working long hours for several months to keep all of the family fields clear of weeds. During droughts, women also carried water to the fields in clay pots.[10]

Bird-scaring was another time-consuming agricultural activity delegated primarily to women. This was necessary as soon as the grains of winter wheat began to appear in October and November, and again when the grains of sorghum and maize appeared in January. Because bird-scaring was necessary both day and night, special huts were built in the fields for bird-scarers, who slept in the fields. This work was critical: an entire field could be devastated by birds in only a few hours.[11] During the month of March the task became so demanding that men also slept in the fields and helped with the work.[12]

Women worked long and hard to harvest the crops, breaking off the heads of sorghum or maize individually and collecting them for threshing. It generally took the women and children of a family one to two months to harvest the sorghum and maize fields depending on how successful the crops had been. The women rose in the dark, went to the fields to begin work before sunrise, and worked all day until tired.[13] An observer at the end of the nineteenth century wrote

> During the two months of the mid-winter harvest the women work very hard. A woman will leave her home a few minutes after dawn, carrying her infant on her back, and a large *Seruto* – a basin-shaped basket – on her head. She will trudge along bravely and patiently until she reaches her corn patch, at perhaps four or five or even seven or eight miles distance. In that corn patch she will work with scarcely any interval of rest until the long slanting rays of the declining sun warn her to return home. Then she piles her basket to the brim with maize cobs or bunches of millet . . .[14]

Work-parties of men were always held for harvesting wheat, because wheat had to be cut and threshed quickly before it was ruined by rain.[15] A field could generally be cleared in a single day at a *letsema*, or work-party, and any crops remaining in the field after the *letsema* were reaped later by the owner.[16]

Work-parties were also held to thresh sorghum if the crop was large, because the work was often too much for a family to do alone.[17] In the past threshing had been women's work, but over time it became more common for young men to do this task.[18] The participation of men in threshing did not really constitute a dramatic shift in the gender division of labor, however. Boys and young unmarried men normally helped their mothers in the family fields, and even married men performed agricultural tasks usually allocated to women when they attended work-parties for chiefs or other people. There was no stigma attached to the performance of agricultural labor by men, and the expanding grain market acted as an incentive for men to help their wives to produce agricultural surpluses for sale to traders.

Men performed the labor of threshing at work-parties using big sticks (knobkerries), while women brewed beer and prepared food for them. Often the work continued through the night and on until mid-day, with the men drinking, eating, threshing, and singing. The work and festivities continued as the women took over the work of cleaning the chaff from the grains with brooms and with their hands, and winnowing.[19] When the winnowing was finished, each woman who had helped was given *moelela*, a little bag or basket of grain, to thank her.[20] Cattle were sometimes driven over the piled grains to thresh them, making the work easier for the men, but then the women had to clean the excrement from the grain afterwards.[21] Women usually processed maize and beans by hand, cutting the grains of maize off the cobs with stones, and picking the beans out of their shells.[22]

The burden of agricultural labor changed for men and women during the nineteenth century because of selective advances in technology which only affected certain stages in the agricultural labor cycle. The ox-plow was adopted to increase the efficiency of field preparation, but no comparable technological innovations were adopted to facilitate cultivation at other stages of the agricultural cycle. Since the number and size of fields under cultivation grew significantly after the introduction of the plow, the work of women in hoeing weeds, bird-scaring, and harvesting using traditional methods and technology increased accordingly. In addition, the annual agricultural labor time for women was no longer evenly distributed over time. Instead, women experienced much higher labor peaks during the seasons for weeding, bird-scaring, and harvesting.

At the same time an attempt was made to reallocate men's labor to use it most effectively to increase production, even when it meant the further breakdown of the sexual division of labor. As the demand for labor increased in activities which were traditionally allocated to women, men began to help women. It became more common to hold work-parties for weeding, harvesting, and threshing, at which men (both married and young unmarried men) helped with the agricultural labor. Some men adopted harrows to help with the weeding process, and men helped with bird-scaring during the most demanding months. All of these strategies were designed to reduce the peak labor seasons of women, while reducing the periods of underemployment of men. The attempt to allocate male labor more efficiently to increase production and reduce periods of underemployment was also reflected in the adoption of winter wheat.

As a rule, innovations which would have decreased the labor time of women were not readily adopted. Some BaSotho learned to make harrows, *ekhe*, to assist with the weeding process, and others bought them from traders, but they were relatively rare. In 1875 there were only 238 harrows in the country, as compared to 2,749 plows.[23] Because the labor of weeding was the work of women, men had no incentive to adopt this technological innovation. Only men could use harrows because they were pulled by oxen, and women were prohibited from handling cattle. The labor time of men was therefore increased with the use of this tool, which was a disincentive for its adoption. On the one hand, men would have no reason for wanting to increase their own workload. But the failure to readily adopt the harrow may have also arisen from the fact that as men worked for longer periods and more frequently as migrant laborers outside the country, they were not present throughout the agricultural cycle to take on new tasks. Most of men's tasks were concentrated in the months of July through November, allowing men to enter into migrant labor contracts during the rest of the year. The labor of weeding took place during precisely those months when men tended to leave the country, and the wages foregone by staying to help weed instead of leaving to work outside the country would have been a high price to pay for the entire homestead. Even when harrows were used, it was necessary for women to rid the field of the remaining weeds by hand.

The transportation of crops from the fields could be done by women on a piecemeal basis, or cooperatively by the whole village, in conjunction with threshing work-parties. When cooperative transport was arranged, everyone in the village contributed his oxen and bags to the effort, and the herd-boys brought the pack oxen with bags out to the threshing floors in the fields to carry the grain to the village.[24]

Local industries and the production of household goods and services

The division of labor in industries was in part determined by gender, and was to some extent determined by the nature of the item being made in a given craft. Women wove some household goods and men wove others. Both men and women also contributed to the building and maintenance of houses and fences. Men prepared oxskins, but women occasionally tanned sheep and goat skins. Only men engaged in iron-working and wood-working. The crafts and industries performed exclusively by women included the manufacture of pottery and ointments and the mining of salt and minerals from which cosmetics were made.

Women were responsible for the processing of food for consumption, and for all related activities. Having harvested, threshed, and winnowed the grains from the fields as part of the agricultural process, BaSotho women then had to prepare the grain for cooking by grinding it on millstones by hand. This was a long tedious job done twice a day to provide enough flour for the morning and evening meals for the entire family. When asked about women's work, the first job mentioned by most informants was *ho sila*, to grind. A European observer in the 1830s noted that a woman's main occupation during the day was cooking and grinding,[25] and the rigorous nature of this aspect of women's work was also reported:

> Each morning one sees [the women] rising before dawn in order to go fetch the water necessary for the day's consumption. This done, they must grind the grain by a very arduous method ... They sit on their heels in front of a flat rock with a surface two feet long by one foot wide. This mill is slightly tilted, with the lower end in contact with a wide basket. The worker takes in her hands a hard oval stone with which, using the whole weight of her body, she crushes the grain which is placed in small quantities on the immobile grindstone. One hour of work provides enough meal for the morning consumption. Then it must still be cooked ... The family had hardly sat down to eat when the mother takes her hoe to go work in the fields. She returns from there, her head weighed down with an enormous faggot of wood, a little before sunset, so she will have the time to fetch water, grind grain, and cook as she did in the morning.[26]

As noted here, it was also necessary for a woman to collect water for cooking and washing twice a day. Because of the time-consuming nature of this work, it was often delegated to young girls, who often walked miles to fetch water for their mothers. The collection of fuel for the cooking fire was just as difficult. In the 1840s and 1850s it was still possible to find wood for fuel along the Caledon, but as early as 1845 fires were being built with dry animal dung.[27] As wood became more scarce, dung became the exclusive fuel for fires.[28] A British military report from 1880 noted that: "The country is destitute of wood, with the exception of some small patches of bush on the western slopes of the Maluti Mountains, and in the Cornet Spruit valley. Cow dung is the only fuel used.[29]

By the 1891 dry dung, *lisu*, was "the ordinary fuel of the country."[30] A second military report in 1905 emphasized the problem and its effect on women:

> The depredations of an ever-increasing population have caused the supply of wood to recede further and further away from the habitations. The women-folk, on whom rests the responsibility of keeping the household in fuel, are often obliged to travel five or six miles every other day to the nearest watered kloof, returning the same distance heavily laden with faggots weighing some 120 lbs ...[31]

There were also seasonal variations in the availability of fuel which affected women's labor time. Dried cattle dung which was dug from the floors of cattle kraals was available only during the winter when the herds were kept at home. For most of the year only dung collected from fields and woody shrubs were available for cooking. The latter fuels required much more time to collect because sources of supply were often far from the villages, and neither burned as efficiently as the dry dung. In the winter, maize cobs provided a temporary source of fuel in the period after threshing.[32]

Few innovations were adopted to lessen the burden of women's work. Two European mills were built in the nineteenth century, but because the

Table 3. *Seasonal distribution of labor for women*

	Aug.	Sept.	Oct.	Nov.	Dec.	Jan.	Feb.	Mar.	Apr.	May	June	July

Agricultural ———————— = = = = = = = = = = = = = = = = =********************
 labour (hoe-planting-weeding ——————— bird-scaring — harvest —— threshing)
Gathering = = = = = = = = = = = = =————————————————————————
Weaving ———————
Building and ———————
 thatching
Ointments from ———————
 animal fats
Fuel collection ——————————————————— = = = = = = = = = = = = =—————
 and preparation
Food preparation =
Home maintenance ——

Note:
Less intensive ——————— = = = = ******** More intensive

costs of having grain ground at these mills was high and they were inaccessible to most people, few BaSotho used them until well into the twentieth century.[33]

The seasonal distribution of labor

Table 3 presents the seasonal distribution of labor for women and demonstrates the interrelationship of the labor demands of agriculture and household production. Women participated in agricultural labor throughout the year, but the amount of time spent daily on agricultural labor increased as indicated. Although exempt from spring plowing after the introduction of ox-drawn plows, women still prepared and planted small fields and gardens. In addition they were responsible for preparing large quantities of food and beer for laborers who came to help with agricultural chores at work-feasts. Gathering activities were highest during the spring when stored grain supplies were used up and new crops were not yet ripe. The weaving of clothing began in February as wild marigold plants became green and ready for use.

The time of peak labor demand for women was in the winter months of May through July. This was the best time for building and thatching because reeds and roofing grasses were harvested at this time. This was also the time of year when animals were slaughtered and ointments from animal fats were prepared. Unfortunately, these activities coincided with the time of peak labor demand in agriculture for women. During the summer and fall seasons of weeding, bird-scaring, harvesting, threshing, and winnowing, most of the daylight hours were spent in the fields, and household jobs were done before sunrise or after sunset.

Table 4. *Seasonal distribution of labor for men*

	Aug.	Sept.	Oct.	Nov.	Dec.	Jan.	Feb.	Mar.	Apr.	May	June	July
Agricultural	= = *******************								= = = = = = = = = = =			
	(Plowing and planting)								(harvest and thresh wheat in mountains)			
Hunting	———											
Tanning skins	= = = =								= = = = = = = = = =			
Weaving									= = = = = = = = = =			
Building and thatching									———			

Note:
Less intensive ——— = = = = ******** More intensive

Men also worked hard. As agricultural innovations made the work of field preparation and sowing easier, the BaSotho cultivated larger and larger areas of land. When not busy with hunting, herding, and plowing, men produced essential household goods: skin blankets and clothing, tools and implements of iron and wood, and woven granaries. Houses were built or repaired, and luxury items, including jewelry, pipes, and musical instruments, were crafted.

Table 4 indicates that there were wide seasonal fluctuations in the demand for men's labor. Herding was an ongoing responsibility, but it was delegated to herd-boys and did not interfere with other activities. Intermittent non-seasonal activities included iron-working, sewing, and carving. The primary demand for men's labor in agriculture came during the spring season of plowing and planting. In the mountains, plowing and planting activities began and ended earlier so that crops would have the longest possible growing season before early frosts came. Men also helped harvest and thresh the wheat promptly in the mountains so the crops would not be ruined.

These activities did not conflict with men's craft activities, which took place in the fall and winter. Granaries were woven in the early fall to be ready for harvested crops, and men helped women with building and thatching in the winter. Skins were also prepared in the winter, because herds were culled and animals slaughtered at this time, and skins from wild animals were brought in after hunts.

Over time the gender division of labor did begin to break down, somewhat to women's advantage. The most significant changes occurred with the introduction of the ox-drawn plow. Men were motivated to increase their contribution to arable production primarily by market opportunities that allowed for the commoditization of agricultural products beginning in the 1840s and 1850s. This does not diminish their contribution toward lightening the burden of women, however. To compensate for women's increasing workload after the adoption of the plow, men's labor was reallocated; that is, they helped the women in the fields.

As land shortages combined with droughts and crop failures forced more men into migrant labor in the 1890s and 1900s, the burden of production increased for those at home, particularly for women. But clearly women were already fully employed in the local economy, so it was impossible for women to increase their labor inputs in agriculture without reducing their labor time in other areas of production. The change in women's workload, then, came not in the number of hours worked but in the way the labor time was allocated among various tasks. Forced to spend more and more time on agricultural tasks, women gave up other activities, such as weaving, pottery, and home-building. Men similarly gave up some tasks or spent less time on them, such as the preparing and sewing of skin clothing, home-building, weaving, and carving. Men used their wages to purchase goods that they had once made, such as blankets, clothing, and wooden and iron tools, weapons, and utensils. They also purchased goods previously made by women, such as skirts, pots, utensils, and cosmetics. In this way women's workload in household production was reduced, allowing them to contribute more time to agricultural labor.

Other tasks were allocated increasingly to the old or the young. Old women and young girls collected dung for fuel and gathered wild vegetables. Young girls fetched water, cared for younger children, and helped with grinding, weeding, and harvesting. Boys and girls helped with bird-scaring. Young boys, who had formerly cared only for small livestock, took over care of cattle as well. Old people cultivated vegetables and tobacco in gardens near the homesteads. In these ways local economies adjusted to losing young men's labor to migrant work.

Toward the end of the nineteenth century the labor burden of women left at home stabilized. Because there was no new land available for new generations of young men, for the first time land-holdings were sub-divided among sons and their wives, and the land held by each household decreased in size. Women were able to sustain agricultural production until the constraints of smaller land-holdings and soil deterioration made it increasingly difficult to produce enough food for subsistence. The twentieth century thus saw women seek alternative forms of employment as migrant laborers to farms in the Orange Free State, as beer-brewers, and when desperate, as prostitutes.

Women, production, and gender oppression

The role of women in production was critical to accumulation and economic growth in Lesotho. There production and maintenance of the labor force has been recognized as one of women's indirect contributions to the accumulation process in the capitalist sector of developing economies. Clearly women's role in the reproduction of the household, through production, was just as important to the economy of nineteenth-century Lesotho. When goods for consumption were produced within the household, scarce

111

resources could either be saved or redirected to the purchase of goods for production, thus aiding in the processes of accumulation and growth.

The distinction that is often drawn between production for consumption and production for exchange is largely irrelevant in the case of nineteenth-century Lesotho, because the organization of labor, including the sexual division of labor, was not significantly affected by whether production was for home consumption or for an external market. Surplus grain was sold both locally and to external markets, but unlike people in other parts of Africa the BaSotho did not adopt the production of new cash crops that primarily involved men's labor. Foods and goods that were exchanged locally and sold to traders for export were surpluses from agriculture or craft production. Men became more involved in agricultural production in response to market opportunities, but they did not displace women as the primary agricultural producers.

BaSotho women made many direct economic contributions to their households during the nineteenth century. Women produced many goods that were traded outside the household. Foremost among these was surplus grain: grain was traded for livestock, and men used the surplus grain that their wives produced in order to increase their herds. The labor of women in cultivation was therefore directly translated into the "capital" (that is livestock) holdings of the household and assisted in the process of "capital" accumulation. These cattle were eventually exchanged as bridewealth to bring more wives into the household, so each wife in fact contributed to the expansion of labor power in the household both by bearing children and by enabling the head of the household to acquire additional wives.

In addition, the surplus grain that women produced was used to buy iron tools and weapons from local smiths, which contributed to the more efficient production of food through hunting and cultivation. In the nineteenth century, food was the "money" of Lesotho, and surplus grain was used to pay for the services of other craftsmen and specialists, including tailors, weavers, shoemakers, and healers. In the latter part of the century, grain was sold to European traders in exchange for a variety of imported goods. Women also produced surplus craft goods for sale outside the household, and traded their labor for grain, which again made a direct economic contribution to the household.

Women's indirect economic contributions were also significant. Work associated with the preparation of food – gathering fuel, fetching water, grinding, and cooking – was essential to the survival and well-being of household members. Although often subsumed under the category of repro-ductive labor, these activities are aptly characterized as productive, because they assist indirectly in the accumulation process. Put simply, if women did not perform these tasks, someone else would have to be paid to do them.

Because the provision of food was the primary means for compensating labor recruited from outside the household, there was sex-based difference in the organization of labor for given agricultural and household tasks. When men were faced with labor-intensive tasks such as clearing and preparing fields or preparing animal skins, they recruited laborers from outside the household (often in the context of a "work-party") and compensated them with cooked food. This labor appears to be an exclusively male contribution to production, but women played a crucial role as well. It was the women who prepared and provided the food and beer to compensate the laborers, which generally involved as much labor time as that of the men. A male head of household could thus exchange the women's labor for the labor of other men, effectively decreasing his own workload.

This "work-party" option for large and difficult tasks was not as readily available to women, however, because they could not compensate workers with cooked food without taking the time to prepare the food themselves. Indeed, they would merely be trading one kind of work (the task itself) for another: preparing food. When women worked in groups to complete agricultural tasks, the "host" reciprocated by agreeing to provide her own labor to the other women who helped in her fields. In this case, women's labor time was not reduced but merely reallocated. When work-parties were held for weeding, harvesting, or threshing, men did help complete work that was normally the responsibility of women. Even so, the women's job of preparing and cooking food and helping with the work itself might amount to several days and nights of labor at one time. This might have been preferable to completing the given tasks on a daily basis over a period of a month or more, but the woman still had to use her own labor to compensate workers who were completing agricultural tasks for her.

The disadvantaged position of women and implicit gender struggle within the household was also evident in the fact that men made decisions about whether to adopt innovative technology, and as a rule they invested only in those technologies that benefitted themselves. There are separate male and female interests inside the household, and consequently households do not constitute homogeneous decision-making units; these separate interests had ramifications for agricultural production and for receptivity to innovation. Men were not receptive to innovation when the benefits accrued to women, as with the adoption of harrows to assist in the weeding process or the acquisition of donkeys to assist in transport. The adoption of related innovations, such as the use of European mills, was resisted by men, who made the decisions regarding the capital expenditures of the household. The adoption of the harrow was further impeded because it increased men's labor at a time when men were being drawn off into migrant labor.

The evidence concerning the benefits accruing from the adoption of the plow is more ambiguous. Both men and women benefitted from the expansion of arable production that the plow made possible, but both were also required to invest more labor time. Late in the century young women began to stipulate that their future husbands have plows and know how to use them.[34] Widdicombe described these changes in the 1880s, but he incorrectly attributed them to the influence of Christianity rather than rational choice and necessity since Christians were still a tiny minority while these changes were widespread. He observed that

> The field work was formerly almost entirely performed by women, but since the introduction of Christianity into the country the men have gradually learnt to take their share in it, and at the present time both men and women work hard in the fields during the ploughing and harvest seasons. The plough is largely superseding the native pick or mattock; indeed, the young girls are already beginning to stipulate that the man who asks them in marriage – that is to say, who asks their father for them – should possess a plough and know how to use it. They say that "a man who has not got a plough has no business to have a wife."[35]

This stipulation was significant for two reasons. First, women's need to insist that their husbands have plows suggests that men did not always perceive that the benefits of the plow were a sufficient incentive for adopting it. Second, women apparently were aware that although their workload also increased with the plow's adoption, the benefit derived from producing a grain surplus was a sufficient incentive for working more hours. Did the reported ability of young women to influence the choice of their marriage partners, based on the prospective husband's possession of a plow, reflect real leverage? Did it indicate a certain amount of control over their lives that normally lay in the hands of their fathers? Probably this leverage was illusory and the young women's stipulations were respected only because their desire coincided with the interests of their fathers, who arranged their marriages. It was evident to the father of a marriageable woman that a man with a plow could bring larger fields under cultivation and would be better able to generate a high income, allowing him to pay off quickly his outstanding bridewealth debt to the wife's family.

Given the subordinate position of women in BaSotho society socio-economically and politically, it seems surprising that women would initiate changes that increased their own workload. I suggest that this occurred precisely *because* of their marginal position in society. Women and children suffered first and foremost during times of food scarcity and were largely left to fend for themselves by gathering wild plants (known as famine foods) when grain stores ran out. This gave women a compelling motive to increase the stores of grain. In nineteenth-century Lesotho, where the population had suffered severe famine in the 1820s and continued to do so in the wake of recurrent severe droughts, the threat of famine was ever-present to stimulate women's efforts in cultivation. Furthermore, women's efforts in cultivating a grain surplus were among the few ways in which they could exercise some control over their own fate.

Women took other initiatives in reducing their vulnerability to hunger and want. The care of pigs fell largely to them, with the help of children, but they apparently took on the task willingly because the new animals could provide extra food. Women voluntarily helped other households with harvesting work, in order to increase the food stores of their own households. Women who specialised in crafts produced more goods than their families needed, in order to trade for other household goods or additional food.

These were voluntary activities, and they arose because women perceived the benefits they would derive from more household wealth. The extent to which women were willing to invest their labor should be viewed in the context of their marginal position in society as a whole. Excluded from ownership or control over land and cattle, women were largely dependent on their husbands and male kin for access to wealth and for protection from hunger and poverty. Thus a woman benefitted when the resources of the household increased, even when she did not control those resources herself. A wealthy household was more likely to have access to food in times of scarcity, making the marginal members of the household – women and children – less likely to be deprived or cast off.

Women were valued largely for their reproductive functions: bridewealth was paid to the woman's family so that the husband's family would receive rights to his children. But women were also valued for their productive labor, which is important with regard to the relation between the economic role of women and their subordination. In Lesotho, women's productive activities failed to provide an avenue for empowerment and instead created a further incentive for men to subordinate them. In nineteenth-century BaSotho society, social and political status derived from wealth and the ability to gain clients and loyalty through the distribution of wealth, which in turn engendered obligations. Men prevented women from having independent access to material resources, especially land and cattle, to ensure women's dependence and to prevent them from building their own networks of sociopolitical power. Only by limiting women's power could men ensure their own control over reproduction and production, from which their own security derived. The effect of preventing women from having access to cattle was to prevent women from owning the most productive resource of the society, which in turn prevented them from building the client relationships that formed the basis of sociopolitical power.[36]

Clearly, women played a critical role in promoting economic growth in nineteenth-century Lesotho. It is important to see women not merely as pawns, but as actors who consciously strove to shape their own destinies. In Lesotho as elsewhere in Africa, male domination manifested itself in male control over the resources of production. Women's participation in production, therefore, took place in the context of a domestic struggle over resources. Given a social structure that left women dependent on men, the interests of women in terms of their material well-being were closely tied to those of their male kin. Male control over resources meant that women's share of household resources was limited, and the only way women could increase the resources available to them for consumption was to increase the total resources of the household. Under these circumstances, women were motivated to produce surpluses with the goal of contribution to the overall wealth of the household. Women's efforts to improve their own material position represented an important internal dynamic generating economic growth and change in nineteenth-century Lesotho.

9

The local exchange of goods and services, 1830–1910

Throughout the nineteenth century there were no formal markets in Lesotho prior to the arrival of European trading stores. Local exchange occurred in the context of individual transactions. Exchanges involving cattle and bride-wealth were arranged between households and involved members of the extended family. The barter of commodities, including agricultural and household products, occurred between households in the same village, or between members of different villages. Trade over longer distances between people from different districts occurred because resources such as iron and salt were not universally available. Long-distance exchanges were also prompted when factors such as crop failure forced people to search further afield for food.

The transfer of women and cattle among households was the most significant socioeconomic transaction in nineteenth-century Lesotho, but the inability of individual households to be completely self-sufficient in the production of agricultural and household goods also prompted the barter of numerous items of lesser value. Some exchanges were prompted by unequal access to scarce resources which were not available throughout the region and could only be acquired by trade, such as iron and copper, salt, and animal products including skins of exotic wild animals, feathers of special birds, ivory, and ostrich eggs. Some resources, including pot clay and roofing grasses, were easily found in the lowlands but were not available in the mountains, so those BaSotho who migrated into mountain districts in the later nineteenth century had no choice but to acquire these materials through trade with their lowland neighbors.

Trade in goods

Craft specialists sold their products. Because only smiths manufactured iron goods, the dissemination of iron tools and weapons could only occur through exchange at the local level. The BaSotho paid smiths for their services with food, animals, or (in later periods) money. Early in the century smiths had to smelt iron from ore, and therefore required greater compensation for finished items than in later years when the customer often supplied the smith with scrap iron of European origin. Ellenberger's evidence suggests that in the seventeenth and eighteenth centuries the ancestors of the BaSotho traded cattle for hoes, at the rate of six hoes per head of cattle.[1] In the early nineteenth century, the scarcity of iron and iron goods continued to enhance the value of the specialist's skills and goods.

Later in the century when European iron was commonly available a spear could be purchased from a smith for one goat or ten shillings.[2] Since European traders did not sell imported spears, many informants remembered that their fathers had owned locally-made spears when they were young, in about 1900. One woman noted that her father and others "bought their spears from people who travelled around [hawking them]."[3] Another explained that his father had

> Spears, not one spear but many spears. His quiver was full of spears, not just one spear. Even I still have spears. They might be two or three, and others which have broken handles.
> They were things that were forged by Basotho, from iron stones that they cooked. They crushed them [the stones] and beat them like hoes which were made in Lesotho, according to SeSotho customs, which are still here now owned by people who have kept them. Even mine is still there.[4]

This demand for spears and hoes kept the iron specialists in business. Asked whether his father made spears himself, Moseeka explained

> No, it was known by the smiths, they were there, those who knew how [to work iron]. Because it [smithing] was not known by everyone. It was known by those who made them. Then he bought a spear with a goat, if he bought it when it was made; a spear [for] a goat, ten [shillings] if you bought it.
> Here at this village right here. Over there near grandmother's before the dam on this side you can still find what remains of iron which came from the [work of the] man who was called Ratjeoa.[5]

The BaSotho paid other craft specialists for their goods or services. Women sometimes sold woven skirts, clay pots, salt, and ointments to other villagers. Digging salt could be quite lucrative for an enterprising woman. The BaSotho used salt as a seasoning and as medicine, and a woman could buy a goat with only a small amount of salt which she had dug up. Asked what women made for themselves, Moseeka answered: "They molded pots of clay. They sold them and they [the pots] were bought. They gathered wild marigold plants, they took the fibres off the plants, they twisted and spun it, and made short skirts."[6]

Similarly, a woman informant explained that women in her home, in particular her aunts, plaited these grass skirts, decorated them with beads, and "they sold them to others" for one shilling.[7] Women sold ointments they had made:

> They were made of buttermilk fat. Fat from the butter of cows which was poured out and churned. Then [when] someone needed some (my child you indeed speak well [ask good questions]) he who needed it bought some, more

than this. A shilling's worth was a large amount, a shilling's worth. It was full, then the ointment was used and at the end of a year it was still being used.[8]

Asked to whom the women sold pots, Moseeka replied, "to those people in villages nearby; those in villages nearby who needed them."[9] Moseeka shed light on the motives of women who made a surplus of pots or other goods, beyond what was needed for their own households, in order to sell them. This was a form of independent economic enterprise by women, controlled by women, from which women benefitted. As he explained,

> Grain was poured into the pots [and that amount of grain was exchanged for the pot]; it was all right if it was sorghum or if it was maize. They helped themselves thus, the women. Then when they had gotten enough grain [by selling pots] they took it to the store there when they needed a blanket or skirt; a yard of cloth was sixpence up to ninepence, ninepence for a yard, or a shilling, and they [the women] made a living this way.[10]

The BaSotho also paid men who specialized in weaving granaries and in tailoring luxurious skin blankets, leather skirts, shoes, and other articles of clothing, with food and beer. In these cases the craftsmen were generally paid for their services, while the customer supplied the materials. After the introduction of European currency, the BaSotho sometimes paid tailors with money. Shoemakers received 1s. per pair of shoes, which later rose to 2s. A specially made leather skirt cost £1 to £1 10s. according to its size.[11]

Compensation for specialized services and labor

Among the most highly valued services were those of traditional healers, or doctors. The BaSotho gave healers a sheep, a goat, or even a cow for their work. When a healer was asked to use his medicine for the benefit of the entire community, such as to prevent hail or bring rain, the whole village contributed to his payment in grain.[12]

The BaSotho gave food as compensation for many other kinds of non-specialized labor as well. They held work-parties for cutting trees, building houses, cultivating, plowing, weeding, harvesting, threshing, and bringing crops in from the fields. The host supplied the people attending a *letsema* or work-party with food and beer to consume while they worked. Similarly, men who were invited to help scrape and tan skins received food and beer as compensation for their labor, and women who helped winnow and thresh someone else's grain received for their work a basket of grain. Women regularly helped other families with agricultural labor in exchange for food. One man explained that

> On the day that they finished thrashing [threshing] that pile of unthreshed grain which I just spoke of, women they come to winnow there, they invite each other from the village ... and when the winnowing is finished, before they can pour the grain into the bags the woman who is the master [*mong*] there takes a

119

basket for carrying grain ... [and] she gives a small quantity to each woman [who came to help].[13]

This small quantity of grain clearly acted as an incentive for women to help each other. One woman stated explicitly that "they used to help each other a lot because there was this thing which is called *moelela*; *moelela* is food which is given to a woman when the work is finished, it is [measured] with a tin dish or a small grain basket and you thank her."[14]

The BaSotho also travelled to other districts to search for food when the crops in their own districts had failed. When they did not have livestock to trade, the BaSotho exchanged their labor for food. During harvest time, people whose crops had failed helped with the harvest in other districts and received sorghum in exchange for their services.[15]

Attendance at the work-parties of the chief was one of the obligations of a subject in exchange for the land and other benefits he received from living in the chief's ward or district. Traditionally people were only required to work the fields of the chief's first wife, and specially designated fields which produced food used for the nation. Missionaries described these huge events in which almost a hundred plows turned over the land holdings of a chief in one or two days. For weeding, hundreds of people brought their hoes, and worked in groups of up to two hundred people, keeping "perfect time with their hoes as they chant ... "[16] Early British administrators tried to undermine the *letsema* system as it was used by the chiefs. Without regard for the chief's obligations to provide for soldiers, travellers, and indigents, the first Governor's Agent characterized the custom of *letsema* as "the compulsory cultivation of the chief's gardens by the enforced labour of any of the common people whom they may call upon from time to time to work for them without wages, without compensation ... "[17]

Griffith ordered the British magistrates to support and protect those people refusing to participate in work-parties for chiefs, and the issue created continuing tensions between the British administration and the chiefs throughout the century. By the end of the century, some chiefs were requiring their people to work the fields of all of their wives, and were failing to provide food as compensation to the workers, prompting many complaints about the system. But the tradition of holding a *letsema* was well-respected, and was not reserved for chiefs.[18] Many farmers recruited labor by holding work-parties, and provided an abundance of meat and beer, which was "the payment for those who worked and also the thanks."[19] One informant stated more generally that "beer is the payment of Lesotho."[20]

It is not clear when people began to sell beer. A British administrator commented in 1876 that beer (*joala*) was "not yet bought and sold, but is mostly obtained at social gatherings or in return for labour given."[21] In 1885 an article in *Leselinyana* stated that in the district of Makhaleng people were making a living by selling beer. The article indicated that these people were buying the beer which they then sold at a profit, however, so it was apparently not locally brewed *joala*.[22] Informants were uniformly insistent that at the turn of the century beer was never sold. By the time Ashton conducted his fieldwork in 1934, beer was widely brewed for sale at canteens.[23]

Commodities as currency

Because food was commonly used to buy other goods, one informant commented that "sorghum was money."[24] A pot's worth of grain was sufficient to purchase a clay pot,[25] and people could pay for hoes or spears with food. Most commonly people used their surplus grain to buy animals. When a man's crops failed he purchased grain for his family with the sale of a sheep, goat, or even a cow, while a man who had surplus grain used this opportunity to increase his herds. This was a common way for a poor man to acquire animals. During years of average harvests a muid bag of grain was enough to purchase a goat or sheep, and a two-muid bag of grain was traded for two goats or sheep, but during a drought the value of grain rose and two muids of grain was worth one cow or ox.[26]

Trade was facilitated by the use of various other items as currency. Beads had been used as currency since the eighteenth century. Because they were fungible, beads and set measures of rare metals could be assigned known values, making them useful as currencies as well as jewelry. The conspicuous display of wealth through ornamentation reinforced social stratification, and jewelry was a useful if non-productive way of hoarding wealth.

Tobacco was also suitable for use as a currency because of its fungibility. The BaSotho grew it specifically for its exchange value as well as for consumption by members of the household. Many groups in the region, including the BaTswana, Griqua, Kora, and San, used tobacco as a medium of exchange, so that its exchange value gave the BaSotho an additional incentive for cultivating tobacco. Because so much labor was required to produce tobacco, it remained a relatively scarce commodity and retained its exchange value in Lesotho throughout the nineteenth century. In 1822 Burchell described the form in which tobacco was sold. After the tobacco plant was dried, and the stalk and mid-rib were removed, the remainder was steeped and twisted into ropes an inch in diameter. These were coiled into rolls weighing five to ten pounds. For trading purposes, spans of about eight inches were cut from these rolls, weighing one and a half to two ounces.[27]

Informants from Lesotho provided similar descriptions. Small portions of tobacco were often given away, especially to those who helped harvest the tobacco, but it was also sold in various quantities. Those who cultivated a lot of tobacco kept it in rolls in small clay houses. A tobacco-grower sometimes wandered to various places selling his or her product. Usually the trader cut a piece off the roll, *semokolo*, and sold it for a small amount of grain, a chicken, or a shilling. At other times traders sold tobacco by the roll, which

121

was worth a goat or ten shillings. Some people cultivated large quantities of tobacco for the express purpose of selling it to people in the mountains in exchange for animals.[28]

The cultivation of tobacco must have been lucrative. Moseeka's grandmother was a tobacco trader, and grew it in great quantities:

> [She grew] tobacco, in [an area surrounded by] little stone walls here behind this house. On this side and there tobacco was grown, rolls of tobacco. There was a house called a molded house which was made by my grandmother. Big rolls of tobacco were put in, tens of rolls of tobacco. Tens of rolls.[29]

Another informant confirmed that tobacco was grown "by those who knew how to," implying that a certain expertise was required. Then

> it was made into rolls of tobacco, then *lesuane* grass was picked [for tying it], then the tobacco was picked when it was thought to be musty, when it had been allowed to turn musty, it was bound in a roll with a grass rope, this tobacco. Then, you know, then when it was just right like that and she had already tied it, she smoked it herself or she then sold it to other people.[30]

Some people sold tobacco as itinerant traders, and "a person would walk from place to place everywhere saying 'I am selling pieces of tobacco.'"[31]

Trade and the BaSotho in the nineteenth century

The initiation of trade contacts and a migrant labor system in the nineteenth century did not represent a radical break from past experience for the BaSotho. There was a clear continuity between early patterns of exchange between the BaSotho and other Africans and later exchange patterns between the BaSotho and the Boers and British. The evidence of trade, the accumulation of wealth, the specialization of labor (albeit at low levels), and the organization of labor outside the family unit are indicative of an evolution within BaSotho society towards an exchange-oriented economy. Contact with Europeans accelerated changes which had already begun before the nineteenth century and which had been further stimulated by the upheavals of the 1820s.

Exchanges in services occurred when the BaSotho provided compensation for labor from outside the family unit. This included the payment of goods to specialists for their services, but the unequal distribution of wealth and tribute-based relations between chiefs and their followers also led to the provision of unskilled labor for compensation in goods or in privileges. Early village settlement patterns indicate a tendency towards political amalgamation and socioeconomic differentiation, suggesting that the distributive system entailed labor exchanges beyond the homestead among SeSotho-speaking people even before the nineteenth century.

Local exchanges of goods and services allowed for the diffusion of wealth in BaSotho society, and individual hard work and enterprise were rewarded. The chiefs accumulated wealth from the payment of tribute in labor and in kind, perpetuating socioeconomic stratification, but there were many ways in which poor people could also acquire and accumulate wealth. When they cared for a rich man's cattle through *mafisa*, they were rewarded with a portion of the natural increase of the animals under their care. Poor men were married through the payment of bridewealth on their behalf, at which time they were allocated land for cultivation. With this allocation of land, families could accumulate wealth through hard work in the fields, because they could purchase livestock with surplus grain and tobacco. Skilled craftsmen such as smiths and tailors augmented their incomes by selling their goods or services for grain and animals. Women voluntarily produced or manufactured woven clothing, pottery, mineral salt, ointments, and cosmetics expressly for purposes of exchange to increase their household income.

Individuals within a household had differential access to and control over different portions of the household wealth, and worked to increase their share of wealth within a household. Both men and women were aware that women's contributions in the provision of household services and in increasing household wealth were indispensible, giving women some leverage to control and trade what they produced. An Anglican missionary described an encounter between the local British magistrate's wife, Mrs. Austen, and two BaSotho men, one of whom was a chief:

> You know, there has been a great drought throughout S. Africa, and the crops of mealies look wretched. Mrs. Austen is sure that the Natives have enough left from last season, to carry through the winter, and she said so to them. They answered – "No, the women would sell it for ornaments!" I suggest that they ought not to let the women have such power over the corn: and they replied; "The women say, *they* have the trouble of planting, so they claim the power of selling." I told them that the *men* ought to do all the hard work, and make the women stay at home, to cook and clean and sew. They answered, "Oh, it is of no use, the women *will* have their own way, and if we thwart them, they will just walk away from us, and then, who is to grind our corn, and cook for us?"[32]

In many ways this is a simplification of the patterns of household control, as men generally controlled the grain from the large plowed fields, and women only controlled the food they planted with hoes in the smaller gardens near their houses. In addition, it is not clear that this report from BaSotho men accurately records the use women made with the proceeds from their grain sales, and may just have been an opportunity for these men to discredit women in the eyes of these Europeans. Nevertheless, the underlying struggle over household resources, and the efforts of women to exercise some control over the products of their own labor, was clearly evident to these men. With their own Victorian view of the world the missionaries discouraged this independent role of women, which was to diminish as the oppressive effects of colonialism gave BaSotho men greater leverage and greater incentives to control BaSotho women.

The evidence of a complex pattern of surplus production for exchange undermines the simplified portrayals of pre-colonial economies as dominated by subsistence household production with exchanges associated only with ritual or kin obligations. Economists subscribing to the substantivist school of thought have insisted that trade was embedded in and governed by kinship obligations and associated rituals, but the evidence from Lesotho suggests far greater independence for men heading homesteads and even women within the households comprising the homestead. Trade was prompted and governed by necessity and the drive for economic security, and was predicated on considerable economic autonomy. As long as tribute obligations to chiefs were fulfilled, homesteads and households controlled the products of their labor. Just as broadly-based kinship, beyond the interaction of two generations, played only an ideological role in politics, it also lacked a substantive role in economic production and exchange.

The evidence from Lesotho also reveals that goods were not exchanged merely for the purpose of acquiring other goods with use value for the household. On the contrary, both men and women engaged in producing surplus food and in manufacturing surplus goods to exchange them for recognized forms of wealth. Even when Marxist anthropologists and historians have acknowledged that some goods were traded outside the household, because of the absence of capitalism they have assumed that these goods were exchanged for their use values only. The oral evidence, combined with miscellaneous anecdotal written evidence, suggests that the BaSotho often initiated trade with the explicit purpose of accumulating household wealth, and transforming that wealth into more durable or productive forms, primarily cattle. Cattle in turn could be used to increase the productive potential of the male-headed homestead comprising several wives and households, since cattle could be exchanged for wives which brought more fields and more children to the husband. Women contributed to the process of accumulating household wealth, because wealth could not be transferred from household to household by a man with several wives, and would be used eventually to pay the bridewealth for a daughter-in-law whose labor would lighten the load of her mother-in-law. As long as women could trade the goods they produced, they had strong incentives for working hard.

The achievement of economic growth by Lesotho in the nineteenth century thus reflects the initiative of individuals motivated by the drive for security which accompanied the attainment of wealth. This motivation reflected not harmonious communal and household interests, but rather emerged as a result of many conflicting interests and a struggle over resources within a society characterized by socioeconomic stratification and the domination of women by men. The growing interaction with Europeans provided further opportunities for ordinary BaSotho as well as chiefs to accumulate wealth through regional trade and labor migration. In the end, however, colonialism fostered and sustained internal political oppression through the elimination of counterbalances to chiefs' powers, and imposed a severe economic burden in the form of direct taxation. The voluntary trade of surplus produce in the pre-colonial era quickly evolved into an involuntary sale of food needed for household subsistence by the end of the nineteenth century. The expanding involvement of the BaSotho in selling grain to Europeans was a spontaneous and natural extension of the earlier exchange economy. High levels of production could not be sustained, however, because of the shrinking size of the country and the deterioration of the soil. The terms of trade declined as a result of deliberate European policies, and in the end the interlocking of the local economy into the regional market, promoted by missionaries as the route to "civilization," became the road to impoverishment.

10

Women, reproduction, and production

The accumulation of people was a driving goal governing politics and society throughout southern Africa in the nineteenth century. The imperative of achieving and maintaining social and economic security motivated individuals, families, and chiefdoms. From defense against outsiders who might appropriate basic resources and wealth, to a working social order in which the welfare of the society as a whole rested on the health and welfare of individuals, the contributions of women in reproduction and production were indispensable. Recognition of the value of women gave men an incentive both to protect them and to control them. As a result, the history of women in southern Africa has been characterized by varying degrees of individual initiative, but always in the context of explicit domination by and subordination to men.

Women played a key role in the dynamics of social, political, and economic change in nineteenth-century Lesotho because of their central functions and activities related to reproduction and production. Their indispensable role in biological reproduction and their central roles in productive activities, ensuring the continued physical welfare and ideological underpinnings of BaSotho society, gave women a recognized value which prompted men to control and dominate them. Men's recognition of women's value was reflected in the payment of bridewealth by the husband's family to the woman's family when she married, to compensate the family for the loss of one of their women. The distribution of women affected the distribution of both wealth and power within and between groups, since through the payment of bridewealth the rights to the progeny of the marriage were obtained and the descent group expanded its numerical strength and continued into another generation.

Laws and social customs were structured to ensure the legal, social, and economic dependence of women upon men. Women were not allowed independent access to the primary means of support, land, nor did they have legal recourse as their access to the courts was only through men. The ability of women to resist domination was further limited by their susceptibility to physical abuse, especially when pregnant, and by their maternal desire to remain with their children even at cost to themselves. Only widows with grown children were able to maintain independent households under the supervision of male relatives. Tied to their homes, which were headed by men, women as daughters, wives, and mothers had a strong incentive to further the interests of the men to whom their interests were tied. Women appear in history as actors in their own right, but the choices they made must be understood in the context of male dominance and control. Women worked to exploit their political, social, and economic importance, as well as their biological functions in reproduction, as leverage to ensure their own well-being, but they never did so in a way which could have overturned the social organization by which men perpetuated their control over women.

The term reproduction has come to be used by extension to refer not only to biological reproduction, but also to the ongoing process of ensuring the continuation of social organization. Women "reproduce" the social order by their domestic labor, that is the production of household goods and services, which by supporting family members serves to "reproduce" labourers. Their domestic work, which is productive and serves an economic function by increasing the wealth of the household, can also be defined as "daily reproduction," with a social function. As women pass on the ideological values of society in raising and teaching their children, they reinforce the ideological underpinnings of social organization, thus playing an important role in "ideological reproduction." In theory, through their role in ideo-logical reproduction women might have controlled the transmission of culture as wives and mothers. In practice men, however, ensured their control over the education process through circumcision schools in which boys were indoctrinated with the ideals and ideologies which were appro-priate to the continuation of the inherited culture.

These "reproductive" functions of women have been analyzed on the basis of an evaluation of women's roles in the internal working of societies, whereas their role in external politics has generally been overlooked. To these varieties of "reproduction" I therefore add the concept of "political reproduction," in which political bonds were forged through marriage alliances, ensuring the political survival of a particular society in a regional context. As wives and sisters, married outside their own chiefdom, women produced and reproduced the regional political order. When they served as "queens," that is regents, the wives and mothers of chiefs ensured political succession and the inheritance of political office, reproducing sociopolitical relations by holding a place for the male heir until his coming of age.

Political marriages were also the vehicle for the dissemination of a common culture. We see a deliberate and well-considered process of forging political alliances through marriage occurring over many generations and across a wide geographic area as the SeSotho- and SeTswana-speaking peoples spread across the region from the fourteenth century or earlier. Periodic migrations and intermarriage sustained common cultural tradi-tions, including traditions of origin, and the natural transference and dissemination of all aspects of culture which may have undergone change and incorporated innovation over time. The languages of all the SeSotho- and SeTswana-speaking peoples have remained mutually intelligible until today, and in Europe would not be classified as separate languages. Modern European linguists have followed the various orthographies, based on phonetic systems from different European languages, which were developed independently by missionaries with different native European tongues working in different regions. This led modern scholars to redefine this common language as several distinct and separate languages in order to conform to the false western notion of distinct and divided pasts, creating "tribalism," whether deliberately or unintentionally. The exaggeration of linguistic differences has furthered the ends of apartheid in fostering divisiveness where historical unity is evident in the most basic element of culture, language. Mothers passed on language and culture to their children, and the intermarriage between groups, distinguished from one another by chiefs representative both of lines of descent and political units, preserved and fostered a common culture over widely dispersed settlements.

The records in the oral traditions of deliberately arranged marriages between different descent groups as far back as the fifteenth century suggest the level of ongoing cultural sharing and dissemination which occurred. Women carried their own cultural heritage with them, and passed it down to their children, who incorporated cultural traditions from both parents. Such marriages often took place following the migration and resettlement of one group near or among another, necessitating political cooperation. Under these circumstances, innovations in both ideas and technology were easily disseminated even as the SeTswana- and SeSotho-speaking populations dispersed over generations. Wives transferred from one group to another over wide geographic areas through marriage were therefore important in reproducing cultural unity and forming or maintaining political unity among widely dispersed groups. Their role as political links also gave them a role in cultural dissemination.

Daughters, sisters, and wives: marriage alliances before 1830

The oral traditions of the BaSotho demonstrate the importance of women in forging political and military alliances among the SeSotho-speaking peoples from approximately the fifteenth century. Women appear in these traditions, by name, because of their importance as daughters, wives, sisters, and mothers. Women secured political and therefore military alliances through marriage which linked a woman's father and brothers with her husband. It is significant that specific women are remembered by name for their importance in just such alliances.

It was customary for a chief to marry the daughter of another chief, with the father incurring an obligation to help the husband of his daughter, and the son-in-law incurring a reciprocal obligation to his father-in-law. The maternal uncle retained social and economic obligations with respect to his sister's children, acting as their protector until they reached adulthood. These obligations created ongoing ties between a woman's own family and line of descent, and the descent line of her husband as the father of her children who became members of her husband's descent line.

Because of this tie, which called for the maternal uncle to help his sister's children marry, a son would often settle near his mother's relatives when he left his father's home. When he first left his father's village, Moshoeshoe asked for and received an allocation of land on which to settle for himself and his circumcision age mates. He received the land from his mother's family, who were BaFokeng, rather than from his own father from the BaKoena descent line.[1] Brothers, thus, could intercede in political and military matters to aid their sisters, their sisters' children, and hence their sisters' new families. Moshoeshoe's maternal uncle Ratsiu became one of the first to bring his people (who were from the chiefdom of Moshoeshoe's mother), to place himself and them under Moshoeshoe's rule before 1822. Ratsiu became one of Moshoeshoe's principal advisors, and "took his place when he was absent or ill."[2] Later the brother of Moshoeshoe's great wife 'MaMohato became a senior advisor to Moshoeshoe.[3]

Similarly the BaTlokoa and the BaSia forged an important marriage link when the BaTlokoa chief Mokotjo married the sister of the BaSia chief Letlala. Each subsequently felt free to call upon the other for help militarily.[4] Maternal uncles bore ongoing responsibilities for their sisters' children, which gave a chief an important ally in his mother's family. The female relatives of chiefs thus represented important political currency, and as such were accorded a certain amount of protection and respect. So important were the alliances forged through the exchange of wives that the widow of a chief, who was not supposed to remarry but rather fall to a male relative under the levirate system, often became the object of dispute because the alliance she represented would strengthen the hand of the male relative who took her in and protected her.

With people from various descent lines settling together and recognizing common political authority, the ancestors of the SeSotho- and Se-Tswana-speaking peoples placed great weight on the tracing of the relative positions of descent lines for determining political ascendancy and legitimacy. BaSotho oral traditions concerning the political importance of the BaFokeng descent line illustrate the political role of women in perpetuating or creating legitimacy in political domination. The BaFokeng have had a preponderant influence east and south of the Limpopo and Vaal. As the senior line of SeSotho- and SeTswana-speaking descent groups the BaFokeng commanded respect and influence. However, they are remembered not as conquerors, but as people of amiable character who dispersed among various other SeSotho-speakers. It was through their women that their influence spread, as "their daughters have always been much sought after as wives, especially by the chiefs of other tribes [sic]."[5] The oral traditions record marriages between chiefs and daughters of other chiefs, and many of these marriages centered either on the BaFokeng or on the BaKoena, who became dominant as Moshoeshoe's line of descent. Over the centuries the BaFokeng forged marriage alliances with the BaKoena, BaKhatla, BaTaung, BaPhuthi, and San. The BaKoena, in addition to marrying BaFokeng wives, also intermarried deliberately with the BaPhuthi and the San. The BaPhuthi, having forged alliances through marriages with the MaPhuthing among whom they first settled, also intermarried with the San who occasionally dominated the BaPhuthi, as well as with the BaFokeng and BaKoena. Another notable marriage alliance was built between the BaTlokoa and the BaSia.[6]

Only the most important political alliances forged by marriage were recorded, especially those which increased the legitimacy of chiefs' claims to seniority and dominance. The marriage alliances recorded in the traditions paint a picture of the intentional use of women to blend descent lines in marriage. Polygamy was a central element of this strategy, as multiple marriages allowed chiefs to ally themselves with as many other people as possible. The BaMonaheng chief Mohlomi (d. 1815), renowned as a rain-maker, healer, traveller, and philosopher, is remembered not only for having married wives wherever he travelled, but also for passing on to Moshoeshoe the advice that marrying many wives was the best strategy for building political alliances. The strategy was clearly not new with Mohlomi, however, as his grandfather Monaheng had built his own strength through many marriage alliances in the previous century.[7] Moshoeshoe pursued this strategy, and already had about thirty wives by 1833.[8]

The oral traditions record in detail some instances in which marriage alliances were critical factors in political contests. For example, at the beginning of the nineteenth century Moletsane did not inherit the chieftainship of the BaTaung, because he came from a junior house of the descent group. Rather, he gained influence when he came to the rescue of his father-in-law Mokheli, the chief, whose sons were conspiring to depose him. At the request of his wife's father, Moletsane raided and punished the sons and "Mokhele gave Moletsane full authority to act for him."[9] Eventually Moletsane extended his power with many marriage alliances, for he married 33 wives and had more than 115 children.[10]

Women did not have any leverage to control their own fates in these marriage alliances. The political bonds forged through marriage alliances were of critical importance in military contests, and the heirs produced through such marriages further cemented the original alliance. Once these heirs had been produced, however, a chief's wife who was left a widow might retain some control over her subsequent fate. Chiefs' widows were not supposed to remarry since their new spouse might be jealous of his stepson who stood to inherit political office and so pose a threat to his life. Normally the chief's widow would fall to the younger brother of the chief through the levirate, and she might produce further children by him. Evidence that this was preferred but not enforced comes from the experience of Moshoeshoe's great-grandmother. When her husband, the chief Motloang, died at the beginning of the eighteenth century, she refused to submit to any of his brothers through the levirate and instead chose an Nguni-speaking UmHlubi man as her lover. Eventually Motloang's family brought such pressure to bear on the couple that the man left, but not before he had fathered Moshoeshoe's grandfather, a child called Peete in reference to his father's stutter when trying to speak SeSotho. Although she had refused to be taken in a *"kenela"* (widow inheritance) relationship by her dead husband's brother Mokoteli and instead had relations with another man, her child Peete was automatically adopted into Mokoteli's line of descent because the family had acquired the right to all of her children by having paid her bridewealth. Here is an example of a woman deliberately choosing a relationship which might have had significant political ramifications, and being subsequently thwarted for this reason. In the end her apparent leverage to control her own fate was revealed as illusory. This relationship between a MoSotho woman and an UmHlubi man also indicates the possibilities for cultural transference which must have always been present between SeSotho- and SeTswana-speaking peoples on the one hand and their distant Nguni neighbors, with whom they traded, on the other hand.

Women as mothers: queen regents before 1830

The role of women as queen regents reveals much about their positions as sisters as well as their potential influence as wives and mothers. The most famous queen regent in BaSotho history was Mokotjo's wife 'Manthatisi, but she was not the first. Two generations earlier the BaTlokoa chief Tsotetsi (born *c.* 1735) died while his heir was too young to rule, and his widow Mamohlahlo proclaimed herself regent. She was opposed by the two brothers of her dead husband, who aspired to the chieftaincy, but was supported by his cousin Motonosi, the powerful chief of another branch of the family. Only because of her persistence did the chieftaincy pass to her son.[11]

In about 1800 the problem recurred, this time in the senior branch of the family, when Motonosi died. His eldest son Montueli having predeceased him, Motonosi's grandson stood to inherit. The mother of the heir did not trust her brother-in-law, however, and protected her son by seeking refuge with her own family. According to oral tradition as reported by Ellenberger, Montueli's widow Ntlo-kholo "after consultation with her relations, the BaSia, went to live with them during the minority of her son [Mokotjo]. She was escorted by a guard consisting of her husband's circumcision mates, who remained with her during her sojourn with her own people, which lasted about three years."[12]

Here we see that women could mobilize help from men based on bonds with their husbands. The initiation mates of a chief became his military strength for life; he needed them as a base for his power, but they also held status because of their relation to him. Hence it was in their interest to protect his wife and heir even if he died, for they became councillors to the new chief, whereas if another claimant took power they lost their status to the new chief's circumcision mates. This was a relationship which the chief's widow could manipulate, and so was part of the strategy of queen regents, who also drew upon their own fathers and brothers for protection of their children. It was in the interests of the queen's family for her son, their kin by marriage, to succeed to the chieftaincy. Montueli's younger brother never contested the chieftainship of his nephew, but when the younger brother died his own widow tried to assert her son's claim against his cousin. In the end, the widows of two brothers were set against each other in pursuing an inheritance for their sons. The young Mokotjo, supported by his age mates, was received back by this branch of the BaTlokoa, and was able to take over his father's position because of the protection he had received from his mother and her family. His mother's family in turn remained allied through marriage to an important chief. So important was his mother Ntlo-kholo considered to be that even her death is remembered in oral traditions.[13]

Perhaps because of his own experience, Mokotjo warned his own wife to beware of his brothers if he died while their son was still a minor. Mokotjo had married his cousin Monyalue, daughter of his mother's brother and therefore a MoSia. When Mokotjo died in 1813 his heir was only nine years old, and his widow became the queen regent known as 'Manthatisi after the name of her eldest daughter. She ruled capably as regent, but always with the intention of securing the chieftainship for her son. When it came time for his circumcision she became suspicious, apparently with justice, of her brother-in-law's intentions and had her son removed from the BaTlokoa circumcision school and sent to her own brother to be circumcised among the BaSia. Eventually her son Sekonyela assumed the chieftaincy, but not before his mother had earned her own important place in history. In this case 'Manthatisi used her position as daughter and sister to reinforce her role as wife and mother: she called upon her blood relations to defend her son's inheritance.[14]

Other women are remembered because of their importance as mothers. The grandmother of Moorosi, who as chief of the BaPhuthi became a subordinate ally of Moshoeshoe, was remarkable. Towards the end of the eighteenth century a MoFokeng woman, Ngoanamokone, was left a widow with five children, two sons and three daughters, on the death of her husband, a BaPhuthi chief. She took her children to live with another branch of the BaPhuthi, where her eldest son worked for the chief's son herding his cattle. Her husband apparently left the family with no property in livestock, presumably because he had fled his home on the Tugela River in a political dispute. On her own initiative Ngoanamokone grew tobacco and hemp which were widely used as currency in the area, and which she traded to the San for skins and ostrich feathers. Ostrich feathers were highly valued as a war ornament for chiefs, and with them she was able to acquire almost enough cattle to provide the bridewealth for her son to marry the chief's granddaughter, who was also the daughter of his employer. In *Basuto Traditions* MacGregor found it hard to believe that she had accomplished this alone, but he nevertheless presented the evidence of her strategy and tactics:

> Meanwhile, Ngoanamang [Ngoanamokone], who had brought with her some tobacco and hemp (dagga) sought to acquire some property by trading these commodities with the Bushmen [San] for skins and ostrich feathers. These, which were much prized, she bartered for cattle, and by this means was able to provide for the marriage of her son Mokuoane with Maidi, daughter of Tsosane. On the other hand, it is said, that Tsosane, in consideration of the services of Mokuoane in herding his cattle, waived the question of dowry. Probably the truth is somewhere between these two statements, and is that Ngoanamang's trade did not produce sufficient for the purpose, and that Tsosane, for the reason stated, remitted the rest. In any case, Makuoane got the girl, and she became the mother of Morosi.[15]

Since the normal reward for herding another man's livestock was only one head of cattle a year, it is most likely that most of the bridewealth portion came from Ngoanamokone. Ellenberger's later collection of traditions indicates that Mokuoane made blankets from the skins and made headgear and ornaments from the ostrich feathers. Mokuoane knew how to make the chiefly battle ornament *Mokhele*, which had ostrich feathers bound to a bamboo pole. Mokuoane sold these ornaments, highly valued because of the skill required to make them and because the feathers were rare, to chiefs at the price of one heifer for each. In this rendition Ngoanamokone barely receives credit for her indispensable contribution of acquiring the skins and ostrich feathers by growing and selling tobacco and hemp, for Ellenberger concludes that "in this way, and with the help of his mother, Mokuoane got together almost enough cattle to enable him to marry the daughter of his master, Tsosane."[16]

Male attitudes and gender relations before 1830

Evidence about attitudes towards women is scanty, and makes such attitudes difficult to discern, especially for the more distant period. What evidence there is indicates that women were valued by men. The recognition of women's value is only occasionally reflected in evidence of respect for women, however. On the contrary, attempts to acquire and control women were sometimes marked by violent disregard for their persons. As in the history of western civilization, the experience of women seems to have been marked by vacillations in their status, but always in the context of generalized subordination to men. When women emerged as influential or powerful, it was as individuals, or "honorary men." They could not pass the high status they had earned on to their daughters or other women.

Evidence of respect for women is embedded in oral traditions referring to perhaps the earliest period remembered, the late fifteenth century, when the BaKoena first subdivided and the BamaNgwato chose a new *seboko*, or totem symbol, to distinguish themselves. Ngwato is said to have chosen the *phuthi*, or duiker (a small antelope variety) "to please his wife, who with her ancestors revered this antelope."[17] This indicates as well the extent to which the cultural traditions of women were respected even after marriage into another descent group. Similarly the MaZizi, who had immigrated into the area of Lesotho from the Tugela river area, are said to have acquired their new name because the chief married a daughter of the MaPhuthing chief in about 1600 and the child of this marriage, a son Tsele, took the totem of his mother's people. Coincidentally their totem was also the *phuthi* or duiker, so that they were called BaPhuthi from then on, although they were not related to the BamaNgwato who observed the same totem.[18]

Women, although sometimes nameless, appear in favorable terms, and sometimes heroic roles, in these traditions. Certainly Mamohlahlo, Ntlo-kholo, Ngoanamokone, and 'Mantatisi were remembered for courage and wisdom as they led their people in the transition between their husbands and their sons. The wife of a MaKholokoe chief escaped from a battle with her son and fled to live with the chief of the Mahlapo, and her son eventually married into a junior branch of the chief's family.[19] A MoTlokoa woman named Maseile rallied her people to resist an attack of Moshoeshoe, and thus turned the tide of battle to save her people.[20] BaPhuthi women were credited with keeping the men supplied with heavy stones to throw down from their mountain stronghold against attackers in a battle against the AmaNgwane.[21] When Matiwane's AmaNgwane were exerting their domi-nance in the region in the 1820s, one of his wives visited Moshoeshoe at Thaba Bosiu and was treated with the respect and courtesy due an important emissary, serving to cement an alliance between the parties.[22] In the early eighteenth century Mokoteli, founder of the BaKoena family branch into which Moshoeshoe was born three generations later, was captured in a battle with some AmaHlubi and only escaped with the help of an unnamed woman.[23] Moshoeshoe's own father Mokhachane was similarly rescued by an unknown woman after being captured in battle in about 1780.[24] She is said to have scraped a hole in the mud wall of the hut where he was being held, expecting to be killed, and to have "released him from his bonds, and let him out." That she is remembered in oral traditions indicates that even the BaSotho of the time recognized that their history might have been very different had it not been for the courageous action of this anonymous woman.

The value of women is indicated by the fact that they were captured deliberately in battle, and that they were ransomed when captured. Several incidents indicate the vulnerability of women as well as the extent to which men did or did not protect them. While Moshoeshoe was still at Butha Buthe two of his wives were captured by a MoFokeng chief, but Moshoeshoe later recaptured them in a counterattack.[25] When Moshoeshoe led his people from Butha Buthe to Thaba Bosiu in 1824 his elder sister and two of his wives fell behind in a difficult pass because "one was ill and the two others far advanced in pregnancy."[26] When they were attacked one man managed to protect them from capture and others returned to help, but the rescuers were too late to save the elderly stragglers including Moshoeshoe's grandfather Peete. Such an attack was foreseeable under the circumstances, and sufficient precautions could have been taken to protect the women all along, but were not. That the women were eventually rescued but the elderly were not also reflects the priority of the times. Later Sekonyela captured many women in an attack at Thaba Bosiu, including two of Moshoeshoe's wives, one of them his great wife 'MaMohato. In the course of the battle the women were rescued, and the BaSotho were said to have been driven to attack furiously because Sekonyela was carrying off their women, including the queen.[27] When some BaKhatla women were captured, their chief ransomed them from their captors with six head of cattle.[28]

The right of men to abduct women without regard for their wishes seems to have been taken for granted. When Moshoeshoe helped his father's people defeat the BaSia he captured three women. Keeping two as wives for himself he gave the third to his brother.[29] In the early eighteenth century a major battle was fought over the fate of a beautiful chief's wife who was coveted by another man, Mokheseng, for her beauty. Mokheseng (son of Monaheng, and also known as Ratlali) is remembered as "a brave warrior and also a poet," who "composed all the national songs of war and of circumcision,"[30] but his desire for women is remembered as causing the death of many people. Apparently he was known for committing adultery, and Ellenberger was told that "he would conceive a desire for the wife of this or that chief, and would never rest until he possessed her by force or fraud."[31] He asked his relations to mount an attack so he could abduct the wife of the MaKhoakhoa (BaHlakoana) chief Liyo, and in the ensuing battle he, Liyo, and another BaKoena chief were all killed.[32]

The treatment of widows, like captured women, could reflect callous disregard for the wishes of the woman. Such an issue arose among the BaKoena several generations before Moshoeshoe's time, in the aftermath of the battle started by Mokheseng. When he died in the early eighteenth century in pursuit of another man's wife Mokheseng left behind his own wives as widows, and they became the objects of dispute among their captors, such that "the question of the widows gave rise to discords and quarrels which were not settled even by the spilling of blood."[33] In another incident in the early nineteenth century Moletsane's brother set in motion a series of battles by committing adultery with one of Moletsane's wives. He was forced to leave and fled to a BaRolong chief, where he was secretly killed as punishment for the adultery. A fierce battle consequently ensued between the BaTaung and the BaRolong.[34] Even Moshoeshoe's father Mokhachane married his wife, Moshoeshoe's mother Kholu, forcibly: Ellenberger recorded the story that "she had been promised in marriage to one Lesia, of

135

her own tribe [sic]; but Mokhachane was not to be denied, and took her by force."[35] Some of the evidence regarding attitudes about women appears directly in the recorded traditions. There is a BaSotho saying that "*morena ke mosali*" meaning "woman is chief." Ellenberger explains this as meaning "that even a chief must respect her, and may not abuse or punish her, though she may have provoked him."[36] In practice, this ideal was not realized, as women were frequently abducted and captured with no respect for their persons. At least some BaRolong men were taught in initiation school "to despise all women, even their own mothers."[37] When the wise philosopher Mohlomi was dying he is said to have told his wife that "the wisdom I have sought in vain will be revealed to thee who art but a woman," displaying his belief in the inferiority of women in general.[38]

Even Moshoeshoe's relationship with his favorite wife, his great wife 'MaMohato, is revealing. Only Sanders has discreetly discussed a case which has received little attention, no doubt because it reflects so poorly on the man who became a hero in all the traditions. According to the missionaries the relationship between Moshoeshoe and 'MaMohato was affectionate, an "apparently perfect union" characterized by "perfect cordiality mingled with respect," but she died in 1834.[39] Generations later Ellenberger was told that Moshoeshoe had discovered that she had been unfaithful, and that "a violent scene with the Queen 'Mamohato followed, resulting in a serious illness and ultimately in her death at childbirth."[40] Normally the punishment would have been inflicted on the other man, as "any man having carnal connection with the great wife of the chief was liable to be driven from the community or strangled."[41] There is no record that the man in this case was punished, suggesting that he was very important and close to Moshoeshoe; Ellenberger referred to him as "one of his chief officers."[42]

How much power and influence did women actually enjoy, whether in public roles or over their own lives? On the one hand we see Peete's mother taking a lover against the wishes of her former husband's relatives, contrary to custom. Her initial rebellion against their control did not last, however: her lover was forced to leave, and she eventually migrated with her dead husband's brother, Mokoteli, with Peete becoming a member of Mokoteli's line of descent. The experience of 'MaMohato shows the ultimate penalty faced by women who rebelled, since she apparently died as the result of a harsh beating inflicted by Moshoeshoe.

Women were legally protected in certain ways, but access to the courts to enforce laws rested in the hands of men and hence women remained dependent on male relatives for protection, including access to means of support. Protection against physical abuse was minimal: a woman could return home and seek a divorce only if she were repeatedly and badly abused, in which case her family could keep the bridewealth as the means for her support. Without evident cause the family had to return the bridewealth, however, which gave the woman's family an incentive to send her back even to an abusive marriage. If the bridewealth had been paid up, the husband retained rights to her children and she would in effect be abandoning them if she left him.[43] Casalis wrote in 1859 that

> The case of divorce is very frequent there where the bridewealth is of low value. Among the Bassoutos, where it is rising rather high, the dissolution of marriage involved great difficulties. The husbands who send back their wives do not intend to leave at the wife's home the cattle which they had sent there. On their side, the relatives of the women are rarely disposed to return a good which they hold, or which is no longer found in their possession. The law authorized them otherwise to refuse all restitution when the marriage has been fruitful. The children already born are deemed to have acquitted the debt.[44]

Women had limited security with regard to their access to any means of support. The wealth accumulated in one household could not be transferred by the husband to the household of another of his wives, and women therefore had rights to the products of their labor, and could help to ensure their own welfare through their own hard work. For the most part property rights were still vested in the husband, but women retained some rights over property attached to their house. For example, the cattle received as bridewealth were attached to the household of the mother of the bride. They could be used to pay the bridewealth for a son from the same household, but they could not be used by the father as bridewealth for the son of a different wife.[45] Women also clearly held some property of their own, although the limitations of the sources for the nineteenth century make it difficult to obtain a complete picture of women's property rights. A woman might own her own animals, for example. Of the bridewealth paid for her daughter, one animal was designated for the mother: usually the mother was given "a good young heifer," and "it is said it belongs to the breast which suckled" the young bride, hence it is called the *"khomo ea letsoele"* or "cow of the breast."[46]

In a sense much of the history of BaSotho women, in terms of their roles and the potential and limitations of their influence, is embodied in the story of 'Manthatisi, the most heroic of all women in BaSotho traditions. Daughter of the BaSia chief Phenya, she was married to the BaTlokoa chief Mokotjo to strengthen their alliance. She was reputed to be tall, slim, and handsome as a young woman, but by the time she became queen regent in 1813 at about age forty she was large, stout and strong, as befitted a person of wealth and leadership, male or female. According to oral traditions she was "affable and social, and very popular with all her people."[47] What is remembered about her in the traditions is revealing of her character and her perspective, which was sometimes distinctly that of a woman. For example, on one occasion "Mantatise sent the fighting men to forage for grain for the children."[48] Providing food for children was the responsibility of women, and men, especially warriors in the field, often had access to meat which was not necessarily shared with women, much less children. At a time when granaries were empty from drought and the traditional foraging and gathering activities of women and children put them in danger of kidnapping by outsiders,

137

women and children were at risk of starvation. In no other place in the traditions is the welfare of children ever a consideration, suggesting that 'Manthatisi's concern reflected a sensitivity to the needs of the more vulnerable members of society which a man might have overlooked.

Her power to send out warriors on an errand of mercy for children also indicates that her authority was respected and effective even though she reigned only as a regent. Indeed, she was accorded the respect normally given to any male ruler, and as such served as an "honorary man." According to traditions, "She used to sit in court with the men on the biggest stone in the circle, hear cases and discuss politics; and the policy of the tribe [sic] during her regency was conducted by her alone."[49] She even devised battle strategies for her warriors although she did not participate in battles herself. In a tradition obviously remembered because it reflected her strategic abilities, 'Manthatisi is said to have saved her people from an attack by the AmaHlubi while her warriors were away. She had lines of women appear at the edge of the top of the mountain stronghold holding mats and hoes in the pose of warriors, behind the few remaining armed men. This appearance of strength held off their attackers until the warriors returned.[50] In 1817 the BaTlokoa conducted a successful battle against the AmaHlubi on the Mzinyati River, which brought 'Manthatisi and her people both a vast herd of cattle and considerable prestige, such that another AmaHlubi chief placed himself under her rule the following year. The raid took place in the wake of a serious cattle epizootic in the region, and control over cattle wealth in a time of scarcity must have given 'Manthatisi considerable political leverage, as it did Moshoeshoe in the years to follow.

Clearly scarcity governed many political and military decisions throughout the region during the 1810s and 1820s, and it is in this context that 'Manthatisi's role in the so-called "*mfecane*" must be judged. After the AmaHlubi attacked the BaTlokoa in 1822, 'Manthatisi's people were faced with destitution. They had weathered the cattle epizootic several years earlier, but had then faced problems of food scarcity because of a drought which lasted several years. When 'Manthatisi's brother, chief of the BaSia, offered to join forces in a joint counterattack against the AmaHlubi she refused, "because, as she said, her people were hungry and might loot the crops of the Basia, and thus cause friction. She judged it better, therefore, to move on, and help herself to the property of less friendly tribes."[51]

At this point 'Manthatisi tried to reclaim cattle which belonged to her dead husband and were being held by a client living among the BaFokeng. He resisted with the support of the BaFokeng, and the BaTlokoa resorted to force to take back their livestock which they now needed so desperately.[52] 'Manthatisi and her people, along with the rest of the SeSotho- and SeTswana-speaking peoples of the region, found themselves competing for food in a time of great scarcity which had initially been caused by drought.[53]

Had 'Manthatisi ruled in her own right, she might have been able to mitigate some of the suffering which ensued in subsequent years. Instead her son

Sekoniela came into his majority, and power passed into his hands. Sekoniela began acting without his mother's approval soon after his initiation ceremony in about 1818, and he had taken control by 1823 or 1824. 'Manthatisi is said to have opposed Sekoniela's attacks on other people, but her son displayed a recklessness and even brutality which she could not control.[54] By the time Andrew Smith met her in 1834 she was behaving in a totally submissive manner towards her son, reportedly out of fear for her life:

> His [Sekoniela's] mother ['Manthatisi], who was present at the time and who was naturally very communicative, was peculiarly reserved in his presence, and not only she herself but others had told us that he was extremely captious with her and she feared if she should seriously displease him he would kill her. Owing to the peculiar position in which she had long been placed she was much respected by the elders of the tribe [sic] and it was only the striplings and others who delighted in mischief that supported him in his proceedings particularly those of them which related to the treatment of his mother.
> It was only shortly before our arrival that he had risen into power, the tribe [sic] having previously been managed by his mother since the death of his father, and such was the faith of most of its members in her judgement that they still insisted on her opinion being ascertained before any matter of importance was decided. The old woman, however, probably better acquainted with the disposition of her son than they were, was fearful of opposing him, and, therefore, the advantages which under other circumstances might have been derived from her superior discretion and understanding were not secured.[55]

Both oral traditions and European eyewitness accounts confirm that contrary to the myth spread by Europeans of a one-eyed giant leading warriors in battle, 'Manthatisi was an astute and popular leader. Ellenberger even reports that "she was afterwards often called Mosayane (the little woman), not by any means in derision, for she was rather tall, but rather in a spirit of admiration similar to that which once inspired Frenchmen to call their great Emperor "the little corporal."[56] 'Manthatisi's life history reveals the pattern in which women were used as daughters and wives to build political alliances and as mothers to ensure inheritance along the direct line of descent. Within prescribed constraints which kept them dependent on male supporters, they could emerge individually into positions of power. This did not happen often, however, and it was always temporary. Powerful women might be able to ameliorate the plight of women and children, but they could not change a system which ensured the perpetuation of male dominance. Because they were forced to rely on male relatives, they pinned their fates to these men and worked on their behalf, while their daughters were married away to face their own fates among their husbands' families.

Cattle as bridewealth in the nineteenth century

The payment of bridewealth was an index of the value placed on women by men. Bridewealth was normally paid in cattle, the most valuable form of transferable property among the BaSotho. Cattle played a fundamental role in the exchange system in BaSotho society. Cattle provided milk and meat for food; hides for blankets, clothing, and bags; transportation; and, after the introduction of the ox-drawn plow, draft power for the cultivation of fields. Cattle had multiple functions in BaSotho society, however, and their value extended beyond their more obvious productive roles. In the absence of alternative investment opportunities, wealth was invested in cattle. Through natural reproduction the size of the original herd increased, providing a return on the initial investment.[57]

The important productive function of cattle and their economic function as "capital" in turn gave cattle an important exchange value. Nineteenth-century missionaries in Lesotho described cattle as capital useful for both investment and exchange, as did Moshoeshoe himself. Writing in 1835, Arbousset reported that Moshoeshoe "understood the utility of money as a means of exchange and is procuring it for himself, saying 'that our *ecus* [currency] are our cows.'"[58]

In 1859 Casalis observed that cattle were "the only form of wealth [valeur] in circulation," and that "Cattle have ceased to be only the equivalent of domesticated game, they are *capital with interest* which one cannot touch except parsimoniously."[59]

More than thirty years later another missionary noted that "the cow ... is the current coin and the only commerce of the country."[60] This was not accurate: by the end of the century there was a considerable commerce using (European) currencies, and barter of less valuable items was common at the local level. Cattle continued to change hands in payment of bridewealth, however, which involved the largest single transfer of wealth in the society.

Estimates of the size of bridewealth payments in the nineteenth century generally ranged from ten to thirty head of cattle. Payments apparently increased over time as the BaSotho accumulated more cattle.[61] They also varied widely according to the woman's social status. In addition, polygamists usually paid less for wives in successive marriages.[62] By the turn of the twentieth century the general consensus of observers was that the typical bridewealth payment included twenty head of cattle, ten sheep or goats, and one horse. A MoSotho pastor in the French Protestant missionary church reported that the payment had increased to this amount only since the establishment of British rule in the country.[63] This scale is still in effect, although now and in the past there has been much variability in the final agreement, which was affected by social rank, and in the schedule of payments.[64]

The devastating destruction of cattle herds in the Rinderpest epizootic did not disrupt the payment of bridewealth. For some marriages the payment was reduced to five from eight head of cattle or twenty sheep or goats.[65] Other marriages were sealed with debts of honor, stones from the kraal representing the cattle which would someday change hands.[66] At some point it became common to accept payment in the form of grain at the market equivalent of the cattle owed. As one informant explained,

A lot of people in the old days were married with food [grain]. Two bags [*methe*] made one cow. They were married with grain, it was not often people were married with cattle, only someone who was very rich could marry by giving his own cattle. If he did not have this great wealth it was two bags instead of each cow. Then three bags and so on and a little more at a time like that so you know that the cows are [paid off] more and more and like that the number of cattle [owed] is reached.[67]

The bridewealth paid on behalf of informants married in the early twentieth century ranged from thirteen to twenty-three head of cattle, with additional small animals and a horse sometimes included or substituted.[68] Bridewealth was normally paid in installments over many years. This meant that the natural increase of the bridewealth cattle was not entirely lost to the husband's family. The social ends of the payment of bridewealth were therefore compatible with the economic interests of the parties involved.

The payment of bridewealth cannot be analytically reduced to mere economic exchange. Much more was at stake in the transfer of resources from the husband's family to the wife's family than the exchange of economic assets. The most important function of bridewealth exchange was the transfer of rights to children from one family or descent group to another.[69] It is also important to recognize, however, that the payment of bridewealth is not economically irrational. The social function of the exchange, in which the reproductive value of the woman was recognized, was entirely compatible with the economic benefits which accrued to both parties in a bridewealth exchange. In paying cattle as bridewealth for wives the BaSotho accorded recognition to the reproductive function of women, and endowed cattle with a reproductive function in the sense that the ownership of cattle made it possible for descent groups to acquire women. But both cattle and women had corresponding productive roles which were also highly valued, making such an exchange economically as well as socially rational. Resources could be transferred from one sphere of production to another through the payment of bridewealth.[70] The productive role of cattle has already been described. Women had an equally significant productive role in the economy. As the principal cultivators, women provided agricultural labor for their husbands. Every man received an additional allocation of land each time he acquired an additional wife, so that his landholdings increased along with the labor that was available to cultivate them. An Anglican missionary observed that "The possession of many wives brings to the possessor of them great wealth and influence. Every wife or concubine has her own hut, works in the fields allotted to her, and supports her own establishment, the husband reaping as he chooses the fruits of her labours."[71]

Bridewealth and children

Women were clearly important for their reproductive capacities. Sons were a source of labor, and increased the strength of the lineage. Daughters provided agricultural labor until they were married, when they brought in income from their bridewealth. The initial payment of bridewealth for a wife therefore represented not only an investment in land and agricultural labor; it also brought a direct return on the investment in the form of children. The BaSotho perspective on bridewealth is reflected in the regional aphorism, "cattle beget children." A man with several daughters eventually received back several times the number of cattle he originally gave for his wife when his own daughters married. Bridewealth paid for his sons could similarly be viewed as an investment which would eventually be returned with the birth of female offspring. If a woman failed to produce children, another woman would be sent by her family for a small payment or no additional payment at all. Adam Kuper correctly states that "marriage payments represent a shift in investment, not a form of consumption."[72]

Chiefs and wealthy men invested not only in wives for themselves, but also paid the bridewealth on behalf of clients too poor to acquire wives on their own. The sociopolitical motivations for providing bridewealth for a subordinate to marry are obvious, as the husband whose bridewealth has been paid and his family are obligated to the payer and become his supporters and allies. Early missionary observers misunderstood this process: they assumed that the woman became the wife of the payer of bridewealth, who then lent or gave these women to his clients. In this case, however, the client was not just receiving the temporary hospitality of a woman. She became his wife, lived at his homestead, and worked the fields that were allocated to him when he married her. Moshoeshoe paid bridewealth on behalf of many young men following the wars of the 1820s when cattle were scarce. He thereby increased the membership of his own descent group, but he also created new domestic productive units: households with land to cultivate.

The payment of bridewealth implied much more than the transfer of a woman from one homestead to another, because it entailed the transfer of the rights to all of the woman's children from her lineage to that of the payer of the bridewealth. Among the BaSotho the person who provided bridewealth for someone else received more than the one hundred percent return on his investment implied by the right to the bridewealth received from the eldest daughter. As was common elsewhere in Africa, he retained the rights to all of the children produced by the marriage, and he remained their nominal father.[73] A person who paid bridewealth on behalf of another man benefitted from all the children of the marriage in the same way that he benefitted from his own children. With each son the patron's lineage expanded, and upon the marriage of every daughter, not just the eldest daughter, the patron, not the father, received the bridewealth payment. Bridewealth was a fruitful economic as well as political investment, and enhanced the power and wealth of chiefs. Kuper correctly concludes that "Marriage payments and polygamy are not equalizing mechanisms. On the contrary, the rich rely on them to maintain their position."[74]

A man who had obtained his wife with bridewealth paid by his patron never held any rights to the children conceived from that marriage. Instead he had to work hard to accumulate his own wealth with which he could acquire a second wife who would bear children belonging to his own lineage. This second marriage, giving a man his own children, was made possible only because the first marriage had given him access to land, from which, with his wife's labor, he could obtain grain surpluses that could be sold to acquire cattle for the second wife's bridewealth payment.

The ramifications of bridewealth for women were mixed in character. Because they had received a bridewealth payment, a woman's family was likely to pressure her to remain in an abusive marriage so that they would not have to return her bridewealth to the husband. Since her children belonged to her husband's lineage by virtue of the bridewealth payment, if she left her husband she had to leave her children. Although a woman might be allowed to keep small children until she was older, in the long run the husband and his family retained custody and the right to keep them or take them at any time. When the bridewealth had been paid by a patron on behalf of a poor man, the patron might claim the children from her upon her husband's death. A serious case involving Moshoeshoe brought this problem to the attention of the early missionaries, who subsequently opposed such clientage relationships. The poignant plight of this woman is described at length by Arbousset, who is quoted extensively by Thompson.[75] Moshoeshoe insisted that the widow of a client on behalf of whom he had paid bridewealth turn her son over to him after her husband died. When she refused after a lengthy argument in front of a circle of people, Moshoeshoe violently attacked one of her defenders and then beat the woman with a stick. The incident reveals the extent to which even Moshoeshoe would go to control the "children of his cattle," and the vulnerability of women who were violently forced to submit to male authority.

BaSotho men and women sometimes held divergent views on bridewealth, its significance, and its ramifications. On the one hand the BaSotho argued against the missionary view that it was a form of selling women, or enslavement, since the husband could not subsequently sell his wife to someone else. Recent informants repeated this argument to defend the practice. As one man explained,

> This marriage by the cattle which white people said was a form of being sold, it was not a sale because even if you are like this and might marry ten women, and then I am your brother but a poor person, you cannot give me one of your wives. You are obliged to go and look for a young woman for me at her home, rather you take out your cattle and bring about the marriage so that she should come from her home in my name, not in yours. Bridewealth [bohali] of cattle of the BaSotho was still with ten cattle up to twenty, but it was not something that was binding so that before you reached [paid] twenty you could take your wife.[76]

A woman's perspective could be entirely different since the payment of bridewealth clearly restricted her choices and actions, tying her to her husband directly and through their children who became part of his line of descent. Hence a women noted that

> These marriages, leading [life in] these marriages was hard because, isn't it so, some people they, they married with cattle and other people they did not marry with cattle, they did not arrange marriage with cattle, because they said to marry your daughter with cattle was to sell her, because although her life might become hard or her husband even die, especially if her husband died she would find that her life was hard. She could not – even if she left their village, she would have her children taken away and continue to be deprived of them like a bird, because it is a child of the cattle. So others had their daughter married only in the church. Because in the church it happens that if your husband dies ... you stay by yourself there with everything and there is no one who can bother your things, if you don't like staying there you must go with everything of yours even the children; the inheritance belongs both to you and the relative of your husband; whereas in the first kind of marriage that with cattle, it is not so.[77]

Misunderstanding the socioeconomic implications of bridewealth trans-actions, one missionary referred to young girls as "the greatest article of commerce." A Catholic priest expressed similar misconceptions about the custom when he wrote that polygamy was "the source of all their revenue and almost the only trade of the country."[78] But in spite of the efforts of the missionaries to eradicate bridewealth practices, the exchange of cattle for women remained a fundamental feature of BaSotho society in the nineteenth century.

Reproduction, production, and bridewealth

The value placed on women because of their roles in reproduction and production was reflected in the payment of bridewealth for women. Women were primarily valued for their capacity for biological reproduction since only in this were they indispensable. If a woman proved infertile her family had to either send a second wife to her husband or return the bridewealth, indicating that her primary purpose was to perpetuate her husband's line of descent. Once she had produced her husband's heirs she had freedom to leave the marriage since her primary function had been fulfilled. In this context it is clear that women's roles in production, while important, were considered secondary in importance to their role in biological reproduction. In their related role as wives and mothers women were also indispensable in reproducing the political order through marriage alliances and by serving as regents when their husbands died leaving sons who were too young to inherit. Men could fulfill most of the other reproductive and productive tasks of women, however. When on their own as herd-boys or warriors men provided food and clothing for themselves and lived for months without the benefits of the daily reproductive activities of their mothers or wives. Boys and young men performed agricultural tasks generally assigned to women; hence women were not indispensable in agriculture. The gender division of labor was socially determined, so that it was only biological reproduction which gave women a unique value.

Given the socially-determined gender division of labor, however, women made an invaluable contribution to the economic welfare of their families and of society as a whole. Evidence from the preceding chapters indicates the significant role played by women in deliberately increasing household wealth. The higher the level of household wealth, the greater the economic security of the woman who ran the household. However many wives a man had, each was entitled to her own house and fields, and the wealth of one could not be transferred by the man to another. If a woman increased the wealth of her household through her own efforts, she maintained control over whatever she brought into the house. Women were surplus producers, and deliberately exchanged their labor and the products of their labor for more durable forms of wealth. Another motive for men to control women, then, was the productive contribution of women by which they not only maintained the household but also increased household wealth. Since the creation of wealth involved the exploitation of natural resources through the application of labor, the accumulation of wealth by some did not necessarily involve the deprivation of others. The overall wealth of the society increased as the wealth of individuals increased.

Various scholars from Marx to the present, however, have questioned whether the accumulation of wealth was a primary goal of pre-capitalist societies. This is difficult to demonstrate or disprove since the concept of wealth is ambiguous. Africans perceived cattle to be a form of stored wealth, which realized a natural increase. They protected their investment in cattle by distributing their herds in different areas to diversify their risk. Grain was also seen as a form of wealth which could be traded for virtually anything, including livestock. On the one hand wealth could bring greater luxuries and comforts in everyday life, from greater consumption of meat to more luxurious clothing and ostentatious shows of wealth such as wearing jewelry. The conspicuous consumption of wealth in turn conferred and reinforced social prestige, which often could be translated into social power.

On the other hand, since livestock could be used as bridewealth to acquire a wife, and various products including grain could be used to acquire livestock, any form of wealth was convertible into people. Guy has assumed that the exclusive control over livestock lay in the hands of elders, allowing them to monopolize that form of wealth which could be used to acquire women and form a household. In fact livestock were accumulated in many ways by young men and even women through the exchange of their labor and produce, and monopolistic control over bridewealth cannot be assumed. This suggests that intergenerational relations between men, as well as gender relations, were much more complex than is commonly recognized, and that they were manipulated by young men and by women in their own work and strategies. Guy, following Meillassoux, correctly identifies women as a keystone in the workings of pre-colonial African societies, since politics, social organization, and economic viability were all determined by the reproductive and productive roles of women. Security was found in large numbers of people, and accumulation of people into larger and larger political and social units was a central goal of African societies in southern Africa during the nineteenth century. It is important to modify the emphasis Guy gives to the various functions of people, however, and to acknowledge that people were valued as much for providing a chief with socioeconomic strength within his chiefdom. As the political guarantor of socioeconomic security, power was an end in itself, and chiefs bartered wealth in kind for wealth in people towards the goal of achieving economic and political security for themselves and their communities.

11

The BaSotho and the rise of the regional European market, 1830–1910

BaSotho participation in regional trade with Europeans was the natural extension of their earlier trading activities locally and regionally. The BaSotho were driven to trade not by new "artificially induced wants," nor by a Christian impulse towards "civilization" as defined by western missionaries, but rather, as always, by their efforts to acquire the livestock and technology which would enable them to achieve economic and military security. As in the past they traded grain for livestock, building their cattle herds which represented an investment in production that could be transformed into a social investment through the payment of bridewealth. They also purchased horses and guns which allowed them eventually to contain the aggression of Griqua and Kora raiders sponsored by white frontier settlers who provided the ammunition and purchased the stolen cattle and children. Horses and guns then proved indispensable in the struggle to defend the territorial integrity of their country against the violent incursions of Europeans. These needs for cattle, horses, weapons, and iron agricultural tools were neither "new" nor "artificial": guns were essential replacements for their now obsolete weapons, and soldiers could be deployed most effectively on horseback when fighting commando raiders on horseback; plows represented an improvement over hoes, and cattle were the source of wealth and power. BaSotho participation in regional trade was spontaneous and widespread.

Kimble and others have mistakenly attributed the rise of BaSotho trade with Europeans in the 1840s to the influence and direction of European missionaries seeking to introduce mechanisms for achieving what the missionaries considered to be "civilization." There is no question that, as Kimble has argued, missionaries in Lesotho, beginning with those of the Société des Missions Evangéliques who arrived in 1833, were interested in promoting simultaneously "Christianity, commerce, and civilisation."[1] Kimble has also argued that in the nineteenth century the BaSotho chiefs controlled trade and were responsible for the commoditization of agriculture. However, the BaSotho were not responding to missionary or Christian or western influences as they steadily increased their trade with Europeans. Nor did the

147

chiefs control trade and commodity production. Kimble's conclusions rest on a series of unfounded assumptions, which she reached using evidence from the end of the nineteenth century that she then projected backwards in time.

Kimble has raised important questions concerning the "internal structural determinants of labour migration" which she appropriately linked to agricultural production and trade. Kimble correctly noted that "in itself, 'new wants' cannot explain why labour migration should develop as the form of market participation," since commodity production can accomplish the same goal of providing a marketable good for acquiring such "new wants."[2] However, Kimble imposed Marxist and substantivist preconceptions of a theoretical African "social formation" and African economy onto the BaSotho society of the nineteenth century. She consequently argued mistakenly that chiefs controlled production and that the notion of a "single, structurally isolated homestead, which operates on the basis of a particular form of economic calculation and rationality, conceptualised in terms of individual 'choice' and voluntary 'response' to market pressures," is "inappropriate" to an analysis of production in nineteenth-century Lesotho.[3] Summarizing her master's thesis, Kimble asserted that "amongst Basotho resident in the area demarcated under royal control, these links [between the homestead head and his chief] were still decisive in determining the patterns of production."[4] Assuming falsely that the chiefs monopolized control over land and cattle, Kimble concluded that

> The emergence of the royal lineage was an important precondition for the extensive development of agricultural commodity production in Lesotho during the years 1830–70. This process in turn served to strengthen and entrench the ruling group, which was thereby able to reproduce its dominance on an expanded scale. The key to consolidation of Koena power lay in the various modes of appropriation or surplus through which the safety and defence of the kingdom was assured, and every homestead granted access to the essential means of production – cattle and land.[5]

BaSotho chiefs did control access to land, but their need to attract followers prevented them from abusing this privilege as their failure to provide adequate land could provoke their followers to emigrate and offer their allegiance elsewhere. Not until after the boundaries of the colony were fixed in 1872 did the commoners begin to lose the leverage over their chiefs which they derived from their ability to emigrate.

Nor did the chiefs have a monopoly on wealth in cattle. Moshoeshoe was the most successful at protecting his herds during the 1820s, allowing him to consolidate his power and emerge with his wealth intact in the 1830s, but he and his BaKoena relatives were not the only people to own cattle. Those of his followers from Butha Buthe who stayed with him in the move to Thaba Bosiu retained their ownership over any cattle they owned previously. Furthermore, Kimble has misrepresented the *mafisa* system as a system of loaning cattle in which clients keeping the cattle of a wealthy person received only the use of the cattle in their care, providing both the labor of herding and other service obligations in return.[6] She was mistaken: the owner of the herd compensated his client by giving him a portion of the herd's increase, at least one head of cattle, every year for his services. The private ownership of one or more animals thus passed completely from the patron to the client every year. Every man thus had the opportunity to begin his own herd, independently from his family and even if he was of a completely impoverished background; future natural increases from his slowly growing, privately owned herd would accrue to him as well. The fact that *mafisa* was not confined to chiefs further suggests that not all wealthy men were chiefs, and that commoners also became wealthy enough to accumulate their own clients. Clearly commoners controlled agricultural production of their own land and pastoral production through their own herds, which they kept on common pasture lands.

BaSotho chiefs did expropriate surplus in labor and in kind, and their wealth and power were mutually reinforcing. However, the expropriation of surplus took the form of requiring tribute labor for several days out of each agricultural season, and of occasionally providing food or animals collected for special purposes such as the payment of bridewealth for the chief's main wife and the payment of fines levied against the chief or his people as a whole. Beyond this, homesteads headed by men, and within these, to a certain extent, households defined in terms of their wives, retained autonomous decision-making powers regarding production and trade, and retained rights to surpluses produced and goods obtained through trade. There is no question that the chiefs were able to perpetuate their socioeconomic advantage and dominance, but at the same time commoners retained considerable leverage over their chiefs until the imposition of colonial rule in the 1870s, and as a result retained considerable economic autonomy. The relative economic independence of homesteads allowed BaSotho commoners as well as chiefs to enjoy the benefits accruing from the expansion of production and participation in trade. All of the evidence produced by Kimble to demonstrate unbridled chiefly control over and exploitation of commoners relates to the colonial period, after the power of the chiefs had received the reinforcement of the colonial power.

Kimble conceded that individual homesteads independent from this supposed chiefly control did participate in trade, but she asserted that these were only the households of Christianized BaSotho who had been freed from chiefly control by residing on missions, and that the missionary influence had induced their participation in production for exchange. Again she was mistaken to assume that all individuals and homesteads independently engaged in production for exchange were Christians and affiliated with mission stations. That she would make this mistake is not surprising for two reasons. First, those BaSotho who took refuge in the French mission stations closest to the Cape Colony frontier exhibited the earliest and most rapid involvement in trade with Europeans and the consumption of European imports. Their incentives for residing on the mission stations related more to security and less to the appeal of Christianity than the missionaries would concede, however, and they naturally took advantage of the trade benefits accruing from their geographic location. Second, almost all of the written evidence about the BaSotho from the 1830s through the 1860s comes from the French missionaries, who claimed (falsely) that it was their influence which was causing the BaSotho to prosper and trade. The missionaries made the claim that African involvement in trade was a sign of Christianization for their own propaganda purposes as they sought to raise money back home, and scholars such as Kimble have subsequently accepted these claims. In fact the evidence contradicts this association of trade with Christianity. Contrary to what Kimble suggested, the missionaries never gained "autonomous control over the surrounding land areas,"[7] and Christians living both on and near the mission stations continued to be subject to fulfilling their obligations to their chiefs, in tribute labor, taxation in kind, and military service. The missionaries could not and did not free their Christian converts from these obligations, and it is a mistake to argue that the homesteads of Christians were therefore more "atomised," with weakened links to the chiefs and greater autonomy in production. All homesteads enjoyed considerable autonomy in production, and the Christians were no different in this, hence the supposed missionary influence was not the decisive factor in determining which households engaged in trade. Finally, it is also evident that the involvement of the BaSotho in trade from the 1840s on was widespread, involving chiefs and commoners, wealthy and poor, whereas Christians constituted only 0.5 percent of the total population in the 1840s, rising to only 3.65 percent in the 1870s.[8] Neither chiefs on the one hand, nor Christians on the other, were primarily responsible for intensified production and trade from the 1830s through the 1870s. On the contrary, it was the initiative of all BaSotho, men and women, from all levels of a socially and economically stratified society, which accounted for the growing volume of trade across the changing borders of Lesotho.

BaSotho trade with Europeans, 1827–1880

Perhaps the most obvious evidence that the BaSotho needed neither chiefs nor missionaries to induce or compel them to trade, is that BaSotho trade with Europeans predated the arrival of European missionaries in Lesotho and the consolidation of Moshoeshoe's power. As early as 1827 BaSotho were making journeys down to the area around the Orange River to trade with scattered groups of BaTswana as well as with white trekboers who occasionally crossed the Orange River to graze their livestock. On one occasion a group of BaSotho travelled down from above the Caledon River with pack oxen carrying corn to trade with the white people.[9] After Pellissier founded the Bethulie mission station in 1833 near the junction of the Orange and Caledon Rivers, BaSotho went there on foot from Thaba Bosiu carrying corn on their shoulders. They purchased goats belonging to the BaTswana living in the area, and sometimes bartered for sheep skins.[10] By 1833 Moshoeshoe was sending expeditions expressly to trade with white farmers.[11] Thus the BaSotho were trading sporadically with their white neighbors by 1827, and more regularly after 1833. The first evidence of extensive trade between the BaSotho and Boers dates from the early 1840s, when there was a large influx of Boers into the area north of the Orange River following the British annexation of Natal.

The market for grain from Lesotho flourished in the Cape Colony and the Orange Free State from the 1840s until the early 1880s. In the early years, the BaSotho hawked their grain themselves among white farmers, as indicated by the trading expedition of 1833. Other groups also sometimes served as middlemen in this trade. In 1841 Backhouse wrote that the BaRolong (BaTswana) were a "trading people," who bought corn from the BaSotho and resold it to the Boers for a good profit.[12] By the 1850s, both BaRolong and Griqua were engaged in this middleman trade.[13] Itinerant European traders who had served the frontier farmers for decades in the Cape Colony and Orange Free State also began trading in Lesotho in the 1840s.[14] The trade proved to be very lucrative, and these hawkers, or *smous*, became numerous as time went on. Some were considered unscrupulous speculators by the missionaries, because they came during famines to offer food at exorbitant prices to the starving BaSotho.[15]

Gradually the Boers began making their own way into Lesotho to trade directly with BaSotho. In 1845 Casalis first reported that "the emigrant farmers who live in the neighborhood of Morija come in crowds to buy grain here," and such reports continued in the 1840s and 1850s, even during border wars.[16] In 1853 a British official reported that the BaSotho "grow almost all the corn that is used in the Sovereignty [Orange Free State], where the burghers only rear cattle."[17] In 1865 Casalis wrote that "Agriculture has made such great progress among the Basutos that one can without any exaggeration call their country the granary of the Orange Free State, and of a part of the Cape Colony."[18]

By the 1860s the Boers were dependent on the grain of the BaSotho for survival; each year they received thousands of bags of wheat and maize for the subsistence of their families.[19] The droughts of the 1860s were devastating to the white farmers as well as to the BaSotho, and prompted the expropriation of much of the agricultural land of Lesotho by the Boers.

Even after the BaSotho lost over half of their arable land in the 1860s, they continued to supply surrounding regions with grain. They were able to do so by intensifying production and converting pastoral land to arable use. The market for grain increased dramatically in the 1870s because of the tremendous influx of people seeking fortunes and work at the Kimberley diamond mines. Estimates for grain exports from Lesotho to the Diamond Fields and Orange Free State were 72,000 muids in 1871 and 100,000 muids in 1873.[20] Many Europeans earned their livelihood purchasing wheat, sorghum, and maize from the BaSotho for re-sale at the diamond mines and elsewhere.[21] In 1874 a British official reported that "Hundreds of wagons enter Basutoland, and traverse it in every direction, collecting and exporting the grain of the country of the Free State and the Diamond Fields."[22]

In 1874 the government of the Orange Free State tried to profit from this commerce by imposing a duty of £1 on every load entering the country from Lesotho, which almost put a stop to the grain trade. Apparently the tax was almost immediately reduced; the following year it was 5s. to 10s. per wagon and 1s. 6d. per pack animal, and trade again increased.[23] The BaSotho became prosperous from this trade, although their dependence on it was apparent as early as 1876, when a regional economic recession caused the diamond mines to close down almost entirely. The slump lasted for a year, but by 1878 the grain trade had resumed. The diamond mines were still dependent on Basutoland produce. Ironically, so was the Orange Free State since, after taking the agricultural lands of the BaSotho in the 1860s, the Boers did not use them. A British official in the Leribe District of Lesotho explained: "even the conquered territory, which adjoins us, buys grain here for its own consumption, as its inhabitants find that they can supply themselves with grain from Basutoland for less than it costs them to produce it . . ."[24]

In addition to grain, the BaSotho exported livestock and wool during the nineteenth century. Having built up their herds during the 1830s and 1840s, they sold cattle to their European neighbors in the 1850s. Lesotho supplied the Orange Free State with "cattle in abundance," and itinerant traders took cattle in exchange for their goods.[25] The wool trade developed slowly, as the BaSotho acquired wooled sheep to replace their fat-tailed sheep and gradually upgraded their flocks. One missionary observed in 1864 that wool constituted a "considerable article for trade," but because the BaSotho did not know how to prepare and clean it well, they received very low prices for it. This remained true, so that the price received for wool from Lesotho always remained low on the world market.[26] In spite of this the export trade in wool grew steadily. There are no figures available showing the quantity or value of wool traded in the years before 1871, when an estimated 2,000 bales were exported.[27]

BaSotho participation in production for the European market was widespread. In the context of regional economic and political competition, BaSotho chiefs were more concerned with maintaining the viability and military strength of the country than with monopolizing wealth within the country. In the early years of trade with Europeans, many people who had lost their livestock during the 1820s were able to sell grain and rebuild their own herds, freeing themselves from dependence on cattle borrowed through the *mafisa* system. As commoners regained their economic independence, however, they did not rebel against their chiefs. The costs of paying tribute were low, and well worth the political stability which had allowed for economic regeneration. Moshoeshoe created a climate of security for both producers and traders, and trade flourished.

Barter and the introduction of currency

Barter remained the most common form of exchange between BaSotho and Europeans throughout most of the nineteenth century. Goods which had been used as media of exchange before the arrival of the Europeans continued in use as forms of currency: tobacco, salt, beads, and copper and brass wire. Andrew Smith used tobacco and metal buttons to buy milk when he travelled through the country; buttons were also used by the first Catholic missionaries in Lesotho to hire a guide in the 1860s.[28] Travellers and traders at shops used beads and brass wire as currency as late as the 1890s. These were in demand for ornamenting leather clothing and making jewelry similar to that manufactured by traditional smiths.[29]

Salt was also commonly used by the missionaries to purchase items such as milk, meat, eggs, fowls, fruit and vegetables, roofing grasses, fuel prepared from dried cow dung, and even drinking water.[30] Walton exaggerates when he claims that "salt in those days was the chief commodity of exchange," but it certainly was one of several goods which were used as currency.[31] As late as 1900 Widdicombe reported that "we usually barter coarse salt to the natives for fuel." Sugar was also sometimes used for this particular transaction.[32]

Although it did not diffuse quickly, money was introduced as soon as the first missionaries arrived in the 1830s. Arbousset reported that Moshoeshoe understood the utility of money and was trying to procure it. A European traveller gave Moshoeshoe 8 Rixdollars (12 shillings) each for two young oxen in 1834.[33] The only other evidence of the early diffusion of money derives from sporadic reports of donations received in collections at mission services. Most church donations were made in kind, but small amounts of cash were received from BaSotho by the missionaries beginning in the early 1840s. Residents of mission stations were in the closest proximity to traders, who established themselves at mission stations because of the welcome reception given them by the missionaries, and because of the security which mission protection offered, so that evidence of the use of cash on mission stations is not necessarily indicative of the availability of money in the country at large. Even so, this evidence does demonstrate that even at an early date traders were giving cash for BaSotho goods.

The availability of currency increased in the colonial period after the market for BaSotho grain expanded in the 1870s. The Governor's Agent reported that the hut tax for 1872 was paid entirely in cash, citing this as "a significant proof of the increasing circulation of specie in the country."[34] The BaSotho had a strong incentive to insist on receiving money from the traders so that they could pay their tax in cash: the average price received for a muid bag of grain was 12 shillings, but the government only valued it at 2s. 6d. for tax purposes.[35] After the bottom dropped out of the market traders refused to give money for grain, and only bartered for it with goods from their stores. As a result, money became scarce after 1885, and the government

153

again received taxes paid in kind. Money did not become plentiful again until the Anglo–Boer War brought opportunities for the BaSotho to work for high wages and sell their livestock at higher prices.[36]

Imports

The BaSotho traded their produce and used their money to acquire a wide variety of imports in the nineteenth century. In the early years of trade with the Boers, when they were still trying to build up their herds after their livestock losses in the 1820s, the BaSotho used their grain to buy cattle and small livestock. This was apparently successful, as they were soon exporting large numbers of cattle to the Cape Colony and Orange Free State. The BaSotho also sought to acquire horses, which they valued at first for their usefulness in raids and wars. The number of horses increased rapidly. Moshoeshoe imported 200 horses between 1833 and 1838, and visited Mekuatling with a cavalry of 200 mounted men in 1842. Arbousset was impressed that most of the warriors arming to fight the British in 1851 were mounted, and in 1858 Letsie's forces included almost 2000 mounted men, with an additional mounted force of eight to nine hundred under Moperi and Moletsane.[37]

Recurrent wars between the BaSotho and their neighbours meant that there was a strong demand for guns in Lesotho throughout the nineteenth century. Atmore points out that the early weapons obtained by the BaSotho were poor, and that the Sand River Convention of 1852 (which prohibited the gun trade) hindered the ability of the BaSotho to acquire the better guns to which the Boers had access. This did not prevent them from building up their arsenal, however; the gun trade flourished illegally, and even high quality rifles were acquired. All the mounted warriors were armed with guns in the 1840s and 1850s. In 1862 a British official from the Cape Colony was concerned about the quality as well as quantity of guns being imported into Lesotho, including breech-loaders costing £35 to £40 each.[38] As Atmore also points out, the acquisition of rifles became a major incentive for labor emigration to the diamond fields, which led to a great improvement in the quality of guns during the colonial period and contributed to the success of the BaSotho in the Gun War.[39] Even during the war itself, the Boers continued to sell guns and ammunition to the BaSotho.[40] The Gun War proved that the concerted effort of the BaSotho to arm themselves was warranted, and the BaSotho continued to value guns. An official Military Report on southern Basutoland in 1905 estimated that half of the "full fighting strength" had serviceable firearms and ammunition, and that the other half had obsolete rifles, thus implying that every man who might participate in a war was armed with a gun of some kind.[41]

Iron goods, especially knives and agricultural implements, constituted an important element of imports. In addition to knives and hoes, traders found a great demand for picks, spades, axes, and plows. A plow in 1885 cost £6, but as they became more common the price dropped to between £2 and £3.[42] Three-legged iron pots also grew rapidly in popularity because of their durability.

European clothing found a market among the BaSotho for various reasons, economic and social in origin. BaSotho resident at mission stations and by definition dependent on missionaries began to wear European clothing in part because the missionaries encouraged church members to wear European clothes as a sign of "civilization." In addition, buying imported clothing was often cheaper than slaughtering animals and spending weeks manufacturing comparable leather articles of clothing, and by the 1850s many people who came to live on mission stations were indigent and had no animals to slaughter for skins. For those wealthy enough to make a choice, European clothing was sometimes avoided because of its association with the missionaries and their attempts to undermine the social order, and was sometimes worn as an attempt to claim prestige outside the traditional social order. Moshoeshoe wore either leopard-skin karosses or European clothing, depending on the nature of the audience he wished to accommodate or impress. Thus various people, Christian and non-Christian, purchased the hundreds of overcoats, vests, pants, shirts, hats, and pairs of shoes which were sold in Morija in 1857.[43] Because they were so cheap relative to leather goods, cotton and wool blankets became the most popular article of clothing, replacing the large skin robes which had previously served as the warmest outer garment. These European blankets began to appear in the early 1870s, and were originally plain, often white. The BaSotho decorated these as they had previously decorated their leather blankets, until the Europeans began manufacturing the blankets in bright colors and designs in the late 1880s and early 1890s.[44] The new blankets had universal appeal, largely because they were less expensive than leather blankets made locally, and were worn both by Christians over their European clothing, and by non-Christians over their traditional leather clothing. European blankets ranged in price from 10s. to 30s. according to quality.[45] For the years in which statistics are available at the beginning of the twentieth century, wearing apparel and cotton and woollen goods account for over half of the value of all imports.

The BaSotho purchased other miscellaneous articles from the traders. Beads, copper wire, tobacco, grain bags and wool packs remained in demand throughout the century. Furniture and building materials including windows and doors were bought by the wealthy, particularly chiefs, but remained rare among the general population.[46] In spite of attempts by Moshoeshoe and the Colonial government at suppression, an illegal liquor trade also flourished. Gerard wrote that when the Catholic missionaries arrived in the 1860s liquor was scarcely known, but soon became common.[47] Other goods available at stores in Lesotho included saddles and bridles, cooking utensils, soap, candles, lamps and paraffin oil, stoves, casks and barrels for brewing, and luxury foods including salt, sugar, tea and coffee, rice, and canned meat and fish.[48] Even so, except for the devastating year of 1866, the BaSotho did not import significant amounts of staple foods until 1903.[49]

Traders and transportation

The export of all goods from Lesotho depended on the availability of transport, and the participation of traders who provided the necessary transportation. Before the advent of British rule, Moshoeshoe favored the establishment of commerce and did not impose taxes or restrict traders in any way.[50] Regional transportation over long distances was carried on by means of covered wagons, approximately 15 feet long and 6 feet wide. Because of the size of the wagons and the nature of the terrain, which was broken up by deep gullies and ravines, fourteen to eighteen oxen were needed to pull a single wagon.

In spite of their high cost, averaging about £120 each, the BaSotho invested in wagons as soon as they were available. Wagons were never manufactured locally by BaSotho or by Europeans in the Orange Free State because of the lack of wood necessary for their construction. Instead they were imported from the Cape Colony. Moshoeshoe already owned three wagons in 1841, and in 1846 the inhabitants of one mission station possessed a dozen wagons among them. During the war in the 1860s, the Boers collected 120 wagons belonging to the BaSotho from one area and burned them all together.[51] Wagons were the most efficient means of transport and therefore of trade, and because the BaSotho recognized their value they were willing to make large capital investments in order to participate in the lucrative transport business and trade.

Over time, European traders began to establish permanent stations in Lesotho. Among the first were three traders who settled at Platberg (near modern Ladybrand), and two or three who established themselves at Thaba Bosiu as early as the 1830s. Traders first settled at Morija in the 1850s, and in the 1860s a European woman established the first store at the site which became Maseru in 1869. When traders' licenses were first issued in 1872, there were twenty of these settled "general traders" in the country, and the number rapidly increased. The diffusion of stores demonstrates that trade expanded rapidly at the end of the century. In 1878 a missionary living in Ste.-Monique wrote that "the country of the Basutu has a multitude of shops and trading stations."[52] The expansion of trade is reflected in the rising number of licenses granted to hawkers and general traders presented in table 5.

Not all of Lesotho was equally served by the traders, however; throughout the nineteenth century trading stations were for the most part confined to locations in the lowlands. By the 1870s there were stores at Molapo's and Advanced Post (near modern Teyateyaneng) to serve the northern districts. Stores in Maseru and its vicinity were opened by Richard Trower and Irvine, Holden & Co. Robinson's and at least five smaller trading stations were

Table 5. *Licenses issued by the colonial government*

Year	General Traders	Hawkers	Mills	Labor Agents
1872	20			
1873	30			
1874	50			
1887	73	166		
1889	79			
1890	119			
1891	120			
1893	129	152		
1894	133	89	2	
1895	132	144	2	
1896	132	287	2	
1897	141	109		
1898	141	149		
1899	140	241		
1900	140	40		
1901	126	83		
1902	125	144		
1903	110	355	2	
1904	161	491	1	77
1905	161	472	2	142
1906	164	617	2	225
1907	168	608	1	298
1908	163	710	3	69
1909	163	692	3	30

Sources: Cape of Good Hope, *Report of the Governor's Agent, Basutoland, for 1872*, G 27–'73; South Africa, *Despatch from Sir Hercules Robinson*, 1887, C.-5238; Her Majesty's Colonial Possessions, No. 31, *Basutoland*, 1887, C.-5249-28; Her Majesty's Colonial Possessions, No. 70, 1889, C.-5897; Great Britain, *Colonial Reports.–Annual, Basutoland*, 1890–1909.

located in the South near Mafeteng. Donald Fraser opened the first of the network of Fraser's stores near Mafeteng in 1877. Prominent stores which appeared in the 1880s and 1890s included Richard A. Wells in Morija; S. C. Collier in Mafeteng and elsewhere; and G. L. Stevens and Maitin Bros. in the Berea District.[53]

The mountain districts remained isolated during this period, with neither roads nor stores to facilitate trade. In the south there were still no trading stations beyond Moorosi's mountain in 1887, and people from the mountains beyond used the market at Matatiele in East Griqualand, which had commercial relations with Natal.[54] The annual Colonial Report of 1892–93 noted that there were no roads in the Qacha's Nek district, and that transport was by pack animals and sledges. From mountain areas it took two days on horseback or four to five days on foot to reach the nearest store. A military report from 1905 indicated that in Southern Basutoland there were

157

only 33 miles of wagon roads and 25 miles of wagon tracks. At that time there were two trading stations in the Qacha's Nek district. Even then it took many people in the mountains three days to descend to the nearest shop, either at Qacha's Nek in the south or Witsieshoek in the north.[55] In 1910 there were still only 463 miles of roads within Lesotho, and bridle paths continued to be the only routes into most of the country well into the twentieth century.[56]

The establishment of permanent trading stations in Lesotho generated a new independent transport business. Unlike itinerant traders who transported their own goods to and from the Cape Colony and Orange Free State, settled traders relied on other transport riders to haul their produce and goods back and forth between Lesotho and the market towns across the borders. This allowed for greater participation by BaSotho, who could serve as transport riders even if they did not have the capital necessary for going into trade on their own. For several reasons the participation of the BaSotho in this enterprise remained limited. The difficulties of acquiring wagons was one factor. After the destruction of hundreds of wagons in the wars of the 1860s, wagons remained rare because the discovery of diamonds put them in such great demand in the Cape Colony. It was at this time that the price of wagons was highest, rising to as much as £500 in 1875.[57] This was a huge amount of money for a MoSotho to acquire, particularly in the aftermath of the destruction and disease of the late 1860s. Along with the wagon, it was necessary to own many spans of oxen, which increased the cost and entailed additional risks. During droughts transport oxen died on the roads, causing severe losses for their owners.

The profitability of the transport enterprise for BaSotho was also hindered by new restrictions in the colonial period, which further inhibited BaSotho participation. In addition to the duty imposed by the Orange Free State on goods coming from Lesotho, the Volksraad levied a tax of one shilling per head on every MoSotho passing through the Orange Free State. The tax was aimed at migrant workers, but it is not clear that any distinction was made according to the destination or purpose of BaSotho entering the Orange Free State.[58] The British also imposed a selective tax on African transport riders, requiring that all BaSotho (but not Europeans) buy a pass for each vehicle and pack-animal carrying grain out of the country for sale, at the rate of 2s. 6d. per vehicle and 3d. per animal.[59] All grain taken out of the country by BaSotho without such a pass was liable to seizure and confiscation. Clearly the purpose was not to provide revenue to the government, but rather to favor white hawkers.

It appears that white Free State citizens dominated the transport business, but they did not monopolize it. Reports from the 1880s indicate that some BaSotho were becoming very wealthy hauling goods for traders who had previously employed Boers. Nevertheless, hawkers from the Free State retained most of the business.[60]

The decline of the export business, 1880–1910

The profitability of the grain trade and the prosperity the BaSotho producers derived from it was short-lived. In 1880 a missionary wrote that, because the Orange Free State had suffered from several consecutive years of drought which did not affect Lesotho, the grain of the BaSotho continued to find a ready market.[61] Commerce was interrupted by the Gun War between the Cape Colony and Lesotho in 1880–81, however, and then by drought and civil war in 1883–85. The entire region also suffered from a severe economic depression which lasted from 1881 to 1886. During this time other sources of grain were found, and Lesotho lost a large share of the market.

The discovery of gold in the Transvaal brought the rest of South Africa out of the economic depression, but Lesotho did not benefit from this new market, and as Kimberley ceased to be as profitable traders in Lesotho turned their attention to the Transvaal. The Colonial Report for 1887 explained that "The market for grain, the staple production of the country, is limited. Kimberley is largely supplied from Basutoland, but the competition from the Orange Free State and Western Province [Cape Colony] is keen."[62]

The completion of the railroad through the Cape Colony to Kimberley and the Orange Free State in 1886 undermined the ability of the BaSotho to sell their grain at competitive prices. Wheat and other grain came not only from white producers in the Cape Colony, Free State, and Transvaal, but also from Australia and America, and could be transported to the diamond mines by wagon.[63] The price of grain plummeted accordingly. A muid of grain, which had once been worth 15s. to 20s. (and much more during bad years), could be sold for only 2s. to 4s. in 1888.[64]

With the cost of transport, neither producers nor traders in Lesotho could make a profit; transport for a sack of grain only to Bloemfontein cost 4s. in 1886, when wheat was selling there for 7s. to 8s. per muid.[65] In 1901 the cost of transporting one bag of grain from the border of Lesotho to the nearest railroad was equal to the cost of carrying the same bag 2,500 miles by railway.[66] Furthermore, the Free State government imposed an import duty on wheat in 1894. These factors prevented the diamond mines from serving as a profitable outlet for the produce of Lesotho after the mid-1880s.

Unfortunately, the newly-discovered gold mines did not become an alternative market for the BaSotho, even though the railways did not reach the Transvaal until 1892. In order to favor Orange Free State produce, the Transvaal imposed a tariff on all grain entering the Transvaal other than that grown in the Free State, virtually closing the market to Lesotho. The Resident Commissioner of Basutoland estimated that in 1887 the trade for the country had been adversely affected by this preferential tariff to the cost of over £20,000.[67]

The disastrous events of the 1890s disrupted the export trade of Lesotho further. Grain production itself suffered from drought and locust invasions,

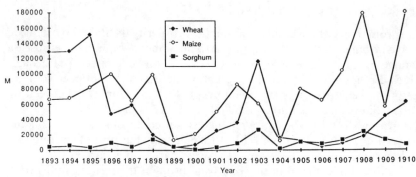

Fig. 8 Cereal exports by quantity (in muids)

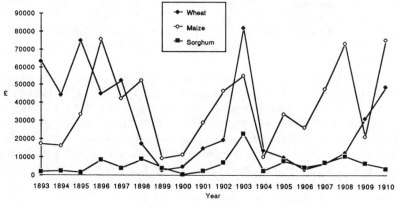

Fig. 9 Cereal exports by value

and then Rinderpest paralyzed commerce entirely. Transport oxen died, the borders were closed in an effort to prevent the spread of the disease, and transport riders were ruined.[68] Before commerce could recover, the Anglo–Boer War broke out, once again closing the borders and cutting off trade temporarily. Cereal exports, presented in figures 8 and 9, reflect the tremendous volatility in grain production and in the grain market during this period.

Although the British brought their food supplies with them from the Cape Colony, the BaSotho profited briefly during the war from the sale of horses to the British army. Livestock exports for the period 1893 to 1909, presented in figures 10 and 11, demonstrate how the war skewed the export market. Because of the disruption of trade in other commodities during the war, the Lesotho economy came to be temporarily based on the export of horses, a commodity with only short-term potential. In 1901 the export of horses accounted for 73 percent of the value of exports.[69]

160

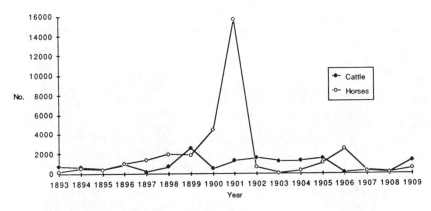

Fig. 10 Livestock exports by quantity

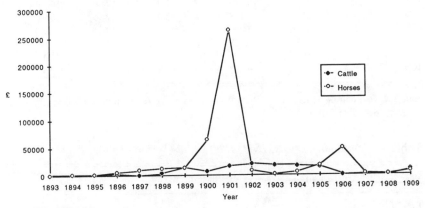

Fig. 11 Livestock exports by value

Commodity prices and the quantity and value of exports reflected changing circumstances in supply and demand in the latter part of the century. Most volatile were grain prices, as shown in table 7. Grain prices were high during years of drought in 1841, 1852, 1859, 1864–66. Prices remained strong throughout the 1870s, but fell dramatically during the 1880s. Figure 12 illustrates that prices rose only during years of poor production in 1885 (drought), 1892 (locusts), 1896–98 (drought), and 1903 (drought). The price of cattle rose steadily through the century, and the price of horses rose dramatically during the Anglo–Boer war. The demand for horses from the German government, fighting in Southwest Africa, accounted for high export figures for horses in 1906. The dramatic growth in the production and export of wool and mohair, illustrated in figures 13 and 14, helped compensate for poor agricultural years, and contributed significantly to the rise in the total value of exports during the first decade of the twentieth century.

Table 6. *Livestock exports*

Year	Number of cattle	£/head	Cattle (value in pounds)	Number of horses	£/head	Horses (value in pounds)
1893	715	3	2,061	220	5	972
1894	639	4	2,072	519	8	2,157
1895	427	4	1,348	409	6	1,964
1896	917	4	3,684	964	5	6,383
1897	227	4	932	1,336	9	9,892
1898	711	6	3,959	1,986	6	12,628
1899	2,555	10	14,282	1,869	6	14,091
1900	522	12	6,997	4,419	16	64,031
1901	1,312	12	16,842	15,684	19	262,991
1902	1,574	13	20,453	656	20	9,049
1903	1,241	14	17,571	81	20	1,227
1904	1,284	10	16,740	347	17	5,496
1905	1,521	10	15,266	1,071	17	18,730
1906	128	10	1,118	2,439	19	50,042
1906[a]	272	10	3,360	125	19	3,238
1907	306	8	3,222	265	17	3,680
1908	144		1,043	88		1,436
1909	1,313		9,813	482		7,638

Note: [a] Year ending 31 Dec. 1906. Previous figures are for years ending 30 June.
Source: See table 5, p. 157.

Table 7. *Commodity prices, 1841–1880*

Year	Grain/muid	Sheep/head	Cattle/head
1841*	18s.		18s.
1844	12s.	3s.-4s.	18s.
1845			18s.-20s.
1852*	£3 4s.		
1854	7s. 6d.	4s.-7s.	17s.
1859*	£4		
1860*		18s.-20s.	£4-£5
1862*		3s.-6s.	£2
1864*	£1 10s.	5s.-8s.	£2-£5
1866*	£3 10s.		
1868	12s.		
1877	7s.		
1880*	£3 5s.		

Note: * Years affected by drought

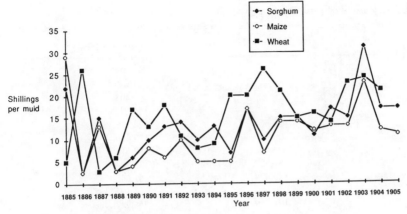

Fig. 12 Grain prices in Lesotho

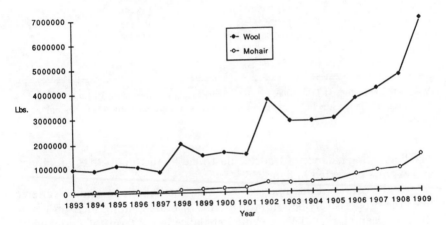

Fig. 13 Wool exports by quantity

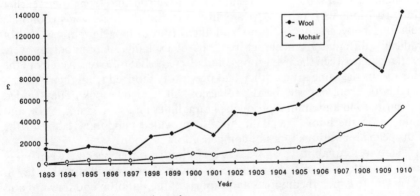

Fig. 14 Wool exports by value

163

Table 8. *Values of imports and exports*

Year	Imports in pounds	Exports in pounds
1893		103,608
1894		83,407
1895		138,495
1896		160,277
1897	135,560	124,911
1898	100,280	138,499
1899	93,683	82,615
1900	85,527	133,864
1901	145,474	361,646
1902	230,680	166,895
1903	191,019	258,927
1904	298,140[b]	127,057
1905	149,821	164,817
1906	191,701	172,496
1906[a]	242,353	185,155
1907	235,084	248,541
1908	237,240	193.122
1909	254,204	349,884

Note: [a] Year ending 31 Dec. 1906. Previous figures are for years ending 30 June.
[b] First year all imports included in figures. Previous figures are for dutiable articles only.
Source: See table 5, p. 157.

The fluctuating balance of trade is illustrated by the total values of imports and exports presented in figure 15.

Over the course of the nineteenth century the BaSotho economy suffered from the progressively deteriorating terms of trade limiting their profits on the European market. The growing imbalance in the terms of trade, which were set by supply and demand factors within the European economy, distinguished BaSotho trade relations with Europeans from their earlier trade relations with other Africans in the region. In some ways economic relations between the BaSotho and their European neighbors were not radically different from earlier patterns of exchange. Commodities were exchanged between the two groups, and often the BaSotho received from the Europeans the same articles they had previously received from their African neighbors: iron, copper, beads, tobacco, salt, and livestock. They traded primarily food and animal products: grain, hides and skins, milk, wool, and animals on the hoof. The BaSotho also provided temporary labor to the Europeans for various types of compensation.

There were qualitative as well as quantitative differences between these early and later patterns of exchange, however. Part of the distinction lay in the extent to which the imports and exports of the BaSotho had forward and backward linkages to production. Early imports had important forward

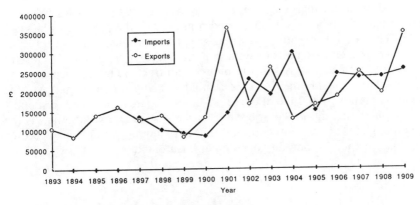

Fig. 15 Values of imports and exports

linkages to BaSotho production: cattle stimulated pastoral production, and iron tools and implements stimulated hunting and arable production. Imports of beads and copper ornaments, tobacco, and salt did not affect the productive sector of the economy, but did facilitate exchange. During the later nineteenth century, Europeans continued to supply the BaSotho with iron goods, particularly agricultural implements, which had forward linkages to production in Lesotho. As time went on, however, articles for consumption constituted a larger and larger proportion of imports. Cotton and woolen goods, leather goods, clothing, and food not only replaced more productive imports, but also replaced locally made goods, undermining household industries and restricting local specialization in production.

The export of livestock and grain to both African and European neighbors also stimulated the productive sector in Lesotho throughout the country, giving these exports backward linkages to production. These exports did not promote specialized industries in Lesotho, however, but instead gradually depleted the natural resources of the country. Raising sheep for wool rather than meat meant that animals themselves were preserved, and it was possible to use areas of rough terrain for sheep-raising which would otherwise have been unproductive. After the land available for cultivation had been restricted by the new Colonial boundaries, however, the intensification of arable production slowly depleted the non-renewable soil resources of the country and reduced the long-term ability of the BaSotho to produce an agricultural surplus for export.

Although labor was exchanged for food or other compensation within BaSotho society, there were important differences between this allocation of labor beyond the family unit and the later migrant labor system which served the Europeans. In BaSotho society a person who provided labor to a patron or chief retained access to his own productive resources, including land or livestock or both. Agricultural labor was provided for others within BaSotho society on a temporary and often reciprocal basis, and a man who received cattle through the *mafisa* system also cultivated his own fields. In both cases, the laborer was supported primarily by the produce of his own land. He worked for others to meet social obligations or to increase his productivity. The attempts of BaSotho migrant laborers to remain close to home and to accept only short-term work contracts reflected their attitude toward labor outside their own household as being supplemental. As time went on, however, and the resources of Lesotho were insufficient to support the population, migrant labor became a necessity for many BaSotho. By the beginning of the twentieth century, the labor of migrant workers had become the major export commodity of colonial Basutoland.

12

The colonial imposition and the failure of the local economy, 1871–1910

In March 1868 Lesotho was annexed to the British Crown and was officially designated Basutoland. After a brief "interregnum," in November 1871 Basutoland was annexed to the Cape Colony. Neither the Imperial authorities nor the Cape Colonists wished to incur any expenses as a result of their new responsibilities in governing Basutoland, and they were therefore primarily concerned with generating enough income from taxation to support the imposition of colonial law and order. Of the estimated £4,500 in revenue for 1871 from Basutoland, £2,500 was allotted for the payment of magistrates, leaving £2,000 for the establishment of a police force; no other expenditures were anticipated. There is no evidence that funding for roads, education, and other projects which might have improved the prospects for development in the country was considered. The only other change was the establishment of a postal service between Aliwal North and Basutoland.[1]

The politics of colonial rule

During the period of Cape Colony rule, colonial officials consciously devised policies designed to weaken the authority and power of chiefs. When possible, policies which had proved successful for dominating Africans within the Cape Colony were extended into Basutoland. The High Commissioner, Henry Barkly, displayed the deliberate strategy of transferring policies from the Cape, and the conscious effort to destroy the power of the chiefs, when he wrote to the Governor's Agent in Basutoland, C. D. Griffith, in 1871:

> to the policy of keeping the Chiefs on bad terms with a view to play off one against another, however successful in Kaffraria where different tribes are to be found, it strikes me as scarcely applicable to Basutoland which is principally inhabited by a homogeneous race long under the sway of one Family alone.[2]

The attempt by the Colonial government to impose Cape Law and to undermine the power of the BaSotho chiefs has been investigated by Burman. Her study illustrates the natural preoccupation of the government with law and order rather than development.[3] The British motive for undertaking to "protect" Lesotho through colonial rule was political rather than economic, and the primary goals of colonial policy were to achieve political stability and economic self-sufficiency, that is to ensure that the new colony was neither a political nor economic burden, but paid for itself.

The BaSotho objected to the fact that they had no influence or control over colonial policies, and over the use of the funds they provided from the payment of taxes. In a petition to the Governor of the Cape Colony, Sir Henry Barkly, twenty-three BaSotho, including Paramount Chief Letsie, expressed this concern:

> It appears also fitting that since Basutos pay taxes they should be represented where the disposal of these is discussed. That it is therefore the humble prayer of Your Excellency's humble petitioners ... that such steps may be taken as may be deemed fitting to procure Basutos some representation in the council of Government, of which their natural country now forms an integral part ...[4]

In fact the status of Basutoland with regard to the Cape Colony was never very clear. The petition of the BaSotho for representation was rejected on the grounds that this would require the country to accept the status of British Kaffraria, which entailed the loss of considerable independence and the acceptance of colonial laws.[5] The magistrates were already imposing some colonial laws in Basutoland, however, and when it was to the advantage of the colonists provisions and acts were extended to Basutoland as if it were indeed an "integral part" of the Colony.

The loyalty of the BaSotho to their new government was soon put to the test. Troops were raised in Basutoland to put down Moorosi's rebellion in the southern part of the country in 1880. Burman explains that the BaSotho cooperated because they were threatened with the confiscation of the Quthing District to reward colonial troops if the BaSotho did not raise their own troops.[6] Instead of rewarding the BaSotho after they had successfully defeated Moorosi, however, the Cape government attempted to impose a number of punitive measures. The Peace Preservation Act, which had been passed by the Cape Parliament in 1878, and which called for the disarmament of Africans in the Colony, was to be applied to Basutoland. The hut tax was to be doubled to £1 per hut annually; £12,500 was to be appropriated from Basutoland to pay for expenses of the Colony; and the Quthing District was to be confiscated and sold to white farmers in spite of BaSotho cooperation in suppressing the rebellion.[7]

Two observations must be added to Burman's assessment of these penalties, which culminated in the Gun War, or Basutoland Rebellion, of 1880–81.[8] First, the BaSotho were upset because they were required, at least in theory, to turn in not only their guns, which they had earned through hard labor in the Cape and Free State, but also all their other weapons, including spears and assegais.[9] This would not only have crippled the BaSotho capacity for territorial defense, but would also have deprived them of the means for hunting and slaughtering animals which provided them with food and clothing. Second, and most important, the confiscation of the Quthing district for white settlement threatened the very integrity of the BaSotho nation by setting a precedent which might allow for further land expropriation in the future. An official War Office document from Great Britain stated explicitly in 1880 that no part of Basutoland was safe from colonial confiscation: "The Cape Government, however, were of the opinion that no pledge had been given to Moshesh that either the Quthing district *or Basutoland at large* would be kept as a reserve, which Basutos only should be allowed to inhabit ..."[10]

Ignoring prevailing regional politics, Kimble has misinterpreted the relationship between the chiefs and their people before and during the Gun War, and the dynamics driving the BaSotho to accumulate guns before the war. Projecting backwards in time the levels of exploitation which came to characterize the relationship between chiefs and commoners after 1884, Kimble assumed that decision-making powers with regard to popular participation in migrant labor, and the choice of buying guns with the money earned, lay with the chiefs rather than with the participants themselves. What is at question here is not whether the chiefs wanted their people to work for wages and buy guns, since it is clear that the chiefs encouraged these activities. At issue is the underlying motive of the chiefs, and whether popular compliance was voluntary or compulsory. Kimble argues that

> It is thus in the context of the increasing dominance of the Koena lineage, and of the importance of military organisation to the reproduction of this dominance, that any 'desire to get guns' on the part of the Sotho labourers should be understood. Beyond this, the character of the colonial threat to Koena power in the 1870s is significant. The various attempts made by the Cape administration to infringe chiefly prerogatives, alongside its overt readiness to work closely with the missionaries, were regarded with great suspicion by Sotho chiefs. The latter were ready to defend their rights of surplus appropriation against the "Queen's government" – a government, moreover, which by 1875 did not remotely resemble the form of administration envisaged by Moshoeshoe in his requests for British "protection" a decade earlier.[11]

Kimble has simplistically reduced the motives of the BaKoena chiefs to their own self-interest in retaining the power to dominate other BaSotho within Basutoland. But this does not explain why BaSotho commoners displayed overwhelming chiefly support in a contest which was geared to ensure their domination by the BaKoena chiefs. Kimble implicitly underestimates the intelligence, perceptiveness, and deliberation of the BaSotho at large, when she attributes the waging of the Gun War to chiefly power and prerogative:

> Not only could the chiefs send their followers to the mines, they could also summon them back at times of crisis in Basutoland, and, furthermore, impose their own system of direct taxation on returning labourers ... in 1880, the impending military confrontation with the colonial government over disarmament led the Koena chiefs to issue a general summons to the mines ... more than 4000 Basotho returned immediately. With this evidence it becomes pos-

sible to interpret the massive national resistance to disarmament in 1880–81: not only were BaSotho exceedingly bitter at yet another broken promise of the British, but the threat to disarm BaSotho struck at the very foundations of royal power, a power which had been considerably strengthened during decades of organising and controlling the movements of labour migration.[12]

Kimble's only evidence of supposed BaKoena coercive control over their people is the responsiveness of the BaSotho in going to the mines, which corresponded with the chiefs' wishes, and popular responsiveness to the chiefs' call to return home as war approached. But there is no evidence that the chiefs ever had to compel their people either to go or return against their will, and it is clear that the BaSotho participation was voluntary and did not reflect, much less demonstrate, chiefly power. The chiefs had not "organised or controlled the movements of labour migration for decades," nor is this demonstrated by their having allowed and encouraged it for decades. If any thing, labor migration had long given the BaSotho considerable ongoing leverage over their chiefs: participation in migrant labor allowed them to accumulate wealth and acquire weapons independently from chiefly control. The portion of wages paid to the chiefs upon their return was a pittance, amounting to several days wages at most, while the BaSotho kept as their own the livestock and the guns which they earned and brought back into Lesotho. When the BaSotho complained about taxation, they complained explicitly about colonial taxes which were levied on every man indiscriminately, regardless of income. Had their chiefs been exercising unreasonable measures of exploitation, the BaSotho would have manipulated their wealth and used their guns to overturn BaKoena rule; surely they would not have willingly participated in defending BaKoena dominance within Basutoland, as Kimble argues they were doing under the coercion of their chiefs. The purpose of the BaSotho at large in waging the Gun War was not merely to keep their arms, but rather to defend the territorial integrity of the country, which could only be ensured by overthrowing Cape Colony rule, and retaining the right to bear arms with which to fight in the future. The dynamics of the Gun War involved considerable strategic planning by both the chiefs and their people, as even those appearing to collaborate as loyalists were part of the conspiracy to overthrow Cape Colonial rule. Oral testimony confirms that the Gun War reflected a conscious and deliberate exercise aimed at achieving national self-determination.[13]

In winning the Gun War, the BaSotho successfully defended their land and their right to bear arms in defense of their nation. They also threw off the burden of rule by the Cape Colony, which, in seeking to expropriate land from Basutoland, had demonstrated that it was motivated purely by European interests. In spite of considerable dissension among the BaSotho concerning the subsequent decision to return to direct Imperial rule instead of seeking full independence, in March 1884 Basutoland was disannexed from the Cape Colony and again came under direct Imperial rule.[14] The British colonial office, now directly responsible for running Basutoland, adopted a policy of indirect rule which required bolstering the powers of the chiefs for the purpose of efficient administration. In the end the BaSotho won freedom from the Cape Colony at the expense of their own liberties at home, and their chiefs, no longer vulnerable to popular opposition, took advantage of their new opportunity to become increasingly exploitative.

Socioeconomic change in the colonial era was thus characterized by increasing socioeconomic stratification and exploitation by the upper layers of BaSotho society, notably the chiefs. The transition to direct Imperial rule brought the BaSotho territorial security at the expense of internal freedom. The BaSotho chiefs had not urged their people to accumulate guns in order to secure their own internal dominance, since their internal position of domination had never been seriously at risk except from the external colonial threat. They had mustered popular support, and allowed their people to accumulate guns, because of the external threat posed to the country by the Cape Colony. As long as the chiefs needed popular support, such as that garnered during the Gun War, they could not afford to alienate their people. With the advent of Imperial Rule, the chiefs no longer depended on popular support to sustain their dominance internally. From 1884 the BaSotho began to pay the price for their external protection, ensured by the British, as the exploitation they experienced at the hands of their chiefs intensified.

Even the chiefs were aware that they abused their subjects under the new colonial order. Chief Jonathan Molapo testified to the South African Affairs Commission in 1904 that

> We [chiefs] are depriving the people of their property and we have no law to protect the people's property ... Yes, I myself. If I am pleased with another man's ox, and if I see it is a big one, I can take it; and I know that no one will take it away from me ... Yes, the other Chiefs are also guilty the same as myself.[15]

Similarly, a European trader who had been in the country for twenty-five years portrayed the abuses of the chiefs at the end of the nineteenth century:

> Many of the Natives have complained to me that when a poor man commits a petty theft, or does something that the Chief does not like, he is made to pay a couple of fowls or a sheep, or something of that sort, but if a man of wealth does something that his Chief does not like he is "eaten up" [has all his property confiscated] or heavily fined. This is not an encouragement to them ... I know the common saying amongst the people is that there are far too many Chiefs.[16]

Many Europeans testifying in 1903–04 repeated the charge that the BaSotho thought there were too many chiefs, and that people feared to make investments in their land for fear their chief would confiscate it as punishment for a false, trumped up charge.[17] In perhaps the worst indictment of the chiefs, a missionary charged that

> Both [British] Government and Native laws with regard to fining for offences lead to grave abuses. If a Chief is fined by Government, he extorts from his people a sum far in excess of the amount he has to pay. The actual amount of

the fine is handed over to the Govenrment, the surplus amounting to more than the fine itself he keeps for himself. Thus the fine inflicted on a Chief becomes a means of enriching him. A Chief is at liberty to fine the people he likes, without any regard being had of the proportion of the fine to the offence committed, or without any regard to the punishment falling on the head of the actual offender. No check is kept on the amount taken by the Chief in fines. This engenders much dissatisfaction and impoverishes the people.[18]

The scarcity of land within Basutoland, evident from the 1880s onwards, eliminated the former leverage represented by the potential to emigrate which had enabled the BaSotho previously to influence their chiefs. After 1884 exploitation intensified as a direct result of British colonial policies designed to bolster the power of cooperative chiefs through whom indirect rule could be maintained. Some chiefs became collaborators. Freed from the constraint of having to seek popular support, they benefitted from colonialism.

Economic policy and practice

Throughout the colonial era, under both Cape Colony rule and direct imperial rule, the object of colonial economic policies was to have the colony pay for itself. Towards this end direct taxes were imposed, and non-essential expenditures, such as those normally associated with any social and economic benefits contributing to "development," were avoided. From the beginning a hut tax was imposed to support the Governor's Agent, magistrates, and police force. Every man was required to pay a tax of 10s. for each hut, with the understanding that each hut represented the establishment of a wife. This tax was levied every year without regard for a family's income, which might fluctuate dramatically from year to year because of climatic factors which affected harvests and market factors which affected profits. The tax was levied in addition to the obligations which the BaSotho already owed their chiefs, primarily labor time. The new subjects in Basutoland thus paid more for the dubious privilege of being governed by the Cape Colony, while their principal chiefs benefitted from the new income which taxation generated: they received 10 percent of the money which they collected. It immediately became obvious that the collection of taxes was only possible with the aid of many subordinate chiefs as well, and from 1872 they too were rewarded financially for their cooperation.[19]

The burden of taxation was not insignificant to the BaSotho. While payments could be made in kind, the value of stock, as noted above, was "purposefully fixed low in order to discourage it as a medium of payment."[20] This had the intended result of bringing in more and more payments in cash each year so long as the BaSotho were able to sell their produce easily. In the first year, 1870, when the tax was only partially paid because of opposition from the Chief Masopha, the third son of Moshoeshoe, £3,700 was collected. The following year the income from Basutoland was £4,753, although this included some funds generated from licenses, fines and marriage registers. In 1872 the hut tax revenue was £5,296, and the total revenues including income from licenses and fines were £5,921. Reported governmental expenditures were £5,499.[21]

The BaSotho had always provided tribute labor as a form of taxation benefitting their chiefs, and this concerned Cape Colonial officials who feared that this interfered with the BaSotho ability to work in their own fields to obtain money to pay colonial taxes. They also perceived that tribute labor represented the backbone of the chiefs' power, symbolizing their ability to tax their subjects and providing concrete wealth to bolster their power. As soon as the Cape Colony took over, the Governor's Agent, Griffith, sent a circular to the British magistrates in the various districts of the country instructing them that "*letsema*," by which he meant the practice of providing tribute labor to chiefs, should be "abrogated as soon as possible." He insisted to the magistrates, who would be handling cases in which such disputes would arise, "I have to request that you will protect natives refusing to take part in this custom."[22] After the 1880s, as the chiefs consolidated their control with the support of the British, the provision of tribute labor to chiefs began to interrupt homestead production significantly and became a burdensome form of taxation. The steady placing of chiefs over one another made people liable to supplying tribute labor to many chiefs, and some chiefs began to require that all of their wives' fields be worked, so that the amount of work required of each subject increased significantly. By the end of the century the allocation of labor to agriculture within homesteads was clearly impeded by the heavy burden of tribute labor.[23] A European trader who had resided in Lesotho for thirty years testified in 1903 about the transformation which had occurred in the obligations due to chiefs after the colony was transferred to direct imperial rule. He explained:

> At the ploughing and weeding seasons the men were called together and were called upon to plough or weed the personal lands of the Chief and that of his first wife, but they were always liberally fed by the Chief during the work. This traditional law of the Ba-Sotho was carried out even under the administration of the Colonial Government. The people were never compelled to work for the "small wives" or for the sons of the Chiefs and petty Chiefs. Since the Imperial Government took over the country the people are compelled to work in the lands of the Chiefs and, in most cases, never get a morsel of food. It often happens that those who want a rest are assaulted, and that those who did not, for one reason or another, attend the work are fined, in most cases arbitrarily. The present tyrannical system causes great dissatisfaction. If only the people were fed they would not feel so much dissatisfied, although they have now to work for so many Chiefs and petty Chiefs. The Chiefs who feed the people who thus work for them are, at present, the great exception.[24]

The economic impact of the change from Cape Colony to direct Imperial rule in 1884 is difficult to assess, since its primary effect was the negation of laws which had never taken effect: no land was confiscated, and the hut tax was not raised from 10s. to £1. It was vital for the BaSotho to retain the land in the Quthing district because of overcrowding in the country, which was already evident and which intensified with the continued influx of other Africans into Basutoland.[25] In light of the economic recession which affected the country beginning in the 1880s,[26] few BaSotho would have been able to pay a doubled hut tax in any case.

In fact, even the tax of 10s. was too heavy a burden under the economic circumstances prevailing at the end of the nineteenth century, and it caused considerable hardship for many BaSotho. The government managed to collect £4,600 in hut tax in 1884 in spite of Chief Masopha's continued refusal to cooperate.[27] In the late 1880s, however, both missionaries and chiefs were complaining that since the commercial crisis even people who had paid their taxes regularly in the past were no longer able to do so.[28] The tax was due in mid-July,[29] after the season's crops had been harvested. This obliged most BaSotho who had no money in reserve to sell enough of their grain immediately to pay the tax, creating a glut of grain which drove down prices. As the size of family land holdings and the size of family harvests declined many households were forced to sell grain which was needed for the family's subsistence in order to pay taxes. When the remaining food supplies ran out, these households had to sell livestock, their "capital" holdings, to purchase food for subsistence at prices which were much higher than those they had received when they sold their crops for tax money.

The problem was exacerbated during agricultural crises such as droughts. On the one hand, the necessity to pay taxes explains why, even after extremely poor harvests, some grain was sold by the BaSotho to traders who exported it to the Cape Colony and the mines. With the prospect of poor harvests looming, traders also used high prices to induce the BaSotho to sell their grain, later reselling grain to the same BaSotho at even higher prices once famine had set in. This happened in 1892, after the crops were destroyed by locusts: BaSotho who had sold their grain for 10s. to 13s. per muid could only repurchase it at 20s. to 28s.[30] During that year £19,000 was collected in hut taxes, but many subsequently survived only by eating wild roots, grasses, and seeds.[31]

At the same time, more and more people were trying to eke out their survival on insufficient allotments of land. The stage was set for ongoing internal political strife associated with competing land claims, and for the appearance of a generation of landless young men. The annual report for 1894 described the dilemma which the BaSotho faced:

> The country is circumscribed, the population is growing, the land suitable for cultivation is all allotted and taken up, and the rising generation of men are no longer able to support themselves on it. When leading chiefs die, a scramble ensues over the inheritance among the children, we having during the year witnessed a serious stage in the scramble over the late Paramount Chief's inheritance.[32]

Fluctuating market conditions made it impossible for the BaSotho to profit even after good harvests. By the late 1880s the traditional markets for grain from Lesotho were being inundated with American and Australian grain: in 1896 there were 300,000 bags of American corn in the Colony, which had to be cleared out by traders before they would consider buying any grain from Lesotho.[33] Between 1893 and 1894, the volume of grain exported rose while the value of these exports declined.[34] The devastation of Rinderpest coincided with several consecutive years of drought, depriving the BaSotho of both their annual income from the sale of crops and their capital assets in the form of cattle.[35] In spite of this, most BaSotho worked hard to pay their taxes. According to the Annual Colonial Report of 1896–7 "They readily adapted themselves to new conditions by using their ponies for ploughing and transport, in many cases turning again to the abandoned hoe rather than groan under the misfortune of being unable to cultivate."[36]

While they continued to pay taxes, the BaSotho were suffering. Gone was the semblance of affluence which missionaries saw symbolized in the consumption of European goods. A French missionary who arrived in January 1899 was surprised by the dismal conditions he found. He ethnocentrically equated "civilization" with the adoption of European customs and goods, and referred to BaSotho culture as "savage." He wrote:

> all that I had heard said about it in France, I believed it [Lesotho] infinitely more civilized.—The indigenous people, dressed in a fashion extremely primitive; the routes perhaps still more primitive, studded with high steep crags, often perpendicular (without exaggeration), do not exist except very vaguely; the pagan villages, without any trace of civilization ... in general, I would never have believed southern Africa still so savage.[37]

Surprised because of exaggerated missionary reports of westernization, his impressions nevertheless accurately reflected widespread economic depression which affected all elements of society: the population was plagued with famine and local war in 1898, partial drought and continued food scarcity in 1899, and typhoid fever, smallpox, influenza, and dysentery. The response of the Imperial government to the apparent devastation of the BaSotho economy wrought by natural factors and poor terms of trade, was not to waive the hut tax, but to double it from 10s. to £1 per hut annually. The only concession of the government was to defer the increase for a year, so that it took effect in 1899. The increase was imposed in order to make Basutoland completely self-supporting: the country had previously received an annual subsidy of up to £22,000 from the Cape Colony.[38] Because of the rate increase, hut tax revenues rose dramatically between 1893 and 1910, as demonstrated in Figure 16 below. The BaSotho also paid taxes indirectly as consumers because of special customs duties which were levied on imported merchandise.

Colonial revenues were used for the payment of officials and chiefs, a mounted police force of BaSotho which numbered 150 in 1891, the construction and repair of roads, and grants in aid to education. Eventually the railway to Maseru was completed in 1905–06. Efforts at reforestation which had begun under the Cape Administration also continued, aided by the

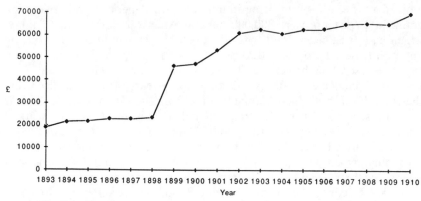

Fig. 16 Hut tax revenue

missionaries.[39] But because the BaSotho paid for these development projects from which they benefitted, their economic interests were not furthered by their colonial status beyond the fact that their territorial integrity was protected. Many BaSotho continued to question the benefits of colonial protection given its high cost to them. After the return to direct Imperial rule in 1884 Chief Masopha remained the most widely-supported chief among the BaSotho because he continued to resist the colonial authorities and the payment of taxes.[40] The era of the chief's resistance to colonialism was waning, however, and died with Masopha in 1898. It is perhaps no coincidence that in this same year the hut tax was finally doubled. Subsequently the Imperial government took further advantage of the BaSotho during the South African War of 1899–1902. The British relied on BaSotho troops to defend their borders from the Boers, commandeered wagons from Lesotho, and used pasture land in the country to keep the confiscated stock of the Boers, while refusing to purchase Basutoland grain for their supplies. As a result, thousands of armed BaSotho guarded the frontiers on British orders, while their pastures and cultivated lands were damaged, Boer refugees flooded the country with their stock, animal diseases were introduced, and more than 325,000 bags of grain were prevented from reaching markets outside the country.[41] It is not surprising that the loyalties of the BaSotho were divided during this war, as the British had just raised the hut tax and were now making new demands on their unwilling subjects.[42]

The high wages earned by the BaSotho working for the British during the war temporarily disguised the economic stagnation of the country, but the weakness of the economy became apparent in the next few years. The country began to import food on a regular basis, as the people continued to sell grain which they needed for their own subsistence in order to pay their taxes, later being forced to repurchase grain at higher prices. As the first decade of the twentieth century came to a close harvests were poor, the people did not have enough food, and work at the mines became hard to

176

obtain because of an oversupply of workers, causing the salaries of migrant workers to fall.[43]

BaSotho in the Conquered Territory: the Orange Free State

After the colonial borders of Basutoland were finally fixed, many BaSotho remained outside the country as permanent or long-term workers and tenants on farms in the Orange Free State, particularly in that portion which became known as the "Conquered Territory." As one missionary noted, many preferred to subject themselves to new masters rather than leave the land of their forefathers, where they had lived their entire lives.[44] The sacrifices they made were great: one European reported that the BaSotho "considered it a fearful degradation to wait upon a 'white man,'"[45] and another observed in the Orange Free State that "the condition of the coloured population is lamentable in the extreme. The white people treat them with more indifference than we in England treat dogs. The Dutch are positively cruel."[46]

While this was especially true of workers employed directly by Europeans either as farm or household workers, many Africans retained considerable independence through the first decade of the twentieth century. Africans theoretically had "communal ownership" of land in the reserves at Witsieshoek (Harrismith District) and Thaba 'Nchu, where some also held individual titles to land outside the reserves, which they registered in the name of a (European) guardian.[47] Most, however, "squatted" on land of European farmers according to various systems which generally entailed share-cropping or "plowing-on-the-half." All Africans were required to pay an annual poll tax of 20s. if they remained in the country for three months. Permanent residents also paid a hut tax of the same amount.[48]

Of the two "Native Reserves," Witsieshoek was primarily inhabited by BaSotho, while Thaba, 'Nchu was the territory which the Boers had allowed the BaRolong to keep. The BaSotho of Witsieshoek came under the rule of the Orange Free State by virtue of a treaty between Paulus Mopeli and the Free State government. An Ordinance passed in 1869 or 1870 regulated land in the location, which was inalienable and held in trust by the government, and which an appointed government Commandant allocated for residence, grazing, and cultivation uses.[49] The BaRolong were absorbed under Free State rule after an internal conflict over succession in 1884, in which the Boer government supported one of two claimants to power. The government's allies were allowed to stay on their land for fifteen more years. Some of the land was held communally and some was held under individual land titles. Many BaRolong migrated into Lesotho in 1884, and the rest were dispersed when they finally lost their rights to the remaining land in 1899.[50]

The majority of BaSotho in the Orange Free State lived on the farms of Europeans, providing various forms of compensation to white farmers for the right to use the land. The Free State government set a limit of five families of squatters per farm in an attempt to mobilize wage labor for towns and for farmers who only had small tracts of land. In an attempt to enforce this limit, an extra tax of £5 was imposed on white landowners for each person above the limit on a farm. Landowners were known to keep farms just for squatters, however, and there was apparently no limit to the number of farms into which their land could be divided. In some cases the African tenants merely paid a heifer a year as rent for the right to use the land for cultivation and grazing, keeping all produce. In other cases the owner provided the seed while the Africans provided the labor, and the produce was equally shared. Alternatively, the land was sometimes divided between the white farmer and the black tenants, with the latter receiving full rights to the produce of the land they cultivated in exchange for providing necessary farm labor for the white farmer on his portion of the land.[51] Finally, many Africans served as wage laborers on farms, receiving cash payments for performing whatever work was required. In addition the wage laborer often received some grazing rights, as well as food and clothing. Their counterparts in the towns, working as house servants and in shops, earned a higher monthly wage but often did not receive any extra compensation in kind.[52]

Arrangements made between white land owners and tenant African farmers could be very flexible. Sometimes different agreements about work and compensation governed different members of the same family on the same farm. Such a possibility was described by a farmer in Smithfield seeking workers from Lesotho. Writing to William Scott, a trader in Mafeteng, he explained:

> You would greatly oblige me if you could get me a good native, I want one that has the span of oxen, as I have a lot of land here that I want to give to a good boy [man] to plow & sow on half shares, if you can get one, I want him to bring with him two boys & a girl [two men and a woman] to hire themselves as farm servants.[53]

Generally the Africans who participated in sharecropping or "farming-on-the-half" enjoyed more permanent status than wage workers. Sharecropping contracts with farmers were of one year's duration, but in practice the BaSotho who farmed on this system remained indefinitely in the Conquered Territory.[54] From the perspective of the BaSotho, payment in labor or in kind for the right to cultivate a portion of land independently was not radically different from providing labor and services to chiefs in Lesotho for a similar privilege. With the advent of colonial rule and taxation, the diminution of the chiefs' power, and the gradual decline in protection and services offered by chiefs to their people, the benefits of living in Lesotho were less obvious. The fertile lands of the Conquered Territory promised far greater returns than the available mountain lands of Lesotho. The prospect of farming richer land, even subject to Boer rule, was clearly an attractive alternative to prospects within Lesotho.

Unfortunately but not surprisingly, the security of the BaSotho tenants farming in the Orange Free State was illusory. The tenant system seemed to offer more security, more independence, and greater profitability to the MoSotho farmer than did wage labor on farms. Wage laborers tended to cross the border into the Orange Free State for shorter periods of time, and their earnings opportunities were limited. On the other hand, most of the wage earners kept homes in Lesotho, where their wives or families worked the family fields. The income earned in the Orange Free State was crucial but supplemental, and if they lost their jobs they had alternative means of meager support.

The more permanent residents of the Conquered Territory discovered their vulnerability only when the white landowners expelled them from the land. When a severe drought affected the area in 1886, BaSotho were sent off the farms on which they lived with only a day's notice because they had too many cattle of their own, which competed with the cattle of the white farmers for scarce pasture during the drought. They were replaced with other African families who had little or no stock.[55] Even when drought was not a factor, sharecroppers were generally expelled when the quantity of their livestock exceeded "the reasonable possibilities of grazing on the farm."[56]

The fortunes of the BaSotho in the Orange Free State suffered dramatically in the 1890s. When Rinderpest came, families were devastated: "The temporal possessions of natives are represented almost exclusively by cattle. Land they have none in the Free State, and all savings are invested in cattle."[57]

Two years later the Boers seized all the sheep, oxen, horses, and wagons of the Africans in the Orange Free State for use in the war.[58] Then drought prevented recovery: a white farmer wrote about the BaSotho in the Orange Free State that

> Their present resources are much less, owing to the fact that they lost all their sheep, cattle and horses in the war, and consequently their whole capital and income. What little funds they collected in the war or had saved were dissipated in the one and half years of famine, and impossible conditions of labour, as it seemed to them, which followed.[59]

Early statistics do not distinguish between different African groups, but later tables show that the BaSotho represented about 60 percent of the African population in the Orange Free State. Moreover, many of the BaRolong and IsiZulu-speakers who constituted the remaining African population also had strong ties to Lesotho, as reflected in their historical political ties as well as in family connections and ongoing immigration to Lesotho. The size of the African population in the Orange Free State, including BaSotho, grew steadily between 1880 and 1910. Census data show that the African population numbered 72,496 in 1881, 129,787 in 1890, and 244,636 in 1906.[60] The contribution of the African population to the economy was proportionately significant. In addition to labor, Africans provided the Orange Free State with £30,000 annually through hut tax and poll tax payments in the early twentieth century.[61]

African farmers in the Orange Free State finally lost the right to farm on the terms described above when the Land Act of 1913 was passed in the newly constituted Union of South Africa. This bill was directly aimed at black squatting and farming-on-the-half, because these options for relatively independent African agricultural production made it difficult for small white farmers and the mines to recruit black wage labor. Although in practice the law was applied only gradually, over time thousands of Africans were finally and irrevocably uprooted from the lands which they had worked for generations. Deprived of access to land, Africans were forced to sell their stock and enter into service as wage laborers. No longer was independent farming in South Africa a viable alternative for the BaSotho and their African neighbors.

The changing borders of nineteenth-century Lesotho meant that the legal status of many BaSotho changed dramatically even when they remained on land which had been in their families for generations. Many BaSotho who had given their allegiance to Moshoeshoe and had been part of the BaSotho nation later found themselves residing in the Orange Free State. Their past was inextricably linked to the history of their neighbors and kin who remained within the limits of colonial Basutoland. But their fate is also important because a comparison of the fortunes of the BaSotho in the Orange Free State with the fortunes of the BaSotho in Basutoland reveals the relative advantages attached to living within Lesotho at the beginning of the twentieth century in spite of growing exploitation by chiefs. The impotence and disabilities experienced by the BaSotho of the Orange Free State fed the nationalism of the BaSotho in Lesotho and perpetuated popular support for chiefs.

Popular tolerance of exploitation by chiefs within Lesotho can therefore only be understood in terms of the regional sociopolitical context. The British colonial rulers of Basutoland were eager to cooperate with white capitalists and the white governments in South Africa on the verge of unification. It is easy to characterize BaSotho chiefs within Lesotho as collaborators as well, but their position was much more complex. At no time in the nineteenth century did the BaSotho feel secure from the threat of direct domination and dispossession by the Boers of the Orange Free State. This BaSotho sense of insecurity was evident in 1898, when Paramount Chief Lerotholi, grandson of Moshoeshoe, was compelled by the British to attack his recalcitrant uncle Masopha who was shielding his son Moeketsi from the law. The British magistrates had ordered Moeketsi arrested because he had fled from punishment for a crime in the Orange Free State. Unwillingly Lerotholi fought against Masopha, not only because of British pressure, but also because the BaSotho sincerely believed that the Orange Free State would wage war on Lesotho to retrieve Moeketsi, and that the Boers would finally expropriate the remainder of BaSotho lands.[62] Except for Masopha and his followers, both the chiefs and the population at large preferred the perceived advantage of protection available through British colonial rule to full independence and the prospect of national disintegration and territorial incorporation into the Orange Free State or a united South Africa. As a result, the BaSotho remained subject to exploitation by their chiefs, and found themselves increasingly compelled by politics and poverty to participate in the exploitative migrant labor system.

13

Economy, politics, migrant labor and gender

The examination of the political and economic forces at work in Lesotho in the nineteenth century provides the context for analyzing the motives of migrant laborers, and the opportunities and constraints, both political and economic, which shaped their choices. Forces shaping the rise of a migrant labor system must be sought not only in the needs of the agricultural and industrial sectors of the emerging capitalist economy, but also in the rural areas from which African laborers hailed. There have been careful and insightful studies of the system of labor migrancy in the late nineteenth and early twentieth centuries, which have focussed on issues such as mine policies, labor recruitment, and colonial interventions. Individual studies have traced the rise of African participation in labor migration for many areas, revealing variations in the degree and timing of participation of people from different chiefdoms, kingdoms and polities including AmaMpondo, AmaZulu, BaTswana, BaSotho, and BaPedi.[1] Incisive analyses of the functions of labor migrancy for mining capitalism have come from Wolpe and Meillassoux. They have each presented the case for the utility of the system to capitalism because miners' families who were left behind in rural areas could theoretically support themselves and the costs of the "reproduction" of the labor force would not be born by the mines via high wages, but by those who remained tilling the land back home.[2] It is clear that the migrant labor system has been functional to capitalism, however this was not the primary determinant leading initially to the use of a migrant, rather than settled, labor force. Africans were motivated to leave home and work for white farmers, on colonial projects such as the railways, or at the mines, but they also chose to maintain their links with their rural homes and actively forged a migrant system through which they maintained considerable independence to come and go based on their own needs for cash or goods, and on the wages offered.

Similarly, the role of women in subsidizing the capitalist system through a migrant labor system by supporting the costs of reproducing the labor force, while functional to capitalism, does not demonstrate that women's subordination derived originally from capitalism. As Bozzoli aptly notes:

Because female oppression performs certain functions for capitalism, this does not mean that it was a pure creation of capitalism. To posit this would be to deny the history of female oppression in other, non-capitalist, societies, and to fail to acknowledge its existence in socialist ones. This functionalist tendency in Marxist attempts to cope with female oppression reflects an anti-historical and economistic bias.[3]

The evidence from pre-capitalist, pre-colonial Lesotho, and from oral traditions concerning the ancestors of the SeTswana- and SeSotho-speaking peoples, demonstrates clearly that the domination of women by men long predated capitalism. Capitalism and the migrant labor system must therefore be seen as perpetuating and making use of pre-existing patterns of women's subordination. Bozzoli has emphasized that it was forces at work in the rural areas, rather than the needs of the capitalist economy, which kept women at home while allowing men to work as migrants. However, her analysis remains largely theoretical for lack of empirical evidence about the history of gender relations in rural areas. The evidence from nineteenth-century Lesotho provides the opportunity to analyze the conditions in a rural area giving rise to and shaping the migrant labor system, with attention to local politics, socioeconomic stratification, gender struggles, and colonial interference.

In the specific case of Lesotho, Kimble concluded that "with the exception of the migration characteristic of Christianized petty commodity producers, the primary structural determinant of migration was the concerted action of the Koena royals to direct their subjects to enter the labour markets at the mines and on the colonial railway works."[4] This interpretation of labor migrancy, in which Kimble identified the political ambitions of the BaKoena ruling family within Basutoland as the important push factor of BaSotho participation in migrant labor, is inadequate. Like Kimble, I argue that the motives and the "structural determinants" within Lesotho governing labor migrancy changed over time, but the evidence indicates that other motives were at work than those which Kimble attributed to the BaSotho. Kimble is incorrect to assume that individual homesteads were so controlled by obligations to chiefs that they were unable to make individual choices concerning participation in migrant labor. Kimble correctly rejected the notion of "new wants" and an unspecific "need" for commodities, but she incorrectly assumed that such supposed, artificially created "new needs" were the only possible reason for individual homesteads to allow or encourage members from their family to migrate abroad for work. As Kimble noted, we need to take into account "how these [needed commodities] were integrated into the circuits of production and reproduction within the total social formation."[5] Her own analysis falls down, however, whereas an analysis of the intersections of production and "reproduction" with reference to gender provides a more insightful starting point for analyzing the causes and effects of migrant labor participation in colonial Basutoland.

The BaSotho and migratory labor

BaSotho responses to migrant labor opportunities and the effects of migrant labor participation changed over time as the agricultural base of the BaSotho economy gradually disintegrated and relations between chiefs and their subjects changed. Socioeconomic differentiation among the BaSotho increasingly prompted a differential response to migrant labor opportunities according to the varying statuses of homesteads. The economic status of the homestead from which a worker came also determined the economic impact of participation in migrant labor for a given household. The study of the allocation of labor between agriculture and migrant labor has important theoretical implications. By providing a careful chronology of changes in the interaction between the local economy and the regional economy, it is possible to reconcile two opposing perspectives on this interaction, one of which views migrant labor as having been a positive source of capital for the BaSotho, and the other of which emphasizes the exploitative nature of the migrant labor system and its failure to provide wages at a level which could benefit the local agricultural economies from which migrant workers hailed.

The BaSotho began working for Europeans as early as the 1820s, when many people found themselves entering the Cape Colony, voluntarily and involuntarily, as a result of regional raids and wars. Certainly the white frontiersmen had been supporting and aiding Griqua and Kora raiders in capturing SeTswana- and SeSotho-speaking people north of the Orange River before the 1820s, and many African women and children became captives entering involuntary servitude in what can be appropriately termed a form of slavery.[6] But the experiences of BaSotho recorded in the 1830s demonstrates that some had gone voluntarily, and many were able to subsequently leave at will, taking with them livestock which they had earned, indicating that not all of the labor provided was involuntary and many BaSotho received compensation for their services. The BaSotho were still unfamiliar to the colonists, however, and their origins were not recognized. Nevertheless, many BaSotho exchanged their services for payment in kind and in cash, building "capital reserves" in the form of livestock which they later imported into Lesotho. In late 1822 some BaRamokhele went to the Cape Colony, and some MaPolane and MaPhetla took service in Somerset East under the supervision of Sir Andries Stockenstrom, where they remained until 1836; many "learned Dutch and became useful interpreters to Government officers and missionaries."[7] The younger brother of a powerful chief, when his people had been devastated by Pakalita and Matiwane, was reduced to working for a farmer in the Cape Colony for several years. He returned with several heifers and a small herd of goats to resettle near Morija where his relatives had already established themselves.[8] Most BaSotho who had gone to the Colony returned home after peace was restored to the area in the 1830s, but a relationship with the colonists had been established which continued through the years. In these early years the BaSotho earned a reputation for honesty and fidelity.

From the beginning of economic recovery in the 1830s until the beginning of colonial rule, BaSotho participation in transient, migratory labor took place in the context of a growing, thriving economy which allowed the BaSotho to dictate their own terms when they provided labor, and to withdraw when circumstances were unfavorable to workers. This allowed them to command wages which they considered adequate. As early as 1847 H. D. Warden wrote that "there are many instances among Moshesh's people of four or five hundred [rix]dollars having been earned in the Colony and expended in the purchase of colonial cattle."[9] By the 1850s estimates of the numbers of BaSotho working for whites in the Cape Colony and Orange Free State ranged from 500 to thousands.[10] It is possible that the number varied seasonally, as it did later in the century; many BaSotho were willing to work for whites only when they were not busy on their own land.[11] Much of the Boer demand for labor was itself seasonal, reaching a peak at sheep-shearing season.

Even before the period of colonial rule, the attitude of the chiefs towards migrant labor was ambivalent. On the one hand, the chiefs benefitted directly from migration by levying a tax on migrant workers when they returned. In addition it was in the interests of the chiefs that the overall wealth of the country increase, that is that capital be brought into the country by these workers. Thus it is not surprising that a deposition from the 1840s reported that Moshoeshoe encouraged his followers to seek work abroad.[12] There were also reasons for chiefs to oppose such migrancy, however. First, working abroad provided any man the opportunity to acquire and accumulate wealth without the aid of the chiefs. Even after the opening of the mines, BaSotho men preferred to enter into agricultural service with Free State farmers, for which they were generally paid in livestock.[13] Commoners could thus take advantage of an alternative source of income which did not put them in debt to the chiefs, threatening the political dominance of the chiefs who depended largely on controlling the distribution of wealth in the country. In addition, whenever there was a military threat the chiefs wanted all BaSotho men at home and ready to serve in war. Thus in the 1860s the chiefs began to use "their utmost exertions to prevent their subjects leaving Basutoland to take Colonial service."[14] The strategy was successful: colonial officials across the border complained that there was a shortage of labor and tried to remedy it by forcing BaSotho refugees either to seek wage employment or to return to Lesotho. Even with thousands of starving refugees on hand in 1866 an official had difficulty in filling one hundred posts for workers in the Cape Colony.[15] Later, as the Gun War threatened to break out, the chiefs again summoned their subjects back from the mines to be available for military service.[16]

Finally, it was clearly in the interests of the chiefs *not* to disrupt agricultural production at home by sending men abroad. Not only did chiefs need to ensure the availability of tribute labor for working their own fields, but they also wished to preserve the economic viability of the homesteads under their jurisdiction. The chiefs' decisions to send or allow men to go abroad or to forbid them from going, and the decisions of their followers to comply, were therefore governed by both economic and political factors at both local and regional levels, and changed according to the circumstances prevailing at any given time.

In the early colonial years of Basutoland, from 1868 to 1880, the economy flourished, to the benefit of both the chiefs and their people. During this period the BaSotho continued to expand grain production to supply the Kimberley diamond mines, and BaSotho participation in migrant labor began to expand with the support and encouragement of their chiefs. Since the chiefs were directly supported and enriched by colonial taxes it is easy to conclude that the chiefs, motivated by self-interest, subordinated the interests of their people to the colonial system from its beginnings in the 1870s. But the relationship of the chiefs with their subjects and with the colonial system was much more ambiguous. Throughout the 1870s and 1880s the powers of the chiefs were constrained by the ability of their subjects to transfer their allegiance to other chiefs, to migrate into the mountains, or to leave the country entirely. The extent to which subjects responded to the will of their chiefs therefore reflected the extent to which chiefs were still acting in the interests of their people. This meant that insofar as the chiefs sought to encourage migrant labor in the 1870s and 1880, compliance on the part of the people was largely voluntary, and BaSotho participation in the migrant labor system in this period reflected a congruence of interests between the people and the chiefs.

There is no question that the economic and political interests of the chiefs were also served: they expropriated a portion of the migrant workers' wages, and they encouraged the migrant workers to buy guns with their wages in order to built up the national arsenal. The acquisition of guns was clearly a powerful incentive, but the desire to build up an arsenal of weapons cannot be reduced to the desire of the BaKoena chiefs to sustain their position of political dominance within colonial Basutoland.[17] If the chiefs had not enjoyed popular support they would not have encouraged the acquisition of guns by a potentially rebellious population. The motive of both the chiefs and commoners in acquiring guns was to ward off the continuing threat emanating from the Cape Colony. Since the BaSotho still retained enough leverage to limit the power of their chiefs at this time, they would not have gone to the mines, or would not have brought back guns instead of livestock, if they had not perceived that guns were vital to the broader interest of national survival. During this period it was not only poor, subordinated homesteads who sent their young men to the mines. Even young men from homesteads of chiefs worked abroad for the purpose of getting guns.

In the 1890s the situation changed dramatically. The chiefs had consolidated their control over their subjects and the political options of individual homesteads were limited. When the new colonial government explicitly began to support the chiefs as their colonial agents after 1884 the chiefs became almost completely independent of the traditional need for popular support. In addition, the growth in population density accelerated as a result of extensive immigration. As the BaSotho were pushed into the mountains and all remaining land within the country was allocated, geographic mobility was no longer a viable option for people who wished to express discontent with their chiefs. As soon as the chiefs' powers were no longer constrained by the independent mobility of their people, a major incentive for ruling justly and generously disappeared. When the Basutoland National Council was created in 1903 it was almost entirely controlled by the chiefs, and in 1906 the codification of the Laws of Lerotholi further reinforced their political control.[18] The chiefs began to take advantage of their new security, becoming in turn more supportive of the colonial system and more exploitative themselves. The turn of the century therefore marked a clear turning point both in relations between chiefs and commoners, and in relations between the chiefs and the colonial power. These changing relationships determined the BaSotho response to the migrant labor system and the effects of the system on agricultural production within Lesotho.

Migrant labor and the Basutoland economy

Prior to the 1890s participation in the migrant labor system benefitted the BaSotho economy because migrant workers could command high wages which were invested in the agricultural economy back home. Men could also work as migrant laborers without hindering production at home. Before the turn of the century it was the young men, sent by their chiefs or their fathers, who supplied the mines with labor which was underutilized at home.[19] An analysis of the local organization of labor shows that in the last quarter of the nineteenth century there was excess labor in the local economy because some members of society were underemployed either regularly or seasonally. Young unmarried men in particular did not have fields of their own and only occasionally helped in cultivation. Instead they worked primarily as herders, who were normally away in the mountains during the months of heavy agricultural labor. Their contribution to agriculture had always been minor and seasonal, and when they went to the mines the herding of cattle was taken over by younger men and boys who already herded goats and sheep. It was thus possible for young unmarried men to go to the mines without depriving the local economy of important labor. In addition, young men were usually still available during the peak agricultural labor season for men – the spring plowing season – because they timed their contracts accordingly.

At the beginning of the colonial period, then, it was possible for the BaSotho to participate in migrant labor without disrupting local production. At first there were few BaSotho at the diamond mines, but gradually the high wages attracted more workers from Lesotho. In 1875 it was possible for a worker at the mines to earn enough money to buy a gun in just one or two months.[20] The pay at public works projects in the Cape Colony, notably on the railways, was also high, at 2 to 3 shillings per day, and higher with piecework.[21]

Because they entered the migrant labor force voluntarily during the early colonial period, the BaSotho were able to refuse to work abroad when wages were low. This was reflected in the labor shortages that plagued both farmers and mine operators throughout the nineteenth century. The difficulty of attracting labor first caused mineowners to compete for labor, and then prompted them to coordinate wage levels and rationalize recruitment.[22] The elasticity in the labor supply indicates that it was wages rather than the inadequacy of local resources and the local economy which mobilized labor before the turn of the century. This in turn suggests that migrant workers from Lesotho represented surplus labor-power. The factors which led the BaSotho to migrate were directly related to the subsequent effect which migration had on agricultural production. As long as the local economy remained strong the BaSotho could always withdraw their labor, which gave them leverage over their employers who had to pay wages high enough to attract workers. These wages were not needed for basic subsistence, but were available for capital investment in agriculture, including the purchase of plows or draught oxen.

The situation began to change after the Disannexation Act was passed in 1884. The BaSotho working abroad had come home during the Gun War, and many stayed through the civil war of 1883–85. With the return of peace, many men were suddenly available to work abroad again. The loss of the lucrative grain market after the war meant that fewer BaSotho could earn a living off their land, and even more men were consequently pushed into the labor market at a time of declining demand. At the same time, the introduction of labor-saving machinery in the agricultural districts of the Orange Free State reduced the demand for labor further. A worker in the Free State or Cape Colony could earn only 10 shillings a month, or as much as a mine worker had previously been able to earn in only three or four days.[23]

The ecological disasters of the 1890s wreaked such havoc on agricultural production that the economic choices of the BaSotho were limited. At this point socioeconomic differentiation within Lesotho began to determine which homesteads sent men to the mines, as poorer families succumbed to the economic disasters sooner than did rich families. The number of passes granted to BaSotho going abroad to seek work rose steadily in spite of declining wages as the BaSotho suffered from successive crop failures and sought alternative sources of income. Official figures for labor passes rose to 28,000 in 1896. In 1896 BaSotho men were still going to the gold and diamond mines primarily during the winter season.[24] Each miner had to save "more or less 10 shillings for his chief, which he slips to him discreetly in his hand in coming to greet him."[25] During the Rinderpest epizootic in 1897 the borders were temporarily closed and temporary restrictions were imposed on

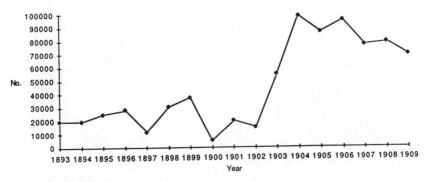

Fig. 17 Migrant labor passes

migrant labor. Participation increased dramatically in 1898 and 1899, however, only to be cut off again during the Anglo–Boer War. Employment on Free State farms and at the mines in Kimberley and Johannesburg ended abruptly when the South African War began in 1899, but thousands of BaSotho quickly found work in non-combatant branches of the British army at very high wages.

In 1903 a trader at Thaba Bosiu testified that when he had first arrived in the country nineteen years before in 1884, only young men left to work as migrant laborers and that few went after they were married. By contrast he noted that in 1903 even married men went because they needed money.[26] By the turn of the century men found they had to go to the mines to get cash to pay the tax, or *khafa*.[27]

In the immediate aftermath of the war, when the Chamber of Mines reduced wages from £3 to 30s. per month, the BaSotho were able to resist returning to the mines because they had accumulated savings by working for high wages during the war.[28] This effect was only temporary, however. By the turn of the century agricultural production in Lesotho had deteriorated so much that migrant labor provided a greater return to men's labor than did agriculture even when wages were low. Men could no longer choose when to go, or for how long, and consequently they lost the leverage which had enabled them previously to demand high wages. The number of labor passes issued to BaSotho jumped dramatically in 1903 and 1904 after crop failures, as can be seen in figure 17. Thereafter the employment options open to BaSotho men were limited, forcing them increasingly to become migrant laborers. The supply of workers was soon more than sufficient to meet the labor demand, and wages dropped. At this point the only choice for migrants was whether to work on Orange Free State farms as wage workers, or to go further to work in the mines.

Recruiting efforts by the mines were strengthened at this time, as labor agents flooded the country. The increase in the availability of migrant laborers from Lesotho was not the result of more extensive recruiting efforts

189

Table 9. *Migrant labor passes*

Year	Mines	Railroad	Farm and domestic	Miscellaneous	Total
1893					19,518
1894					20,000
1895					25,384
1896					28,115
1897[a]					11,778
1898					30,274
1899			24,175		37,371
1900	720		4,424		5,144
1901	585		7,995	11,477[b]	20,057
1902	2,427		3,920	8,847[b]	15,194
1903	13,914	6,054	34,042	376[b]	54,386
1904	14,214	12,132	23,667	48,009	98,022
1905	18,492	8,402	19,623	39,618	86,135
1906	20,241	8,698	18,802	47,261	95,002
1907	23,847	6,778	12,797	33,363	76,785
1908	22,438	6,958	15,528	33,972	78,896
1909	22,554	5,487	12,046	28,783	68,870

[a] Temporary restrictions imposed on migrant labor because of Rinderpest.
[b] Employment with British army.
Source: See table 5, p. 157.

in Lesotho, however, but rather the result of the collapse of the local economy. In fact, there is a negative correlation between the number of labor agents who recruited in Lesotho during these years and the number of BaSotho who left the country as migrant laborers. In 1902–03, nineteen industries were represented in Basutoland by recruiters. During the peak year of migrant labor from Lesotho, 1904, there were 77 labor agents in Lesotho. This rose to 142 in 1905, but migrant labor actually dropped off in that year. The number of labor agents in the country increased over the next two years but then dropped off dramatically, from 298 in 1907 to 69 in 1908 and 30 in 1909, in response to new regulations governing recruitment in Lesotho. Regulations requiring labor agents to deposit a substantial sum of money with the Basutoland government effectively reduced the number of unscrupulous agents after 1907.[29] However, at this point the number of BaSotho leaving the country as migrant laborers remained steady in spite of the decreasing numbers of recruiters. The BaSotho had always resisted the efforts of local recruiters, whom they did not trust. Labor agents commonly lied to potential recruits, and when workers did not receive the wages they expected at the mines, they were falsely told that their chiefs had already been paid a portion of the money. When BaSotho men did go to Johannesburg, they preferred to go and engage themselves to employers directly, without the intervention of labor agents.[30]

The mines had difficulty competing with Orange Free State farmers for workers from Lesotho. The BaSotho were reluctant to go underground, forcing advertisers to promise work at the mines which was above ground only.[31] The length of contracts was also an important factor for the BaSotho. Men were unwilling to enter into contracts for long periods of time because of their commitment to agricultural labor in their own fields. It was therefore difficult to hire men for the six-month contracts required by the mines; agents were more successful when contracts were restricted to three or four months.[32] Relative wages were also at issue. During the war the BaSotho had earned as much as £6 per month in the British army, but after the war the Chamber of Mines reduced wages from £3 to 30s. per month. This soon reverted to 50s. to 60s. per month to match the wages paid by farmers. Even then the BaSotho preferred farm work, in part because it was closer to home; mine work only became competitive with farm work as farm wages fell to the level of 15s. to 30s. per month.

Agricultural production and migrant labor: the dilemma of diminishing returns

The BaSotho managed to sustain agricultural production even as they entered into migrant labor and were increasingly dominated and exploited by their chiefs and by regional capitalist interests. Men and women employed many strategies in their endeavors to maintain the viability of their homesteads in the face of this exploitation. After the turn of the century older married men as well as young unmarried men had to migrate to earn an income. Once again the BaSotho demonstrated flexibility in terms of the allocation of labor at home, in order to accommodate the loss of the labor of men who headed homesteads. This was possible because the indispensable labor of men in cultivation was concentrated in the late winter and spring plowing season. Married men arranged their contracts so they could be home for land preparation. Labor shortages at the mines tended to be seasonal, reflecting the temporary withdrawal of the labor of married men at plowing season. Men were no longer available to help women throughout the rest of the year, but they lightened the burden on women by using their wages to buy durable iron pots, cloth skirts, utensils, oils, cosmetics, and salt, so that women no longer had to produce these themselves. Participation in migrant labor was not inspired by new desires for imported commodities or by changing tastes, but by the fact that imported commodities were cheaper than the cost represented by the labor time required to produce these goods locally.

The BaSotho were able to resist going to the mines when wages were low as long as local economic conditions made it possible for them to find productive employment at home. Because of limited natural resources this labor could not be used to sustain agricultural production however, and men were compelled to seek alternative forms of employment in the capitalist sector. The availability of surplus labor made the BaSotho more vulnerable to exploitation abroad and earnings declined.

At the same time the earnings of the migrants were increasingly needed merely for subsistence at home because agriculture alone was no longer capable of supporting many homesteads. Whereas previously labor had been invested abroad for the sake of earning surplus wages, because agricultural production at home could support the homestead, after the turn of the century agriculture was no longer capable of supporting the members of the homestead itself, much less the needs of the worker who went away. The benefits accruing to the local economy from earning capital abroad virtually disappeared. No longer did the wages, now lower, provide surplus income to the homestead which could be invested in agriculture, but were instead needed for taxes and mere subsistence.

The BaSotho then faced the dilemma of diminishing returns to their labor. Both men and women worked harder and harder; women worked harder so men could leave, and men worked harder to help at home and work abroad. The returns to this labor nevertheless declined over time. The land holdings of individual homesteads grew smaller and poorer, which precluded the possibility of continued agricultural expansion. The fact that participation in migrant labor was now necessary led to an increase in the number of migrants and a fall in wages, which in turn caused the migrants to rely more heavily on local agricultural production. The result was a vicious cycle of impoverishment. The BaSotho were able to benefit temporarily from high wages earned abroad, but this was possible only so long as the local economy was viable. Subsequently they were compelled to work as migrant laborers for wages too low to contribute to the diversification and expansion of the local economy.

Migrant labor and gender

Underlying the new allocation of labor which accompanied rising participation in the migrant labor system was the ability of BaSotho men to dominate and control women. Cherryl Walker has provided a useful overview of the important issues in understanding the intersection of gender struggles with labor migrancy in southern Africa.[33] Using Bozzoli's seminal article, Walker notes that "what allowed these societies to export male labour was the system of homestead production in which women were the primary producers."[34] Bozzoli's work raised important theoretical questions about internal domestic struggles over resources, and how the outcomes of these struggles were affected by external forces, which created what she terms a second layer of "external domestic struggle."[35] By analyzing both "internal domestic struggles" and "external domestic struggles" it should be possible, she suggests, to determine why or how "these societies possessed a capacity to subordinate women's labour," which later allowed men to leave as migrant laborers.[36] As Bozzoli notes, "pre-capitalist domestic relations are crucial determinants of the pace and sequence of proletarianisation," but she did not have the data to pursue empirically the nature of these domestic relations and their role in shaping labor migrancy. Bozzoli's discussion is therefore descriptive rather than explanatory, which led Peters to criticize her for presenting a circular argument, that is, that their tight control over women allowed African men to migrate, yet the proof that African women were subject to greater subordination is that men left the land.[37] Bozzoli has indeed failed to explain why and how African men were able to subordinate their women, settling for a mere demonstration that they did so.

The question remains, why did men force women to remain behind on the land while they went out as migrant laborers? It is not sufficient to argue that women were the agricultural workers, since this was a socially-determined gender division of labor which could have been changed, and indeed men, especially young men, had always helped with a significant proportion of agricultural labor. It would have been possible to assign all farming tasks to young men in order to allow women to leave, and agriculture would have been similarly sustained. Women were kept at home not only because of their productive roles, but also because of their indispensable role in biological reproduction.

Women represented for men the provision of social security throughout their lives, especially in their old age. Only upon marriage did men acquire land. This reflected the reasonable social goal of providing land to someone for cultivation, which was to encourage the formation of families which would produce children and strengthen society at large. Once a man had land allocated to him, he retained the use of the land only as long as the land remained under cultivation. If the land remained uncultivated for two years the chief had the right to reallocate the land to someone else. A man's permanent right to land was virtually guaranteed as long as he kept using it, so when he left as a migrant laborer he relied upon his wife to keep his land under cultivation. Even after it became impossible for women to sustain the economic viability of their households through agriculture, and families came to rely more and more upon their portion of the migrant laborer's meager wages, it was essential for the family to work the land to avoid becoming landless.

Migrant workers to South Africa always faced insecurity because of the insidious combination of capitalism and racism. Capitalists did not foster labor migrancy because the supposed self-sufficiency of migrant's families "allowed" them to pay low wages: they did not care about the welfare of these families. The feature of the migrant labor system which allowed the capitalists to pay low wages was that it prevented the stabilization of a labor force which could organize, demand higher wages and better working conditions. Permanent residence in cities would have allowed workers to achieve the political clout of an urban working class and to demand costly social security services, such as health, education, and welfare benefits. The economic cost to employers of labor migrancy was twofold: they bore the

193

costs of continually training new replacement workers, and they bore the cost of paying high wages to white workers because they prevented black workers from becoming skilled. These costs were more than outweighed by the economic advantages of preventing labor organization which would have eventually led to high wages and costly benefits for all workers regardless of color. Apartheid was not only compatible with capitalism, it reduced costs and increased capitalist profits. Apartheid and the migrant labor system compelled Africans to retain links to the land as a form of social security in the event of unemployment, disability, and old age.

African men and women could count on social security in their old age only if they had land and children. The association of children with social security in old age is universal, and even modern welfare systems do not provide adequate security for elderly people without children. Gaining control over biological reproduction in order to have children was a compelling reason for BaSotho men to control their wives. This control was best assured when women were kept at home on the land, which served the dual purpose of ensuring the man's land rights. Some women resisted male control and migrated across the border into South Africa against the will of BaSotho men, but most acquiesced to male control and stayed behind, working the land and bearing and raising children. Why did these women acquiesce? The choices for BaSotho women were even worse than those of the men. Across the border were no opportunities for advancement, but a brutal system of exploitation which left women exposed and unprotected against the abuses of racism and sexism.[38] The price for personal independence and autonomy from the control of a MoSotho husband was high, and implicitly entailed the potential of violent subjection to any and all men at their will in the cities. Life in rural areas was difficult for women, but the ravages of overwork and hunger were balanced by the promise, however elusive, of the security implicit in access to land and bearing children to provide for one's old age.

Labor migrancy became intricately interwoven into the life stages of the BaSotho. Young men worked to earn their bridewealth which in turn gave them access to land. For a man, the application of his wife's labor to his land brought at least the promise of social security and at best the potential for surplus grain which could be traded for livestock that in turn would become bridewealth for a son one day. Even as BaSotho economy and society were increasingly governed both by the interference and burden of colonial rule, and by the regional political economy through the tentacles of the migrant labor system, the cycle of production and reproduction which provided security and potential for wealth continued.

14

In pursuit of security

Throughout the nineteenth century the BaSotho strove to protect and improve the quality of their lives. Political and economic developments within the country reflected a universal pursuit of security. The BaSotho were successful in innovating and adapting as necessary, and in achieving political and social unity and economic growth. However, given a political context marked by overt conflicts over land, their efforts to sustain prosperity, achieve a rising standard of living, and reduce their economic insecurity were doomed to failure. The hard work of the BaSotho could not possibly overcome the long-term negative economic effects of their loss of arable land despite their short-term successes. Because of events outside their control the BaSotho ultimately failed to sustain the economic viability of their households and their nation into the twentieth century. Nevertheless, it is important to recognize that the BaSotho adapted to meet every challenge, from their adoption of plows and firearms and horses to their move into the mountains.

The struggle to achieve and sustain economic and social security in the face of environmental and human threats was a constant feature in the experience of the BaSotho and their ancestors. The BaSotho did not begin to work hard only with the advent of European markets and Christianity; the work patterns of the BaSotho clearly pre-dated the nineteenth century. The political context changed, however, which required new strategies in the pursuit of security. The BaSotho emerged from the widespread disruption of the 1820s by forging a kingdom through the consolidation of chiefdoms under Moshoeshoe. Throughout the middle of the nineteenth century the BaSotho sought both to restrain the power of chiefs and to protect the kingdom's sovereignty. The creation of colonial Basutoland represented a compromise with regard to both goals, as the people lost leverage and the chiefs' powers were reinforced, and territorial integrity was retained only under British colonial protection. Just as many BaSotho had sacrificed political independence to acquire Moshoeshoe's protection, so they now won British protection at the price of independence. The choices of the BaSotho in the nineteenth century reflected a universal human dilemma, in which security – whether military, economic, or social – could only be achieved through trade-offs which entailed social, economic, and political costs. The BaSotho achieved political security only by supporting a strong centralized government which demanded taxation, tribute, and the sacrifice of individual and group autonomy.

The BaSotho continually demonstrated their resilience, surviving taxation, tribute labor, migrant labor, and the depredations of their precolonial and colonial rulers. On their own initiative they turned mountainous land into pastures and villages, adapting agriculture to a harsh climate and rocky terrain as they pushed into the mountains. Moshoeshoe and his sons made use of missionary support and guidance in their conduct of international politics, and the missionaries expanded their influence over time. The body of converts remained small throughout the nineteenth century, and their concerns were sidelined by the traditional concerns of chiefs, but Christianity provided a new ideology for a small western-educated elite which emerged in the twentieth century as an effective force in politics and society.

The political achievements of the BaSotho were remarkable. In one form or another, the polity built around Moshoeshoe's chiefdom survived from the 1820s to the present day. Small chiefdoms gave way to a large nation in which the supreme political authority, Moshoeshoe, was accepted as representing and protecting the interests of the nation at large. The nationalism of Moshoeshoe was not an ethnically-exclusive nationalism, but one that cut across linguistic and cultural boundaries. People from many chiefdoms speaking many languages offered their allegiance to Moshoeshoe, and became BaSotho by virtue of the fact that they identified themselves as BaSotho and as subjects of Moshoeshoe. Moshoeshoe himself symbolized the cultural openness and breadth which Europeans in South Africa have so long sought to deny, and prevent, among black South Africans. A man of his times, when the cultural, linguistic, social, and political boundaries between Africans were fluid, Moshoeshoe was fluent in both SeSotho and IsiZulu, and could speak directly with every one of his followers hailing from every corner of the region.[1] Beneath the apparent cultural unity of modern Lesotho there are still traces of these diverse, multicultural origins: IsiXhosa is still spoken in parts of the South, and IsiZulu is still spoken in various mountain areas. Symbolic and representative of the historic processes of incorporation, amalgamation, and nation-building is the village of HaChopo (Thaba Phutsoa) in the mountainous Mokhotlong district. Almost one hundred years after he migrated as a youth, in the 1880s, from the Natal area into Lesotho, Chief Moetsuoa Mohlahloe Mzwane (b. 1873) continued to insist that his people speak to him in IsiZulu, even though he was fluent in SeSotho which had become the language of his people.[2] Different styles of building evident in different parts of the country also reflect the diverse cultural origins of the BaSotho. In spite of their diverse regional and cultural origins, the BaSotho achieved national unity and cultural assimilation in the nineteenth century. Civil wars in the nineteenth century and political tensions in the twentieth century have reflected power struggles within the ruling elite, but there have never been any internal struggles originating from "ethnic" rivalry.[3]

Political power in Lesotho in the early nineteenth century was based on the unequal distribution of wealth which in turn was engendered by many factors: control over natural resources, skill in raiding cattle, success in defending cattle and crops, and ultimately, control over people. Success in raids and defense was often a function of a chief's ability to organize many people in military expeditions, which reflected his level of political power. Thus political power and control over wealth were mutually dependent and mutually reinforcing; moreover, both were predicated upon and facilitated the achievement of control over people. Socioeconomic stratification and exploitative relationships within BaSotho society caused conflicts of interest between the rich and the poor and between men and women. Degrees of socioeconomic inequality and exploitation varied over the course of the century, however. As people from all levels of society worked hard to accumulate wealth through production and trade following the disruptions of the 1820s, the gap between rich and poor narrowed. The specialization in craftwork and concomitant trade in locally-produced goods, as well as the consumption of selected imports appropriate to the given economic conditions reflected deliberate BaSotho efforts to enhance their productivity through careful choices in production and trade activities. At the same time, social and political links were forged through marriages, as bridewealth obligations tied together the kin groups of husbands and wives and tied clients to their patrons.

Only when further economic growth became impossible at the end of the nineteenth century did the chiefs acquire both the incentive and the opportunity to monopolize wealth and exploit their people more harshly. The BaSotho resisted their chiefs by using the missionaries and colonial authorities to protect themselves from heavy demands for tribute labor from chiefs. The BaSotho nevertheless made a conscious choice to submit to their chiefs rather than to rebel entirely, because they saw that only through the collective authority imposed by the chiefs could their nation survive.

Temporary economic expansion and subsequent economic failure in Lesotho occurred in the context of changing relations between the chiefs and their people, and also in the context of changing relations between the nation and the European settler population. After the turmoil of the 1820s, as before, the BaSotho worked hard to produce enough food to ward off famine and chronic hunger. They had always produced surpluses for storage as a means to avoid famine in times of crop failure, and the BaSotho expanded agricultural production in the late 1820s and the 1830s initially to increase their food security rather than in response to market incentives. During this period they also built up their herds of cattle by trading part of their surpluses to other Africans. Later in the 1840s agricultural expansion

197

was further fuelled by the demand for grain and cattle among Europeans. The willingness of the BaSotho to work hard is underlined by the fact that the early agricultural boom took place in the absence of technological innovation: the BaSotho did not begin to use plows until the 1850s.

Both market expansion and the ox-drawn plow arrived at an opportune time for the BaSotho. Extensive land expropriation had not yet taken place, so that the continued expansion of cultivation was possible through the conversion of land from pastoral to arable use. The adoption of the plow did not decrease labor but rather increased it. Both men and women had to work longer and harder as larger and larger fields were brought under cultivation, and they did so willingly to increase the level of household production. Women eventually came to insist that their future husbands have plows and know how to use them, in the full knowledge that their own work would increase as more fields were brought under cultivation.[4] They were motivated by the desire to increase the overall resources of the homestead and thereby reduce their own vulnerability to famine or hunger, since women and children were often the first to be deprived of food in times of scarcity.

Early BaSotho participation in migratory labor reflected a choice based on fluctuating economic and political incentives and disincentives. When the decision to work abroad was made based on household needs, as opposed to political goals decided at a higher level, rational economic decision-making is evident. The BaSotho did not choose to work as migrant laborers because they had developed new tastes for European-made goods. Rather, the BaSotho could acquire the goods they needed more easily and cheaply by earning cash wages to buy them from traders, than by producing the goods themselves or getting them from local craft specialists. The BaSotho did not prefer European clothing. Leather clothing and blankets were more durable and much warmer than European clothes, but they were expensive and difficult to acquire. The first to wear European clothes were the indigent, who gathered at mission stations and were given clothing by the missionaries. European dress was initially associated not only with foreign white missionaries, but also with the poor. The association of European clothing with Christianity actually inhibited the wider adoption of European dress at an early date.

To acquire a skin garment a person had to own an animal, slaughter it, spend the equivalent of a month preparing the skin, and probably pay a specialist to sew it into an article of clothing. By selling surplus grain or working abroad on European farms or at the mines, a MoSotho could earn enough cash to buy a comparable article of imported clothing in much less time. As a result, the cost of supporting local craftsmen was too high for BaSotho consumers to bear willingly. The import of cheap European goods hurt BaSotho craft specialists, but it also allowed many poorer people to acquire goods which they could not have afforded otherwise. Local producers stayed in business by specializing further. Instead of manufacturing items that were available from traders, they avoided direct competition and made custom-designed and luxury goods. Buying goods which had previously been made at home allowed some members of the household to reallocate their labor either to agricultural production or to migrant labor.

In addition, traditional BaSotho military technology offered little protection against rifle-bearing horsemen. The accumulation of horses and guns was therefore a priority for all Africans throughout the years of direct military confrontation with Europeans.

BaSotho participation in the migrant labor system was initially voluntary, but it did not remain so for long. The story of the BaSotho in the nineteenth century is the story of a people increasingly unable to sustain the political and economic viability of their nation. At the same time that Africans were reaching the limits of agricultural expansion because European conquest limited the land resources of African societies, the same Europeans also closed off other options and opportunities to Africans. Africans were legally deprived of the right to stake out claims to the newly-discovered mineral wealth of southern Africa, as European speculators flooded the area of the diamond diggings and gold reefs. Africans were allowed to participate in the exploitation of South Africa's natural wealth only as wage laborers. Mining was consolidated in the hands of white industrialists at the same time that the BaSotho were losing their ability to choose the terms and conditions under which they would work.

In South Africa, a white-dominated society characterized by deeply-rooted racism decreed that the primary victims of capitalist exploitation should be black Africans, and white workers would be protected against the worst effects of industrialization. As in other societies, workers who provided the labor for the emergence of capitalist industry worked long hours for wages too low to support a family. Elsewhere, however, workers settled permanently in cities and organized unions to demand higher wages and better working conditions. In South Africa, white capitalists in the late nineteenth century had been willing to hire black workers for jobs that were later designated as skilled labor, as long as they remained powerless and therefore cheap. Racism and the evolving apartheid system ensured that these better jobs and higher wages were protected for white workers by social decree and white solidarity, but black workers were unable to withdraw their labor in response to low wages once farming at home was no longer viable. The migrant labor system, like apartheid later, then came to suit the capitalists well, for it ensured that black South African workers would remain temporary, unorganized, and powerless.

Because their nation was politically and economically weak, the BaSotho were faced with the choice of submitting to British colonial rule which offered them some measure of protection, or risking the forced incorporation of Lesotho into the Orange Free State, with the consequent loss of their territorial integrity and limited sovereignty. Colonial rule never did provide the security that Moshoeshoe had been seeking when he requested British protection. Under Cape Colony rule, the BaSotho were threatened

199

with land expropriation by their own "protectors." Greater security was achieved with the return to direct Imperial rule in 1884, but the price was high. The BaSotho were forced to cooperate with their British rulers in every way or risk abandonment. After the British victory over the Boers in 1902, British strategic interests in Basutoland came to an end. The Boer interest in the remaining fertile land of Lesotho never disappeared, however, and most BaSotho believed that they could resist incorporation into South Africa only with the continued support of the British. This dependence further constrained their ability to resist exploitation at home and in the regional economic system.

Subject to British colonial rule and enmeshed in the vagaries of labor migrancy, men more than ever felt the need to control women. Women provided men with children, with agricultural labor, and with household goods and services. They ensured that men, compelled by political and economic forces to join the migrant labor system, would always have the security of land and family waiting at home when they were unemployed, sick, or old. If the resources at home were scarce and inadequate, they were more than was available across the border where all social and economic security was denied to Africans. The imperatives of production and reproduction within Lesotho became more apparent to men as men's vulnerability became more and more evident in South Africa. Men's dependence on women prompted their efforts to control women, which suited the goals of British officials who wanted only to ensure the social and political stability and economic viability of Basutoland. The economic viability of the colony was already an illusion by the turn of the twentieth century, as individual households and the colonial government relied on migrant worker wages for household sustenance and colonial taxes. The interests of British colonial officials, South African officials, and BaSotho men converged in seeking to institute greater controls over BaSotho women. The choices available to women were even more restricted: with few legitimate or legal employment opportunities for women outside of Lesotho, they faced a bleak life at home or an insecure life in the cities of South Africa; in both cases their health and welfare were always at risk. There was no security and no escape for women.

The recognition of exploitation did not cause the BaSotho to rebel against their chiefs, nor women against men, in the nineteenth century and since. This acquiescence was not the result of ignorance or complacency. The failure to rebel can only be understood with reference to BaSotho perceptions of their circumstances and limited options. People's actions are guided by their consciousness, and when they make decisions to acquiesce in oppression it is not necessarily because they fail to recognize their own interests or are the unwitting dupes of leaders or rulers. When conflicts between social classes lead to change they are readily identifiable as dynamic historical forces. When underlying socioeconomic and political conflicts do *not* lead to change, however, it is not sufficient to attribute this lack of change either to a lack of consciousness on the part of the people or to a monopoly of power in the hands of the ruling classes. The imperative of national security has also been a driving force in history because societies do not develop in isolation. National allegiance may impede or retard class struggle, but it is not just a propaganda tool used by rulers to manipulate their subjects. Recognizing that all BaSotho were vulnerable in the face of white unification in South Africa, the BaSotho made conscious choices to support their chiefs which shaped their destiny in the nineteenth century and after. Similarly, most BaSotho women continued to believe that their interests were best served by loyalty to male kin and family structures even though these were restrictive and exploitative of women.

The unification of Lesotho in the nineteenth century shows what has been and can be achieved by black South Africans. The linguistic and cultural diversity of Africans in South Africa has been used to question the ability of Africans to maintain unity and stability in a democratic state based on universal black suffrage. However, it has been necessary for the white government to reinforce and strengthen ethnic and linguistic divisions among the black population systematically and artificially, precisely because the historical tendency of Africans in South Africa since the nineteenth century has been towards unification and assimilation. In the nineteenth century political boundaries were fluid and were not constrained by language divisions or by descent group affiliation. The concept of ethnicity is ambiguous in this context; "tribalism" or "ethnicity" became an artificially-created tool of white domination. The capacity of Africans to overcome a narrow sense of identity and build African nationalism in South Africa was already evident in nineteenth-century Lesotho. Segregation and apartheid in South Africa attempted to freeze social and cultural boundaries which had previously been open and ambiguous, and deliberately hindered African unification and organization which would have allowed Africans to attain power. The past, present, and future of the BaSotho are consequently tied to the fate of all black South Africans. Moreover, the ancestors of the BaSotho hailed from every corner of South Africa, so that the BaSotho of today are kin with all black South Africans. Over one hundred years later, many BaSotho of Lesotho retain their knowledge of and yearning for ancestral homes across a border which was established under alien colonial rule. As regional transformation occurs, the severe restraints imposed by regional politics on the choices and actions of the BaSotho at home will be eased, and the people can finally begin to overcome the poverty and political oppression which have plagued them for over a century.

Appendix

Oral sources

The criteria I used for finding informants for oral research in economic history were necessarily different from criteria employed in choosing informants knowledgeable about political history or specific events. For this fieldwork I was not primarily interested in retrieving oral traditions, which are transmitted over generations and tend to contain limited information, such as genealogies and chronicles of migrations or wars. Rather I was interested in creating a body of evidence of oral history, collected from living eyewitnesses to the events and periods and evidence they discussed, which generated information relevant to the study of economic and social history not available in the public record, whether written or oral. People interviewed for the purposes of this study did not need to have any specialized training or information about the past, nor did they have to be eyewitnesses to a specific event. Instead, people were chosen primarily on the basis of age: because they were being interviewed about their own families, as far back as they could remember, informants could be virtually any willing old people who were still clear in their memories and present perceptions.

The use of old age as a criterion for the selection of informants may have influenced the data if, for example, rich people outlive poor people because they have better access to food and health services throughout their lives and in old age. Unfortunately this bias could not be remedied, but I gathered evidence from the informants which might allow me to determine a bias based on socioeconomic status. To some extent this information was evident in the answers to general questions designed to identify the person interviewed; for example, who were your parents and grandparents? where did they come from? how many wives did your father have? how many fields did your grandparents and parents have? how much livestock did they have? These data provided a profile of the informant's background and ultimately a profile of the entire pool of informants which suggests that among my informants wealthy people were disproportionately, but not exclusively, represented. This information has to be carefully assessed and used to determine its accuracy and legitimacy, since it could have been biased by the unwillingness of an informant to reveal the poverty of his or her family. However, my experience suggests that informants did not hesitate to indicate when their fathers owned little or no livestock, a key indicator of wealth in Lesotho for the period under investigation.

My experience strongly suggests that ordinary people made the best informants of this kind of study, and it was in some ways difficult to interview people who had specialized knowledge in oral traditions or recent historical events. It was sometimes difficult to convince such people that information about their families and early lives was as important to me as information about the early political history of the country. For example, whereas most people did not question the wisdom of discussing agriculture, one person who had played a prominent role in politics offered the dismissive comment, "agriculture is agriculture; ask me something important!"

I made a considerable effort to interview people from as many different geographic regions as possible. Regional similarities can confirm the applicability of information from one area to another, while regional variation sometimes reflected the diffusion of economic change I was attempting to trace. The need to interview people from many different places meant it was necessary to interview a relatively large number of people, even if the information in the end tended to be duplicated many times over. Because the evidence of a single person cannot be taken alone as representative of a given area, I interviewed several people from each area. The size of my pool of informants does not allow for statistical analysis, but does confirm the extent to which generalizations can, and sometimes cannot, be drawn from the sample. During my fieldwork in 1981 and 1982 I interviewed over eighty informants, but several interview tapes were subsequently discarded because it was obvious that the memories of the informants were impaired. Because the information sought was neither threatening nor controversial, I encountered no problems with tape recording every interview. All interviews were conducted orally by myself and my assistant, Malete Mokhethi, in SeSotho, and the interviews took the form of unstructured discussions with no pre-determined questions or sequence of questions. Questions which were used to initiate discussions were open-ended, and people were encouraged to talk as long as they wished about the material aspects of the lives of their families when they were young, with only occasional questions to elicit further explanations or details about the subject under discussion, or to raise a new line of enquiry when appropriate. The length of interviews thus varied from less than an hour to several hours depending on the responsiveness of the person being interviewed. Copies of all tapes have been deposited at the BOLESWA Archives, Library of the National University of Lesotho. Subsequent interviews conducted in 1988 and 1989 were part of a later study with a different focus, and have not been used for this book.

Appendix

Informants

The following people were interviewed in 1981 and 1982. Dates of birth are approximate, determined by the known events associated with the year of birth.

1 'Mamphoho Peshoani, f., b. 1904 at Phameng, Maseru District. Interviewed at HaMaama, Maseru District, December 14, 1981.

2 'Mamoerane Rakhele, f., b. 1912 at Masitise, Quthing District. Interviewed at HaMaama, Maseru District, December 14, 1981.

3 'Masekotoana Lelakane, f., b. 1900 at HaJobo, Maseru District. Interviewed at HaMaama, Maseru District, December 14, 1981.

4 Lefaufau Maama, f., b. 1896 at HaMaama, Maseru District. Interviewed at HaMaama, Maseru District, December 14 and 16, 1981.

5 'Mantele Mishaka, f., b. 1899 at HaMishaka, Maseru District. Interviewed at HaMaama, Maseru District, December 16, 1981.

6 'Masebabatso Theko, f., b. 1903 at Matebeleng, Maseru District. Interviewed at HaMaama, Maseru District, December 16, 1981.

7 Tsehla Maime, m., b. 1896 at HaMishaka, Maseru District. Interviewed at HaMotanyane, Maseru District, January 12, 1982.

8 Lintso Motanyane, m., b. 1905 at HaMotanyane, Maseru District. Interviewed at HaMotanyane, Maseru District, January 12, 1982.

9 Dixon Rafutho, m., b. 1890 at Thabu Bosiu, Maseru District. Interviewed at Thaba Bosiu, Maseru District, January 14, 1982.

10 Azael Lehau, m., b. 1902 at HaKhoabane (Thaba Bosiu), Maseru District. Interviewed at Thaba Bosiu, Maseru District, January 14, 1982.

11 'Mathakane Matooane, f., b. 1890 at Thupa-Khoali, Maseru District. Interviewed at Thaba Bosiu, Maseru District, January 14, 1982.

12 Moleko Thateli, m., b. 1898 at Thaba Bosiu, Maseru District. Interviewed at Thaba Bosiu, Maseru District, January 14, 1982.

13 Lineo Koromo, f., b. 1916 at HaRamabele (Matsieng), Maseru District. Interviewed at Matsieng, Maseru District, January 29, 1982.

14 'Maisaka Mokeke, f., b. 1912 at HaTake (Matsieng), Maseru District. Interviewed at Matsieng, Maseru District, January 29, 1982.

15 Lipolelo Ramonyai, f., b. 1911 at Matsieng, Maseru District. Interviewed at Matsieng, Maseru District, January 29, 1982.

16 'Matsuonyane Malefane, f., b. 1903 at Thaba Tsoeu, Mafeteng District. Interviewed at Ha Mantsebo, Maseru District, January 30, 1982.

17 Sekaute Letle, m., b. 1896 at Makeneng, Maseru District. Interviewed at HaMantsebo, Maseru District, January 30, 1982.

18 Lehlohonolo Kele, m., b. 1913 at Makhoakhoeng, Butha Buthe District. Interviewed at HaMantsebo, Maseru District, January 30, 1982.

19 Moeketsi Moseeka, m., b. 1898 at HaSebete, Maseru District. Interviewed at HaToloane, Maseru District, February 6, 1982.

20 Nkane Azariel Kaka, m., b. 1908 at Thaba Chitja (Morija), Maseru District. Interviewed at Thaba Chitja, Maseru District, March 3, 1982.

21 Tsoeu Temeki, m., b. 1882 at HaTemeki, Maseru District. Interviewed at HaTemeki, Maseru District, March 3, 1982.

22 Joel Pharoe Moeno, m., b. 1908 at Masite, Maseru District. Interviewed at HaMajane, Maseru District, March 8, 1982.

23 Kopano Jeremiah Telo, m., b. 1910 at HaMokaoli, Maseru District. Interviewed at HaMokaoli, Maseru District, March 8, 1982.

24 Molikeng Motseki, m., b. 1899 at HaBereng, Maseru District. Interviewed at HaMokaoli, Maseru District, March 8, 1982.

25 'Mamothobi Mphosi, f., b. 1891, Quthing District. Interviewed at Tsupani, Maseru District, March 26, 1982.

26 Francina Phalatse, f., b. 1899 at Hermon, Mafeteng District. Interviewed at HaMphobe, Mafeteng District, March 26, 1982.

27 'Mamotoai Letsosa, f., b. 1892 at Thaba Pechela, Mafeteng District. Interviewed at HaNtanyele, Mafeteng District, March 26, 1982.

28 'Mampeo Ranteme, f., b. 1896 at Rabeleng, Mafeteng District. Interviewed at HaNtanyele, Mafeteng District, March 26, 1982.

29 'Mamolikeng Motoai, f., b. 1890 at Phoqoane, Mafeteng District. Interviewed at Ha Rapaulo, Mafeteng District, March 26, 1982.

30 'Makoloti Koloti, f., b. 1902 at HaLebona, Mafeteng District. Interviewed at Likhotlong, Mohale's Hoek District, March 30, 1982.

31 'Mabatho Serobanyane, f., b. 1894 at Kubake, Mohale's Hoek District. Interviewed at Likhotlong, Mohale's Hoek District, March 30, 1982.

32 Selbourne Moeketsi Lefoka, m., b. 1906 at Lithoteng, Mohale's Hoek District. Interviewed at Likhotlong, Mohale's Hoek District, March 30, 1982.

33 Moselantza Sehloho, f., b. 1890 at HaMapetla, Maseru District. Interviewed at Likhotlong, Mohale's Hoek District, March 30, 1982.

34 'Malibote Makoetlane, f., b. 1891 at Thabana Morena, Mafeteng District. Interviewed at Likhotlong, Mohale's Hoek District, March 30, 1982.

35 Thabo Fako, m., b. 1898 at Sefikeng, Berea District. Interviewed at Tsoelike, Qacha's Nek District, April 14, 1982.

36 Mpinane Makhaola, f., b. 1890 at Tebetebeng, Berea District. Interviewed at Makhaola, Qacha's Nek District, April 14, 1982.

37 'Mafesi Makhaola, f., b. 1890 at Thaba Maboloka, Mafeteng District. Interviewed at Makhaola, Qacha's Nek District, April 14, 1982.

38 'Mamapote Kobile, f., b. 1890 at HaMohlapiso, Qacha's Nek District. Interviewed at Makhaola, Qacha's Nek District, April 14, 1982.

39 Lira Motlhotlo Khalala, m., b. 1899 at Kubung, Quthing District. Interviewed at Makhaola, Qacha's Nek District, April 14, 1982.

40 Rosalia Tlali, f., b. 1900 at Moyeni, Quthing District. Interviewed at White Hill, Qacha's Nek District, April 15, 1982.

41   Kichinane Ratoronko, m., b. 1899 at HaRatoronko, Qacha's Nek District. Interviewed at HaRatoronko, Qacha's Nek District, April 15, 1982.

42   Ntobobaki J. Matabane, m., b. 1898 at HaRatoronko, Qacha's Nek District. Interviewed at HaRatoronko, Qacha's Nek District, April 15, 1982.

43   'Mafrancina Matabane, f., b. 1902 at Thaba Tsoeu, Mafeteng District. Interviewed at HaRatoronko, Qacha's Nek District, April 15, 1982.

44   'Malipere Tjamela, f., b. 1898 at Makhaola, Qacha's Nek District. Interviewed at HaBulara (HaRafolatsane), Mokhotlong District, April 21, 1982.

45   Monyoe Makibitle, m., b. 1891, Leribe District. Interviewed at Thabang, Mokhotlong District, April 22, 1982.

46   'Matsekoa Motleleng, f., b. 1880 at Thabang, Mokhotlong District. Interviewed at Thabang, Mokhotlong District, April 22, 1982.

47   Moetsuoa Mohlahloe Mzwane, m., b. 1873, Natal. Interviewed at HaChopo (Thaba Phutsoa), Mokhotlong District, April 23, 1982.

48   'Matsitso Mosoang, f., b. 1899, Mafeteng District. Interviewed at Salang, Mokhotlong District, April 26, 1982.

49   'Matsela Tooai, f., b. 1891 at Matsieng, Maseru District. Interviewed at Moyeni, Quthing District, May 31, 1982.

50   'Mathotoane Mpobole, f., b. 1882 at HaJankie, Quthing District. Interviewed at HaJankie, Quthing District, May 31, 1982.

51   Morai Moeletsi, m., b. 1900 at Pontseng-HaNkuebe (Sebapala), Quthing District. Interviewed at HaNkuebe, Quthing District, June 1, 1982.

52   'Mamohloli Nkuebe, f., b. 1889 at Hamohajane, Quthing District. Interviewed at HaNkuebe, Quthing District, June 1, 1982.

53   Mohau Nkuebe, f., b. 1889 at HaNkuebe, Quthing District. Interviewed at HaNkuebe, Quthing District, June 1, 1982.

54   Miriam Mothata, f., b. 1891 at HaMaunyane (Fort Hartley), Quthing District. Interviewed at Pokane (Fort Hartley), Quthing District, June 1, 1982.

55   Setabele Morahanya, m., b. 1901 at Qabanyane, Mohale's Hoek District. Interviewed at Pokane, Quthing District, June 1, 1982.

56   Maria Tsekuoa, f., b. 1892 at Kubung, Quthing District. Interviewed at Masitise, Quthing District, June 2, 1982.

57   'Makhetsi Khetsi, f., b. 1891 at Mohale's Hoek (Camp), Mohale's Hoek District. Interviewed at HaPotsane, Mohale's Hoek District, June 2, 1982.

58   Masimphole Mokoaleli, m., b. 1898 at HaPotsane, Mohale's Hoek District. Interviewed at HaPotsane, Mohale's Hoek District, June 2, 1982.

59   'Mamoeketsi Mokoaleli, f., b. 1899 at HaPotsane, Mohale's Hoek District. Interviewed at HaPotsane, Mohale's Hoek District, June 2, 1982.

60 'Mateba Sokosoko, f., b. 1898 at Maboloka, Mohale's Hoek District. Interviewed at HaPotsane, Mohale's Hoek District, June 2, 1982.

61 Moratehi Jankie, m., b. 1890 at Hatitipana, Leribe District. Interviewed at Hatitipana (Leribe), Leribe District, June 7, 1982.

62 Marika Mosuoe Kukame, m., b. 1896 at Nqechane, Leribe District. Interviewed at Nqechane, Leribe District, June 7, 1982.

63 'Mataelo Nkhethoa, f., b. 1890 at Tsikoane, Leribe District. Interviewed at Leribe, Leribe District, June 8, 1982.

64 'Mahoki Mokitlane, f., b. 1892 at Lekhalo la Mantsi, Qwaqwa. Interviewed at Leribe, Leribe District, June 8, 1982.

65 Malefetsane Motiea, m., b. 1892 at HaSekhunyana, Leribe District. Interviewed at HaSekhunyana, Leribe District, June 8, 1982.

66 'Majoseph Molapo, f., b. 1891 at Lekhooana, Leribe District. Interviewed at HaMopeli, Butha Buthe District, July 12, 1982.

67 Setene Lenela, m., b. 1899 at HaMopeli, Butha Buthe District. Interviewed at Majakaneng, Butha Buthe District, July 12, 1982.

68 'Mamopeli Sello f., b. 1896 at Mohalinyane, Mohale's Hoek District. Interviewed at HaMopeli, Butha Buthe District, July 12, 1982.

69 'Mataelo Ramotoka, f., b. 1899 at Marakabei, Maseru District. Interviewed at HaMopeli, Butha Buthe District, July 12, 1982.

70 Joshua Kengkeng Marake, m., b. 1902 at Thabana Mokhele, Butha Buthe District. Interviewed at Makopo (Camp), Butha Buthe District, July 12, 1982.

71 Mahlatsoane Seboche, m., b. 1896 at HaJonathane, Leribe. Interviewed at HaSeboche, Butha Buthe District, July 13, 1982.

72 'Mapula Letsika Matela, f., b. 1902 at Qholaqhoe, Butha Buthe District. Interviewed at HaSeboche, Butha Buthe District, July 13, 1982.

73 'Mateko Mpoka, f., b. 1883 at HaRasebitsoa, Leribe District. Interviewed near HaSeboche, Butha Buthe District, July 13, 1982.

74 'Masekhokoane Fani, f., b. 1881 at Fobane, Leribe District. Interviewed at HaPokane, Butha Buthe District, July 13, 1982.

75 Nerea Molapo, f., b. 1891 at Makhoakhoeng, Leribe District. Interviewed at HaRampai, Leribe District, July 13, 1982.

76 Leemisa Mpiti Tsosane, m., b. 1879 at Witsieshoek, Qwaqwa. Interviewed at Ha Rampai, Leribe District, July 13, 1982.

77 Teko Lebeoa Mainoane, m., b. 1893 at Levi's Nek, Leribe. Interviewed at HaNkhasa, Leribe District, July 14, 1982.

78 'Mankaea Mohatlane, f., b. 1886 at HaMasupha, Berea District. Interviewed at HaMamathe, Berea District, July 14, 1982.

79 'Masekake Thamae, f., b. 1887 at Thupa Kubu, Maseru District. Interviewed at HaMamathe, Berea District, July 14, 1982.

80 'Mamotopo Lephema, f., b. 1894 at HaNotsi (HaKoali), Berea District. Interviewed at HaLebusa, Berea District, July 14, 1982.

Notes

1 Introduction

1 The name Lesotho was the indigenous term referring to the nation of Moshoeshoe in the nineteenth century. It continued in use among both BaSotho and Europeans even after the British substituted the name Basutoland in the colonial period.

2 Andrew Manson, "Conflict on the Eastern Highveld Southern Kalahari, c. 1750–1820." Paper presented at the University of the Witwatersrand, conference on "The 'Mfecane' Aftermath: Towards a New Paradigm," 6–9 September 1991, *passim.*

3 Eldredge, "Slave-Raiding across the Cape Frontier." This information emerges from San and SeTswana oral history and oral traditions reported by early British travellers in the area.

4 These developments remain a fertile ground for further historical exploration and analysis. I reject the Eurocentric slave-raiding thesis put forth by Cobbing to explain Zulu state formation and conflicts in the interior because of strong evidence which indicates that extensive slave-trading out of Delagoa Bay began only after 1823. However, like Cobbing, I reject earlier misinterpretations of the causes of disruptions in the early nineteenth century, which besides other problems were falsely Zulucentric. I consequently reject the term *"mfecane"* because it is misconceived, of ambiguous origins, and supports false renditions of southern African history, with serious damaging consequences in modern South Africa. Unlike Cobbing I seek an explanation for dramatic sociopolitical change in this period in a complex interplay of environment, production, trade, and politics over a longer time frame. See Cobbing, "The Mfecane as Alibi"; and Eldredge, "Sources of Conflict in Southern Africa."

5 Peires, "The British and the Cape."

6 Eldredge, "Drought, Famine and Disease."

7 I have borrowed this idea and perspective from Feierman, *Peasant Intellectuals.*

8 Kimble, "Labour Migration in Basutoland."

9 I use the term reproduction loosely here, acknowledging the dangers set out by Harris and Young on the other hand, but finding the term appropriate and useful, albeit intentionally ambiguous, on the other hand. I do not mean to imply acceptance of any underlying meanings other than those explicitly stated here. See Harris and Young, "Engendered Structures."

10 Eldredge, "Women in Production."

11 My argument differs from that of Colin Bundy and others who have described a rise and subsequent fall in South African "peasant" production which they attributed to trans-formations in African agricultural production that arose in the context of the European presence and influence. Bundy described a positive African reaction to the European market for agricultural produce (the "rise" of the peasantry), followed by European expropriation of land and an inevitable "fall" in African productivity. I am concerned to show the

208

intricacies of the African economy, including production and inter-African trade in cattle and grain, and in metals and manufactured goods, before European contact. The evidence of early African production and trade demonstrates a continuity in the innovativeness and responsiveness of Africans, which is interpreted in the existing literature as an African reaction to Europeans. For an example of the criticisms aimed at Bundy for his lack of attention to the internal dynamics of African societies, see the review by Judy Kimble in *Journal of Peasant Studies*, 9, 4 (1982), 286–290.

12 Notable works which incorporate oral research and strong empirical evidence into their analyses include Pieres, *The House of Phalo*; Bonner, *Kings, Commoners and Concessionaires*; Beinart, *Political Economy of Pondoland*.

13 Kahn, "Marxist Anthropology"; and Kahn and Llobera, "Towards a New Marxism"; and Bloch, *Marxism and Anthropology*, pp. 141–172.

14 Guy, "Analysing Pre-Capitalist Societies," p. 19.

15 *Ibid.*, p. 21.

16 *Ibid.*, p. 22.

17 *Ibid.*, p. 27. For Guy, the only value which could be increased in pre-capitalist societies was labor-power. He sees labor-power, rather than a material product, as the only value which could be produced in surplus, thereby increasing, cyclically, the productive and reproductive capacities of women at a man's disposal. Guy, "Gender oppression," p. 39. In trying to offer a broad, general analysis of "the oppression of women amongst southern African farming peoples south of the Limpopo, in the era before colonial subjugation" Guy is even less empirical and historical in this article than in his earlier work, and his assertions and conclusions are even more tenuous.

18 Meillassoux, *Maidens, Meal and Money*, p. 72. Meillassoux reasserted the validity of his 1981 arguments about the domestic community in his more recent work, *The Anthropology of Slavery*, p. 24 and *passim*.

19 For a discussion of this process in central Africa see Vansina, *Paths in the Rainforests*, pp. 105–106. Note that Vansina seeks to determine the relevance of kinship terminology to sociopolitical organization, but does not see kinship as determining these relations nor kinship terms necessarily reflecting these relations.

20 Meillassoux himself acknowledges the potential significance of outside factors, but only in passing without pursuing the issue. Hence when asking whether the contradictions he identified in pre-capitalist societies based on gender and struggles for control over reproduction were sufficient to generate change and transform "domestic society," he answers that "this latent contradiction in the social system is not in itself sufficient to transform it." Instead he admits that "changes are more often observed as a result of peaceful or brutal confrontation with foreign populations, rather than of internal transformation." He notes that the vulnerability of communities to raids generates a need for protection, that protection usually derives not from mutual agreements but from domination, and that the relations of domination are then masked by an ideology of kinship. He concludes that "the will to dominate must interfere for history to be made." Meillassoux, *Maidens, Meal and Money*, pp. 73, 84, 85–86. Meillassoux's mistake, then, is only one of emphasis, that is, he minimizes these last points of his which are in fact central.

21 In challenging "invalid cross-cultural assumptions about a universal drive towards accumulation and male power," Guy seems to be seeking a better, more humane social goal in early southern African societies than what he sees as merely the pursuit of wealth and power. Guy insists that "the concept of wealth in these precapitalist societies is not comparable to that of wealth in capitalist societies," which may well be true although he has not demonstrated it with evidence of African perceptions of wealth. But Guy further infers from his assumptions that a difference in the concept of wealth creates a fundamental difference in human motivation. See Guy, "Gender oppression," p. 37.

22 Thompson, *Survival in Two Worlds*; Sanders, *Moshoeshoe*.

23 Burman, *Chiefdom Politics and Alien Law*; Burman, *Justice of the Queen's Government*; Burman, "Fighting a Two-Pronged Attack."
24 Kimble, "Towards an Understanding of the Political Economy of Lesotho." Unpublished M.A. thesis.

2 Settlement and trade patterns before 1830

1 Kuper, "The Social Structure of the Sotho-Speaking Peoples of Southern Africa," *Africa*, XIX, 1 (1975), pp. 69, 80; Legassick, "The Sotho-Tswana People," p. 120.
2 Maggs, *Iron Age Communities*, p. 159.
3 Delius, *The Land Belongs to Us*, pp. 11–19.
4 Sansom, "Traditional Economic Systems," p. 142.
5 Burchell, *Travels in the Interior*, II, p. 160.
6 D. F. Ellenberger, *Leselinyana*.
7 Harinck, "Interaction Between Xhosa and Khoi," pp. 160, 164.
8 Wilson, "The Sotho, Venda and Tsonga," pp. 143, 148–149.
9 Borcherds, *An Autobiographical Memoir*, pp. 81, 124.
10 Barrow, *Travels into the Interior*, p. 396; Campbell, *Travels in South Africa*, pp. 213, 311; Burchell, *Travels in the Interior*, II, p. 311.
11 Burchell, *Travels in the Interior*, II, pp. 340, 420.
12 D. F. Ellenberger, *Leselinyana*.
13 Mamadi, "Copper Miners of Musina," p. 81.
14 Alan Smith, "Delagoa Bay," p. 286.
15 Burchell, *Travels in the Interior*, I, p. 119.
16 *Ibid.*, vol. 2, p. 288.
17 *Ibid.*, vol. 2, p. 289.
18 E. Casalis, 4 Oct. 1833, Journal des Missions Evangéliques (*JME*), pp. 143–144; Backhouse, *Extracts from the Journal*, p. 25.
19 Smith, *Andrew Smith's Journal*, p. 297.
20 Motebang, "Sefaga"; for information about Mohlomi see Ellenberger, *History of the Basuto*, pp. 90–98.
21 Motebang, "Sefaga"; Sechefo, *Old Clothing*, pp. 17, 19; Interviews with 'Mamphoho Peshoani (1), Lineo Koromo (13), 'Matsuonyane Malefane (16), Nkane Azariel Kata (20), 'Makoloti Koloti (30), 'Mamoeketsi Mokoaleli (59).
22 Sechefo, *Old Clothing*, pp. 17, 19.
23 A. Mabille, "Quelques Traits de la Vie Missionaire: Extraits de la Correspondance Particulière de M. et Mad. Mabille." Unpublished MS. copy, edited by Betsy Celerier, Appendice, pp. 403–404; my translation.
24 Moshoeshoe to the Secretary of Native Affairs, Natal, 8 Nov. 1861; *Basutoland Records* (*BR*), edited by George M. Theal (Cape Town, 1883; reprinted 1964), III, p. 109.
25 Arbousset and Daumas, *Narrative*, pp. 164–165. The difficulties in identifying these early groups is made evident by Marks in her examination of Nguni traditions. The Thonga who inhabited this area included many groups of various origins, but served primarily as middlemen in regional trade. I have found no evidence that the Thonga worked iron or copper, leading me to believe the "Makasana" were a Nguni group. See Marks, "The Traditions of the Natal 'Nguni'," pp. 126–44; and Alan Smith, "Delagoa Bay," *passim*.
26 Autobiography of Elie Mapike Taole, *JME* (1843), p. 201.
27 Chiefs Sekwati, Toulouane, Ladaba, Patla, and Katla. Arbousset, 28 June 1844, *JME* (1844), pp. 460–461; Arbousset and Daumas, *Narrative*, p. 169.
28 Thompson, "Cooperation and Conflict," pp. 403, 439–440; Lye, "The Distribution of the Sotho," pp. 193–194.
29 J. Austin, 21 March 1868, *BR*, VI, part I (unpublished), pp. 44–45; Atmore and Sanders,

"Sotho Arms and Ammunition," p. 538; A. Mabille, 1984, "Quelques Traits," Appendice; Peter Delius, "Migrant Labour and the Pedi, 1840–80," in Marks and Atmore (eds.), *Economy and Society*, pp. 293–312.

30 Arbousset and Daumas, *Narrative*, pp. 170, 179.

31 *Ibid.*, p. 175.

32 Andrew Smith, *Diary*, vol. 1, p. 347.

33 Lye, "The Distribution of the Sotho," pp. 200, 202.

34 Ellenberger, *History of the Basuto*, 3rd Period (unpublished), vol. 1, p. 3.

35 Arbousset and Daumas, *Narrative*, pp. 87, 90, 98.

36 *Ibid.*, p. 90.

37 Ellenberger, *Leselinyana*; Motebang, "Lesela" [Cloth]; Motebang, "Sefaga" [Breads].

38 Moshoeshoe to the Secretary of Native Affairs, Natal, 8 Nov. 1861, *Basutoland Records (BR)*, edited by G. M. Theal (Cape Town, 1964) III, p. 109.

39 Nehemiah Sekhonyana Moshoeshoe, SeSotho MS., sent to J. M. Orpen, 4 Dec., 195, p. 17; my translation.

40 E. Casalis, 18 July 1843, *JME* (1843), p. 82.

41 Nehemiah S. Moshoeshoe, MS. to J. M. Orpen, 4 Dec. 1905, p. 17; my translation.

42 E. Casalis, "Histoire," 26 May 1834, *JME* (1835), p. 38.

43 Casalis, *Les Bassoutos*, p. 215.

44 Lieutenant Governor of Natal R. W. Keate to High Commissioner, 14 Feb. 1872, *BR* VI, part II (unpublished), p. 391; C. H. Bell to Governor's Agent, 17 Jan. 1872, *BR* VI, part II (unpublished), p. 355.

45 Letter from "Investigatus" dated 30 Jan. 1834; *Graham's Town Journal*, 6 Feb. 1834; Archbell, 4 Sept. 1833, in Thompson, *Survival in Two Worlds*, p. 110.

46 Moshoeshoe, "A Little Light from Basutoland," part 11, p. 282. This man, Adam Krotz, has been remembered for his role in informing Moshoeshoe about the value of white missionaries. Thomson, *Survival in Two Worlds*, p. 70.

47 Arbousset, 28 June 1836, *JME* (1837), p. 34.

48 Arbousset, 26 June 1838, *JME* (1839), p. 60.

3 Political consolidation and the rise of Moshoeshoe in the 1820s

1 D. F. Ellenberger, *History of the Basuto*, p. 24.

2 *Ibid.*, p. 78.

3 *Ibid.*, p. 86.

4 Legassick, "The Griqua, the Sotho-Tswana, and the Missionaries," Ph.D. Dissertation; Lye, "The Sotho Wars in the Interior of South Africa," Ph.D. dissertation. Although emerging scholarship demonstrates the inadequacy of some of the analyses of Legassick and Lye, who accepted distorted historical versions of a so-called "*mfecane*," both studies contain important empirical evidence of the early SeTswana-speaking peoples which has not been duplicated elsewhere.

5 Parsons, "Economic History of Khama's Country," pp. 114–15.

6 Burchell, *Travels in the Interior*, II, p. 248.

7 Casalis, *Les Bassoutos*, pp. 198–99.

8 Interviews with (14) 'Maisaka Mokeke, (17) Sekaute Letle, (19) Moeketsi Moseeka, (21) Tsoeu Temeki, (22) Joel Pharoe Moeno, (35) Thabo Fako.

9 Interview with Malefetsane Motiea (65). Moshoeshoe's father Mokhachane was only the second son of Moshoeshoe's grandfather, so the succession to the chieftancy would not normally have fallen to Moshoeshoe's line. But Mokhachane, and Moshoeshoe in his turn, gained influence because they were generous, unlike Mokhachane's elder brother Libe.

10 Moshoeshoe, "A Little Light from Basutoland," vol. 2, (Jan–June 1880), p. 282.

11 Casalis, *Les Bassoutos*, p. 271.

12 Casalis, 24 July 1837, *JME* (1838), p. 2.
13 Casalis, *Les Bassoutos*, p. 199.
14 E. S. Rolland, "Notes on the Political and Social Position of the Basuto Tribe," 30 March 1868, *Basutoland Records (BR)*, IV, part 1, 1868 (unpublished), p. 129.
15 See chapter 10 below.
16 Interview with Moeketsi Moseeka (19).
17 "Extracts from the Journal of a Traveller," *Graham's Town Journal*, 18 December 1845; Rolland, "Notes on the Political and Social Position," pp. 132–133; Casalis, *Les Bassoutos*, p. 203; Molelekoa Mohapi, *Temo ea Boholo-holo Lesotho*, pp. 21–22; Widdicombe, *Fourteen Years*, p. 43; Interviews with fourteen informants.
18 Porte, "Réminiscences," p. 320.
19 Ellenberger, *History of the Basuto*, p. 298.
20 Arbousset, Morija, 30 Dec. 1852, *JME* 1852, p. 240; Kimble, "Aspects of Economic History." Unpublished paper (1976), pp. 3–6.
21 Interview with Maisaka Mokeke (14).
22 Interview with Sekaute Lethe (17).
23 Interview with Tsoeu Temeki (21).
24 Interview with Morai Meoletsi (51).
25 Letter from the Chief Moshesh to the Secretary to Government, 15th May 1845, *BR*, I, p. 83; quoted in part in Thompson, *Survival in Two Worlds*, p. 130.
26 *Ibid.* For more extensive discussion of the formation of the BaSotho nation under Moshoeshoe, see Thompson, *Survival in Two Worlds, passim*, and Sanders, *Moshoeshoe, passim*. In addition, in his comparative study of the BaSotho and BaTloka, Sanders underlines the importance of cattle reserves for the expansion of political power. He observes that in 1828 the BaTloka and BaSotho were "roughly equal in strength," but the balance of power "swung dramatically in Moshweshwe's favour after he had conducted two extraordinarily successful cattle raids against the Thembe below the Drakensburg. The resultant acquisition of wealth was of vital importance to him, for many Sotho who had previously been attached to the Ngwane now turned to him for sustenance and were granted cattle under the *mafisa* system." Sanders, "Sekonyela and Moshweshwe," p. 443.
27 Arbousset, *Missionary Excursion*, p. 107.
28 *Ibid.*
29 *Ibid.*

4 The land of the BaSotho: the geographic extent of Moshoeshoe's authority, 1824–1864

1 Letter of J. M. Orpen to Nehemiah Sekonyana Moshoeshoe, 8 Sept. 1905, Ellenberger Papers, PEMS Archives, Morija, Lesotho.
2 Letters of J. M. Orpen to D. F. Ellenberger, 9 Dec. 1905 and 22 Dec. 1905, Ellenberger Papers.
3 "Memorandum Drawn up by Joseph Millard Orpen . . .," *BR*, V, part 1, 1869 (unpublished), pp. 69–71; D. F. Ellenberger papers, Grand Format II #14: excerpt from page 10 of Bluebook "Caffir War . . . " printed 12 July 1837 . . . Enclosure no. 3 in Despatch of Sir B. D'Urban No. 5 of 14 Oct. 1835, Government Notice: Colonial Office, Cape Town, 21 June 1836; letter from J. M. Orpen to N. S. Moshoeshoe, 8 Sept. 1905.
4 Letter from J. M. Orpen to D. F. Ellenberger, 11 April 1913, Ellenberger Papers.
5 Letter from J. M. Orpen to N. S. Moshoeshoe, 8 Sept. 1905, and "Memorandum Drawn up by Joseph Millard Orpen. . . ."
6 *Ibid.*
7 Letter from J. M. Orpen to D. F. Ellenberger, 29 Aug. 1905; and "Memorandum Drawn up by Joseph Millard Orpen. . . ."
8 Extracts from "A Sketch of the Principal Events Relative to the Government of the Basutos since 1833." Paper supplied by the Chief Moshesh to the British Authorities in 1852, *BR* I, p. 1.

9 Letter from E. Casalis to the Civil Commissioner of Colesberg, Thaba Bosiu, 19 March 1844, *BR* I, p. 65.
10 Arbousset and Daumas, *Narrative*, p. 32.
11 Letter from Chief Moshesh to the Secretary to Government, Thaba Bosigo, 15 May 1845, *BR* I, p. 84.
12 F. Daumas, 15 Feb. 1837, *JME* (1837), 333.
13 J. M. Orpen to D. F. Ellenberger, 25 Jan. 1906 and 3 Feb. 1906, Ellenberger Papers.
14 F. Daumas, 18 June 1840, PEMS Archives (Paris), AL215: 3288.
15 Dyke *et al.*, "Précis des circonstances ...," 18 July 1851, *JME* (1852), pp. 14–20.
16 Letter from Moletsane to the High Commissioner of Mekuatling, 1 Oct. 1864, *BR*, III, p. 298; see also F. Daumas to Governor George Grey, 26 Aug. 1858, *BR*, II, pp. 414–415.
17 D. F. Ellenberger, "Histoire Ancienne et Moderne des Basotho," I, p. 3; letter from N. S. Moshoeshoe to J. M. Orpen, 4 Dec. 1905, p. 17, Ellenberger Papers; Information told to J. M. Orpen by Jan Fick; letter from J. M. Orpen to N. S. Moshoeshoe, 8 Sept. 1905, Ellenberger Papers.
18 Letter from E. Casalis to British Resident, 11 June 1853, *BR*, II, p. 56.
19 "Memorandum of information ... from the chief ... at Beersheba," 20 June 1861, *BR*, II, p. 591–592.
20 Casalis, *Les Bassoutos*, pp. 198–199.
21 *Ibid.*
22 *Ibid.*
23 *Ibid.*

5 The European intrusion and the competition for land, 1834–1868

1 For a more detailed analysis see Eldredge, "Drought, Famine and Disease."
2 Smith, *Andrew Smith's Journal*, p. 63, 10 Oct. 1834.
3 The export of ostrich feathers, hides, skins and horns accounted for £25,000 of this total, with the sale of cattle and horses accounting for only £1,000 in the year. Collins, *Free Statia*.
4 "Sensus van Bevolking ...," Bylaag 59, 1865, V.P. 187, 127–169.
5 Letter from Moshesh to Secretary of Government, 15 May 1845, *BR*, I, pp. 85–86, italics mine. See also the letter from Rev. Casalis on behalf of Moshesh, to Sir H. Pottinger, High Commissioner, 14 April 1847, *BR*, I, pp. 131–132.
6 Letter from Moshoeshoe to Lieutenant Governor, 26 Nov. 1839, *BR*, I, p. 36. See also the letter from Moshoeshoe to Secretary to the Government, 15 May 1845, *BR*, I, p. 86.
7 Original petition, in Dutch, Caledon, 19 Aug. 1845, Orange Free State Archives, BRI/I, pp. 215–218. Also quoted in Sanders, *Moshoeshoe*, p. 79, with additional evidence.
8 P. T. Botha, Cradock, 15 April 1850, to Lieutenant Governor Sir Harry George Wakelyn Smith, (unpublished), Orange Free State Archives, BRI/I, p. 139. Italics mine.
9 Sir George Clerk, Bloemfontein, 14 Jan. 1854 to Duke of Newcastle, *BR*, II, p. 94.
10 British Agent John Burnet to the High Commissioner of Aliwal North, 15 Sept. 1856, *BR*, II, p. 237. Also quoted in Sanders, *Moshoeshoe*, p. 219.
11 Prosper Lemue, Sept. 1839 in Germond, *Chronicles of Basutoland*.
12 Sir George Napier, 7 Sept. 1842, *BR*, I, p. 48.
13 Sir George Napier to Lord Stanley, 15 Sept. 1842, *BR*, I, p. 49.
14 S. Rolland, 10 Aug. 1843 in Germond, *Chronicles of Basutoland*, pp. 157–158.
15 Sanders *Moshoeshoe*, pp. 159–60.
16 Orpen, *Reminiscences of Life in South Africa*, p. 187.
17 *Ibid.*, p. 247.
18 Thompson, *Survival in Two Worlds*, pp. 218–252.
19 For details of the above discussion see Thompson, *Survival in Two Worlds*, maps and descriptions, pp. 124, 146, 248, 290, 314.

20 "Sensus van Bevolking . . ."
21 Special Commissioner S.C. 4/1/2: Documents re The Land Board 1853 June – 1854 June, Free State Archives, Orange River Sovereignty Depot.
22 Theron, "Die Ekonomiese en Finansiele Toestand." Unpublished M.A. thesis.
23 *Ibid.*
24 *Ibid.*
25 Orpen, *Reminiscences of Life in South Africa*, p. 51.
26 Free State Archives, S.C. 5/13 and S.C. 4/1/2.
27 Orpen, *Reminiscences of Life in South Africa*, pp. 221–222.
28 Letter from the British Resident to Secretary to the High Commissioner, 18 Aug. 1850, *BR*, I, p. 315.
29 Letter from Sir George Clerk to the Duke of Newcastle, 10 Nov. 1853, *BR*, I, p. 72.
30 Free State Archives, S.C. 4/1/2: Free State Archives, S.C. 5/9, claimant no. 36; S.C. 5/10; S.C. 5/13; S.C. 4/1/2.
31 Schedules of Confiscated Farms sold by Government During the Period of the Orange River Sovereignty 1848–1852, Free State Archives S.C. 5/18; S.C. 5/19; S.C. 5/20; Collins, *Free Statia*, p. 182. Collins offers several other similar examples of the rise in farm prices.
32 Letter from Rev. J. Daniel to the Civil Commissioner of Aliwal North, *BR*, II, p. 578.
33 Letter from the President of the Orange Free State to the High Commissioner P. E. Wodehouse, 2 April 1868, *BR*, IV, part I, (unpublished), p. 172.

6 Food and politics: feasts and famines

1 For example, the French revolution of 1789, and the Russian revolution of 1917.
2 Bawden and Carroll, *Land Resources*, pp. 27–57; Smit, *Lesotho*, pp. 3–4.
3 *Ibid.* Temperature extremes range from 14 degrees Fahrenheit to 98 degrees Fahrenheit in the lowlands, with a decrease of approximately 3 degrees Fahrenheit for each increase in altitude of one thousand feet. The first frost comes in the mountains on about April 10, and in the western lowlands on May 1, and lasts about 140 days in the lowlands and 180 days in the mountains.
4 F. Maeder, 4 March 1856, Société des Missions Evangéliques (PEMS), Archives (Paris), ALM52; C. Gosselin, 30 Aug. 1852, PEMS Archives (Paris), ALG52; C. Gosselin, 5 Jan. 1863, PEMS Archives (Paris), ALG71; Frederic Porte, 29 June 1884, Correspondence Files (unpublished), Archivum Générale, OMI, (Rome, Italy); C. Christeller, 27 May 1902, PEMS Archives (Paris), 1902.
5 Germond, *Chronicles of Basutoland, passim.*
6 Bawden and Carroll, *Land Resources*, table 1, p. 86.
7 P. Berthoud, 19 March 1873, *Lettres Missionaires de M. et Mme. Paul Berthoud de la Mission Romande, 1873–1879*, (Lausanne: Georges Bridel, 1900), p. 60.
8 Arbousset and Daumas, *Narrative*, pp. 71–2.
9 "Extracts," *Graham's Town Journal; The Little Light of Basutoland*, no. 2 (February 1872); Segoainyana, "Tsa Masimo."
10 L. Duvoisin, *JME* (1883), p. 113; Marcellin Deltour, OMI, "Histoire du Lesotho." Unpublished MS. (*c.* 1888), p. 4; Widdicombe, *Fourteen Years*, p. 5; Martin, *Basutoland*, pp. 6–7; F. Christol, *Petit Messager* (1895), 154; Great Britain, *Colonial Report.– Annual*, (*CRA*), *Basutoland*, 408, Cd. 1768–13; *Leselinyana la Lesotho*, August 1902.
11 Casalis, *Les Bassoutos*, p. 204.
12 Circular from the Governor's Agent, Charles D. Griffith, to the Magistrates in Basutoland, 30 Jan. 1872, *BR*, VI, part II, 1871–72 (unpublished), 367.
13 Letter of J. P. Kennen, Assistant Commissioner for Mafeteng, 3 March 1905, Scott Papers, 1/9/8.

14 Interviews with (9) Dixon Rafutho, (19) Moeketsi Moseeka, (38) 'Mamapote Kobile, (41) Kichinane Ratoronko, (42) Ntorobaki J. Matabane, (46) Matsekoa Motleleng.
15 Arbousset, 4 Aug. 1836, PEMS Archives (Paris), AL129.
16 William Crisp, 5 July 1869, "Letters of William Crisp," (unpublished typescript), Library, Society of the Sacred Mission, Schrumpf, 23 Oct. 1845, PEMS Archives (Paris), ALS21.
17 This was common knowledge among my elderly informants.
18 Casalis, 20 June 1846, PEMS Archives (Paris), AL355 [1846–47: 115].
19 Backhouse, *Extracts from the Journal*, p. 25; Annual Conference Report, *JME* (1848); Report of Commandant Gideon D. Joubert, 1845, *BR*, I, p. 109; Despatch of Sir H. G. Smith to Earl Grey, 3 Feb. 1848, *BR*, I, pp. 163–164; J. Fredoux, 13 Oct. 1852, *JME* (1853), p. 55; F. Meader, "Notice Sur la Nation des Bassoutos," *JME* (1855), p. 43.
20 Sanders, *Moshoeshoe*, p. 245.
21 *Ibid.*
22 Arbousset, 26 May 1854, *JME* (1854), p. 445; L. Maitin, 7 Aug. 1854, *JME* (1855); Maeder, 2 Jan. 1842, *JME* (1860); *Sou Missionnaire*, no. 7 (1858); *JME* (1862), 56; *JME* (1865); Maitin, 16 July 1866, PEMS Archives (Paris), AL902 [1866–7: 93]; *JME* (1903), p. 107; "Reports & Official Correspondence, Missionaries of Lesotho, in Aliwal North, to Comité de la Société …," (May 1866 – 22 February 1869), unpublished MS. (L. J. Cochet, secretaire), PEMS Archives (Morija), April 1869; *Assemblée Générale de la Société des Missions Evangéliques*, (April 1883), p. 15; J. H. Bowker to the High Commissioner, 20 August 1869, *BR*, V, part I (unpublished), p. 280; T. Jousse, 7 Jan. 1870, PEMS Archives (Paris), AL1181 [1869–70: 137].
23 John Burnet, Civil Commissioner of Aliwal North, to the High Commissioner of Aliwal North, 17 Dec. 1865, *BR*, III, p. 571; *JME* (1873), p. 456.
24 Bishop Jean Francis Allard, OMI, 3 March 1866, *Missions de la Congrégation des Oblats de Marie Immaculée (Missions)*, no. 22 (June 1867), pp. 214–219.
25 E. Jacottet, 2 July 1855, PEMS Archives (Paris), 1885; Annual Conference Report, *JME* (1886), p. 263; Widdicombe, *Fourteen Years*, pp. 250–251; South Africa, *Despatch from Sir Hercules Robinson*, C.–5238; Great Britain, Her Majesty's Colonial Possessions, No. 31, *Basutoland, Report of the Resident Commissioner for 1887*, (London, 1887), C.–5249.–28.
26 Widdicombe, *Fourteen Years*, p. 40; *CRA*, 186, 1895–96, C. 8279.–10, 32.
27 *Missions*, no. 118 (June 1892); *CRA*, 152, 1894–95, C. 7944–4; *CRA*, 444, *Report for 1903–4 With Returns of the Census*, 1904. Cd. 2238–21.
28 François Lebihan, OMI, Report to H. Davies, Assistant Resident Magistrate, Maseru, 23 Dec. 1879, in Marcel Ferragne, OMI, *Au Pays des Basotho, les Cent Ans de la Mission St. Michel*, I, 1868–1899, (Roma, Lesotho, n.d.).
29 South Africa, *Further Correspondence Respecting the Affairs of Basutoland*, C.–4907, 18.
30 Jacottet, *JME* (1885), p. 55; Adolphe Mabille, 28 May 1885, *JME* (1885), p. 404.
31 South Africa, *Despatch from Sir Hercules Robinson*; Henri Marzolff, 11 March 1889, *JME* (1890), pp. 55–56; F. Porte, "Les Fondateurs des Missions du Basutoland," *Petites Annales de la Congrégation des Missionaires Oblats de Marie Immaculée*, III (1893), 302; Jacottet, "L'Oeuvre des Maloutis," *JME* (1894), p. 8; Alexandre Baudry, *Petites Annales*, VII (July 1897), 232; Marzolff, 20 Dec. 1896, PEMS Archives (Paris), 1896; D. F. Ellenberger, 18 April 1900, PEMS Archives (Paris), 1900.
32 D. F. Ellenberger, 26 Nov. 1890. *JME* (1891), 47.
33 Widdicombe, *Fourteen Years*, p. 43; Cape of Good Hope, Ministerial Department of Native Affairs, *Blue-Book on Native Affairs* (*BBNA*), 1879, (Cape Town, 1879), G33–79, 13; *CRA*, 152, 1894–95, pp. 5–6.
34 Barkly, *Among Boers*, p. 119.
35 Casalis, *My Life in Basutoland*, p. 191; Andrew Smith, *Diary*, entry dated 27 Nov. 1834; François Daumas, 10 May 1839, *JME* (1839), p. 410.
36 Jean Fredoux, 13 Oct. 1852, *JME* (1852), p. 55; Maeder, 5 Jan. 1859, *JME* (1859), p. 127;

Government Secretary of the Orange Free State to Fieldcornets on the Border, 11 March 1869, *BR*, V, part I (unpublished), p. 116; Paulus Moperi to the President of the Orange Free State, Sept. 1869 *BR*, V, part II (unpublished), 289; H. Hanger to the Government Secretary of the Orange Free State, 9 Sept. 1869, *BR*, V, part II (unpublished), p. 299.

37 Great Britain, *Basutoland* (Great Britain: War Office, 1880), 9; Widdicombe, *Fourteen Years*, p. 46.

38 François Maeder, "Notice Sur La Nation Des Bassoutos," *JME* (1856), p. 206; *Diary of Father Joseph Gerard*, entry dated 16 May 1865, p. 27; Lelinguana, interviewed by Job Moteane, *JME* (1888), p. 305; Widdicombe, *Fourteen Years*, p. 3; D. F. Ellenberger, 18 April 1900, PEMS Archives (Paris), 1900; Henri Lebreton, OMI, "A Travers les Montagnes du Basutoland," *Les Missions Catholiques* (Lyon), 1907, 262. Interviews with twelve informants.

39 Interviews with nine informants; N. Moshabesha and H. E. Jankie, "Mosotho." Unpublished MS., PEMS Archives (Morija), revised version (1939), pp. 133–40.

40 Daumas *JME* (1843), p. 323; J.-P. Pellissier, 15 May 1851, *JME* (1852), p. 31; A. Mabille, 3 Dec. 1866, "Quelques Traits," p. 281; Spencer Weigall, 4 Jan. 1899, *Quarterly Paper of the Orange Free State Mission*, (*Quarterly Paper*), 124 (1899), 78.

41 Barkly, *Among Boers*, p. 45; Interview with (20) Nkane Azariel Kaka; François Laydevant, OMI, "La Misère au Basutoland," *Les Missions Catholiques* (1934), 336.

42 Arbousset and Daumas, *Narrative*, p. 35.

43 Mohapi, *Temo*, pp. 17–20.

44 Interviews with (8) Lintso Motanyane, (22) Joel Pharoe Moeno.

45 *Ibid.*, 21; Casalis, *Les Bassoutos*, p. 203; *Melao ea Lerotholi* (Laws of Lerotholi), (Morija, revised edn. 1959), p. 6.

46 Mohapi, *Temo*, p. 22.

47 Interview with (8) Lintso Motanyane.

48 Interviews with (1) Mamphoho Peshoani, (8) Lintso Motanyane, (14) Maisaka Mokeke, (15) Lipolelo Ramonyai, (22) Joel Pharoe Moeno, (31) 'Mabatho Serobanyane.

49 Mohapi, *Temo*, pp. 38, 41.

50 *Ibid.*, 39, 41; Casalis, *Les Bassoutos*, p. 213.

51 Moshabesha and Jankie, "Mosotho." Unpublished MS., p. 116; Mohapi, *Temo*, p. 46; Casalis, *Les Bassoutos*, p. 214. Both Sanders and Thompson conclude that maize arrived in the area in the 1820s: Thompson, *Survival*, p. 9; Sanders, *Moshoeshoe*, pp. 9, 71.

52 Mohapi, *Temo*, pp. 46–49.

53 *Ibid.*, pp. 51–56; E. Casalis, 31 July 1833, *JME* (1834), p. 53; E. Casalis, June 1840, *JME* (1841), p. 164; Arbousset and Daumas, *Narrative*, p. 35.

54 Annual Conference Report, *JME* (1845), p. 14.

55 Arbousset, 3 Dec. 1835, *JME* (1836), p. 151; Annual Conference Report, *JME* (1850), p. 332; *Petit Messager*, pp. 338–340; Christian Schrumpf, *Sudafrikanische Cap- und Atlantische Gee-Bilder*, mit Unhang: *Die Bassuto Wie Sie Sind*, p. 45; Annual Conference Report, May 1844, in Germond, *Chronicles*, p. 66.

56 Fredoux, *Petit Messager* (1853), p. 336; Mohapi, *Temo*, p. 50; Daumas, 2 April 1843, *JME* (1844), p. 87; Annual Conference Report, *JME* (1845), p. 26; Prosper Lautre, 15 May 1846, *JME* (1847), p. 247; Maeder, 15 July 1846, *JME* (1847), p. 48; Arbousset, 9 Dec. 1846, *JME* (1847), p. 207; Gosselin, 12 July 1850, *JME* (1850), p. 457; Widdicombe, *Fourteen Years*, p. 8.

57 Clarke, "Unexplored Basutoland," p. 523; Maeder, 22 Jan. 1873, *JME* (1873), p. 129; E. Casalis, 2 Dec. 1880. *JME* (1881), p. 170; Widdicombe, *Fourteen Years*, p. 47; Lelinguana, Interviewed by Job Moteane, *JME* (1888), p. 305; *CRA*, 89, 1892–93, Cd.–6857–39; *Her Majesty's Colonial Possessions*, 31, (1887), C.–5249.–28.

58 Gosselin, 9 Nov. 1833, *JME* (1835), p. 46; Arbousset, 28 June 1836, *JME* (1837), p. 34; Maeder, 15 July 1846, *JME* (1847), p. 48; Arbousset, 9 Dec. 1846, *JME* (1847), p. 207;

C. Schrumpf, *Die Bassuto*, p. 45; Maeder, 22 June 1873, *JME* (1873), p. 129; Gosselin, 16 Jan. 1837, *JME* (1837), p. 236.

59 Mohapi, *Temo*, pp. 48–49, 52, 56–57; Widdicombe, *Fourteen Years*, p. 8.

60 Mohapi, *Temo*, p. 60; Interviews with twenty-two informants; *Petit Messager* (1853), pp. 338–340; Tlali, *Mehla ea Boholo-holo*, pp. 11–12.

61 Mohapi, *Temo*, pp. 60–61.

62 Arbousset, 26 June 1838 in Germond, *Chronicles*, p. 438.

63 "Extracts," *Graham's Town Journal*; Casalis, *Les Bassoutos*, p. 114.

64 *BBNA*, 1876; census returns of 1891 in *Leselinyana*, 1 Nov. 1891, 7–8.

65 *Her Majesty's Colonial Possessions*, 70, 1889, C.–5897, p. 19; Balfour, *Twelve Hundred Miles*, p. 57; *CRA*, 1894–95, p. 11.

66 Andrew Smith, *Diary*, entry dated 25 Nov. 1834, p. 145.

67 Arbousset, "Excursion Missionaire." Unpublished MS., p. 33.

68 Maeder, 15 Jan. 1858, *JME* (1858), p. 133; Cape of Good Hope, *Report of the Governor's Agent, Basutoland, for 1872*, G27- 73; W. Crisp, *Quarterly Paper*, 23 (Jan. 1874).

69 *BBNA*, 1876.

70 Casalis, *My Life*, p. 235.

71 *BBNA*, 1876; Fredoux, 27 Dec. 1861, *JME* (1862), p. 128; Interviews with eleven informants.

72 Sanders, *Moshoeshoe*, p. 46, cf. D. F. Ellenberger, *History of the Basuto*, p. 195; "Extracts," *Graham's Town Journal*. From other evidence, Sanders concludes that Seidenstecher arrived at Thaba Bosiu in December 1832.

73 Fredoux, 27 Dec. 1861, *JME* (1862), p. 128; *BBNA*, 1876; census returns of 1891 in *Leselinyana*.

74 Rinderpest therefore had a different effect on the distribution of wealth than did the destruction of the 1820s. During the 1820s, wealthy chiefs were able to use their influence to control remaining herds as livestock were killed off, and this reinforced disparities in wealth between the rich and the poor.

75 Segoete, "Leeto la Malingoaneng."

76 Interviews with twenty-four informants.

77 Sen, *Poverty and Famines*; Eldredge, "Drought, Famine and Disease."

78 Crochet, 5 Feb. 1863, PEMS Archives (Paris), AL746 [1863–4: 2].

79 Sen, *Poverty and Famines*.

80 Barrow, *Travels into the Interior*, II, p. 55.

81 Ellenberger, *History of the Basuto*, p. 42.

82 Mabokoboko, informant, in letter of D. F. Ellenberger, 1 July 1884, *JME* (1884), p. 420.

83 F. Laydevant, OMI, "La Misère au Basutoland," p. 336.

84 Ellenberger, *History of the Basuto*, pp. 30, 95.

85 *Ibid.*, pp. 96, 295.

86 Letter of D. F. Ellenberger, 1 July 1884, *JME* (1884), p. 420; *Almanaka ea BaSotho*, Selemo sa 1894; *Litaba tsa Lilemo*; N. S. Moshoeshoe, "A Little Light from Basutoland," 2, 10, pp. 221–233 and 2, 11, pp. 280–292.

87 Ellenberger, *History of the Basuto*, pp. 131, 144, 151, 174. The oral reports and traditions regarding specific conflicts over crops and grain are likely to be accurate, even though Ellenberger's renditions of related events must be treated with caution and his interpretations of attitudes and causes, explicit and implicit, are often very wrong. See also MacGregor, *Basuto Traditions*, pp. 41, 49, 51, 52, 53, 62, 66.

88 Ellenberger, *History of the Basuto*, p. 88.

89 *Ibid.*, p. 74.

90 *Ibid.*, p. 130.

91 *Ibid.*, p. 125; MacGregor, *Basuto Traditions*, p. 25.

92 Ellenberger, *History of the Basuto*, pp. 144, 151.

93 MacGregor, *Basuto Traditions*, p. 41.

94 Moffat, *Missionary Labours*, p. 309.
95 George Thompson, *Travels and Adventures in Southern Africa*, (London, 1827). Reprinted (Cape Town, 1968), II, pp. 30–33.
96 Moffat, *Missionary Labours*, p. 315.
97 *Ibid.*, p. 316.
98 Ellenberger, *History of the Basuto*, p. 174.
99 Eldredge, "Sources of Conflict in Southern Africa."
100 Pellisier, Bethulie, 1 Oct. 1849, *JME* (1850), p. 42; *JME* (1851), p. 408; *JME* (1852), p. 31; C. Gosselin, 10 Jan. 1851, PEMS Archives (Paris), ALG 50 #381; C. Gosselin, 30 August 1852, PEMS Archives (Paris), ALG 52; Assemblée Générale de la Société des Missions Evangéliques chez les Peuples non-Chrétiens (Paris), 29 April 1852.
101 *JME* (1855), p. 179; Chief Paulus Moperi to Landdrost of Winburg, 6 Nov. 1855, *BR*, II, p. 163.
102 Cochet, 6 Feb. 1863, PEMS Archives (Paris), AL 746 [1863–4: 2].
103 *Almanaka ea BaSotho*; D. F. Ellenberger, 3 Sept. 1862, *JME* (1862), p. 405; "Notes et Souvenirs du Missionaire L. J. Cochet," (unpublished), edited by R. Ellenberger, 2 Oct. 1862, 27 Oct. 1862, 3 Nov. 1862: 2e cahier, 68, PEMS Archives (Morija); C. Gosselin, 5 Jan. 1863, PEMS Archives (Paris), ALG 71.
104 P. Lemue, 6 Feb. 1863, *JME* (1863), p. 41; *JME* (1865), p. 289; "Rapport de la Conférence," 1864, PEMS Archives (Paris), Al 805 [1864–5]; E. Casalis jun., 1 Sept. 1864, PEMS Archives (Paris), Al 805 [1864–5]; Civil Commissioner of Aliwal North to Secretary to the High Commissioner, 18 Sept. 1865, *BR*, III, p. 476.
105 P. Lemue, Feb. 1863, in Germond, *Chronicles*, p. 459.
106 Jousse, 29 Dec. 1860, *JME* (1861), p. 125; *JME* (1865), p. 289; "Rapport de la Conférence," 1864, PEMS Archives (Paris), AL805 [1864–5].
107 M. Schuh, 16 Jan. 1855, *JME* (1855), p. 179; Fredoux, 12 Jan. 1856 and 5 April 1856, *JME* (1857), p. 160; Cochet, "Notes et Souvenirs du Missionaire C. J. Cochet." Unpublished collection, edited by René Ellenberger, PEMS Archives (Morija), 2e cahier, 31–2; E. Casalis jun., 1 Sept. 1864, PEMS Archives (Paris), AL805 [1864–5]; Annual Conference Report, *JME* (1865), p. 289.
108 Civil Commissioner of Aliwal North to Secretary to the High Commissioner, 18 Sept. 1865, *BR*, III, p. 476.
109 L. Cochet, "Notes," 7 Dec. 1868 and 20 Dec. 1869; Adolphe Mabille, *Correspondance Missionaire*, 4, 19 Jan. 1870; Gosselin, 10 Dec. 1869, PEMS Archives (Paris), AL1176 [1869–70: 132]; L. Duvoisin, 31 Dec. 1868, PEMS Archives (Paris), AL1128 [1869–70].
110 Adele Mabille, extracts from "Souvenirs, 1864–5," in Siordet, *Adele Mabille*, pp. 125–127.
111 Thompson, *Survival in Two Worlds*, pp. 290–293.
112 Adolphe Mabille, letter to Betsy Cellerier, "Correspondance Missionaire", no. 16, Morija, 30 Oct. 1877, 4. Translation mine.
113 *Quarterly Paper of the Orange Free State Mission*, no. 49, July 1880.
114 See discussion in chapter 12 below.
115 *JME* (1884), 44, p. 128; E. Casalis, 6 Dec. 1888, PEMS Archives (Paris), 1888; D. F. Ellenberger, 6 March 1889, PEMS Archives (Paris), 1889; *Missions*, 118 (June 1892), 221. For a discussion of how drought-induced migration fosters the spread of epidemic disease see Eldredge, "Drought, Famine and Disease", pp. 83–84.
116 Adolphe Mabille, 6 Feb. 1892, PEMS Archives (Paris), 1892; L. Dieterlen, 16 Dec. 1892, PEMS Archives (Paris), 1892; *JME* (1893), pp. 11, 19; E. Mabille, 29 Jan. 1892, PEMS Archives (Paris), 1892; *Missions*, 118 (June 1892), 226; R. Christol, 24 Jan. 1893, PEMS Archives (Paris), 1893; PEMS Archives (Paris), 1896: H. Marzolff, 13 Jan. 1896 and 17 Feb. 1896; D. Jeanmarait, 8 April 1896; F. Kohler, 12 March 1896; *JME* (1897), pp. 136, 140; *JME* (1898), pp. 17, 91, 244, 298, 880; *JME* (1899), p. 104; *Quarterly Paper*, 119 (25 Jan. 1898), 11, 16, and 121 (25 July 1898), 97–102; *CRA*, 224, 1896–97, C.-8660–22; *JME*

(1898), pp. 243, 880; *CRA*, 255, 1897–98, C.–9046.–23; *Quarterly Paper*, 121 (25 July 1898), 97–102; R. H. Dyke, 22 Nov. 1898, *Gospel Work in Basutoland by Native Agency*, (1898). Unfortunately, there are no specific mortality figures available for this period or for previous famines and epidemics. Population data for the BaSotho in the nineteenth century are limited to the few references, mostly estimates, cited earlier.

117 *CRA*, 288, 1898–99, C.–3–11; Marzolff, PEMS Archives (Paris), 1899; M. A. Reading, *Quarterly Paper*, 126 (25 Oct. 1899), 166; M. A. Reading, 27 Dec. 1899, *Quarterly Paper*, 128 (25 April 1900), 64; G. Lorriaux, 27 Oct. 1899, *JME* (1900), p. 43; *CRA*, 343, 1900–01, C. 788–13; J. & T. Robertson Co., 10 Dec. 1901 and 11 Jan. 1902, Scott Papers, 1/3/19; *CRA*, 313, 1899–1900, Cd.431–5; *CRA*, 380, 1901–02, Cd.1388–4.

118 Basutoland Government Archives S3/1/5/1, S3/1/5/10, S3/1/5/6; H. Dieterlen, *JME* (1902), II, p. 336; D. Jeanmarait, 15 Sept. 1901, PEMS Archives (Paris), 1901; G. Lorriaux, 8 Jan. 1901, PEMS Archives (Paris), 1901; Paul Ramseyer, 17 June 1902, PEMS Archives (Paris), 1902; *CRA*, 1901–02; *CRA*, 408, 1902–03, Cd.–1768–13; *CRA*, 444, 1903–04, C. 2238–21; Joseph M. Helbourg, OMI, 1 May 1903, *Missionary Record of the Oblates of Mary Immaculate*, XIII (1903), p. 380; Marzolff, 12 May 1903, PEMS Archives (Paris), 1903; Jacottet, 14 Oct. 1903, PEMS Archives (Paris), 1903; B. Pascal, 27 Nov. 1903, *JME* (1904), I, p. 106; R. Henry Dyke, 23 Nov. 1903, PEMS Archives (Paris), 1903; *Leselinyana*, June 1903, 3.

7 The rise and decline of craft specialization

1 Sheddick writes incorrectly that "the practice of metal-work seems to have been restricted to the Tlokoa and among them to one or two individuals only." (Sheddick, *The Southern Sotho*, p. 24). Ashton acknowledges early iron-working. (Ashton, *The Basuto*, pp. 158–159.)
2 Arbousset and Daumas, *Narrative*, pp. 77–78.
3 Arbousset, 19 Jan. 1839, *JME* (1839), p. 295.
4 Casalis, *Les Bassoutos*, p. 175; D. F. Ellenberger, *Leselinyana*; Porte, "Réminiscences," pp. 189–190; Bianquism, "La Question Economique," p. 3; François Laydevant, OMI, "Le Basutoland." Unpublished MS., n.d. (written *c*. 1930s and updated *c* 1951), Archivum Générale, Oblats de Marie Immaculée (Rome, Italy), 137.
5 Interviews with (9) Dixon Rafutho, (19) Moeketsi Moseeka, (25) Mamothobi Mphosi, (33) Moselantza Sehloho, (55) Setabele Morahanya, (58) Masimphole Mokoaleli, (59) Mamoeketsi Mokoaleli, (65) Malefetsane Motiea, (77) Teko Leboea Mainoane, (80) Mamo-topo Lephema; Sekese, *Mekhoa ea Basotho*, p. 73.
6 J. M. Orpen to Civil Commissioner of Aliwal North, 25 Nov. 1864, *BR*, III, p. 316.
7 Martin, *Basutoland*, p. 30.
8 *Graham's Town Journal*, 17 October 1833. Other Europeans testified to the presence of coal deposits and mining activities. Andrew Smith, *Diary*, I, p. 153; Casalis, 19 July 1833, *JME* (1834), p. 12; Martin, *Basutoland*, p. 14; *BBNA*, G21–'75, 8; Charles D. Griffith to D. F. Ellenberger, 21 May 1880, Ellenberger papers, Petit Format II.
9 Fagan, "The Later Iron Age," p. 59.
10 Sekese, *Mekhoa ea Basotho*, p. 73; Sechefo, *Old Clothing*, p. 11.
11 Ellenberger, *Leselinyana*; Ellenberger, *History of the Basuto*, pp. 26, 350–353.
12 C. Schrumpf, *Die Bassuto*, p. 45; Moshabesha and Jankie, "Mosotho," p. 45; Interviews with (19) Moeketsi Moseeka, (79) Masekake Thamae.
13 Interview with (41) Kichinane Ratoronko.
14 Casalis, *Les Bassoutos*, p. 173.
15 Interviews with (9) Dixon Rafutho, (19) Moeketsi Moseeka, (24) Molikeng Motseki, (41) Kichinane Ratoronko, (49) Matsela Tooai, (58) Masimphole Mokoaleli, (59) Mamoeketsi Mokoaleli, (70) Joshua Kengkeng Marake, (71) Mahlatsoane Seboche, (72) Mapula Letsika Matela.

16 Backhouse, *Extracts from the Journal*, p. 24.
17 Casalis, *Les Bassoutos*, p. 175.
18 Sekese, *Mekhoa ea Basotho*, p. 73; Sechefo, *Old Clothing*, p. 11.
19 Laydevant, "Basutoland," p. 137.
20 Interviews with (9) Dixon Rafutho, (19) Moeketsi Moseeka, (25) Mamothobi Mphosi, (33) Moselantza Sehloho, (41) Kichinane Ratoronko, (58) Masimphole Mokoaleli, (61) Moratehi Jankie, (62) Makrika Mosuoe Kukame, (77) Teko Leboea Mainoane, (79) Masekake Thamae.
21 J. Merriman, Cape of Good Hope. Report of the Select Committee ... to consider the Provisions of the Basutoland Annexation Bill. Cape Town, 1871. C.1–'71; in *BR*, VI, I, p. 166; Widdicombe, *Fourteen Years*, p. 49; Porte, "Réminiscences," pp. 189–90.
22 Great Britain, War Office, *Military Report and General Information Concerning Southern Basutoland* (1905), p. 36; E. Segoete, *Raphepheng*, p. 12; Interviews with (41) Kichinane Ratoronko, (58) Masimphole Mokoaleli; Fredoux, *JME* (1862), p. 129; William Reed, 30 Sept. 1865, *BR*, III, p. 484; J. M. Orpen to Civil Commissioner of Aliwal North, 25 Nov. 1864, *BR*, III, p. 316.
23 Martin, *Basutoland*, p. 32.
24 Segoete, *Raphepheng*, pp. 5, 12; Sechefo, *Old Clothing*, p. 11, 14; Porte, "Réminiscences," p. 191; Moshabesha and Jankie, "Mosotho," p. 224; Interviews with nine informants.
25 Backhouse, *Narrative of a Visit*, p. 378; Backhouse, *Extracts from the Journal*, p. 25.
26 Martin, *Basutoland*, p. 30.
27 Casalis, *Les Bassoutos*, p. 174.
28 Interviews with (1) Mamphoho Peshoani, (14) Maisaka Mokeke; Tlali, *Mehla ea Boholo-holo*, p. 7; Segoete, *Raphepheng*, p. 14; Moshabesha and Jankie, "Mosotho," p. 45; Sechefo, *Old Clothing*, p. 16.
29 Andrew Smith, *Diary*, p. 114.
30 Interviews with (20) Nkane Azariel Kaka, (24) Molikeng Motseki; Porte, "Réminiscences," p.. 191; Sechefo, *Old Clothing*, p. 13. Note that the BaSotho distinguish between "flaying" and "fraying", referring by the latter not to just beating the skin but rather to giving it a frayed surface, or nap.
31 Interviews with (9) Dixon Rafutho, (12) Moleko Thateli, (13) Lineo Koromo, (1) Mamphoho Peshoani, (7) Tsehla Maime, (17) Sekaute Letle, (51) Morai Moeletsi, (65) Malefetsane Motiea; Moshabesha and Jankie, "Mosotho," p. 185; C. Schrumpf, *Die Bassuto*, p. 45; Sechefo, *Old Clothing*, p. 12; Tlali, *Mehla ea Boholo-holo*, p. 17.
32 Widdicombe, *Fourteen Years*, pp. 50, 81.
33 Interviews with (11) Mathakane Matooane, (15) Lipolelo Ramonyai, (27) Mamotoai Letsosa, (42) Ntorobaki J. Matabane.
34 Interviews with ten informants; Segoete, *Raphepheng*, pp. 11–14; Casalis, *Les Bassoutos*, p. 178; Sechefo, *Old Clothing*, p. 18; "Visit to the Basutu Country", *Graham's Town Journal*, 12 June 1845; *BBNA*, G.13–'80, 21.
35 Interview with (11) Mathakane Matooane.
36 Sechefo, *Old Clothing*, p. 16; interviews with twelve informants.
37 Interview with (31) 'Mabatho Serobanyane; Moshabesha and Jankie, "Mosotho," p. 43.
38 Interviews with (21) Tsoeu Temeki; (50) Mathothoane Mpobole.
39 Backhouse, *Extracts from the Journal*, p. 18; Martin, *Basutoland*, p. 34.
40 Sechefo, *Old Clothing*, p. 6.
41 Interviews with ten informants; Tlali, *Mehla ea Boholo-holo*, p. 16; C. Schrumpf, *Die Bassuto*, p. 45; Porte, "Réminiscences," p. 192; Barkly, *Among Boers*, p. 46.
42 Interviews with sixteen informants; Segoete, *Raphepheng*, pp. 7, 13; Sechefo, *Old Clothing*, p. 16; Tlali, *Mehla ea Boholo-holo*, p. 5; Porte, "Réminiscences," p. 178.
43 Interviews with (1) Mamphoho Peshoani; (11) Mathakane Matooane.

44 Tlali, *Mehla ea Boholo-holo*, p. 13.
45 Sechefo, *Old Clothing*, pp. 26–27.
46 Ellenberger, *History of the Basuto*, p. 294.
47 Interview with (25), Mamothobi Mphosi.
48 Great Britain, *Basutoland*, p. 11; Frank Puaux, *Les Bassoutos*, p. 15; Casalis, *Les Bassoutos*, pp. 187–188; Giacomo Weitzecker, "La Donna Fra i Basuto," p. 466.
49 Ellenberger, *History of the Basotho*, p. 294.
50 Interviews with (6) Masebabatso Theko; (14) Maisaka Mokeke; Sechefo, *Old Clothing*, p. 16.
51 Interviews with seventeen informants; Martin, *Basutoland*, p. 14.
52 Interview with (65) Malefetsane Motiea.
53 *Ibid.*
54 Casalis, 31 July 1833, *JME* (1834), p. 54; Arbousset, 28 Jan. 1834, PEMS Archives (Paris), AL80: 1579.
55 Interviews with (10) Azael Lehau, (45) Monyoa Makibitle, (66) Majoseph Molapo, (69) Mataelo Ramotoka, (70) Joshua Kengkeng Marake; Tlali, *Mehla ea Boholo-holo*, p. 3.
56 C. Schrumpf, *Die Bassouto*, p. 45.
57 Interviews with (15) Lipolelo Ramonyai, (31) Mabatho Serobanyane; *Le Petit Messager des Missions Evangélques* (1895), 38.
58 Marcelin Deltour, OMI, "Histoire du Lesotho." Unpublished MS., n.d., Archivum Générale, Oblats de Marie Immaculée, p. 16.
59 Interviews with (42) Ntorobaki J. Matabane, (46) Matsekoa Motleleng, (47) Moetsuoa Mohlahloe Mzwane, (23) Kopano Jeremiah Telo, (31) 'Mabatho Serobanyane, (32) Selbourne Moeketsi Lefoka, (66) Mamopeli Sello.
60 Interview with (18) Lehlohonolo Kele.
61 Interview with (41) Kichinane Ratoronko.
62 Interviews with (17) Sekaute Letle, (18) Lehlohonolo Kele, (22) Joel Pharoe Moeno, (47) Moetsuoa Mohlahloe Mzwane, (44) Malipere Tjamela.
63 C. Schrumpf, *Die Bassuto*, p. 45.
64 See the discussion in Thompson, *Survival in Two Worlds*, pp. 70–104; Perrot, *Les Sotho*, pp. 36–41.
65 Perrot, *Les Sotho*, p. 36. Translation mine.
66 *JME* (1839), p. 52, quoted in Perrot, *Les Sotho*, p. 36. Translation mine.
67 *JME* (1845), p. 7.
68 Perrot, *Les Sotho*, p. 39.
69 *Ibid.*, p. 41.
70 *Ibid.*, pp. 38, 76–77.
71 *Ibid.*, pp. 110–111.
72 *Ibid.*, pp. 113–114.
73 Lagden, *The Basutos*, II, p. 670. According to the 1904 Census, congregation sizes and membership (communicants) broke down among the church denominations as follows:

	Belonging to the congregation	Number of Communicants
PEMS	40,956	13,555
Church of England	3,383	1,725
Roman Catholic	5,701	3,626
African Methodist Episcopal	798	652
Seventh Day Adventist	40	19

74 Including the African church members at Bethulie until 1862 and at Beersheba until 1868, the following are the figures for the total number of adult Christians in the PEMS church. These

221

figures are compiled from information in V. Ellenberger, *A Century of Mission Work in Basutoland, 1833–1933*.

1843	393
1844	507
1845	1246
1857	1788
1864	2211
1871	3261
1872	3502
1876	4740
1880	5984
1884	5986
1885	6536
1887	7770
1894	13733

The percentages are at best crude estimates, given that the population figures as presented in chapter 6 *supra* are themselves crude estimates, with the possible exception of the one for 1891, which comes from the first official Basutoland Census. The figure for 1904 is derived from the 1904 Census figures of a total (BaSotho) population of 347,731 and a total church membership of 19,577. Lagden, *The Basutos*, II, p. 669–670.

75 F. Coillard, Leribe, 5 Dec. 1864, *JME* (1865), p. 135.

76 C. Coillard, quoted in Favre, *Francois Coillard*, p. 29.

77 The analysis that follows is based on Williamson, "Transaction-Cost Economics," pp. 233–261.

78 I am grateful to James Riddell, University of Wisconsin-Madison, for suggesting the usefulness of transaction-cost economics in explaining the decline of craft production.

79 Williamson, "Transaction-Cost Economics," pp. 238–245.

80 Porte, "Réminiscences," p. 189.

81 Mabille, "The Basuto of Basutoland," 5, 19, p. 240.

82 Weitzecker, "La Donna Fra i Basuto," p. 466.

83 This reflects the process described by Williamson: "As generic demand grows and the number of supply sources increases, exchange that was once transaction-specific loses this characteristic and greater reliance on market-mediated governance is feasible. Thus vertical integration may give way to obligational market contracting, which in turn may give way to markets." Williamson, "Transaction-Cost Economics," p. 260.

84 F. Maeder, 15 Jan. 1858, *JME* (1858), p. 133. Also referred to in Thompson, *Survival in Two Worlds*, p. 191.

85 *CRA*, 1893–1909.

8 The allocation of labor, 1830–1910

1 Interviews with eleven informants.

2 Casalis, *Les Bassoutos*, pp. 209–210.

3 Arbousset, *JME* (1838) p. 215; Tlali, *Mehla ea Boholo-holo*, pp. 16–17; Segoete, *Raphepheng*, p. 5; Fredoux, 13 Oct. 1852, *JME* (1853), p. 55; Moshabesha and Jankie, "Mosotho," p. 46.

4 Moshabesha and Jankie, "Mosotho," p. 46.

5 Samuel Rolland, 19 March 1855, *JME*, (1855), p. 202; F. Maeder, 4 March, 1856, PEMS Archives (Paris), ALM 52.

6 Interviews with (12) Moleko Thateli, (13) Lineo Koromo, (18) Lehlohonolo Kele, (42) Ntorobaki J. Matabane, (52) Mamohloli Nkuebe, (64) Mahoki Mokitlane, (67) Setene Lenela.

7 Interviews with (38) 'Mamapote Kobile, (42) Ntorobaki J. Matabane, (49) Matsela Tooai.
8 Interviews with fourteen informants.
9 Martin, *Basutoland*, p. 33; Mabille, "The Basuto of Basutoland," p. 242.
10 Martin, *Basutoland*, p. 32.
11 Adolphe Mabille, 24 May 1860, *JME* (1860), p. 283; A. Mabille, 1863, "Quelques Traits," p. 58; Gerard, 15 March 1865, *Missions*, 5, 17 (March 1866), pp. 23–24.
12 Mohapi, *Temo*, pp. 34–37.
13 Interviews with (24) Molikeng Motseki, (26) Francina Palatse, (27) Mamotoai Letsosa, (29) Mamolikeng Motoai, (31) 'Mabatho Serobanyane, (20) Nkane Azariel Kaka.
14 Widdicombe, *Fourteen Years*, p. 48.
15 Interviews with (22) Joel Pharoe Moena, (31) 'Mabatho Serobanyane.
16 Interviews with (23) Kopano Jeremiah Telo, (24) Molikeng Motseki.
17 Interviews with ten informants.
18 Segoete, *Raphepheng*, p. 7; Mohapi, *Temo*, p. 41.
19 Interviews with (20) Nkane Azariel Kaka, (27) Mamotoai Letsosa; Segoete, *Raphepheng*, p. 8; Mohapi, *Temo*, pp. 41, 48, 50; Martin, *Basutoland*, p. 40; John Gay, "Field Notes," (unpublished); personal observation.
20 Interviews with (22) Joel Pharoe Moeno, (44) Malipere Tjamela.
21 Interviews with (23) Kopano Jeremiah Telo, (28) Mampeo Ranteme, (30) Makoloti Koloti, (32) Selbourne Moeketsi Lefoka, (71) Mahlatsoane Seboche; Mohapi, *Temo*, p. 50; Widdicombe, *Fourteen Years*, p. 48; Martin, *Basutoland*, p. 40.
22 Interview with (22) Joel Pharoe Moeno; Mohapi, *Temo*, pp. 48, 56; Widdicombe, *Fourteen Years*, p. 48; Martin, *Basutoland*, p. 40; personal observation.
23 *BBNA*, 1876. G.27-'76, 19; interviews with (5) Mantele Mishaka, (17) Sekaute Letle, (18) Lehlohonolo Kele, (22) Joel Pharoe Moeno, (23) Kopano Jeremiah Telo, (35) Thabo Fako, (46) Matsekoa Motleleng.
24 Interviews with nine informants; Martin, *Basutoland*, p. 40; Moshabesha and Jankie, "Mosotho," p. 43.
25 Andrew Smith, *Diary*, p. 114.
26 Casalis, *Les Bassoutos*, pp. 183–184. Translation mine.
27 Casalis, 20 June 1846, PEMS Archives (Paris), AL 355, 1846–47, 115; Casalis, 8 July 1853, PEMS Archives (Paris), AL 529, 1853–54: 179.
28 Schrumpf, 23 Oct. 1845, PEMS Archives (Paris), ALS 21.
29 Great Britain, *Basutoland*, p. 4.
30 Widdicombe, *Fourteen Years*, p. 50; See also Martin, *Basutoland*, p. 38.
31 Great Britain, *Military Report*, p. 25.
32 Rebecca Huss-Ashmore, "Seasonality in Rural Highland Lesotho." Unpublished paper, p. 14.
33 Interviews with nine informants.
34 Widdicombe, *Fourteen Years*, p. 47; *Quarterly Paper*, 75 (15 Jan. 1887); Adeline Melato, 4 June 1896, *Petit Messager* (1896), p. 95.
35 Widdicombe, *Fourteen Years*, p. 47.
36 For another perspective of these issues in the context of southern Africa, see Guy, "Analysing Pre-Capitalist Societies," and Guy, "Gender Oppression."

9 The local exchange of goods and services, 1830–1910

1 Ellenberger, *History of the Basuto*, p. 353; Ellenberger, *Leselinyana*.
2 Interview with (19) Moeketsi Moseeka.
3 Interview with Masekotoana Lelakane (3).
4 Interview with Moeketsi Moseeka (19).
5 *Ibid.*

6 *Ibid.*
7 Interview with 'Masebabato Theko (6).
8 Interview with Moeketsi Moseeka (19).
9 *Ibid.*
10 *Ibid.*
11 Interviews with fourteen informants.
12 Interviews with (25) Mamothobi Mphosi, (42) Ntorobaki J. Matabane, (47) Moetsuoa Mohlahloe Mzwane.
13 Interview with Nkane Azariel Kaka (20).
14 Interview with Malipere Tjamela (44).
15 Dyke, 1 Oct. 1843, *JME* (1843), p. 362; *Sou Missionnaire*, No. 7, 1858; Cochet, "Notes," 17 July 1858, p. 42; *BBNA*, 1876, G1–'76; *BBNA*, 1879, G33–'79; Fredoux, 27 Dec. 1861, *JME* (1862), p. 126; H. Marzolff, 21 July 1896, *JME* (1897), p. 140.
16 Annual Report, *JME* (1844), p. 7; Widdicombe, *Fourteen Years*, pp. 47–48; A. Mabile, "Quelques Traits," Appendice I; *Leselinyana*, Dec. 1874; Porte, "Réminiscences," p. 184.
17 Circular from the Governor's Agent, Charles D. Griffith, to the Magistrate in Basutoland, 30 Jan. 1872, *BR*, VI, part II (unpublished), pp. 369–370.
18 Moshabesha and Jankie, "Mosotho," p. 51.
19 Porte, "Réminiscences," p. 184.
20 Interview with (19) Moeketsi Moseeka.
21 *BBNA*, 1876, G16–'76.
22 *Leselinyana*, Feb. 1885.
23 Ashton, *The Basuto*, p. 95.
24 Interview with (71) Mahlatsoane Seboche.
25 Interview with (19) Moeketsi Moseeka; Ashton, *The Basuto*, p. 160.
26 Interviews with (8) Lintso Motanyane, (21) Tsoeu Temeki, (41) Kichinane Ratoronko, (42) Ntorobaki J. Matabane, (44) Malipere Tjamela, (47) Moetsuoa Mohlahloe Mzwane, (58) Masimphole Mokoaleli.
27 Burchell, *Travels in the Interior*, II, p. 36.
28 Interview with 'Mamphoho Peshoane (1).
29 Interview with Moeketsi Moseeka (19).
30 Interview with Mahlatsoane Seboche (71).
31 Interview with Mamotopo Lephema (80).
32 Rev. E. W. Stenson, letter, *Quarterly Paper of the Orange Free State Mission*, no. 36, April 1877.

10 Women, reproduction, and production

1 MacGregor, *Basuto Traditions*, p. 17.
2 Sanders, *Moshoeshoe*, pp. 23, 134.
3 *Ibid.*, p. 134.
4 Ellenberger, *History of the Basuto*, p. 124.
5 *Ibid.*, p. 17. Because of the need for regularizing political and social relations using traditions of descent, circumcision was a decisive factor in social and political organization and power. At circumcision schools historical traditions were taught and thus perpetuated. In particular genealogies were rigorously maintained and all boys were circumcised according to genealogical rank and precedence: sanctions for violating this were severe. This aided in the preservation of the influence, if not power, of members of higher-ranking lines of descent, such as the BaFokeng, who retained influence but not often power; hence the importance of BaFokeng women as tools of legitimation of junior lines of descent.
6 *Ibid.*, pp. 17, 18, 20, 22, 24, 26, 27, 42, 60, 75–6, 104; MacGregor, *Basuto Traditions*, p. 21.
7 Ellenberger, *History of the Basuto*, pp. 76–78.

8 Sanders, *Moshoeshoe*, p. 58.

9 Ellenberger, *History of the Basuto*, p. 59. Note that Moletsane's father and his wife's father were first cousins, so that Moletsane had married in this instance his second cousin, from a house senior to his own.

10 *Ibid.*, p. 369.

11 *Ibid.*, p. 40.

12 *Ibid.*, p. 41.

13 *Ibid.*, pp. 41, 145.

14 *Ibid.*, pp. 41–42; MacGregor, *Basuto Traditions*, pp. 34–35.

15 MacGregor, *Basuto Traditions*, p. 48.

16 Ellenberger, *History of the Basuto*, p. 27.

17 *Ibid.*, p. 17.

18 *Ibid.*, p. 24.

19 MacGregor, *Basuto Traditions*, p. 39.

20 Ellenberger, *History of the Basuto*, p. 126.

21 *Ibid.*, p. 187.

22 *Ibid.*, p. 171.

23 *Ibid.*, p. 100.

24 *Ibid.*, p. 103.

25 *Ibid.*, p. 123.

26 *Ibid.*, p. 146.

27 *Ibid.*, p. 194.

28 MacGregor, *Basuto Traditions*, p. 54.

29 *Ibid.*, p. 18; Ellenberger, *History of the Basuto*, p. 129.

30 Ellenberger, *History of the Basuto*, p. 80.

31 *Ibid.*

32 See also MacGregor's account: MacGregor, *Basuto Traditions*, p. 24.

33 Ellenberger, *History of the Basuto*, pp. 83–84, 101. Ntsane's people got Ratlali's widow Mamosongoa but Mokoteli's people later carried her off.

34 *Ibid.*, p. 166.

35 *Ibid.*, p. 104.

36 *Ibid.*, p. 298.

37 *Ibid.*, p. 283.

38 *Ibid.*, p. 96.

39 Casalis, quoted in Thompson, *Survival in Two Worlds*, p. 7. See also Sanders, *Moshoeshoe*, p. 140.

40 Sanders, *Moshoeshoe*, p. 50. The authenticity of this incident was reinforced by further related information I received at an interview in 1989, which I was asked not to record.

41 Ellenberger, *History of the Basuto*, p. 269.

42 Quoted in Sanders, *Moshoeshoe*, p. 50.

43 For an elegant and incisive analysis of women's changing legal rights in the early colonial period which addresses all of these issues in depth, see Sandra Burman, "Fighting a Two-Pronged Attack." Burman uses court records to find women's voices which are otherwise notably absent in the historical record; these cases offer considerable insight into matters of marriage, property, and divorce with regard to women's rights. The legal history of Lesotho is difficult to trace since cases were not systematically recorded until the colonial period, by which time European customs (reinforced by the Christian missionary influence) and colonial law influenced legal decisions even in traditional courts. Although Burman does not try to derive evidence of women's legal status from pre-colonial sources, she nevertheless captures much evidence of women's pre-colonial legal status by examining court cases in the 1870s when the two legal systems directly confronted each other. All evidence from this early period is particularly important since the main source used by

scholars studying traditional SeSotho law has been the *Laws of Lerotholi*, but since they were first codified in 1903 (and subsequently amended and augmented) it is extremely difficult to sort out actual tradition from what might have been the "invention of legal tradition" by the wealthy chiefs who presented the laws to the colonial rulers. In spite of the evident Christian bias in it, Ellenberger's discussion of "Some Ancient Laws" and of family life and marriage in *History of the Basotho* (pp. 267–280) is useful in that it was based on earlier sources, including Casalis, *Les Bassoutos* and articles written in *Leselinyana* by various BaSotho men, especially Sekese.

44 Casalis, *Les Bassoutos*, p. 231.
45 See the discussion of property rights in Ashton, *The Basuto*, pp. 177–185.
46 Interviews with Kichinane Ratoronko (41); Mamphoho Peshoane (1); SeSotho transcript, translation mine. See also Ashton, *The Basuto*, pp. 177–178.
47 MacGregor, *Basuto Traditions*, pp. 34–35.
48 *Ibid.*, p. 33.
49 *Ibid.*, p. 35.
50 Ellenberger, *History of the Basuto*, p. 127.
51 *Ibid.*, p. 124.
52 *Ibid.*
53 Eldredge, "Sources of Conflict in Southern Africa."
54 Ellenberger, *History of the Basuto*, pp. 48, 141.
55 Smith, *Andrew Smith's Journal*, p. 92.
56 Ellenberger, *History of the Basuto*, p. 42.
57 Kuper estimates that a cattle herd doubles in twenty-four years. Kuper, *Wives for Cattle*, p. 168; cf. G. Dahl and A. Hjort, *Having Herds: Pastoral Herd Growth and Household Economy*, Stockholm Studies in Social Anthropology, 2 (Stockholm, 1976). This would seem to be a conservative estimate, presumably taking into account losses from diseases and other natural disasters; high mortality rates would certainly have offset natural birthrates among cattle in southern Africa.
58 T. Arbousset, 3 Dec. 1835, *JME* (1836), p. 144.
59 Casalis, *Les Bassoutos*, p. 202. His italics.
60 F. Porte, "Au Basutoland," *Petites Annales*, III (1893), p. 652.
61 Poulter, *Family Law*, pp. 94–95.
62 Sheddick, *The Southern Sotho*, p. 33.
63 Evidence of J. Halifax, South Africa, *South African Native Affairs Commission 1903–5* (*SANAC*), V, Index and Annexures to Minutes of Evidence Together with Written Replies to Questions and Additional Memoranda by Witnesses, p. 396; C. Motebang, *SANAC*, V, p. 417.
64 Poulter, *Family Law*, pp. 91–93.
65 E. Blyth, *SANAC*, V, p. 380.
66 *Ibid.*; C. Motebang, *SANAC*, V, p. 417; Alfred Casalis, 15 Sept. 1897, PEMS Archives (Paris), 1897; Jingoes, *A Chief is a Chief*, p. 23; Christeller, *JME* (1902), I, p. 103; Interviews with (11) Mathakane Matooane, (58) Masimphole Mokoaleli.
67 Interview with Maisaka Mokeke (14).
68 There is little evidence that any other goods were acceptable as substitutes, although one informant indicated that a poor person could give bags of grain, with two traditional two-muid bags equal to one head of cattle. Oral tradition reports that once Mokhesang, son of Thibela, chief of the BaPhuthi of Ntlo-Kholo, got a wife with hoes, but the very notice of this incident implies that it was exceptional. Interviews with eleven informants; Ellenberger, *Leselinyana*.
69 This has led Sheddick to suggest that a more appropriate translation of the term *bohali* is "child-price" instead of "bride-price" or "bridewealth". Sheddick, *The Southern Sotho*, p. 33.

70 Kuper, *Wives for Cattle*, p. 169.
71 Widdicombe, *Fourteen Years*, p. 53.
72 Kuper, *Wives for Cattle*, p. 168.
73 Gerard, *Missions*, 3, 9 (March 1864), in *Records*, p. 105; E. S. Rolland, "Notes on the Political and Social Position of the Basuto Tribe," 30 March 1868, *BR*, IV, part I (unpublished), p. 130; Orpen, *History of the Basutus*, p. 20; Poulter, *Family Law*, pp. 153–154.
74 Kuper, *Wives for Cattle*, p. 168.
75 Thompson, *Survival in Two Worlds*, pp. 96–97.
76 Interview with Morai Moeletsi (51). SeSotho transcript; translation mine.
77 Interview with Matsitso Mosoang (48), SeSotho transcript; translation mine.
78 Schrumpf, 18 May 1847; *JME* (1848), p. 93; Gerard, 4 Feb. 1864, *Missions*, 5, 17 (March 1866), in *Records*, II, p. 5.

11 The BaSotho and the rise of the regional European market, 1830–1910

1 Kimble, "Lesotho and the Outside World," p. 8; Judy Kimble, "Labour Migration in Basutoland, pp. 133–136. Keegan adopts Kimble's interpretation in "Trade, Accumulation and Impoverishment," pp. 197–198.
2 See Chapter 7.
3 Kimble, "Labour Migration in Basutoland," p. 129.
4 *Ibid.*, p. 130.
5 *Ibid.*, pp. 130–131.
6 *Ibid.*, p. 131, and n. 53.
7 *Ibid.*, p. 134.
8 Above, pp. 93–95 and n. 74.
9 These BaSotho were referred to as "Kaffirs," but from the description and location were clearly BaSotho and not AmaXhosa. Deposition of Mr. L. J. Fourie, *BR*, II, p. 438.
10 Deposition of Lena Sang Lepui, *BR*, II, pp. 437–438.
11 Autobiography of Elie Mapike Taole, *JME*, (1843), p. 210.
12 Backhouse, *Extracts from the Journal*, p. 42.
13 Freeman, *A Tour of South Africa*, p. 307; Rolland, *JME* (1855), p. 202.
14 Annual Report, 15 May 1844, *JME* (1845), p. 6; Arbousset and Daumas, *Narrative*, p. 211.
15 Cochet, "Notes," 25 May 1857; Maeder, *JME* (1857), p. 52; Maeder, 5 Jan. 1859, *JME* (1859), p. 127.
16 Annual Report, *JME* (1845), pp. 6, 26; Maeder, *JME* (1846), p. 48; Maeder, 15 July 1846, PEMS Archives (Paris), ALM 38; Arbousset, 9 May 1849, *JME* (1849), p. 392; Cocher, "Notes," 27 July 1858.
17 George Cathcart, 13 Jan. 1853, *BR*, II, p. 8. Also quoted in Thompson, *Survival in Two Worlds*, p. 190.
18 E. Casalis, 24 Oct., 1865, *BR*, III, p. 500. See also Casalis, *Les Bassoutos*, p. 216.
19 Daumas, 5 Feb., 1863, *JME* (1863), p. 120.
20 Governor's agent C. Griffith, 26 Aug. 1872, *BR*, IV, part II (unpublished), p. 499. *BBNA*, 1874, G. 27-'74. A muid as used in South Africa in the nineteenth century was a measure of weight equal to 204 pounds, although some sources equate it to 200 pounds.
21 *JME* (1873), pp. 249, 409; *BBNA*, 1876, G.16-'76.
22 *BBNA*, 1874, G.21-'74.
23 *BBNA*, 1875, G.21-'75; *BBNA*, 1876, G.16-'76.
24 *BBNA*, 1878, G. 17-'78.
25 Arbousset, 26 May 1854, *JME* (1854), pp. 446–447; J. Austen, 28 Feb. 1861, *BR*, II, p. 580.
26 Allard, 15 April 1864, *Missions*, 5, 17 (March 1866), in *Records*, p. 15; Scott Papers, *passim*. Wool from Lesotho was referred to as "Basuto Grease," and was distinguished from higher

quality Cape wool. Even Cape wool was of a low quality relative to wool from Australia and elsewhere. See Thom, *Die Geskiedenis*, pp. 173–177, 318ff.

27 C. Griffith, 16 Aug. 1872, *BR*, VI, part II, (unpublished), p. 499.

28 Andrew Smith, *Diary*, 13 Oct. 1834, I, p. 105, and 25 Nov. 1834, p. 146; F. G. LeBihan, *Daily Despatch*, Article in Correspondence Files, Archivum Générale, OMI, *c.* 1909.

29 Crisp, *Quarterly Paper* 23 (Jan. 1874); Crisp, 25 August 1870, "Letters," III, p. 14; Barkly, *Among Boers*, pp. 31, 46; C. Schrumpf, *Die Bassuto*, p. 45; Widdicombe, *Fourteen Years*, p. 56; E. Vollet, *JME* (1893), p. 423.

30 F. Coillard, 29 Oct. 1863, PEMS Archives (Paris), AL 768 [1863–64: 120]; Barkly, *Among Boers*, pp. 66–67; Widdicombe, *Fourteen Years*, p. 86; Porte,"Réminiscences," p. 192; G. Lorriaux, 27 Oct. 1899, *JME* (1900), p. 44; Marzolff, 15 Nov. 1901, *JME* (1902), p. 32.

31 Walton, *Father of Kindness*, p. 28.

32 Widdicombe, *Quarterly Paper* 129 (25 July 1900), p. 139; Barkly, *Among Boers*, p. 32; Miss Woodman, *Quarterly Paper* 46 (Oct. 1879).

33 Andrew Smith, *Diary*, 22 Oct. 1834, I, p. 117. For early currency use and exchange rates in South Africa see Arndt, *Banking and Currency Development*.

34 Cape of Good Hope, *Report of the Governor's Agent Basutoland for 1872*, G.27-'73.

35 A. Mabille, unpublished letter, 24 June 1870, PEMS Archives (Morija).

36 Dyke, *Basutoland Evangelist Aid Fund*; *Leselinyana*, 1 June 1885; Dr. E. Casalis, 4 Feb. 1886, PEMS Archives (Paris), 1886; A. Mabille, 7 Oct. 1887, "Letters to the British and Foreign Bible Society" (unpublished), PEMS Archives (Morija); Mms. Kohler, 3 Oct. 1887, Correspondance Missionaire 23 (Jan. 1887); *Assemblée Générale* (1887); *CRA* 343, 1900–01, Cd. 788–13; *SANAC*, V, p. 380.

37 Arbousset, 26 June 1838, *JME* (1839), p. 60; Daumas, 29 Jan. 1842, *JME* (1842), p. 321; Arbousset, 6 Aug. 1851, *JME* (1851), p. 412; J. Austen, 22 March 1858, *BR*, II, p. 332.

38 Atmore and Sanders, "Sotho Arms and Ammunition," p. 538; Cochet, "Notes," 26 Feb. 1859; J. Austen, 28 Feb. 1861, *BR*, I, p. 580; Fredoux, *JME* (1862), p. 128; F. Coillard, *JME* (1862), p. 409; Mabille, letter, 1864, "Quelque Traits," p. 412; Dr. E. Casalis, unpublished letter, 1 Oct. 1864, PEMS Archives (Morija); Superintendent of the Wittebergen Native Reserve, 4 Jan. 1862, *BR*, III, p. 114; Civil Commissioner of Aliwal North, 14 July 1862, *BR*, III, p. 174.

39 Atmore and Sanders, "Sotho Arms and ammunition," p. 538; F. Douglas, 14 Oct. 1880, *Quarterly Paper* 51 (Jan. 1881), p. 12.

40 Barkly, *Among Boers*, p. 147.

41 Great Britain, *Military Report*, A.1035.

42 Interviews with (19) Moeketsi Moseeka, (21) Tsoeu Temeki; Scott Papers, items 1/18/14, 1/14/19, 1/14/22, 1/1/10, 1/15/3, 1/3/6, 1/19/1, 1/20/31, 1/10/2, 1/6/9, 1/19/4.

43 Meader, 15 Jan. 1858, *JME* (1858), p. 133; Annual Report, *JME* (1840), p. 370; Fredoux, 27 Dec. 1861, *JME* (1862), p. 128; Gerard, Dec. 1863, *Records*, p. 102; Allard, 15 April 1864, *Records*, p. 15.

44 *Report* 1872, G27-'72; Eugenie Berthoud, 16 Feb. 1874. *Lettres Missionaires*; J. Deacon, *Quarterly Paper* 88 (15 April 1890), p. 237; Widdicombe, *Fourteen Years*, p. 55; Walton, *Father of Kindness*, p. 42.

45 Balfour, *Twelve Hundred Miles*, p. 44; Porte, "Réminiscences," p. 178.

46 Correspondent of the *Friend of the Free State*, 13 Dec. 1861, *BR*, II, p. 609; Allard, 26 March 1862, *Missions*, 1, 3 (Sept. 1862), in *Records*, p. 71; Barkly, *Among Boers*, p. 118; Balfour, *Twelve Hundred Miles*, p. 50; Lebreton, "A Travers les Montagnes du Basutoland," p. 299; Gerard, unpublished letter, 5 March 1914, Special Archives, OMI.

47 Mabille, 30 June 1866, "Quelques Traits," p. 251; *JME* (1885), p. 407; Gerard, unpublished letter, 31 Jan. 1913, Special Archives, OMI.

48 Arbousset, 2 Jan. 1860, *JME* (1860), p. 218; Griffith, 26 Aug. 1872, *BR*, VI, part II, p. 498; *Little Light*, 8 (1874); Balfour, 19 Nov. 1878, *Quarterly Paper* 43 (Jan. 1879); E. Mabille, 26

Sept. 1887, *Petit Messager* (1887), p. 222; Scott Papers, *passim*; Martin, *Basutoland*, p. 39; *SANAC*, IV, p. 399, V, p. 410; Everitt Segoete, *Leselinyana*, 25 Sept. 1909.

49 Letsie, 12 Oct. 1866, *BR*, III, p. 730; Moshoeshoe, 29 Oct. 1866, *BR*, III, p. 730; Secretary for Native Affairs, Natal, *BR*, III, p. 803; R. Henry Dyke, 23 Nov. 1903, PEMS Archives (Paris), 1903; Louisa Cochet, 28 Jan. 1905, *Gospel Work in Basutoland in Native Agency 1904–5*, p. 26.

50 Moshoeshoe promulgated "The Law for Trade," Bethesda, 6th Sept. 1859. In it he stated that "Trade to me and my Tribe is a good thing; I wish to promote it." The law protected the right of traders to establish shops with permission, but denied them the ownership of all and any buildings, and prohibited them from plowing any fields or cultivating more than a small vegetable garden. Quoted in Lagden, *The Basutos*, I, p. 304. Also quoted in Thompson, *Survival in Two Worlds*, p. 200.

51 Allard, *Missions*, 6, 21 (March 1867), pp. 67–77, in *Records*, p. 49; Great Britain, *Basutoland*, 1880; p. 9; *JME* (1897), p. 14; P. Lautre, 15 May 1846, *JME* (1847), p. 247; Assemblée Général, 29 Avril 1841; Evidence of J. Merriman, in Cape of Good Hope, *Report of the Select Committee Appointed by the Legislative Council to consider the Provisions of the Basutoland Annexation Bill*, (Cape Town, 1871), C.I-71; *BR*, VI, part I, p. 166. The price of a wagon was £70 in 1844, and ranged from £40 to £500 during the remainder of the nineteenth century, with scanty evidence suggesting an average price of about £120. *JME* (1855), p. 202; *Missions*, pp. 52, 507; *JME* (1876), p. 205; *Petit Messager*, 1891; *Leselinyana*, February 1878.

52 Gerard, unpublished letter, 17 July 1878, Special Archives, OMI, Rome, Ecrits du R. P. Gerard; Walton, *Father of Kindness*, p. 14.

53 Grant, "A Journey from Qacha's Nek to Advance Post." Unpublished MS., PEMS Archives (Morija), p. 47; Barkly, *Among Boers*, p. 34; F. H. Kruger, *JME* (1883), p. 89; *Little Light*, Oct. 1875, Dec. 1875; *Leselinyana*, Dec. 1875 (first advertisements for Irvine Holden & Co.); W. H. R. Bevan, March 1874, *Quarterly Paper* 28 (April 1875), p. 3; *Leselinyana*, 1 Nov. 1882, May 1883, August 1883, October 1889; *CRA*, 380, 1901–02, Cd. 1388–4.

54 Preen, 9 June 1875, *JME* (1875), p. 368; South Africa, *Despatch from Sir Hercules Robinson*, 1887, C.-5238.

55 *CRA*, 89, 1892–93, C. 6857-39; Dieterlen, 26 Oct. 1893, *JME* (1894), p. 108; Christol, *Petit Messager*, (1895), p. 203; Great Britain, *Military Report*; Lebreton, "A Travers les Montagnes de Basutoland," p. 268; Segoete, "Leeto la Malingoaneng."

56 South Africa, *Military Report on Basutoland*, II, Routes (1910), A.1384.

57 *JME* (1872), p. 83; *Missions* 52 (Dec. 1875), p. 507; *JME* (1876), p. 205. Census returns from 1891 listed 808 wagons in the country.

58 *BBNA*, 1875, G21-'75.

59 "Additional Trading Regulations for Basutoland," P. E. Wodehouse, High Commissioner, Cape Town, 1 May 1870, article 6, *BR*, V, part II, p. 491.

60 *Despatch*, 1887, C.-5238; F. Christol, 15 July 1889, *JME* (1889), p. 369; *CRA*, 123, 1893–94. C.-7629-6.

61 *Quarterly Paper* 49 (July 1880), p. 10.

62 Great Britain, Her Majesty's Colonial Possession, No. 31, *Basutoland, Report of the Resident Commissioner for 1887*, C.-5249.-28.

63 Germond, 8 March 1887, *JME* (1887), p. 61; T. Jousse, *JME* (1888), p. 87; Ellenberger, Oct. 1887, in Germond, *Chronicles*, p. 470. According to Merk, in the United States in the 1870s, "scores" of agricultural machines "produced a revolution in farming comparable in extent and insignificance to the Industrial Revolution ... Its effect was to neutralize the high labor costs of the West, which had previously been one of the chief handicaps in competing in the food markets of the world." Other factors, including land grants through the 1862 Homestead Law, a free immigration policy, the expansion of railroads across the Middle West of the United States, and the introduction of the elevator system of transferring and

storing grain "made possible effective competition with foreign growers." Between 1866 and 1891 the American wheat crop increased from 152 to 612 million bushels; the improvements in transportation made it possible for these surpluses to be sold competitively abroad. See Merk, *History of the Westward Movement*, pp. 431–438; and Morison, *Oxford History*, pp. 743–747.

64 R. Henry Dyke, *The Basutoland Evangelist Aid Fund* (Morija: Morija Mission Press, 1888), p. 4; Jousse, *JME* (1888), p. 87. See table 6.

65 E. Cassalis, 4 Feb. 1886, PEMS Archives (Paris), 1886.

66 *CRA*, 380, 1901–02, Cd. 1388–4.

67 *Her Majesty's Colonial Possessions*, No. 31, 1887, C.-5249.-28. These duties were apparently removed when Orange Free State supplies were inadequate to meet demand after a period of drought. Letter of H. Oldefield and Co., Johannesburg, 28 Jan. 1896, Scott Papers 1/18/4.

68 D. F. Ellenberger, 22 June 1897, *JME* (1897), p. 487; C. Reading, *Quarterly Paper* 118 (25 Oct. 1897), pp. 148–150, 157.

69 *CRA*, 313, 1899–1900, C.431-5; *CRA*, 343, 1900–01, Cd. 788-13; Dieterlen, 14 Sept. 1900, PEMS Archives (Paris), 1900; G. Lorriaux, *JME* (1900), p. 459.

12 The colonial imposition and the failure of the local economy, 1871–1910

1 Cape of Good Hope, *Report of the Select Committee Appointed by the Legislative Council*, C. 1–71.

2 Letter from High Commissioner Henry Barkly to C. D. Griffith, Cape Town, 2 Sept, 1871, *BR*, VI, part II, p. 289.

3 Burman, *Chiefdom Politics and Alien Law*.

4 Petition to His Excellency Sir Henry Barkly K.C.B., Governor, High Commissioner, Cape of Good Hope, 25 Feb. 1872, *BR*, VI, part II, p. 402. See also Burman, *Chiefdom Politics and Alien Law*, p. 68.

5 Burman, *Chiefdom Politics and Alien Law*, p. 68.

6 *Ibid.*, p. 129.

7 *Ibid.*, pp. 133–136.

8 *Ibid.*, p. 136.

9 Lagden, *The Basutos*, p. 599.

10 Great Britain, *Basutoland*, pp. 16–17, italics mine.

11 Kimble, "Labour Migration in Basutoland," p. 131.

12 *Ibid.*, p. 133.

13 "Echoes of the Past," Paper presented at the African Studies Association.

14 Burman, *Chiefdom Politics and Alien Law*, pp. 180–181.

15 Jonathan Molapo, 26 Sept. 1904, *SANAC*, IV, p. 394.

16 George Richard Hobson, 26 Sept. 1904, *SANAC*, IV, p. 508.

17 L. Barrett, Assistant Commissioner, Quthing, *SANAC*, IV, p. 379; J. W. Bowker, Assistant Commissioner, Mohale's Hoek, *SANAC*, IV, p. 381; Guy Hallifax, trader, Quthing, *SANAC*, IV, p. 394; E. Jacottet, missionary Thaba-Bosiu, *SANAC*, IV, p. 403.

18 Rev. Canon Weigall, Masite, *SANAC*, V, p. 421.

19 C. D. Griffith, 15 Jan. 1872, *BR*, VI, part II, p. 354; Bell, 22 Jan. 1872, *BR*, VI, part Ii, p. 360; C. D. Griffith, 7 Feb. 1872, *BR*, VI, part Ii, p. 382.

20 Unpublished letter, A. Mabille to L. J. Cochet, 24 June 1870, PEMS Archives (Morija); Despatch from Governor Henry Barkly, 1 May 1872, *BR*, VI, part II, p. 455.

21 Lagden, *The Basutos*, II, p. 470; "Return, showing the total amount of Revenue received for British Basutoland since the assumption of British Authority over the Basutos up to 31 May 1871, and specifying by whom and under what head collected," *BR*, VI, part II, p. 123; C. D. Griffith, 26 Aug. 1872, *BR*, VI, part II, p. 500.

22 Circular from the Governor's Agent C. D. Griffith, to the Magistrates of Basutoland; Maseru, 30 Jan. 1872, *BR*, VI, part II, p. 368.
23 C. J. Maitin, *SANAC*, V, p. 414; Alfred Casalis, 1 Nov. 1892, *JME* (1893), p. 19; G. R. Hobson, *SANAC*, IV, p. 401.
24 Mr. C. J. Maitin, trader, Boqate, *SANAC*, V, p. 414.
25 Above, pp. 62–65.
26 Above, p. 159.
27 Lagden, *The Basutos*, II, p. 470.
28 E. Mabile, 18 March 1886, PEMS Archives (Paris); interview with Lelinguana, *JME* (1888), p. 305.
29 Unpublished letter, A. Mabille to L. J. Cochet, 24 June 1870, PEMS Archives (Morija).
30 Alfred Casalis, 1 Nov. 1892, *JME* (1893), p. 19; *JME* (1892), p. 19.
31 Lagden, *The Basutos*, II, p. 470; D. F. Ellenberger, 21 Dec. 1892, *JME* (1893), p. 122; *CRA*, 89, 1892–93, C.-6857–39.
32 *CRA*, 152, Basutoland, for the year 1894–95 [C.7944–4].
33 Jousee, *JME* (1888), p. 87; letters from Dunnell Eden & Co., Aliwal North, 21 August 1896, Scott Papers, 1/6/9 and 18 Sept. 1896, 1/6/7, *BOLESWA* Collection, National University of Lesotho.
34 *The Board of Trade Journal of Tariff and Trade Notices and Miscellaneous Commercial Information*, vol. 20 (London, January to June 1896).
35 Above, p. 80.
36 *CRA*, 224, 1896–7, C.-8650–22.
37 G. Lorriaux, Thaba-Bosiu, 10 January 1899, *JME* (1899), p. 190.
38 Jacottei, 13 June 1898, *JME* (1898), p. 552–553; Kohler, 20 Oct. 1898, *JME* (1898), p. 880; Marzolff, 2 Dec. 1898, *JME* (1899), p. 104; Lagden, *The Basutos*, p. 611; Alfred Casalis, *JME* (1899), II, p. 234; Widdicombe, *Fourteen Years*, p. 43.
39 *CRA*, 513, 1905–06, cd.3285. Although fruit trees rapidly became popular, the BaSotho did not actively cooperate in the efforts at tree-planting for two reasons. One European observer who inquired why the BaSotho did not plant more was told that trees attracted birds which destroyed the nearby crops. The more common reason given, however, was that tree planting constituted an improvement to the land which inspired confiscation by chiefs. Planting of the eucalyptus globus was particularly encouraged because it grew quickly and had numerous uses. *JME* (1876), p. 461; *Military Report*.
40 Geoffrey Lagden, *The Basutos*, II, p. 470; *JME* (1883), p. 86; Burman, *Chiefdom Politics and Alien Law*, pp. 181–184.
41 Christol, 16 April 1900, *JME* (1900), I, p. 457; Jacottet, 15 June 1900, *JME* (1900), II, p. 111; *CRA*, 343, 1901–02, Cd. 788–13; letter from Baker, Baker & Co. (East London and King Williamstown), 27 July 1900, Scott Papers 1/14/4l; Memorial of William Scott to Sir Godfrey Lagden, Sept. 1900, Scott Papers, 1/14/13; letters from Dunnell Ebden & Co., (Aliwal North), 4 Dec. 1900 and 22 Dec. 1900, Scott Papers 1/14/27 and 1/14/28; Alfred Casalis, *JME* (1902), II, p. 241.
42 Letter of Dieterlen, 23 Dec. 1899, PEMS Archives (Paris).
43 *CRA*, 634, 1908–09, Cd.4964–8; Christeller, 28 June 1908, PEMS Archives (Paris).
44 Keck, 19 March 1870, PEMS Archives (Paris), AL1194 [1870–71: 3].
45 Barkly, *Among Boers*, p. 33.
46 Crisp, "Letters," Oct. 1867, Book A, 17.
47 M. A. DeBeer, *SANAC*, V, p. 161.
48 James Scott, *SANAC*, IV, p. 327; Robert Dickie, *SANAC*, IV, p. 305; J. G. Fraser, *SANAC*, IV, p. 280.
49 J. G. Fraser, *SANAC*, IV, p. 270.
50 Widdicombe, *Fourteen Years*, p. 250; F. Coillard, 20 Feb. 1899, *JME* (1899), p. 376; J. G. Fraser, *SANAC*, IV, pp. 270–273.

51 F. Coillard, 20 Feb. 1899, *JME* (1899), p. 376; J. G. Fraser, *SANAC*, IV, p. 278; Alec Wilson, *SANAC*, IV, p. 311; G. H. Turvey and J. M. van Reneen, *SANAC*, IV, p. 339; M. A. DeBeer, *SANAC*, V, p. 161; A. R. Walker, *SANAC*, V, p. 179; T. P. Kennan, *SANAC*, V, p. 410; Archdeacon Vincent, 13 Sept. 1910, *Quarterly Paper*, 170 (15 Oct. 1910), p. 134.

52 Caroline Van Heyningen, *Orange Days: Memoirs of Eighty Years Ago in the Old Orange Free State*, (Pietermaritzburg, 1965), p. 25; Sister Emma, 29 April 1875, *Quarterly Paper*, 28 (28 April 1875); C. D. Hall, *SANAC*, V, p. 165; H. Hanger, *SANAC*, V, p. 167; Robert Dickiep, *SANAC*, IV, p. 303; D. Hertzog, *SANAC*, V, p. 167; C. E. Manley, *SANAC*, V, p. 170.

53 Letter from R. C. Prior, 22 Aug. 1903, Scott Papers, 1/15/6.

54 Keck, 19 March 1870, PEMS Archives (Paris), AL1194 [1870–71: 13].

55 Annual Report, *JME* (1886), p. 299.

56 Crisp, *Quarterly Paper*, 124 (25 April 1900), p. 66.

57 H. Crosthwaite, *Quarterly Paper*, 118 (25 Oct. 1897), p. 160.

58 H. Crosthwaite, *Quarterly Paper*, 128 (25 April 1900), p. 160.

59 C. J. Bornman, *SANAC*, V, p. 161.

60 Census van den Oranj Vrijstaat, Opgeromen op 31 Mart, 1880; Census ... 1890; Census statistics in *Quarterly Paper*, 153 (25 July 1906).

61 J. G. Fraser, *SANAC*, IV, p. 280.

62 Interview with (19) Moeketsi Moseeka. See also Eldredge, "Echoes of the Past", for evidence which confirms widespread acceptance of this view based on my subsequent archival and oral research in 1988 and 1989.

13 Economy, politics, migrant labor and gender

1 For example Kimble, "Labour Migration in Basutoland"; Beinart, *Political Economy of Pondoland*; Delius, *The Land Belongs to Us.*

2 Wolpe, "Capitalism and Cheap Labour Power"; Meillassoux, *Maidens, Meal and Money.*

3 Bozzoli, "Marxism, Feminism and South African Studies," p. 142.

4 Kimble, "Labour migration in Basutoland", p. 136.

5 *Ibid.*, pp. 129–130.

6 Eldredge, "Slave Raiding Beyond the Cape Frontier".

7 Ellenberger, *History of the Basotho*, p. 132.

8 Arbousset, Morija, 30 Dec. 1851, *JME* (1852), p. 240: biography of Simeone Bignane.

9 Letter from the British Resident [Bloemfontein] H. D. Warden to the Secretary to the High Commissioner, 27 Oct. 1847.

10 Dyke, Casalis, *et al.*, "Précis des Circonstances," *JME* (1852), p. 16; T. Arbousset, 26 May 1854, *JME* (1854), p. 446; F. Maeder, "Notice Sur la Nation," *JME* (1856), p. 204.

11 *JME* (1862), p. 329.

12 Council for World Missions/London Missionary Society Papers, South Africa, 1841–1842, Box 18, Folder 4, Jacket b, 1, "Memorial of the Missionaries" [copy].

13 C. Griffith, *Little Light of Basutoland*, 2, 7 (July 1873).

14 Civil Commissioner of Aliwal North, 22 Oct. 1866, *BR*, III, p. 730.

15 Civil Commissioner of Aliwal North, 28 May 1866, *BR*, III, p. 701.

16 Kimble, "Labour Migration in Basutoland," p. 123. This is an excellent article dealing with some of the main issues surrounding early labor migration from Lesotho, but Kimble makes no attempt to assess the impact of the migrant labor system on the local BaSotho economy. In addition, I question the extent to which landlessness stimulated labor migration in this early period. This does not seem to have been a significant factor until the late 1890s, and even her evidence for this comes from 1903.

17 *Ibid.*, pp. 119–141.

18 Judy Kimble, "'Clinging to the Chiefs,'" pp. 46–47.

19 Kimble, "Labour Migration in Basutoland," pp. 132–133.
20 Gerard, 10 Sept. 1875, *Missions*, 52 (Dec. 1875), p. 497.
21 *Circular no. 5 of 1873: Native Labour From Missionary Institutions in Kaffraria, For Public Works*. Office of the Secretary for Native Affairs, Cape Town, 11 Nov. 1873.
22 Kimble, "Labour Migration in Basutoland," *passim*; Alan H. Jeeves, *Migrant Labour in South Africa's Mining Economy, passim*.
23 *Leselinyana*, January 1888; Dyke, *The Switzerland of South Africa*, p. 37; Dyke, *The Basutoland Evangelist Aid Fund*, p. 5.
24 *Missions de la Congrégation des Oblats de Marie Immaculée*, 135 (Sept. 1896), p. 274.
25 *Ibid.*, p. 275.
26 J. S. Yeats, trader, Thaba Bosiu, *SANAC*, V, p. 431.
27 Interview with (12) Moleko Thateli.
28 Guy Halifax, *SANAC*, V, p. 394.
29 Proclamation no. 27 of 1907, *CRA*, 595, 1907–08, Cd.4448–4.
30 Jonathan Molapo, *SANAC*, IV, p. 459; C. J. Maitin, *SANAC*, V, p. 414; E. Maitin, *SANAC*, V, p. 416; *CRA*, 255, 1897–98, C.–9046.–23.
31 *Leselinyana*, 1 August 1897.
32 *CRA*, 408, 1902–03, C.1768–13; C. J. Maitin, *SANAC*, V, p. 414.
33 Walker, "Gender and the development of the migrant labour system," pp. 168–196.
34 *Ibid.*, p. 179.
35 Bozzoli, "Marxism, Feminism and South African Studies," pp. 146–147.
36 *Ibid.*, p. 151.
37 Peters, "Gender, Developmental Cycles and Historical Process," p. 102.
38 For the fate of BaSotho women in the cities as female migrancy increased in the 1930s see Bonner, "'Desirable or undesirable Basotho women?'" pp. 221–250.

14 In pursuit of security

1 Arbousset, *Missionary Excursion*, p. 110. Moshoeshoe could thus converse with anyone speaking any of the mutually-intelligible dialects of SeSotho- and SeTswana-speakers and of IsiXhosa- and IsiZulu-speakers. This of course included all of the immigrants coming from east, west, north, and south over the decades in which he ruled: AmaHlubi, AmaNgwane, BaPedi, AmaSwazi, BaTlokoa, BaTaung, BaRolong, BaPhuthi, AmaThembu, AmaXhosa, AmaMpondo, AmaNdebele, and so on.
2 Personal observation during visit and interview with Moetsuoa Mohlahloe Mzwane (47), at HaChopo, May 1982.
3 Moroosi's rebellion was a rebellion of the BaPhuthi to colonial rule; BaSotho troops fought only under the threat of land expropriation if they failed to cooperate. Therefore, although the African forces fighting were divided along ethnic lines, with non-BaPhuthi BaSotho forces fighting BaPhuthi (BaSotho) rebels, the origin of the conflict was not ethnically-derived.
4 Widdicombe, *Fourteen Years*, p. 47; *Quarterly Paper*, 75 (15 Jan. 1887); Adeline Melato, 4 June 1896 in *Petit Messager* (1896), p. 95.

Bibliography

Archives

Société des Missions Evangéliques de Paris (PEMS), Paris, France

Letters from Lesotho, 1834–1910.

Société des Missions Evangéliques de Paris, (Lesotho Evangelical Church), Morija, Lesotho

Arbousset, T. "Excursions Missionaire de M. T. Arbousset dans les Montagnes Bleues."
   Unpublished MS., 1840.
Ellenberger, D. F. "Histoire Ancienne et Moderne des Basotho, 3ième Periode," Unpublished
   MS.
Ellenberger Papers.
Correspondence between J. M. Orpen and D. F. Ellenberger.
Correspondence between J. C. MacGregor and D. F. Ellenberger.
Documents Historiques.
Grant, J. M. "A Journey from Qacha's Nek to Advance Post, Dec. 7–25, 1873." Unpublished MS.
"Lettres de la Conférence (Lesotho) au comité et à Divers," 1848–1865, Unpublished MS.
Moshabesha, N. and Jankie, H. E. "Mosotho." Unpublished MS., revised version, 1939.
Moshoeshoe [Moshesh], Nehemiah Sekhonyana. Sesotho MS., sent to J. M. Orpen, 4
   December 1905.
"Notes et Souvenirs du Missionaire L. J. Cochet."
"Quelques Traits de la Vie Missionaire: Extraits de la Correspondance Particulière de M. et
   Mad. Mabille." Unpublished MS. copy, edited by Betsy Celerier.
Reports and Official Correspondence, missionaries of Lesotho, to Comité de la Société des
   Missions Evangéliques.
Unpublished letters of T. Arbousset, Dr. Casalis, R. Daumas, Adolphe Mabille, N. S.
   Moshoeshoe, J. M. Orpen, E. S. Rolland, S. Rolland, Azariel M. Sekese, G. M. Theal.

Archives of the Diocese of Bloemfontein, Bloemfontein, South Africa

Crisp, William. Log Book and Letters. 2 vols. 1867–1876.
Crisp, William. Letterbook. (Copies). 1879–1893.

Archivum Générale, Oblats de Marie Immaculée, Rome, Italy

Correspondence Files.
Deltour, Marcellin, OMI "Histoire du Lesotho." Unpublished MS., n.d., *c.* 1888.

234

Gerard, Joseph, OMI "Ecrits de R. P. Gerard." Originals and typescripts.
Laydevant, François, OMI "Le Basutoland." Unpublished MS., *c*. 1951.

London Missionary Society (Council for World Missions), School of Oriental and African Studies, London, England

J. J. Freeman Deputation 1849–1850. Two boxes.
Miscellaneous letters: South Africa: 1841–1842, Box 18; 1843, Box 19.

Lesotho National Archives, National University of Lesotho, Roma, Lesotho

Theal, G. M. "Basutoland Records," vols. IV–VI, unpublished.
Agriculture and Veterinary: Rinderpest Papers 1896–1937.

Library of the National University of Lesotho, BOLESWA Collection, Roma, Lesotho

Scott Papers, miscellaneous, 1889–1905, Judy Kimble Collection.

Free State Archives, Bloemfontein

British Resident. Letters Received by the British Resident from the Native Chiefs and Missionaries, 1836, Aug. 4 – 1853, Nov. 7.
British Resident. Meetings and Interviews with Native Chiefs, 1848, Nov. 8 – 1852, Dec. 15.
Special Commissioner. Board of Claims.
Special Commissioner. Documents re the Land Board, 1853 June – 1854 June.

Newspapers and periodicals

Assemblée Générale de la Société des Missions Evangéliques
The Basutoland Evangelist Aid Fund
Correspondance Missionaire
Gospel Work in Basutoland by Native Agency
Graham's Town Journal
Journal des Missions Evangéliques
The Little Light of Basutoland
Leselinyana la Lesotho
Missionary Record of the Oblates of Mary Immaculate
Les Missions Catholiques (Lyon)
Missions de la Congrégation des Oblats de Marie Immaculée
Le Petit Messager des Missions Evangéliques
Petites Annales de la Congrégation des Missionaires Oblats de Marie Immaculée
Quarterly Paper of the Orange Free State Mission
Sou Missionaire

Official publications

Basutoland Government. *Melao ea Lerotholi (e hlophisitsoeng)*. (Laws of Lerotholi augmented.) Morija: Morija Sesuto Book Depot, 1959; reprinted 1981.
Cape of Good Hope. Government Gazette Extraordinary, Tuesday March 18, 1884. *Proclamation of Disannexation.*

Bibliography

Cape of Good Hope. *Report of the Select Committee Appointed by the Legislative Council to consider the Provisions of the Basutoland Annexation Bill.* Cape Town, 1871, C.1–71.

Cape of Good Hope. *Report of the Governor's Agent, Basutoland, for 1872.* G.27-'73.

Cape of Good Hope. *Blue-Book on Native Affairs.* 1874, G.27-'74. 1875, G.21-'75. 1876, G.16-'76. 1877, G.12-'77. 1878, G.17-'78. 1879, G.33-'79. 1880, G.13-'80. 1881, G.20-'81. 1883, G.8-'83.

Cape of Good Hope. Ministerial Department of the Secretary of Native Affairs. *Basutoland. Annual Report for the Year 1882, on the Leribe District.* G.9-83.

Cape of Good Hope. Ministerial Department of the Secretary of Native Affairs. *Annual Report for 1882, of the Acting Governor's Agent for Basutoland.*

Circular no. 5 of 1873: Native Labour From Missionary Institutions in Kaffraria, For Public Works. Office of the Secretary for Native Affairs. Cape Town, 11 Nov. 1873.

Great Britain. *Her Majesty's Colonial Possessions. No. 31. Cape of Good Hope. Report of the Resident Commissioner* for 1887, C.-5249.-28. No. 70, 1889, C.-5897. No. 114, 1889–90, C.-6221.-3.

Great Britain. *Colonial Reports.-Annual. Cape of Good Hope.* No. 20 for the year 1890–91. C.-6563-4. No. 62, 1891–92, C.-6857-12. No. 89, 1892–93, C.-6857-39. No. 123, 1893–94, C.-7629-6. No. 152, 1894–95, C.-7944-4. No. 186, 1895–96, C.-8279-10. No. 224, 1896–97, C.-8650-22. No. 255, 1897–98, C.-9046-23. No. 288, 1898–99, Cd.3-11. No. 313, 1899–1900, Cd.431-5. No. 343, 1900–01, Cd.788-13. No. 380, 1901–02, Cd.1388-4. No. 408, 1902–03, Cd.1768–13. No. 480, 1904–05, Cd.2684-26. No. 513, 1905–06, Cd.3285. No. 556, 1906–07, Cd.3729-20. No. 595, 1907–08, Cd.4448–4. No. 634, 1908–09, Cd.4964-8. No. 677, 1909–10, Cd.5467-13. No. 710, 1910–11, Cd.6007-10.

Great Britain. *Colonial Reports.-Annual.* No. 444. *Basutoland.* Report for 1903–1904 with Returns of the Census, 1904. Cd.2238-21.

Great Britain. *Military Report and General Information Concerning Southern Basutoland.* Prepared for the General Staff, War Office, 1905. A.1035. Confidential.

Great Britain. War Office. *Basutoland.* 1880.

South Africa. *Despatch from Sir Hercules Robinson, with Report of the Resident Commissioner, Basutoland, for the Year ending 30th June 1887, and the Secretary of State's Reply Thereto, 1887,* C.-5238.

South Africa. *Further Correspondence Respecting the Cape Colony and Adjacent Territories.* 1883, C.-3717. Appendix: "Annual Report for 1882, of the Acting Governor's Agent for Basutoland."

South Africa. *Further Correspondence Respecting the Affairs of Basutoland* (London, September 1886). C.-4907.

South Africa. *Further Correspondence Respecting the Cape Colony and Adjacent Territories.* 1884, C.-3855. 1884, C.-4263. 1885, C.-4589. 1886, C.-4644. C.-4838.

South Africa. *Military Report on Basutoland.* Vol. I, General. Vol. II, Routes. 1910. A.1384.

South Africa. *South African Native Affairs Commission 1903–5.* Volume IV, Minutes of Evidence. Volume V, Index and Annexures to Minutes of Evidence Together with Written Replies to Questions and Additional Memoranda by Witnesses. Cape Town: Cape Times, Government Printers, 1904.

Books and articles

Almanaka ea Basotho. Selemo sa 1894. Khatiso ea A. Mabille. Morija, 1894.

Andrew Smith's Journal of his Expedition into the Interior of South Africa, 1834–36. Edited by William F. Lye. Cape Town: A. A. Balkema, 1975.

Arbousset, Thomas, *Missionary Excursion into the Blue Mountains.* Edited and translated by David Ambrose and Albert Brutsch. Morija: Morija Archives, 1991.

Arbousset, T. and Daumas, F. *Narrative of An Exploratory Tour to the North-East of the Colony of the Cape of Good Hope*. Translated by John Crumbie Brown. Cape Town, 1846. Reprinted, Cape Town: C. Struik, 1968.

Arndt, E. H. D. *Banking and Currency Development in South Africa (1652–1927)*. Cape Town: Juta, 1928.

Ashton, Hugh. *The Basuto*. Oxford: Oxford University Press, 1952.

Atmore, Anthony. "The Passing of Sotho Independence 1865–70," in Thompson (ed.), *African Societies in Southern Africa*, pp. 282–301.

Atmore, Anthony and Sanders, Peter B. "Sotho Arms and Ammunition in the Nineteenth Century," *Journal of African History*, 12, 4 (1971), 535–544.

Backhouse, James. *Extracts from the Journal of James Backhouse, whilst engaged in a Religious Visit to South Africa, accompanied by George Washington Walker*. Part IX. London: Harvey and Darton, 1841.

A Narrative of a Visit to the Mauritius and South Africa. London: Hamilton, Adams, 1844.

Balfour, Alice B. *Twelve Hundred Miles in A Waggon*. London: Edward Arnold, 1895.

Barkly, Fanny A. *Among Boers and Basutos*. London: Remington, 1893.

Barrow, John. *An Account of Travels into the Interior of Southern Africa in the Years 1797 and 1798 . . .* London: A. Straban, 1801. Reprinted, Johnson Reprint Corporation, 1968. 2 vols.

Basutoland Records. Collected and Arranged by George M. Theal. Cape Town: W. A. Richards & Sons, Government Printers, 1883. Reprinted Cape Town: C. Struik, 1964. Vols. I–III.

Bawden, M. G. and Carroll, D. M. *The Land Resources of Lesotho*. Tolworth, England: Land Resources Division, Directorate of Overseas Surveys, 1968.

Beinart, William. *The Political Economy of Pondoland 1860–1930*. Cambridge: Cambridge University Press, 1982.

"Production and the Material Basis of Chieftanship: Pondoland, 1830–80," in Marks and Atmore (eds.), *Economy and Society in Pre-Industrial South Africa*, pp. 120–147.

Bianquis, Jean. "La Question Economique au Lessouto," in *Le Christianisme Social*. Paris: Maison des Missions Evangéliques, 1909.

Bloch, Maurice. *Marxism and Anthropology: The History of a Relationship*. Oxford: Clarendon Press, 1983.

Bonner, Philip. "'Desirable or undesirable Basotho women?' Liquor, prostitution and the migration of BaSotho women to the Rand, 1920–1945," in Walker (ed.), *Women and Gender*, pp. 221–250.

Kings, Commoners and Concessionaires: The Evolution and Dissolution of the Nineteenth-Century Swazi State. Cambridge: Cambridge University Press, 1983.

Borcherds, Petrus Borchardus. *An Autobiographical Memoir*. Cape Town: A. S. Robertson, 1861. Facsimile Reproduction, Cape Town: Africana Connoisseurs Press, 1963.

Bozzoli, Belinda. "Marxism, Feminism and South African Studies," *Journal of Southern African Studies*, 9, 2 (1983).

Bundy, Colin. *The Rise and Fall of the South African Peasantry*. Berkeley and Los Angeles: University of California Press, 1979.

Burchell, William J. *Travels in the Interior of Southern Africa*. 1822. Reprinted with an introduction by I. Schapera. London: Batchworth Press, 1953. 2 vols.

Burman, Sandra B. *Chiefdom Politics and Alien Law: Basutoland under Cape Rule, 1871–1884*. New York: Africana Publishing Co., 1981.

"Fighting a Two-Pronged Attack: the changing legal status of women in Cape-ruled Basutoland, 1872–1884," in Walker (ed.), *Women and Gender*, pp. 48–75.

The Justice of the Queen's Government: The Cape's Administration of Basutoland, 1871–1884. Cambridge: African Studies Center, 1976.

Campbell, John. *Travels in South Africa, undertaken at the request of the Missionary Society*. London, 1815. Reprinted, Cape Town: C. Struik, 1974.

Casalis, Eugene. *Etudes sur La Langue Sechuana, précédés d'une Introduction sur l'origine et les Progrès de la Mission Chez les Bassoutos*. Paris: Sociéte des Missions Evangéliques, 1841.

237

Bibliography

Les Bassoutos ou Vingt-Trois Années d'Etudes et d'Observations au Sud de l'Afrique. Paris: Société des Missions Evangéliques, 1859. Reprinted, Paris, 1933.

Mes Souvenirs. Paris: Société des Missions Evangéliques, 1933. First published c. 1880.

My Life in Basutoland. Translated by J. Brierley. London, 1889. Reprinted, Cape Town, 1971.

Clarke, Marshall. "Unexplored Basutoland," *Proceedings of the Royal Geographical Society* (UK), 10 (1888), 519–530.

Clavier, Henri. *Thomas Arbousset: Recherche Historique sur son Milieu, Sa Personalité, Son Oeuvre.* Paris: Société des Missions Evangéliques, 1965.

Cobbing, Julian. "The Mfecane as Alibi: Thoughts on Dithakong and Mbolompo," *Journal of African History*, 29 (1988), 487–519.

Collins, William M. *Free Statia: Reminiscences of a Lifetime in the Orange Free State.* 1907. Reprinted, Cape Town: C. Struik, 1965.

Delius, Peter. *The Land Belongs to Us: The Pedi Polity, the Boers and the British in the nineteenth-century Transvaal.* Berkeley: University of California Press, 1984.

Diary of Father Joseph Gerard, OMI at Roma Mission, Lesotho, December 1864 – February 1875. Roma, Lesotho, 1978.

Dove, Canon R. *Anglican Pioneers in Lesotho: Some Account of the Diocese of Lesotho, 1876–1930.* Maseru, 1975.

Dutton, E. A. T. *The Basuto of Basutoland.* London, 1923.

Dyke, R. H. *The Switzerland of South Africa.* London: Morgan & Scott, 1893.

Eldredge, Elizabeth A. "Drought, Famine and Disease in Nineteenth-Century Lesotho," *African Economic History*, 16 (1987), 61–93.

"Land, Politics, and Censorship: The Historiography of Nineteenth-Century Lesotho," *History in Africa*, 15 (1988), 191–209.

"Women in Production: The Economic Role of Women in Nineteenth-Century Lesotho," *Signs: Journal of Women in Culture and Society*, 16, 4 (1991), 707–731.

"Sources of Conflict in Southern Africa, ca. 1800–30: The 'Mfecane' Reconsidered," *Journal of African History*, 33 (1992), 1–35.

"Slave-Raiding Across the Cape Frontier," in Elizabeth A. Eldredge and Fred Morton (eds.), *Slavery in South Africa: Captive Labor on the Dutch Frontier.* Westview Press, forthcoming.

Ellenberger, D. F. "History ea Basotho: Tsa tsepe le ho qala ha tsoelo-pele," *Leselinyana* (16 July 1911).

History of the Basuto: Ancient and Modern. Edited and translated by J. C. MacGregor. London: Caxton, 1912.

Histori ea Basotho, Karolo I: Mehla ea Boholo-holo. Morija: Morija Sesuto Book Depot, 1917, 4th edn 1956. Reprinted 1981.

Ellenberger, Victor. *A Century of Mission Work in Basutoland, 1833–1933.* Translated by E. M. Ellenberger. Morija: Morija Sesuto Book Depot, 1938.

Sur Les Hauts-Plateaux du Lessouto. Paris: Société des Missions Evangéliques, 1930.

Elphick, Richard and Hermann Giliomee (eds.). *The Shaping of South African Society, 1652–1840.* Middletown: Wesleyan University Press, 1989.

Etherington, Norman. "African Economic Experiments in Colonial Natal 1845–1880," *African Economic History* 5 (1978), 1–15

Fagan, Brian. "The Later Iron Age in South Africa," in Thompson (ed.), *African Societies in Southern Africa*, pp. 50–70.

Fako, Simeon, "Lijo tsa Tlaling," *Leselinyana* (16 November 1911).

Favre, Edouard. *Francois Coillard: Missionaire au Lessouto.* Paris: Société des Missions Evangéliques, 1910.

Les Vingt-Cinq Ans de Coillard au Lessouto. Paris: Société des Missions Evangéliques, 1931.

Feireman, Steven. *Peasant Intellectuals: Anthropology and History in Tanzania.* Madison: University of Wisconsin Press, 1990.

238

Ferragne, Marcel, OMI. *Au Pays des Basotho, les Cent Ans de la Mission St. Michel*, I, 1868–1899. Roma, Lesotho, n.d.

Freeman, J. J. *A Tour of South Africa*. London: John Snow, 1851.

Gallienne, Georges. *Thomas Arbousset (1810–1897)*. Paris: Société des Missions Evangéliques, 1933.

Gerard, Joseph. *Le Père Gerard Nous Parle*. Vol. 2. "Son Premier Séjour à Roma." Edited by Marcel Ferragne, OMI. Roma, Lesotho: The Social Centre, 1969.

Germond, R. C. *Chronicles of Basutoland*. Morija: Morija Sesuto Book Depot, 1967.

Gluckman, M. "The Rise of a Zulu Empire," *Scientific American*, 202 (1963).

Guy, Jeff. "Production and Exchange in the Zulu Kingdom," *Mohlomi: Journal of Southern African Historical Studies*, 2 (1978), 96–106.

"Analysing Pre-Capitalist Societies in Southern Africa," *Journal of Southern African Studies* 14, 1 (1987).

"Ecological Factors in the Rise of Shaka and the Zulu Kingdom," in Marks and Atmore (eds.), *Economy and Society in Pre-Industrial South Africa*, pp. 102–119.

"Gender Oppression in Southern Africa's Pre-capitalist Societies," in Walker, (ed.), *Women and Gender*, pp. 33–47.

Harinck, Gerrit. "Interaction Between Xhosa and Khoi: Emphasis on the Period 1620–1750," in Thompson (ed.), *African Societies in Southern Africa*, pp. 145–170.

Harris, Olivia and Kate Young. "Engendered Structures: Some Problems in the Analysis of Reproduction," in Kahn and Llobera (eds.), *The Anthropology of Pre-Capitalist Societies*, pp. 109–147.

Irvine, T. W. *British Basutoland and the Basutos*. London: H. J. Infield, 1881.

Jacottet, E. "Moeurs, Coutumes et Superstitions des Ba-Souto," *Bulletin de la Société Neuchateloise de Géographie*, 9 (1896–1897), 105–151.

Jeeves, Alan H. *Migrant Labour in South Africa's Mining Economy: The Struggle for the Gold Mines Labour Supply 1890–1920*. Kingston, Canada, 1985.

Jingoes, J. J. *A Chief is a Chief by the People: The Autobiography of Stimela Jason Jingoes*. Recorded and compiled by John and Cassandra Perry. Oxford: Oxford University Press, 1975.

Jousse, Theophile. *La Mission Française Evangéliques au Sud de l'Afrique: Son Origine et Son Developpement Jusqu'à Nos Jours*, vols. 1 and 2. Paris: Librairie Fischbacher, 1889.

"Moshesh, Roi des Bassoutos," *Le Chrétien Evangélique*, Revue Religieuse de la Suisse Romande (Lausanne: Bureau du Chrétien Evangélique), 1867, pp. 7–17, 67–78, 122–132.

Kahn, Joel S. "Marxist Anthropology and Segmentary Societies: A Review of the Literature," in Kahn and Llobera (eds.), *The Anthropology of Pre-Capitalist Societies*, pp. 57–88.

Kahn, Joel S. and Joseph R. Llobera (eds.). *The Anthropology of Pre-Capitalist Societies*. Atlantic Highlands, N.J.: Humanities Press, 1981.

Kahn, Joel S. and Joseph R. Llobera. "Towards a new Marxism or a New Anthropology?" in Kahn and Llobera (eds.), *The Anthropology of Pre-Capitalist Societies*, pp. 263–329.

Kay, Stephen. *Travels and Researches in Caffraria*. New York: Harpert Brothers, 1834.

Keegan, Timothy. "Trade, Accumulation and Impoverishment: Mercantile Capital and the Economic Transformation of Lesotho and the Conquered Territory, 1870–1920," *Journal of Southern African Studies* 12, 2 (1986), 196–216.

Kimble, Judy. "Labour Migration in Basutoland, c.1870–1885," in Shula Marks and Richard Rathbone (eds.), *Industrialisation and Social Change in South Africa*, pp. 119–141. London: Longman, 1982.

Kunene, Daniel P. "*Leselinyana la Lesotho* and Sotho Historiography," *History in Africa*, 4 (1977), 149–161.

Kuper, Adam. "The Social Structure of the Sotho-Speaking Peoples of Southern Africa," *Africa*, 19, 1 (1975), 67–81 and 19, 2 (1975), 39–49.

Wives for Cattle: Bridewealth and Marriage in Southern Africa. London: Routledge & Kegan Paul, 1982.

Lagden, Godfrey. *The Basutos: The Mountaineers and Their Country.* London: Hutchinson, 1909. 2 vols.

Laydevant, F. "La Misère au Basutoland," *Les Missions Catholiques* (1934), 333–337.

Lebreton, F. "A Travers les Montagnes de Basutoland," *Les Missions Catholiques* (1907), 268.

Legassick, Martin. "The Sotho-Tswana Peoples Before 1800," in Thompson (ed.), *African Societies in Southern Africa,* 86–125.

Lettres Missionaires de M. et Mme. Paul Berthoud de la Mission Romande, 1873–1879. Lausanne: Georges Bridel, 1900.

Litaba tsa Lilemo. Morija: Morija Sesuto Book Depot, 1931.

Lye, William F. "The Difaqane: the Mfecane in the Southern Sotho area," *Journal of African History,* 8 (1967), 107–131.

"The Distribution of the Sotho Peoples after the Difaqane," in Thompson (ed.), *African Societies in Southern Africa,* pp. 191–206.

Mabille, A. and H. Dieterlen. *Southern Sotho – English Dictionary.* Reclassified, revised and enlarged by R. A. Paroz. Morija Sesuto Book Depot, 1950. Reprinted 1974.

Mabille, H. E. "The Basuto of Basutoland," *Journal of the African Society* 5, 19 (April 1906), 233–251 and 5, 20 (July 1906), 351–376.

MacGregor, J. C. *Basuto Traditions; being a record of the traditional history of the most important of the tribe which form the Basuto nation of today up to the time of their being absorbed.* Cape Town: Argus, 1905. Reprinted, Willem Hiddingh Reprint Series, no. 12, 1957.

Machobane, L. B. J. "Mohlomi: Doctor, Traveller and Sage," *Mohlomi: Journal of Southern African Historical Studies,* 2 (1978), 5–27.

Maggs, T. M. O'C. *Iron Age Communities of the Southern Highveld.* Pietermaritzburg: Council of the Natal Museum, 1976.

"Iron Age Patterns and Sotho History on the Southern Highveld: South Africa," *World Archaeology,* 7, 3 (1976), 318–332.

Malan, C.-H. *La Mission Française du Sud de L'Afrique.* Translated by G. Mallet. Paris: J. Bonhoure, 1878.

Mamadi, M. F. "The Copper Miners of Musina," in Van Warmelo (ed.), *The Copper Miners of Musina and the Early History of the Zoutpansberg.*

Marks, Shula. "The Traditions of the Natal 'Nguni': a Second Look at the Work of A. T. Bryant," in Thompson (ed.), *African Societies in Southern Africa,* pp. 126–144.

Marks, Shula and Atmore, Anthony (eds.). *Economy and Society in Pre-Industrial South Africa.* London: Longman, 1980.

Martin, Minnie. *Basutoland: Its Legends and Customs.* London: Nichols, 1903. Reprinted New York: Negro Universities Press, 1969.

Meillassoux, Claude. *Maidens, Meal and Money: Capitalism and the Domestic Community.* Cambridge: Cambridge University Press, 1981.

The Anthropology of Slavery: the Womb of Iron and Gold. Translated by Alide Dasnois. Chicago: University of Chicago Press, 1991.

Merk, Frederick. *History of the Westward Movement.* New York: Alfred A. Knopf, 1978.

Moffat, Robert. *Missionary Labours and Scenes in Southern Africa.* New York: Johnson Reprint Corporation, 1969. First published 1842.

Mohapi, Molelekoa. *Temo ea Boholo-holo Lesotho.* Morija: Morija Sesuto Book Depot, 1956.

Morison, Samuel Eliot. *The Oxford History of the American People.* New York: Oxford University Press, 1965.

Moshoeshoe, Nehemiah Sekhonyana. "A Little Light from Basutoland," *Cape Monthly Magazine,* 3rd series, 2, 10 (April 1880), 221–233; 2, 11 (May 1880), 280–292.

Motebang, Carlisle. "E ngue ea lintho tse tlisitsoeng Le-sotho: Sefaga," *Leselinyana* (15 February 1892).

Motebang, Carlisle. "Lesela," *Leselinyana* (15 August 1891).

Murray, Colin. "The Symbolism and Politics of *Bohali*: Household Recruitment and Marriage by Installment in Lesotho," in Eileen Jensen Krige and John L. Comaroff (eds.), *Essays on African Marriage in Southern Africa*, pp. 112–131. Cape Town: Juta, 1981.

Neumark, S. Daniel. *Economic Influences on the South African Frontier, 1652–1836*. Stanford, Conn.: Stanford University Press, 1957.

Omer-Cooper, J. D. *The Zulu Aftermath: A Nineteenth Century Revolution in Bantu Africa*. Evanston: Northwestern University Press, 1969.

Orpen, Joseph M. *History of the Basutus of South Africa*. 1857. Reprinted Mazenod: Mazenod Book Centre, 1979.

Reminiscences of Life in South Africa from 1846 to the Present Day. 2 vols. Durban: B. Davis and Sons, 1908. And articles in *Natal Advertiser*, 1916. Reprinted together, Cape Town: C. Struik, 1964.

Palmer, Robin and Parsons, Neil (eds.). *The Roots of Rural Poverty in Central and Southern Africa*. Berkeley and Los Angeles: University of California Press, 1977.

Parsons, Neil. "The Economic History of Khama's Country in Botswana, 1844–1930," in Palmer and Parsons (eds.), *The Roots of Rural Poverty in Central and Southern Africa*, pp. 113–143.

Peires, J. B. *The House of Phalo: A History of the Xhosa People in the Days of Their Independence*. Berkeley: University of California Press, 1981.

"The British and the Cape 1814–1834," in Elphick and Giliomee (eds.), *The Shaping of South African Society*, pp. 499–511.

Perrot, Claude H. *Les Sotho et les Missionaires Européens au XIXe Siècle*. Annales de l'Université d'Abidjan. Series F, vol. 2, part 1. 1970.

Peters, Pauline. "Gender, Development Cycles and Historical Process: a Critique of Recent Research on Women in Botswana," *Journal of Southern African Studies*, 10, 1 (1983), 100–122.

Phillipson, David W. "Early Iron-Using Peoples of Southern Africa," in Thompson (ed.), *African Societies in Southern Africa*, pp. 24–49.

African Archaeology. Cambridge: Cambridge University Press, 1985.

Porte, Frederic. "Préfecture Apostolique du Basutoland: Les Réminiscences d'un Missionaire du Basutoland," *Missions de la Congrégation des Oblats de Marie Immaculée*, 134 (June 1896), 166–221 and 135 (September 1896), 269–357.

Poulter, Sebastian M. *Family Law and Litigation in Basotho Society*. Oxford: Oxford University Press, 1976.

Puaux, Frank. *Les Bassoutos: Une Mission Française au Sud de l'Afrique*. Paris: G. Fischbacher, 1881.

Puaux, Frank, H. Dieterlen, F. Kohler, E. Jacottet, J. Bianquis. *Livre D'Or de la Mission du Lessouto*. Paris: Maison des Missions Evangéliques, 1912.

Records from Natal, Lesotho, Orange Free State and Mozambique concerning the History of the Catholic Church in Southern Africa. Edited and translated by Leo Sormany, OMI Lesotho Documents. Roma, Lesotho: The Social Centre, n.d.

"Report of the Expedition for Exploring Central Africa under the Superintendence of Dr. A. Smith," (abridged), *The Journal of the Royal Geographical Society of London*, 6 (1836), 394–413.

Sanders, Peter. "Sekonyela and Moshweshwe: Failure and Success in the Aftermath of the Difaqane," *Journal of African History*, 10, 3 (1969).

Moshoeshoe: Chief of the Sotho. London: Heinemann, 1975.

Sansom, Basil. "Traditional Economic Systems," in W. D. Hammond-Tooke (ed.), *The Bantu-Speaking Peoples of Southern Africa*. 2nd edn. London: Routledge and Kegan Paul, 1974.

Bibliography

Schrumpf, Christian. *Südafrikanische Cap- und Atlantische See-Bilder*, mit Unhang; *Die Bassuto Wie Sie Sind*. Strasbourg, 1861.

"Sessuto, Ein Beitrag zur Sud-Afrikanischen Sprachenkunde," in F. A. Backhouse (ed.), *Zeitschrift der Deutschen morgenlandischen Gesellschaft*, vol. 16, part 3, pp. 448–481. Leipzig, 1862.

Schrumpf, Rosette. *Autobiographie de Mme Rosette Schrumpf*. Strasbourg, n.d.

Sechefo, Justinus. "The Twelve Lunar Months among the Basuto," *Anthropos* 5, 1 (1910), 71–81. Reprinted, Mazenod, n.d.

The Old Clothing of the Basotho. Mazenod: The Catholic Centre, n.d. (*c.* 1910).

Segoainyana, "Tsa Masimo," *Leselinyana* (February 1884).

Segoete, Everitt. "Leeto la Malingoaneng," *Leselinyana* (25 September 1909).

Raphepheng: Bophelo ba Basotho ba Khale. Morija: Morija Sesuto Book Depot, 1915. Reprinted 1981.

Sekese, Azariel. *Mekhoa le Maele a Basotho*. Morija: Morija Sesuto Book Depot, 1907. Reprinted 1968 and 1978.

Mekhoa ea Basotho. Morija: Morija Sesuto Book Depot, 1953. Reprinted 1979.

Sen, Amartya. *Poverty and Famines: An Essay on Entitlement and Deprivation*. Oxford: Oxford University Press, 1981.

Sheddick, V. G. J. *The Southern Sotho*. London: International African Institute, 1953.

Soirdet, J. E. *Adele Mabille née Casalis (1840–1923), D'Après ses Souvenirs et sa Correspondance*. Paris: Société des Mission Evangéliques, 1933.

Un Siècle en Afrique et en Océanie: Revue de nos Champs de Mission en Afrique et en Océanie, 1822–1922. Paris: Société des Mission Evangéliques, 1923.

Smit, P. *Lesotho: A Geographical Study*. Pretoria: Africa Institute, 1967.

Smith, Alan. "The Trade of Delagoa Bay as a Factor in Nguni Politics, 1750–1835," in Thompson (ed.), *African Societies in Southern Africa*, pp. 171–190.

"Delagoa Bay and the Trade of South-Eastern Africa," in Richard Gray and David Birmingham (eds.), *Pre-Colonial African Trade*, pp. 265–289. Oxford: Oxford University Press, 1970.

Smith, Andrew. *The Diary of Andrew Smith, director of the "Expedition for Exploring Central Africa" 1834–1836*. Edited by Percival R. Kirby. Cape Town, 1939.

Andrew Smith's Journal of his Expedition into the Interior of South Africa, 1834–36. Edited by William F. Lye. Cape Town: A. A. Balkema, 1975.

Smith, Edwin O. *The Mabilles of Basutoland*. London: Hodder and Stoughton, 1939.

Streit, Robert, OMI and Johannes Dindiger, OMI. *Bibliotheca Missionum*, vols. 17 and 18: Afrikanische Missionsliteratur. Rome, Italy: Verlag Herder Freiburg, 1952.

Thom, H. B. *Die Geskiedenis van die Skaapboerdery in Suid-Africa*. Amsterdam: N. V. Swets & Zeitlinger, 1936.

Thompson, Leonard. "Cooperation and Conflict: The High Veld," *Oxford History of South Africa*, vol. 1, pp. 391–446. Oxford: Oxford University Press, 1969.

Survival in Two Worlds: Moshoeshoe of Lesotho 1786–1870. Oxford: Clarendon Press, 1975.

(ed.), *African Societies in Southern Africa*. London: Heinemann, 1969.

Tlali, S. S. *Mehla ea Boholo-holo*. Morija: Morija Sesuto Book Depot, 1951. Reprinted 1972.

Tylden, G. *The Rise of the Basuto*. Cape Town: Juta, 1950.

Van Heyningen, Caroline. *Orange Days: Memoirs of Eighty Years Ago in the Old Orange Free State*. Pietermaritzburg: University of Natal Press, 1965.

Vansina, Jan. *Paths in the Rain Forests: Toward a History of Political Tradition in Equatorial Africa*. Madison: University of Wisconsin Press, 1990.

Van Warmelo, N. J. *The Copper Miners of Musina and the Early History of the Zoutpansberg*, vol. 8. Union of South Africa Department of Native Affairs Ethnological Publications. Pretoria: Government Printer, 1940.

Walker, Cherryl (ed.). *Women and Gender in Southern Africa to 1945*. London: James Currey, 1990.

242

"Gender and the development of the migrant labour system *c*. 1850–1930: An overview," in Cherryl Walker (ed.), *Women and Gender*, pp. 168–196.

Walton, James. *Father of Kindness and Father of Horses: The Story of Frasers Limited*. Morija: Morija Printing Works, 1958.

Watson, R. L. "The Subjection of a South African State: Thaba Nchu, 1880–1884," *Journal of African History*, 21 (981), 357–373.

Weitzecker, G. "La Donna Fra i Basuto," *Archivio per l'Antropologia e la Etnologia* (17), 31 (1901), 459–478.

Widdicombe, John. *Fourteen Years in Basutoland: A Sketch of African Mission Life*. London: Church Printing Co., 1891.

In the Lesuto: A Sketch of African Mission Life. London: Society for Promoting Christian Knowledge, 1895. (Second revised edition of previous item.)

Memories and Musings. London: Allen & Unwin, 1915.

Willet, Shelagh M. and David P. Ambrose. *Lesotho: A Comprehensive Bibliography*. World Bibliographical Series, vol. 3. Oxford: Clio Press, 1980.

Williamson, Oliver E. "Transaction-Cost Economics: The Governance of Contractual Relations," *The Journal of Law and Economics*, 22 (1979), 233–261.

Wilson, Monica. "The Sotho, Venda and Tsonga," in Wilson and Thompson (eds.), *Oxford History of South Africa*, vol. 1 (1969), pp. 131–182.

Wilson, Monica and Thompson, Leonard, (eds.), *The Oxford History of South Africa*, vols. 1 and 2. Oxford: Oxford University Press, 1969 and 1972.

Wolpe, Harold. "Capitalism and Cheap Labour Power in South Africa: From Segregation to Apartheid." *Economy and Society*, 1, 4 (1972), 425–426.

"Zwanzig Jahre unter den Basuto-Kaffern. Erlebnisse eines Missionars in Südafrika." Reported by P. J. N. Meyer, OMI, *Marie Immaculata*, II (St. Karl, 1894/95), pp. 57–59, 84–86, 114–118, 149–152, 174–177, 211–215, 245–248, 302–305, 340–343, 368–373.

Unpublished theses and papers

Eldredge, Elizabeth A. "An Economic History of Lesotho in the Nineteenth Century." Ph.D. dissertation, University of Wisconsin-Madison, 1986.

"Echoes of the Past: Dilemmas of Accommodation and Resistance in Lesotho." Paper presented at the African Studies Association, Atlanta, Georgia, 5 November 1989.

"Slave Raiding Beyond the Cape Frontier, ca. 1800–1860." Paper presented at the African Studies Association, St. Louis, November 1991.

Gay, John. Field Notes, 9–17 July 1976. Unpublished typescript.

Huss-Ashmore, Rebecca. "Seasonality in Rural Highland Lesotho: Method and Policy." Unpublished paper, Feb. 1982.

Kimble, Judy. "Aspects of the Economic History of Lesotho, 1830–85." Paper presented at a History Workshop, National University of Lesotho, 23–25 July 1976.

"Lesotho and the Outside World, 1840–70: Prelude to Imperialism." Paper presented at the International Conference on Southern African History, National University of Lesotho, 1–7 August 1977.

"Towards an Understanding of the Political Economy of Lesotho: The Origins of Commodity Production and Migrant Labour, 1830–1885." Unpublished M.A. thesis, National University of Lesotho, 1978.

Legassick, Martin. "The Griqua, the Sotho-Tswana, and the Missionaries, 1780–1840: the Politics of a Frontier Zone." Ph.D. dissertation, University of California at Los Angeles, 1969.

Leys, Roger. "Some Observations on Class differentiation and Class Conflict Within the Labour Reserve of Basutoland." ICS Collected Seminar Papers, Oct. 1979 – June 1980, 87–95.

Bibliography

Lye, William F. "The Sotho Wars in the Interior of South Africa, 1822–1837." Ph.D. dissertation, University of California at Los Angeles, 1970.

Manson, Andrew. "Conflict on the Eastern Highveld Southern Kalahari, *c.* 1750–1820". Paper presented at the University of the Witwatersrand, Conference on "The 'Mfecane' Aftermath: Towards a new paradigm," 6–9 September 1991.

Theron, J. D. "Die Ekonomiese en Finansiele Toestand nav die Oranje-Vrystaat Republick, 1854–1880." Unpublished M.A. thesis, Unisa, 1943.

Index

Index

bridewealth (*bohali*), 10, 124, 133, 136,
    139–46, 147, 226n. 68
British, 62, 63, 122, 123, 152
    land speculation, 53–7
    relationship with Boers, 3, 48
    see also Great Britain
Burman, Sandra, 15, 167, 225n. 43

Cape Colony, 48, 68, 78
    and Boers, 3, 48
    drought in, 75, 80
    frontier populations and relations, 1–2, 41,
        62–3, 184–5
    rule in Basutoland, 8, 17, 167–70, 173, 175,
        199
    trade, 48, 70, 75, 151, 154, 158, 159
Casalis, Eugene, 21, 35, 60, 84, 137
Catholic missionaries, 85, 94–5, 144, 155
cattle
    Boer herding, 47–8
    bridewealth, 139–41
    disease, 78–81, 138, 179, 188, 190, 212n. 74
    and drought, 75
    mafisa (loan cattle system), 34–5, 37, 38,
        123, 148, 152, 165–6
    ownership, 34, 71–2, 133, 137, 148
    raiding, 49, 70
    Rinderpest epizootic, 72, 81, 104
    trade in, 70, 133, 152, 154
    as wealth, 34, 115, 123, 127, 140
    and women, 137
    see also agriculture, pastoral production;
        bridewealth; clientage; plow (ox-)
chiefdoms
    political incorporation, 1–2, 18, 19, 28–46,
        196
    political relations, 10, 26, 42–6; marriage
        alliances, 128–31
    internal dynamics, 12–15
chiefs
    abuses, 171–3, 187, 195
    collaboration with colonialism, 9
    and colonial rule, 167–74
    and followers, 8–9, 34–9, 41, 120, 152,
        169–73, 180–1, 186–7, 197, 201
    inheritance and descent, 30–1, 128–31
    and migrant labor, 185–6
    placing and land allocation, 63, 67
    resistance to Europeans, 8, 172, 174, 176
    and trade, 147
    and wealth, 8, 34–6, 72, 152, 155
    and women, 36, 132–3
    see also BaKoena; clientage; cattle, *mafisa*;
        Gun War; Moshoeshoe; taxes; women,
        queen regents
children
    and descent, 10, 126–8
    enslavement by Europeans, 26, 184

and famine, 10, 137–8
inheritance, 67
labor of, 102, 106, 108, 111, 187
and mothers, 9, 127–8, 194
rights to, 142–3, 194
Christianity, 11, 93–5 *passim*, 113–14, 147,
    149–50, 153, 155, 195, 198, 221n. 73,
    221n. 74
    see also Paris Evangelical Missionary
        Society; Anglican missionaries; Catholic
        missionaries
class relations, 12, 16
clientage, 33, 37, 142–3
    see also cattle, *mafisa*; chiefs
climate, 59–60
clothing, 87–9, 94–5, 155, 198
copper, 20–1, 25
crafts
    production, 82–100, 109–10;
        leather-working, 87–9, 97; pottery,
        89–90, 99; weaving (plant fibres), 89, 98
    trade in, 117–19
    see also industries, iron-working; labor,
        specialization; trade
culture, 19, 43, 49, 127–8
    see also language
currency, *see* trade, currency; beads; money

demography, 18, 19, 28–9, 33, 40, 44
    immigration into Lesotho, 62–3
    population: Lesotho, 61–5; Orange Free
        State, 55, 179
    settlement, 1–3, 18–33 *passim*, 40, 44–6, 77
disease, 78–81, 185
drought, 47, 58, 62, 73, 75–81, 111, 138, 151,
    158, 159, 175

Ellenberger, D. F. E., 90, 133, 135, 136, 139,
    225n. 43
environment, 19, 28–9
    politics and food, 72–81
    vegetation, 60
    see also land, resources (Lesotho); land,
        soils; climate

family, *see* bridewealth; children; gender
    relations; households; marriage; women
famine, 58–81, 114, 137–8, 175
food, 10, 39, 53, 58–81, 102–7, 114, 137–8,
    160–1
    entitlements, 74, 76
    hunting and gathering, 65–6, 102
    imports, 155–6
    labor, 102–7
    as payment, 87
    processing, 107–9
    production, 585–9
    storage, 89

246

Index

Other books in the series